Food Safety in the Hospitality Industry

Food Safety in the Hospitality Industry

Tim Knowles

Senior Lecturer in Hospitality Management
Sheffield Hallam University
United Kingdom

OXFORD   AMSTERDAM   BOSTON   LONDON   NEW YORK   PARIS
SAN DIEGO   SAN FRANCISCO   SINGAPORE   SYDNEY   TOKYO

Butterworth-Heinemann
An imprint of Elsevier Science
Linacre House, Jordan Hill, Oxford OX2 8DP
225 Wildwood Avenue, Woburn MA 01801-2041

First published 2002

British Library Cataloguing in Publication Data
A catalogue record for this book is
available from the British Library

Library of Congress Cataloguing in Publication Data
A catalogue record for this book is
available from the Library of Congress

ISBN 0 7506 5349 3

For information on all Butterworth-Heinemann publications
visit our website at www.bh.com

Composition by Genesis Typesetting, Rochester, Kent

Transferred to digital printing 2006

Contents

Preface

The European hospitality industry is large and fragmented. Due to the diversity of the sector, which largely comprises small independent businesses, it is alleged that communicating with caterers is difficult. The lack of any representative trade organization which covers more than a small part of the industry compounds this view. This book seeks to address all sectors of the industry with the aim of providing a framework around which any business can build a food hygiene system, thus ensuring its proper operation.

Fundamental to any consideration of food hygiene is an understanding of the relevant legal requirements on the subject. This book therefore examines current food safety and hygiene legislation in some detail across a number of European countries, using practical examples where possible to explain the legal language.

Part One of this book (Chapters 1–3) gives the legal background to food safety within a number of European countries and sets it within the context of the influences coming from the European Union.

Part Two (Chapters 4–8) gives a comprehensive breakdown of safe food handling practices, with emphasis on practical rather than theoretical matters. The aim of this section is to provide an easy to use reference source for all areas of a catering operation that have a direct influence on the overall hygiene of the business on a day-to-day basis.

Part Three (Chapters 9–10) explores the concept of food hazard analysis in some detail as it provides an important framework for the application of proper food safety policies within the catering firm. This section also offers guidance to those caterers wishing to take the opportunity of establishing the basis for a due diligence defence. However, the intention behind this section goes further than simply providing a legal defence but rather seeks to encourage responsibility for correct food hygiene within a business.

Caterers have a responsibility to their customers to prepare food safely and hygienically. The introduction of the Food Safety Act 1990 in the UK, with its improved enforcement powers and increased penalties for some offences, has caused some to improve their procedures due to pressure from enforcement agencies. Such improvements, based on compulsion rather than an understanding of the principles involved, may only be transitory. Businesses that pay scant regard to hygiene may find themselves locked into a cycle of forced improvements followed by a period of gradually deteriorating standards leading to further legal action. It must make more sense to view these legislative changes in the law as an opportunity to plan hygiene into the operational policies of a business. Any proprietor using a system that achieves specified standards of hygiene and ensures compliance with the relevant legislation can be reassured that they have nothing to fear from a visit by an environmental health officer and can concentrate on the main business of satisfying their customers.

Food safety legislation changes almost on a monthly basis. Legislation quoted in this book is at 1 January 2002.

Tim Knowles
March 2002
E-mail: timknowles@email.msn.com
Tel: +44 (0)1204 708421
Fax: +44 (0)1204 708421

Food Legislation, Consumers and the Hospitality Sector

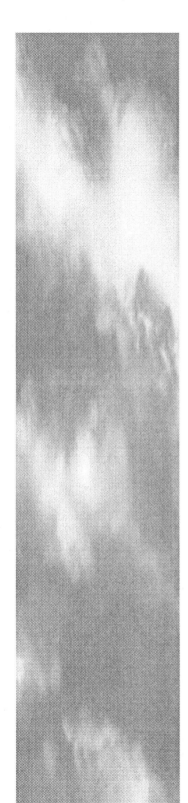

European foodstuffs law and the consumer

Background

On 1 January 1993, the Single European Internal Market was established within the European Union (EU). The focus of this and the following chapter is on how the literature views common foodstuffs law within the EU's internal market, the enforcement practices within individual member states and the implications the internal market has had, or will have, for both the consumer and the hospitality firm (Fallows 1988, 1991; Friedhof, 1991).

In the ensuing discussion the five following key areas are considered:

1 Current legal environment and enforcement in the EU and individual countries.
2 Food safety in the foodstuffs industry.
3 Supply/distribution.
4 Effects on the hospitality industry.
5 Opinions of the consumer.

It is the last point on this list that is the initial focus of attention in this chapter. In identifying the general adopted framework, the specific objectives of this and the following chapter are:

- to investigate the role of the EU foodstuffs law;
- to consider the different food law and enforcement practices in the EU;
- to analyse the law's influence on the foodstuffs industry and supply within the internal market;
- to focus particularly on the law's influence within the hospitality industry;
- to identify relevant aspects that affect the consumer; and
- to identify the extent to which the law fulfils its function towards the consumer.

Harmonization

While both the EU and the Single European Act (SEA) have already been mentioned, the practical basis of the SEA was that move to harmonize EU standards and practices, because during the 1960s and 1970s the community had come up against the obstacle of national protectionism, and there was a need for mutual recognition of each other's standards. This situation culminated in the famous *Cassis de Dijon* ruling after a celebrated case in the European Court of Justice in 1979.

The case arose when a German firm found that it was prevented from importing *Cassis de Dijon* because it allegedly did not conform to German standards for liqueurs. The court ruled that the Germans could only prevent importation if they could prove that the liquid was harmful to health or contravened tax or consumer protection laws – which it did not. In *Cassis de Dijon*, the Court of Justice took a very pragmatic approach to EU food law and the free movement of goods in general. In essence, the court held that member states should recognize that other member states had already regulated health and safety for food products sold in their markets. Importing member states should not therefore have used differing health and safety standards to prohibit the free movement of those goods into their territories.

The Community legislature reacted to the *Cassis doctrine* by adopting a horizontal, rather than a vertical, approach to food law. The legislature reasoned that, with mutual recognition, there was no need for common recipe standards for each product. Rather, it was necessary to set common health and safety standards so that member states and consumers would be confident in mutual recognition. Since then, many exceptions to the *Cassis principle* have been litigated, and the EU Commission has provided its interpretation of some of these cases, including the issue of goods produced and marketed in the same country (Lister, 1992; O'Connor, 1993). Within this *Cassis principle*, it was recognized, therefore, that some supranational way was required in which to achieve harmonization of standards. Hence the need for the SEA (O'Connor, 1993).

Another matter worthy of comment here is qualified majority voting. Each member state is given a number of votes, approximately consonant with its size and importance in the EU. The question of this voting system regarding internal market issues is sensitive as it strikes at the heart of a member state's national veto. However, it only takes two or three of the larger countries in the EU to muster enough votes in order to block a decision.

Another factor within the SEA is what is known as the democratic deficit *vis à vis* the European Parliament's influence on the EU Commission. This situation existed to a great extent prior to the SEA, but was reduced in 1987, a process which has continued to some extent with the ratified Maastricht Treaty.

The entry into force of the Maastricht Treaty on 1 November 1993 increased the powers of the European Parliament in a way that will have important implications for key pieces of food legislation (Agra Europe, 1993; Jackson, 1990), all of which are part of the progress towards a Single European Market (Saunders, 1991).

An extension of EU food law can be seen within the European Economic Area (EEA), which brings together the member states of the EU and three from the European Free Trade Association (EFTA). The EEA is an improved free trade area, rather than a customs union. Whereas the EU member states have transferred sovereign powers to the EU, they and the EFTA countries have not yielded those rights to the EEA. Thus, the mechanisms by which the EFTA countries adopt EEA laws differ from those of the EU institutions, and only certain areas of existing EU laws and principles have been adopted (Inglis and Amaducci, 1994). The bulk of existing EU legislation on food is extended by the EEA agreement to cover the EFTA states. This legislation includes not only specific food legislation, but also certain measures concerning consumer protection. The EU keeps its decision-making processes intact and includes the EFTA states only in measures that have an EEA relevance. The EFTA states play a role which is far weaker than their EU counterparts, in that they may only express their own views. Indeed, they cannot actually influence the decisions of EU members regarding the adoption of legislation applicable in the EU, but may only prevent their application by means of suspension of that legislation in the EFTA states. Where they suspend a measure from application in the EEA, the dispute must be subject to arbitration.

With the proposed accession of EFTA member states to the EU (with the exception of Iceland), the disparities in the representation of the EFTA states in the legislative process should be resolved. Nevertheless, the practicalities of juggling national opt-outs, likely to be attached at their entry, as there have been in the Maastricht Treaty, provide the EEA states with a considerable challenge if an enlarged EU is to be workable (Roberts, 1991, 1992).

The need for foodstuffs law

The comments so far serve as a background for discussing the need for foodstuffs law. Such a requirement is best understood by viewing its historical development, closely linked to the evolution of consumer habits and practices.

When looking at the consumer habits of primitive (hunter–gatherer) societies, a direct link between the foodstuffs supplier and the consumers can be observed. Within these specializations (supplier and consumer), a further development within the eighteenth and nineteenth centuries was that one group concentrated on arable or pastoral farming in order to exchange the food products with the intermediate supplier/distributor, and finally to the consumer (Freidhof, 1991). It is in this respect that the separation widened between the producer and the consumer, a trend that continues today.

Over time, a market developed that was characterized by the different interests of consumers and suppliers, one that can be set within the context of a price–value relationship. The interest of the suppliers, i.e. high price per provided unit of value, stands in contrast to the consumer's interest, i.e. low price per unit of value. This conflict of interest, it is suggested, could disadvantage consumers, since the price–value relationship may be influenced by suppliers to their benefit. The price for a food product can easily be seen by the consumer; the value unit cannot. Thus, the producer can vary the value per unit without the consumer's knowledge. It is precisely this conflict that resulted in a demand for foodstuffs legislation.

The historical development of food legislation is discussed in greater depth in the following chapters but, by way of illustration, it is useful at this point to consider such issues within a UK context.

Before the latter part of the nineteenth century, there was little national legislation to control the adulteration of food. It was not until 1860 that the Adulteration of Food and Drink Act was passed by the UK Parliament, legislation that was concerned with weight and quantity measures. The Act made it illegal to sell food that was not of the nature, substance or quality demanded by the consumer (Roberts, 1993a, 1993b), as for instance, the problem of dilution could arise, e.g. the addition of water to wine (Jukes, 1991). In the latter case, the transparency of the price–value relationship would be revealed, by determining the quality and quantity of the value unit, with the objective of such an approach being to guarantee the consumer standardization and consistency. Statutory control originally focused on bread and other basic products, i.e., consumer protection (Act, 1860; Act, 1872; Act, 1938). During the twentieth century, further refinements have seen food law initiatives considered under the subheadings of either *Food*

Safety or *Consumer Protection*. This distinction focuses on two elements, namely: the protection of the health of the consumer and the prevention of fraud. It was only with the Food and Drugs Act 1938 that these twin themes were consolidated, and then further developed after the Second World War (Act, 1955; Act, 1956; Act, 1984). Such an approach has continued today in the UK with the Food Safety Act 1990 (Act, 1990a; see also MAFF, 1976).

The argument so far has been that, in the Middle Ages, a foodstuff was relatively easy to identify, and hence its quality easy to estimate, since it was usually in its original form (Jukes, 1991). In the twentieth century, food processing of agricultural raw products has created new problems. Given that the products undergo a variety of technical changes before they finally reach the consumer, the real composition of the value unit cannot be clearly identified. It is within this resulting uncertainty that the buyer can be misled by the producer. Consequently, such a source of uncertainty has to be eliminated by the legislative authorities.

These changes of processing methods in agriculture represent a further risk for consumers. Since they must not be neglected, legislation becomes necessary.

Taking into account all these reasons, foodstuffs law has been built up over a time, on a country by country basis, and is of interest to producer, retailer and consumer. Such legislation imposes duties that can be summarized under the four following aspects, namely:

1 Protection of consumer health.
2 Protection from deception and fraud.
3 Producer protection.
4 Integrity of trade.

The central focus of foodstuffs law is to guarantee the health of the consumer. Additionally, however, a very important function has been the standardization and definition of foodstuffs, their production, distribution and sale – particularly at the European level. Only products that comply with these requirements should enter the market and, in so doing, a level playing field is established. This situation ensures a transparency of the price–value relationship for all the products on the market (particularly important with the Single Market), and protects the consumer from deception and fraud. At the same time, foodstuffs law provides the producer with the integrity to trade, and hence engenders consumer confidence.

This historical development of food legislation throughout the EU, and within member states, can today be captured within seven categories (Jukes, 1993). These categories have been classified by the present writer, as shown in Table 1.1.

Food hygiene	Consumer protection	Common processes for control
Hygiene, health and microbiology	Compositional standards	Primary legislation
	Additives	Regulations/statutory instruments
	Contaminants	Enforcement structure
	Processing and packaging	EU legislative dimension
	Labelling	
	Weights and measures	

Table 1.1
Categorization of EU food legislation

The differences and similarities in these categories are considered in this and subsequent chapters, both on an EU basis and within individual member states.

Foodstuffs law and the internal market

The purpose of internal market foodstuffs law is that it attempts to unify foodstuff producers, food service firms and up to 340 million consumers in one market. It is in this respect that the EU Commission seeks to ensure that economic resources are used where they are of greatest need (optimal resource allocation). This situation was not possible before 1992 because of the separation of the market from the consumer, a dislocation that created the burden of additional cost. According to research by the Commission, these expenses of the *non-EU* amounted to 500–1000 million ECU for the European food industry (Cecchini, 1989). The report showed that the removal of trade barriers within the single market would intensify competition, extend trade and cause a structural adaptation at all levels of production and commercialization. The consumer would benefit from comparable prices and products at the same quality levels. Intensified competition would oblige firms to produce at a lower cost, and the consumer would enjoy both lower prices and a greater variety in supply (Cecchini, 1989).

This report has been criticized as it is only based on figures from the seven highly industrialized northern EU countries. It should therefore be regarded with caution. Arguably, the report is biased in a way that suits EU officials who, understandably, wish the single market plan to succeed.

On the positive side, the Cecchini report does give an indication of some of the benefits to be gained from a single internal market. Costs, it is suggested, will be saved through the creation of an internal market with the following effects:

1 The direct savings effect
   - Diminishing the additional costs of export through the elimination of physical barriers, i.e. no bureaucratic procedures at borders, no waiting time at frontiers, reduced transport costs.
   - Reducing the extra costs of transforming production to comply with the regulations of production in the import country. This situation especially relates to national vertical regulations that deal with production methods, raw materials, labelling, packaging etc.
   - The possibility of using cheap raw materials: less rigid regulations of other member states are expected to be applied on the national level of each country.
2 Indirect savings effect
   - With increasing competition between businesses, it will be in the interest of firms to minimize production costs.
   - Competition will eliminate inefficient businesses, which will then be absorbed by more efficient businesses. This savings effect may lead to a reduction in price.

So far, only cost savings have been analysed. To make a judgement on the economic use of the internal market, one issue that needs to be examined is: if the single internal market imposes additional costs, which of these costs will outweigh the savings effect just identified? New costs can arise if, for example, national regulations require additional labelling of goods. Moreover, further costs will arise because firms will require an efficient marketing strategy in order to survive in the emergent fierce competition. It also can be suggested that the quality, and not the quantity, of the marketing is of importance, and therefore additional costs may arise, all of which may have price implications for the consumer.

This approach to analysing costs and benefits in the single market can also be applied to the hospitality industry. A resulting savings effect may arise due to less rigid raw food material regulations, with the consumer basically receiving lower quality but benefiting from low prices. Adding to this debate, it is often suggested that consumers ask for high quality food products, so that in a free market, only producers of high quality goods can survive. This push/pull tendency between price and quality may be an appropriate explanation in times of economic expansion, but might change during a period of recession. In the latter case, the consumer will be price sensitive and will usually tolerate a decrease in quality. It can therefore be questioned whether foodstuffs law should be allowed to endure such fluctuations in the price/quality relationship, and whether it should always set the lowest common denominator in terms of standards (Freidhof, 1991).

In order to achieve integrity of trade within the food industry, there will need to be transparency in the price–value relationship. In ensuring this balance, all products of a similar kind have to be issued to the market under the same legislative benchmarks so that their transparency will be evident to the consumer. It is this specific line of argument that is central to the development of EU food legislation.

EU foodstuffs legislative framework

While a more detailed discussion of EU legislation occurs later in this chapter, at this stage it should be pointed out that the EU Commission classifies its foodstuffs law into two main categories:

1 Horizontal directives.
2 Vertical directives.

All EU Directives have to be translated into national law before they can become effective (the usual timetable being 30 months from adoption).

The horizontal directives deal with aspects that concern all foodstuffs and industry sectors. It is the EU Council of Ministers that ratifies directives, a requirement that is conducive to a harmonization of all national foodstuffs legislation. This stipulation provides legislation concerning all questions regarding health and consumer protection. They refer specifically to additives, hygiene, labelling and nutritional information etc. The issue of food labelling and the caterer is considered in greater detail by other writers (CECG, 1987; Morris, 1991; Clarke, 1993).

Adoption of vertical directives takes a product specific approach, i.e. meat, meat products, milk, milk products and fish. In the case of the principle of mutual acknowledgement, each country of the EU has the obligation, following the *Cassis de Dijon* judgement, to allow sale of an imported product if it has been legally produced and issued in another member state (Anonymous, 1990). On the other hand, with domestic production, the national foodstuffs law is fully applied. An example of this approach can be seen in Germany's beer legislation, where that country's beer has to conform to strict purity criteria, whereas beers imported into Germany do not (Anonymous, 1990).

If imported goods do not comply with product specific regulations, there is a danger of confusion, a situation that can, to some extent, be eliminated by using adequate labelling. It may be seen from this last point that there is a strong relationship between the consumer and the foodstuffs industry. As for the marketing oriented business, knowledge of the needs, wants and characteristics of the consumer is vital to ensure that the four elements of the marketing mix (Product, Price, Promotion, Place) can be effectively applied. For the consumer it is essential to know what effects the common foodstuffs laws have on the market and its products, since demand is directly influenced by both supply and the legislative framework.

The initial approach of the Commission to food law was based on the concept that a national law needed a Community law in order to ensure the free circulation of goods. For many years, Community food legislation pursued the path dictated by this approach, using article 100 of the EEC Treaty which called for unanimity. However, the unanimity rule was not the main obstacle to progress. Although food law in member states had common objectives, the approach and structure were rooted historically in the culinary traditions of member states. The diversity of climate and agriculture in the EU meant that the nutritional needs of the different populations were met in a number of ways and, even in areas having access to the same raw materials, methods of preparation of food varied widely. As labelling was only in its infancy, the interests of consumers and also producers were served by using a food name to inform the consumer by way of specification or recipe. It was inevitable that the ideas of *good beer, good sausages and good bread*, should conflict, in a 'society' as diverse as the Community. Early attempts to legislate were focused on the harmonization of product specifications. They met with little success since they were perceived as a direct assault by bureaucrats on long hallowed traditions. It took some time to understand that the root of the problem lay in the realization that, if recipes were embodied in law, then the point of attack should be on the law not on the food.

In the Communication of 8 November 1985 (EC Commission, 1985a), the Commission stated that the legislative approach followed in the past needed to be revised by drawing a distinction. On the one hand there were matters which, by their very nature, should continue to be the subject of legislation. On the other, were those items whose characteristics were such that they did not need to be regulated. The communication went on to state that it was neither possible nor desirable to confine in a legislative straitjacket the culinary riches of the (twelve) European countries. The Communication from the EC Commission (1985a) argued that it was not a case of applying minimum rules, but of applying the necessary rules more strictly. This division of responsibilities between the Community and the member states contained within the 1985 communication was a direct application of the principle of subsidiarity to food-law-making. In pursuit of this policy, the Commission proposed a number of framework directives dealing with the essential requirements (Gray, 1993).

Consumer protection

The protection of consumers from fraud and deception is ensured when there is no danger that the consumer will confuse two food products because of their similarity, e.g., in packaging and labelling, processes that essentially focus on the origin of food products (Painter, 1991; Anonymous, 1992e; MAFF, 1993a). One approach through EU foodstuffs law to avoid the danger of confusion is the use of adequate labelling, a point addressed in its original directive on the Labelling, Presentation and Advertising of Foodstuffs 1979, as amended. It has to be questioned, however, if this solution is adequate and applicable in order to attain its objectives.

If confusion arises, it is surely because the consumer is either unable or unwilling to identify differences between two similar products. The latter case would result in an attitude that would cause difficulty for the market, partially resolvable, perhaps, through education. Reasons for the former situation might be lack of understanding or perceptual difficulties. Whereas the labelling of additives using E-numbers on food products might be understood by a foodstuffs technologist, it is far less likely to be comprehended by a consumer who, in most cases, does not appreciate or understand their significance, the actual number and often their full names. This situation is problematic for the consumer to make an objective choice, a state of affairs that blurs the boundaries between fraud/deception and knowledge/education. The initial thought that adequate information will suffice to eliminate the danger of confusion is put in serious jeopardy when consumer behaviour is taken into account. The decision to buy is made quickly and allows little room to assimilate information, to analyse it and act accordingly. The decision process is also hindered by difficulties that might arise when confronted with labelling in a language other than the mother tongue, a problem of particular importance in the single market.

In conclusion it can be said that the intention of the EU Commission to eliminate deception and fraud of the consumer regarding food is to be commended. However, in reality, the principles for tackling the situation are inadequate (LACOTS, 1991a; 1991b).

Food Safety

The protection of the health of the consumer through food safety measures is ensured through both horizontal and vertical directives adopted by the EU Council, an example being the Official Control of Foodstuffs Directive (Anderson, 1991). This aspect of food safety legislation will be expanded further in this chapter, with a link being established to the hospitality industry.

Additionally, the Council is advised by an independent Scientific Foodstuffs Committee (CECG, 1991b) and, in this way, bias can be avoided. For instance, a particular piece of foodstuffs legislation supporting national economic interests may not have much in common with health protection, e.g. the regulation that only milk fat should be the fat component of ice cream to support the German milk industry. Hence, a committee that takes into consideration scientific research as a basis for its judgement is an ideal partner for the development of health protection in the internal market.

Each legislative act is only as good as its control, and it can be said that with common foodstuffs law all products in the internal market will have the same level of health protection. It is then up to consumers to choose what products they wish to buy. Being an internal market issue, it is solely the task of the EU authorities to ensure that the health of consumers will be protected irrespective of their decisions (CECG, 1991c).

The trend in traditional purchases from a food retailer, while still important, has to be balanced in foodstuffs law by the fact that more and more meals are taken away from home. In terms of the protection of health, theoretically no difficulties should arise, since naturally all products have to comply with the food safety directives of the EU. Problems concerning deception, fraud and food safety, however, may occur through enforcement and control within individual member states (Eckert, 1991). Another example, within Germany, is the issue of whether consumers are made aware that the beer they are drinking in a restaurant has been brewed according to that country's brewing regulations (*Reinheitsgebot*) or has been imported from other member states.

The Commission has noted within its *free trade of foodstuffs in the community principle* that the issue of adequate labelling can also be applied to restaurants. The information can, for example, be conveyed through labelling items on a menu. One criticism is that this system is not feasible in reality, for reasons of menu space and the complexity of the catering product, points that have been taken into consideration by the UK Government (Anonymous, 1992a). Equally, this approach could lead to information overload and thus irritate the consumer. Conversely, it should be noted that a lack of information often occurs where, due to a restricted budget, ingredients of inferior quality are being used and in such a situation consumers may be willing to trade quality for price.

EU consumers in 2002 are faced with situations of uncertainty, and while they have opportunities to find guidance in foodstuffs laws of the internal market, realistically they cannot be expected to do this. It is more likely that they will prefer domestic products and known brands. National producers and catering retailers will benefit from the realization that a domestic product will usually be preferred to an unknown foreign product, because consumers know what they can expect (sometimes referred to as the halo effect). International producers and retailers will have to intensify their brand policy to compensate for the preference to buy a national product.

Foreign producers will only survive in international markets with an effective usage of the marketing mix and, in particular, their communications policy. This point is particularly pertinent whenever a wide range of products are launched into the market under the same name which used to be reserved for a specific item, for example, cheese from a region other than the area indicated in the name. The political and legal enforcement authorities will have an important new role in ensuring that the consumer is fully informed, not only as to the geographical origin of foodstuffs on the market, but about their composition as well.

Besides the labelling and compositional issues just discussed, 1993/1994 (and subsequently) saw the EU Commission starting to apply EU-wide directives to the subject of food safety.

Developments in European food legislation affecting the hospitality industry during the past 15 years have been determined mostly by the requirements of the Single European Act 1987 (EC Commission, 1986).

While EU legislation provides the broad framework in which member countries must operate, for a number of reasons, different inspection systems for food safety have been in operation in member states. An inspection system tends to be determined by the overall organizational structure of the relevant enforcement authorities and, to this extent, the UK seems to differ considerably from its European partners, a point explored in the following chapters. Issues such as size of inspectorate, number of inspections and effectiveness all seem to vary and impinge on the enforcement process (a high profile issue being the meat enforcement controls on BSE). The question of sanctions against breaches of food legislation and how they are applied can be related back to measuring the effectiveness of the inspectorate. Perhaps one such effectiveness measure would be the number of reported food poisoning outbreaks, an issue that would raise doubts as to how such statistics are gathered and categorized. These and other areas will be explored, along with a study of both food legislation and enforcement within a number of the EU's member states, in Chapters 2 and 3. The focus of this chapter, by contrast, is on the broader EU picture.

With the implementation of the internal market (1 January 1993), national foodstuff laws are now subject to EU-wide regulation. The first steps in the direction of this essentially consumerist policy took place in 1973, with the establishment of an EU department for environmental and consumer protection. This department was later transformed into the Consulting Consumer Council (CCC) with the mandate to represent the consumer's interests at the EU (Anonymous, 1990). Its first programme was submitted in 1975, and the need to promote five issues was identified:

- The right to protection of health and security.
- The right to protection of economic interests.
- The right to compensation.
- The right to instruction and enlightenment.
- The right to representation.

This programme was continued in 1981, 1983 and 1984. The positive consequences of this consumer-oriented policy clearly find expression in a number of guidelines, e.g. in aspects of food, cosmetics, medicine, advertising and product liability. Many of these guidelines have already been incorporated into national law. In 1979 and in the 1980s, for example, the duty of labelling food was introduced. However, it has to be pointed out that the evolution of consumer-oriented policies, as identified in the Second Consumer Programme of 1981, progressed very slowly.

The possibilities for consumer associations to advance consumer-oriented policies at a European level are limited. Since 1973, the existing Consumer Consulting Council (CCC) has had the task of providing statements on EU draft directives. It can also issue statements on its own initiative. Since late 1989, this Council was given a new statute, which brought about its renaming as the Consumer Consultative Council (Conseil Consultatif des Consommateurs). It is composed of 39 members appointed by the EU Commission. There are six experts and four representatives from each of the four major consumer organizations, the BEUC (European Consumer Association), COFACE (EU Committee of Family Association), Euro Coop (European Cooperation of Consumer Associations) and the EGB (European Union Association). Additionally, there are 17 representatives of national consumer organizations, i.e. two from Germany, Spain, France, Italy, Great Britain, and one from Belgium, Denmark, Greece, Luxembourg, Ireland, the Netherlands and Portugal.

Development of EU food legislation

In the context of food safety, the harmonization process has taken two directions, namely: horizontal measures across a wide range of foods and industry sectors, and vertical measures applying to specific food categories (Fallows, 1991). Within the European Community, the mid 1980s saw the establishment of five framework directives (Saunders, 1991), which were introduced on a range of food matters (EC Commission, 1985a). These directives included the following three main ones of relevance to the hospitality industry:

1 Official Control of Foodstuffs Directive (EC Commission, 1989a)
2 Materials in Contact with Food Directive (EC Commission, 1989b)
3 Food Labelling Directive (EC Commission, 1979)

thus establishing general principles and controls.

While the issue of labelling has already been discussed, it is important to set the topic within an overall EU framework. Since 1985, work has progressed on some of the *daughter directives* under this approach. Such directives have generally taken a vertical, or product specific approach, and have governed such areas as: game meat (EC Commission, 1991a), fresh meat (EC Commission, 1991c), poultry (EC Commission, 1971a), meat products (EC Commission, 1977), fish (EC Commission, 1991d), milk (EC Commission, 1971b), along with many others, and have been, or are gradually being, adopted by the European Union (EC Commission, 1962, 1977, 1991b). What these directives are essentially doing is introducing rules into the marketplace, rules that are supplemented by decisions in the European Court (Roberts, 1991).

Another key issue identified within these directives is seen in Article 13 of the Official Control of Foodstuffs (Anderson, 1991). This article focuses on the system of education for food control officers, and identifies the requirement to define the number of officers and their competence. Also in need of consideration is equivalence of enforcement and the training needs of officials. This matter has already been addressed in the UK. With all such EU directives, legislation is required at the national level in order to bring them into force in each member state.

In addition to the five main framework directives established in the 1980s, a range of food measures was identified as having priorities towards the end of the 1980s. These measures are being introduced gradually, and cover such subjects as labelling (EC Commission, 1990a), additives (EC Commission, 1989c), food hygiene (EC Commission, 1991b, 1993a) and food quality (EC Commission, 1993b). Indeed, with such an interest in food issues, it is perhaps only a matter of time before a community food inspectorate will be created (Painter, 1991).

Consumer confidence and the confidence of the hospitality industry is key to the success of the sector in Europe and in the global marketplace. However, many of the concerns within the Community arise because there have been a number of high profile food safety crises over recent years. The BSE crisis highlighted, in particular, that food safety issues transcend borders and need Community-wide public health responses. Indeed, the 2001 foot and mouth disease crisis in the UK, even though it was not a public health issue, again brought into sharp relief the need for coordinated and concerted action to address the animal health and economic issues involved. Everyone within the community has a role to play in the drive towards higher food safety standards, and better production methods, thereby ensuring higher quality foodstuffs.

Indeed, these unprecedented waves of public concern have highlighted the need for all those involved in producing, manufacturing or supplying food, on the one hand, and the official bodies responsible for regulating and controlling food safety standards on the other, to play their part in ensuring that the highest standards are maintained. A safe food chain from farm to fork, correctly regulated and effectively controlled, is the road to building this confidence. Hospitality businesses have their role to play in this regard, as ultimately it is the responsibility of every business to ensure the safety of the foods they produce, manufacture or sell.

Throughout Europe, the Commission is committed to ensuring that consumers have access to the safest possible food supply. Its focus is to establish a comprehensive legal framework with effective and open organizational structures so that it can rebuild the fragile confidence in the food supply. Food safety has to be the driving force in the regulation of the food supply. In addition, its legislation must be modern and flexible enough to regulate a highly technologically advanced European food and hospitality industry while at the same time provide sufficient safeguards in smaller more traditional food businesses. Not only does it have to consider the food law itself but also it needs to ensure that its procedures are efficient. For example, where it has approval mechanisms for products, the scientific assessments must be carried out thoroughly and comprehensively, and without undue delay. Where food safety is assured, the community must not needlessly block industrial innovation, through over-bureaucratic requirements.

The Commission's White Paper on Food Safety was published during 2000. Originally heralded in the White Paper was the Commission's proposal for a regulation laying down the general principles and requirements of food law and establishing a European Food Authority as the cornerstone of its overall strategy. This proposal was subject to scrutiny in the European Parliament and in the Council during 2000–2001, with great progress made towards political agreement on this vital piece of legislation. The European Council in Stockholm, 2001 requested that the Food Authority be up and running from 2002 an objective that was achieved. Rather than go into the detail, it is important to illustrate some of the major concerns and reasoning in putting forward such a far-reaching proposal, which the Commission adopted on 8 November 2000.

First, there is a need to include within a single regulation the principles of food law, the basic necessity for food law to be developed following the principles of risk analysis and to provide the organizational structures and procedures to deliver this. The proposed regulation therefore not only establishes the general principles of food law but also proposes the establishment of the European Food Authority which will be responsible for ensuring that the scientific risk assessment, part of the overall risk analysis process, is carried out to the highest world standards. When Europe decides to establish a Food Authority, this Authority should represent one of the elements of the wider food safety policy, which Europe will want to make more effective, more transparent and more coherent.

Second, the proposal establishes the basic principles that food law must provide a high level of health protection and that only safe food may be placed on the market. Within this principle there are also responsibilities, that is, that the primary responsibility for safe food rests with industry, producers and suppliers, and it is the responsibility of the competent authorities in the member states to ensure that food legislation is complied with. This is achieved through effective enforcement controls at all points in the chain from farm to fork, including in animal feed manufacturing establishments.

Third, recent food safety problems have shown the need for comprehensive traceability of food along the food production chain. The proposed regulation will make it mandatory for businesses to have in place systems to trace at least from whom they have purchased foods and to whom they have supplied them.

Fourth, to increase consistency and legal security, clear definitions are proposed including those for 'a foodstuff' and 'placing on the market'. In the proposal, the precautionary principle is for the first time included in a legislative act regarding food, with an attempt to fix a frame to give some clear definition of what is this precautionary principle. It is a management tool but it should be used within certain well-defined limits. In short, the precautionary principle cannot be used as a political expedient or a disguised distortion to trade. If the public cannot understand the reasoning behind a proposal then how can we expect them to have confidence in the system making such proposals or the legitimacy of the basis for them? The only way to face the controversy surrounding many matters relating to food law and particularly in relation to such innovative matters as biotechnology applied to food is to promote an open-minded and balanced dialogue between all stakeholders – scientists, industry, farmers and consumers – and by ensuring maximum transparency in the risk/benefit assessments.

Furthermore, it is important to accept and respect the consumer's right to have clear information in order to take informed decisions on which products they want to buy. Compromising on food safety is not a way for a farm or a company to reduce costs.

It is actually a very dangerous path, not only for consumers, but also for the farm or company itself and for the whole sector involved.

In an industry worth 535 billion Euros annually in the European Union, that is about 15 per cent of total manufacturing output, even a slight dip in confidence can have significant effects. Between the agri-food sector and the farming sector, there are about 10 million employees in Europe. High levels of confidence are necessary to boost job numbers and competitiveness. Confidence and predictability are also essential elements to boost trade.

The public's demands and expectations have never been higher and confidence is very fragile. To this end, the White Paper proposal also establishes the European Food Authority, which will be based on the principles of independence, scientific excellence, transparency and accessibility. The 'Authority' should be 'authoritative', in that it should be seen as the European reference in terms of scientific assessment, the European voice that should be heard by all member states. The European Food Authority will provide an authoritative body of expertise to the European food safety system. It will become the foremost scientific body of expertise on food safety and will be responsible for the scientific opinions on which the community bases legislative proposals.

The Authority will have a wide remit and, in parallel with the general principles of food law, will also cover all scientific matters that may have a direct or indirect effect on the safety of the food supply. It will cover all stages of production and supply, from the level of primary production, including assessing the safety of animal feeds, right through to the supply of food to consumers.

The second important task of this Food Authority will be to give advice on technical issues; such tasks may include in particular the establishment or evaluation of technical criteria, the development of technical guidelines or guides to good practice. Again, this is work to be developed in common using existing expertise in Europe.

The third important task of this Food Authority is the collection of data. There is an enormous amount of data in Europe, of all kinds. The Commission does not always have the resources to compile, to analyse and to compare in order to have a tool for better legislation. The objective will be a better exploitation of data, which already exist. By better exploiting the information, the food authority could better identify possible emerging risks, and draw the attention of policy-makers before the problem arises.

Finally, the European Food Authority will be a major risk communicator providing information on food safety to the general public, and scientific opinions and risk assessments to those responsible for proposing food law in the European Commission. It will be separate from the European Commission, being a legal entity in its own right, and have its own budget. The vision is that the Authority will be an automatic first port of call on all questions relating to food safety. This is a task that has not always been well understood, because of the fear that by giving away this competence will produce an independent body with a different message to the one issued by European legislators. To be clear, the Authority will have the mission to communicate in the field of its competence, i.e. in the scientific area. It will try to make European consumers understand what is science and to have more confidence in science. For example now, with the BSE crisis, many have different messages about the risks. By having a strong voice, which will say what is the risk, it is possible to avoid disproportionate reactions, which are at times exaggerated.

The Authority will have a Director, and a Management Board. There will also be an Advisory Forum where the member states' national agencies or analogous bodies will have a seat. This will be the instrument by which the community will ensure that the Authority works in collaboration with national agencies. It will oblige national authorities to work together with the Food Authority. And finally, it will have a Scientific Committee with a coordinating role and scientific panels.

These far-reaching proposals in the White Paper are the cornerstones of a new food safety policy, but another very important challenge for the EU is food quality. European consumers will settle for no less than safe food – and they are right. But they expect the food that they eat and feed to their children to be more than just safe. Consumers expect food to meet their nutritional needs, to be wholesome and tasty. They expect to be able to choose amongst a wide variety of foods. They expect their food to be produced and processed in accordance with good farming practices, with greater respect for the environment and for the welfare of animals. And they expect to be informed, in a precise and accurate manner, about the composition, the nutritional value, the durability, the origin and, in certain cases, the method of production of the food offered to them. This all means that food safety is an intrinsic element of food quality.

EU food hygiene legislation and the hospitality industry

One significant directive that has implications for the hospitality industry is the Directive on the Hygiene of Foodstuffs (93/43/EEC), usually referred to as the General Food Hygiene Directive. It was adopted in June 1993 by the EU, and member states had 30 months in which to introduce its requirements into national legislation.

It was finally adopted and published in the EU Official Journal in June 1993 (EC Commission, 1993a). Directorate-General III is responsible for this internal market and issued this horizontal directive under Article 100A of the Treaty of Rome. It was therefore subject to qualified majority voting. The nature of this horizontal directive is that it is wide-ranging in content, and covers *all* sectors of the food industry. The final stages of this draft directive's legislative process, i.e. its second reading in the EU Parliament, took place in April 1993. It was adopted 2 months later.

This Food Hygiene Directive has had wide-ranging implications for the hospitality industry. The often used sector by sector approach, covered by vertical directives, focusing on some foods or stages in the food chain, has created inconsistencies. This directive applies to all food products from the farm gate to the consumer. In taking this horizontal approach, reference is made to the principles of Hazard Analysis Critical Control Point (HACCP). Such principles recognize that what is applicable to manufacturing and cook–chill methods and products, needs modification for smaller catering outlets. It is Article 3 of the Directive which requires all stages of production to be carried out hygienically, with hazard assessment and control procedures being implemented by food business operators to ensure that adequate food safety is obtained (Fogden, 1995a, 1995b). The control procedures must be developed and applied in accordance with the principles used to develop the HACCP system, although that system is not required to be employed, nor will such a formal approach be appropriate or necessary to ensure hygiene in most food businesses. A related issue to HACCP is the importance of EN 29000, the European equivalent of the ISO9000 series. Most of the European food industry has not chosen such a system, and its influence in the hospitality industry is minimal (Gorny, 1992). This lack of enthusiasm is evident, despite the fact that the Directive allows member states to recommend its use.

Article 3 (3) requires specific annexed positions to be met and implements a very broad protection, following a precedent found to work effectively in British legislation, using words to the effect that 'actions should be taken against any contamination likely to render the food unfit for human consumption, injurious to health or contaminated in such a way that it would be unreasonable to expect it to be consumed in that state' (EC Commission, 1993a). Chapter IX of the annex continues this theme by requiring *appropriate* temperature controls to be implemented to guard against microbiological hazards and the formation of toxins. Fogden (1995b) comments that pragmatic but safe regulatory provisions are generally more welcome than a rigid approach. However, the problem is that they may not be easy to enforce.

Another area of interest within the Directive is the requirement that member states encourage the development of *Guides to Good Hygiene Practice* that may be used voluntarily by food businesses as a guide to compliance. This requirement could (the Directive recognizes) be the precursor for developing European-wide Codes if agreement is reached and coordinated by the European standards-making body – Community European Normalization (CEN). What the Directive in actuality is proposing is a hierarchy of codes at national and European levels within the general framework of the Codex document *General Principles of Food Hygiene* (Codex, 1985). Such codes could, by default, effectively become law, as they will probably be regarded by enforcement authorities as acceptable and routine ways of achieving food hygiene standards.

Apart from a reference to food hygiene training within the Directive's annex, the Directive also prompts an interesting question about Europe-wide temperature control regulations. While the horizontal directive does not specify temperatures, the vertical directives (already referred to) are often quite specific on this issue. These inconsistencies between the vertical and horizontal approach to EU legislation, along with differences throughout the EU and pressures from the food industry, led to a review of temperature controls (DOH, 1993c, 1993d, 1993e, 1993f). The UK and the Netherlands have chosen to go it alone in introducing new temperature regulations. It remains to be seen whether these regulations will be superseded at the EU level.

Food businesses are put under varying obligations in each of the directives just discussed. They are intended to give assurances that the foods they produce are processed hygienically and in accordance with the provisions made in the relevant legislation, with sufficient monitoring being undertaken to assure this conformity. These provisions may be part of, or accompany, critical control point systems. In these and other directives, operators are placed under duties generally or specifically, or as an explicit or implied condition of approval of the premises and activities therein. The ultimate responsibility for the safety aspects of food under their control always lies with operators, not with the competent authority that monitors and permits those activities. The authority's responsibility resides in directly ensuring that public health is not put at risk, and only indirectly in the practical aspects of the control measures effected in individual premises to achieve this outcome. However, this distinction is subtle and there is a very large overlap of interest.

Common food law: problems and issues

The food/hospitality industry is one of the few sectors that directly affects all citizens of the Union, and the risk is that directives adopted through qualified majority voting may be adjusted to the lowest common denominator. Consequently, the quality and safety of food will be affected.

It can also be observed that the transformation of EU directives into national legislation is accorded different priority levels within each member state. While the nature of the Union is that common interests have to be taken into consideration, unnecessary directives have to be omitted and necessary directives have to be improved. The central questions in this point are whether or not a directive is necessary for a particular country, and whether or not the concept of subsidiarity applies. When assessing the success of EU food policy, the legislator needs to think in terms of *positive* or *negative* harmonization. Negative harmonization occurs if European changes cause a significant disadvantage or decline in existing standards. Examples of positive harmonization are highlighted below.

One area of common food law regarded as positive harmonization, which also has implications for the protection of health, is the topic of additives. When processing food, a variety of additives are used, and four reasons can be identified:

- to protect the nutritional value of food;
- to improve the consistency of food;
- to guarantee the safety of food, i.e. to prevent the growth of micro-organisms; and
- to improve the flavour, colour and taste of food.

In this respect, food additives serve both the consumer's and the producer's interest. The life of food can be extended, and therefore the production costs of food can be minimized. Additionally, the consumer can profit from a lower price and the longer durability of food. However, an absolute guarantee that food additives, in combination with other ingredients, are harmless cannot be given. This topic requires intensive control of the regulations dealing with the application and admission of such additives into the food chain.

Directives have already been adopted that control the quantity, labelling and purpose of the additives. It is, however, possible that certain additives that are not permitted in a particular member state may be imported. Therefore, an EU Directive passed in 1988 directs the use of additives for the internal market. Additives will only be admitted if:

- their use does not affect health;
- a technological need can be proved;
- the objective aimed at cannot be reached without the use of certain additives; and
- the information provided to the consumer has to be scientifically confirmed.

Additionally, maximum quantities, scope of application and purity criteria are regulated within the EU. The harmonization of the directive on additives is seen as necessary to guarantee a free trade of food. Products that do not comply with one country's regulation may comply with that of another. They can therefore be imported, as long as a danger to health cannot be proved.

The issues just discussed concerning additives play an important role in the protection of the customer and any solution should not be to find a compromise at the lowest level, but to act in the interest of the consumer's health.

Concerning the internal market, clear labelling will minimize deception of the consumer and, at the same time, achieve competition based on quality and consumer protection. Only with clear labelling of all products has the consumer the opportunity to choose the right product. To achieve an objective comparison, the consumer has to be informed of all ingredients, their composition and quantity. This information applies to national products as well as to imported goods. It is also essential to be informed about the country of origin. The naming of the packager is not sufficient.

However, even though the over-informed consumer is often irritated by a surfeit of information, only a clearly regulated labelling policy can assist in achieving maximum consumer protection.

Food labelling has also become a central task for the internal market. The aim in this respect is to allow the consumer to identify all supplied products, to make an appropriate choice and to use the products satisfactorily.

To tackle one of the main causes of death within the Union – heart disease – distinctive labelling of some components, such as energy, fat, sugar and salt is required on all foods. The European guidelines, established in 1990, provide for only voluntary labelling in a standard mandatory format in case a nutritional claim is made. If a product has nutrient characteristics, such as energy, fat, proteins or low sodium, the labelling in most cases must be presented in the required format.

Future trends in harmonization

A clear distinction can be drawn between two principal types of legislated controls on the hygienic production of food. Traditionally, but only for the production of foodstuffs of animal origin, prescriptive requirements have been laid down in considerable detail to ensure that all stages are closely regulated. This listing resulted in a wealth of provisions that were not always appropriate, or necessary, in particular establishments and, to this extent, can be considered as being disproportionate or over-regulatory. Steps should be taken to eliminate such excesses, where practicable. More recently, it has become acceptable to rely on the operators of businesses, approved and monitored appropriately by the competent authority, and to provide adequate hygiene controls within a framework of varying complexity, often based on critical control points. Almost inevitably at this early stage in the development of this type of control system, member states have felt obliged to supplement its sophisticated elements with a limited number of basic obligations. Thus, limited, detailed rules are to be found connected to provisions based on generalities, routine monitoring is associated with irregular auditing, and flexibility is surrounded by historic rigidity. The next generation, it is hoped, will be able to rely on a greater degree of audited self-regulation and less on specific fundamental discipline. As developments continue, the opportunity must be taken at each phase to challenge every rule, and to eliminate provisions that can be safely left to be applied flexibly by responsible businesses, while ensuring that the process can be monitored and controlled by the competent authority.

Within this context, it is suggested that, while there is a useful trend towards adopting risk assessment and monitoring controls based on critical control point techniques, uniformity could be improved. A reference in individual directives to common provisions would achieve this goal. Also, ensuring safety in production leads on naturally to the next stage – controls on finished products (Fogden, 1995b).

Many of the hygiene controls on finished products are similar in principle, suggesting that common basic legislative provisions should be achievable, although there are certainly differences in detail and presentation. In general, foodstuffs are required to be handled, stored and transported hygienically, and with due attention to the maintenance of temperature and time controls. Some of the latter are introduced definitively into the legislation, while others are to be established by the person responsible (manager) for the food and/or the manufacturer. In some cases, restrictions are applied to the means by which such temperatures must be achieved, but generally cooling must be performed as quickly as is reasonably practicable. The diversity of the temperature maxima indicates, no doubt, that the hygiene circumstances resulting from the potential for microbial activity vary significantly between food types. Perhaps more correctly, such diversity suggests that measures have been introduced in this way for reasons other than technical need. It would be an exaggeration to imply that these maxima have been adopted arbitrarily, but certainly several of them would be difficult to justify in the context of a logical hygiene policy based on scientific evidence. The relationship of these maxima to time controls is not clear sometimes, and these factors should ordinarily be considered together. It may also be questioned whether it would not be more appropriate in some, if not all cases, to apply more flexible risk-based systems.

As has already been noted, the latest legislation has an overall tendency to introduce requirements leading to the introduction and implementation of appropriate risk assessment and control procedures. These criteria are generally intended to be developed taking the principles of the HACCP system into consideration, although this stipulation does not always include the documentation procedures of that system. This observation applies most notably in the case of the general hygiene directive, where it can be argued most strongly that a legislated necessity for the application of rigid and formal risk assessment procedures would be disproportionate to the desired outcome.

In summary, numerous differences are to be found, with complex circumstances existing sometimes at the interfaces between provisions in the vertical directives and those in the horizontal rules. However, in general, the principles that are applied are shared; it is the precise legislative form or the practical detail that varies.

With the completion of the internal market, the protection and the health of the consumer should have the highest priority, with all other achievements subordinated to this principle. In order to achieve this aim, consumer representatives have to uphold the following issues:

- Clear and distinctive labelling of food.
- Sufficient identification of products with non-corresponding ingredients from other member states and naming of the country of origin.
- EU-unified quality assurance of basic food supplies and processed foods.
- Encouragement of environmentally friendly production and processing of food.
- Better organization, standardization, intensification of national and Europe-wide food supervision.
- Guaranteed product security by the manufacturers of food.
- Introduction of EU-wide maximum quantity of contaminants.

The protection of the health of consumers is already provided by various EU directives, but clearly these regulations can only be deemed successful if they are followed. Hormones found in meat, or deteriorated ingredients in convenience food, can only be investigated with an effective supervision of food. However, variations in laboratory testing methods, different educational systems and language problems complicate this Europe-wide cooperation. Furthermore, the legal action of the public authorities differs significantly throughout member states. This state of affairs has also been recognized by the EU. The purpose of directives emanating from Brussels is to establish corresponding regulations for all member states. Random tests will need to be carried out by all member states at all levels, i.e. from the producer to the consumer, and should cover raw materials, additives and technical resources, as well as internal reports of the businesses, recipes, and hygiene training of staff.

The opening of the trade barriers in 1993 leaves many consumers uncertain about food and essential commodities that have been imported without the necessary national control. The consumer has to rely on the controls of the producing country, and therefore a reliable basis between the member states has to be developed. This interest has occurred at the same time as intensified publicity in the field of food supervision. Food supervision reports have to be published by the authorities responsible for these controls. Additionally, the EU Commission and the governments of all member states will need to bring their food supervision up to an EU-wide level. This requirement implies that the staff dealing with these controls should have the same level of education, standardized analysing methods and regulations dealing with best laboratory practice.

An effective food supervision programme is an essential requirement for a future internal market with all its implications regarding an enlarged supply of food products.

Summary

The initial approach of the EU Commission to food law was based on the concept that a national law needed a Community law to ensure the free circulation of goods. For many years, Community food legislation pursued a path dictated by this approach, using Article 100 of the EEC Treaty which called for unanimity. However, the unanimity rule was not the main obstacle to progress. Although food law in member states had common objectives, its approach and structure were rooted historically in the culinary and cultural traditions of member states. The diversity of climate and agriculture in the EU meant that the nutritional needs of a given population were met in a variety of ways and, even in areas having access to the same raw materials, methods of preparation of food varied widely. As labelling was only in its infancy, the interests of consumers and also producers were served by using a food name or denomination based on these traditions. This method both informed the consumer and legally reserved the name for a particular specification or recipe. While early attempts to legislate were focused on the harmonization of product specifications, they met with little success. It took some time to understand that the root of the problem lay in the fact that, if recipes were embodied in law, the point of attack should be on the law not on the food.

It was for this reason that there was a shift away from product-specific directives towards general horizontal directives, an example being the EC Directive on the Hygiene of Foodstuffs 1993.

The problems of consistent enforcement of this directive are ongoing throughout the EU, and can be related to the structure of the national authorities – matters that are considered in the following two chapters.

These are the differences in enforcement that make it difficult to introduce EU directives into national legislation. It could be argued that there is a need for a transparent and simpler EU food policy with a preference for horizontal legislation and only limited vertical legislation. Accordingly, it is argued that deregulation and subsidiarity should be the leading principles, in such a way that the EU regulates the main issues clearly and with one voice, and that member states are responsible for the application and more detailed provisions. Another aspect is the use of instruments, regulations and directives. One view is that regulations should be considered more often, first, because a regulation does not need to be transposed into national law, and second, because a regulation promotes a more unified application of community rules in the EU, especially where community legislation does not leave any discretionary power to member states.

In considering the implementation of food law, its enforcement and effects on both the caterer and the consumer, an obvious first step is to consider the legislative environment. This analysis of legislation can be considered at two levels, namely the EU and its member states. This chapter has considered the need for foodstuffs legislation. Both vertical and horizontal EU directives were discussed and their relevance to the hospitality industry was highlighted. Implications for the consumer within the legislative environment were also explored.

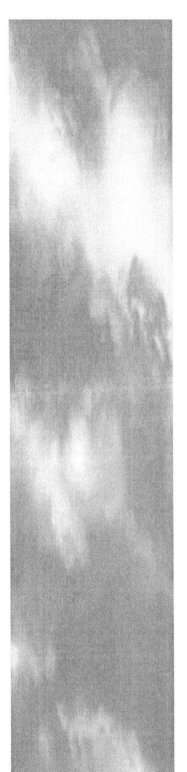

Food legislation and enforcement in EU member states

The framework and reasons for EU foodstuffs legislation has been discussed in Chapter 1. The focus in this chapter is on how the related literature views existing food legislation and enforcement in member states. The countries considered here are the United Kingdom, Germany, France, Denmark and the Netherlands. The purpose for choosing these countries is that they are key players in influencing the development of food safety within the Community. It will also become self-evident that each country approaches the subjects of food safety, consumer protection and enforcement in different ways, while at the same time seeking to ensure the provision of safe food. Further discussion of these issues as applied in practice is presented in Chapter 3.

The United Kingdom

Background

In the UK, the 1980s witnessed a rising trend in the number of reported food poisoning cases, with evidence from the Communicable Disease Surveillance Centre suggesting that food poisoning caused by caterers was greater than in any other sector of the food industry (Shepard *et al.*, 1990). Industry views during this period (Crawford, 1987) revealed apparent weaknesses within the legislation of the day. The topic of food hygiene training, while generating much discussion within the wider hospitality sector, is not new to industry specialists, and was identified by the UK government in the mid 1980s as an area that needed attention.

Present day issues, such as registration of food premises and the powers of environmental health officers, were also debated around that time, along with the need to bring statutory defences into line with other consumer protection legislation, i.e. section 24, Trades Descriptions Act 1968 – *the due diligence defence* (Act, 1968). It was, however, the wider political and media environment that provided the impetus for government to act. Concern over a minister's (Edwina Currie) comments on Salmonella in eggs (Sherman, 1988), Listeria contamination of chilled foods (in particular unpasteurised soft cheeses and pâté), meat products and BSE, and an outbreak of botulism associated with hazelnut yoghurt, created the tense atmosphere within which the government issued its White Paper *Food Safety: Protecting the Consumer* (MAFF, 1989). Soon after, the Food Safety Act 1990 was passed (Aston and Tiffney, 1993; Jukes, 1988a, 1988b, 1989, 1991).

The rise in incidents of food poisoning since the 1990 Act must be regarded as a legitimate cause for consumer concern. While the figures show that there has been an increase in food poisoning, alternatively this trend could be due to a greater level of reporting by GPs or even the growing popularity of eating out. Consequently, a clear reason for the escalation in food poisoning has not been determined. Notwithstanding this confusion, the Steering Group on the Microbiological Safety of Food, established since the Richmond Committee's Report on the Microbiological Safety of Food (1989), conducted a study during the period 1994/95 in order to establish how many people visited their doctors on a food-related complaint (Jukes, 1993).

In the UK, enforcement of health and hygiene issues is generally undertaken by environmental health officers (EHOs) and fraudulent trading practices are the concern of trading standards officers (TSOs). This division is discussed in greater detail within the Code of Practice No. 1 issued under section 40 of the Food Safety Act 1990 (Code of Practice, 1990a). The work of both the TSO and EHO was considered within the Ministry of Agriculture Fisheries and Food's (MAFF) Food Safety Directorate (FSD) and its monthly bulletin (FSD, 1993a; FSD, 1993b), a situation which changed in April 1999 with the establishment of the *Food Standards Agency* (MAFF, 1998). The appointment of such *authorised officers* is a statutory requirement under the Food Safety Act 1990 s.5. Specialist advice is available from the Public Analyst and the Laboratory of the Government Chemist (FSD, 1993c,

1993d, 1993e; Jukes, 1988b). Regulations prescribing the qualifications of these specialists have been enacted (Regulation, 1990a).

Much of the legislation generated by either the EU or Whitehall, and directed at the hospitality, catering or food-service industries, overlaps with the wider food industry, and this overlap is reflected in the duties of both EHOs and TSOs. The link with EU legislation is contained within section 7 of the Food Safety Act 1990. This section empowers ministers to make regulations for the implementation of EU directives.

Principal legislation

The Food Safety Act 1990

Despite the steady stream of criticisms, some misinformed (Booker, 1993; Toner, 1993), directed at one or two seemingly overzealous environmental health officers, the Food Safety Act 1990 has generally been regarded as focusing caterers' minds on their central responsibility to provide safe food and, in that sense, it has created a positive awareness of food safety issues.

In terms of definition (Act, 1990a: ss.1 and 2), most *offences* within the Act refer to sale or supply, possession for sale, offer or exposure for sale and advertisement for sale. The term *business* is also defined to include any undertaking or activity carried out by a public or local authority, with or without profit. The Act now extends to Crown premises. *Food* is defined as including drink, as well as articles and substances of no nutritional value that are used for human consumption. Following on from this definition, the term *human consumption* is important, as the Act is concerned with food that has been sold or is intended for sale. It encompasses food during preparation and food ingredients.

The Act repealed most of the Food Act 1984 and introduces the idea of a food safety requirement (Act, 1984). It encompasses requirements as to food rendered injurious to human health and food that is unfit for human consumption, and speaks of a new principle of contaminated food (Act, 1990a: s.8). Section 8 creates the umbrella offence of selling food that does not comply with food safety requirements and is similar to the general requirement of the Consumer Protection Act 1987 (Act, 1987). The term 'unfitness' in this context brings within the offence most occurrences that might deter the ordinary consumer from eating a food (*David Grieg* v. *Goldfinch*, 1961). The wide application of section 14 (basic to the successful control of food) is evident; offences of substance or quality may be an alternative to proceedings under section 8. One key element in section 14 is sale, referring to retail sale. This aspect explains why authorized officers purchase goods before commencing sampling procedures, an approach which contrasts with that of some European countries.

Section 15 of the Act covers the offence of selling or displaying food with a label that is false, or one that is likely to mislead as to the nature, substance or quality of the food in question. Section 1 of the Trades Descriptions Act 1968 (Act, 1968) is frequently used as an alternative to proceedings under this section. For instance, to describe a menu item as vegetarian, when clearly it has a meat ingredient within it, would result in prosecution under this section. Any false or misleading statement as to food for human consumption, however given, is an offence. There is within this section a difference between 'false' and 'likely to mislead', the former being a stronger expression, and hence more difficult to prove. In the latter case, it is possible to be factually correct and still mislead. An example is 'Scottish Smoked Salmon' and 'Smoked Scottish Salmon'. The latter product comes from Scotland while the former is only smoked there. The offences contained within sections 14 and 15 are mainly consumer protection offences that are enforced by Trading Standards Officers in the UK.

Besides the sometimes high level of fines (Anonymous, 1992a; 1992b), authorized officers have a range of enforcement powers contained within sections 9, 10, 11 and 12 of the Act. These powers cover such subjects as inspection and seizure of suspected food, improvement notices, prohibition notices and emergency prohibition notices. If food fails to comply with food safety requirements (section 9), it may be seized with the issue of a prescribed notice (Regulation, 1990b). Referral to a Justice of the Peace is normally within two days of seizure (Code of Practice No. 4, 1990b). The purpose of improvement notices, as detailed in section 10 of the Act, is to deal with situations where there is a breach of the relevant regulations (Code of Practice No. 6, 1990d). Improvement notices can be issued against processes, equipment or treatments, and are modelled on section 21 of the Health and Safety at Work Act 1974 (Act, 1974a). Examples of circumstances where use of an improvement notice would be appropriate are considered in Code of Practice No. 5 (Code of Practice, 1990c). The contents and nature are to be in the prescribed form (Regulation, 1991a), and a person who is aggrieved may appeal to the Magistrates Court under section 37 of the Act.

Under section 11 of the Act, the courts are empowered to make prohibition orders of two classes. The court, before which the proprietor has been convicted, can prohibit the use of premises, processes or equipment, if it is satisfied that the health risk condition is fulfilled regarding that business. Also, the courts under this section have the power to prohibit any proprietor or manager from participating in the management of a food business.

In the case of emergency prohibition notices (section 12 of the Act), the authorized officer has the power in certain circumstances to close a business immediately and confirm that notice, within three days, by an order before a magistrates court. In these circumstances the health risk condition has to be imminent (not immediate), although no definition is available as to what precisely is meant by the term.

One continuing problem of enforcement is that of consistency in interpretation throughout the UK. Attempts have been made to resolve this difficulty through the issue of section 40 codes of practice (under the Food Safety Act 1990), which can be regarded as guides to enforcement practices; 21 so far have been issued. Authorized Officers are required to have regard to these codes and ministers are empowered to direct food authorities to take specific steps to comply with a code through mandamus (Act, 1990a: s.42). The revision of Codes of Practice 5 and 9 (DOH, 1993a) emphasizes the distinction between *good hygienic practice* and a *legal requirement* which aids this consistency approach. In particular, the revision of code of practice No. 9, Food Hygiene Inspections, reflects the requirements of the EC Directive on the Hygiene of Foodstuffs, a point discussed in the previous chapter (EC Commission, 1991b; Economic and Social Committee, 1992; EC Commission, 1992b; EC Presidency, 1992; European Parliament, 1992). The mission of the Local Authority Coordinating Body on Trading Standards (LACOTS, 1990), the coordinator of the *Home Authority principle*, will also promote consistency and uniformity in interpretation (FSD, 1993a; IEHO, 1992). During January 1996 a draft copy of Code of Practice No. 10, *Enforcement of the Temperature Control Requirements of Food Hygiene Regulations*, was issued for comment (DOH, 1996). It was noted by the Department of Health that a review of all codes of practice issued under the Food Safety Act 1990 was under consideration. It is possible that this general review will result in further changes to Code of Practice No. 10.

The seriousness with which the courts view the enforcement of food safety legislation can be judged, to some extent, by the level of fines imposed on catering premises. Penalties in excess of £10,000 are not uncommon, with the record to date being some £44,000 imposed on a take-away catering outlet (later reduced on appeal to the Crown Court) (Anonymous, 1992b; Anonymous, 1992c). Even when offences are not proven, as in the case of a hamburger outlet in Preston after the outbreak of food poisoning caused by *E. coli* (FSD, 1993e), the resultant bad publicity (in that particular incident) inevitably focused the minds of catering managers.

The Food Safety Act 1990 contains enabling powers throughout, linked with the main provisions to which they relate. The main enabling powers are contained in sections 16–19 of the Act. Regulations already issued cover such topics as the registration of food premises (Regulation, 1991b) and food irradiation (Regulation, 1990c,e). Section 16 of the Act gives powers to issue regulations on food hygiene training. The 1992–1997 Conservative government committed itself to the wording regarding training included within the EC Directive on the Hygiene of Foodstuffs (DOH, 1993b), an approach that was introduced into legislation in September 1995. Training is an important element of the defence of *due diligence* identified in section 21 of the Act.

The concept of *due diligence and all reasonable precautions* lies at the heart of the Act, and examples can be seen of this defence in other statutes, such as section 24 of the Trades Description Act 1968. It was because absolute or strict liability offences are anathema to most lawyers, since they are regarded as oppressive, that the concept of due diligence was introduced into food safety law (Roberts, 1994).

It is a manager's responsibility to ensure that a safe and efficient system of food handling exists and that all reasonable precautions are taken to avoid food contamination during handling. Proprietors have little to fear from food safety law if they can show that the due diligence system is effective in operation, and that it can withstand the critical scrutiny of the enforcement authorities. The type of due diligence system in an establishment must be geared to the size and type of the particular operation. Further discussion of this issue is included in Chapter 10.

The objective contained within section 21 of the Food Safety Act was to modernize the system of defences and bring it into line with other consumer protection legislation. In legal terms, offences of absolute liability are employed in trading legislation. Similarly, it would be virtually impossible to secure a conviction if the prosecutor were obliged to prove guilty intent in every case. However, ever aware that absolute liability could bear down harshly on traders, a series of statutory defences has been introduced over the years which would, subject to proof that the criteria in each case had been fulfilled, enable a court to acquit a trader, even though an offence had been committed. Statutory defences have evolved over time, and the Food Safety Act 1990 (Act, 1990a) brought those relating to food offences up to date.

Such a defence can be extended to persons who neither prepare nor import the food, and who are accused under sections 8, 14 or 15. Within this offence, the objective is to place responsibility for the quality and safety of food upon those persons who have the greatest influence over the product.

Nobody can escape conviction simply by producing a warranty from a supplier. There is, however, a difference between guarantees and written assurances from suppliers. It is the duty of a food business to seek written statements from suppliers that the products being supplied comply with all legal requirements. Such assurances are an essential first step in the establishment of a due diligence system, but are not warranties as defined within the Food Act 1984 (Act, 1984). Such assurances should not go beyond the competence of the supplier.

The burden of proof rests with the defendant. While there is no requirement for a due diligence system, it is, however, *recommended good practice* that every food business should establish and maintain an adequate due diligence system. A control system that is not written down, and not recorded, creates great difficulties of proof in court, no matter how comprehensive it may be.

While the decision of the courts cannot be predicted, case law on due diligence under other consumer protection legislation provides some clues. First, past experience has shown that the courts have expected defendants to prove that they have *actively* taken some steps. The amount of checking necessary has depended on the size and nature of the business. It was not until 1994, some three years after the Food Safety Act came into force, that a law report was published on the due diligence defence, namely *Carrick District Council* v. *Taunton Vale Meat Traders Ltd* (1994) (Food Hygiene Briefing, 1994). The case reached the High Court in London. The key point in this decision was that the company relied on a meat inspector's inspection without having a separate system of checking. The court found that the company's claim of due diligence was proven. While going against the trend of previous case law on due diligence, this decision may also affect an officer's willingness to give specific advice to caterers, since such willingness to give advice may eventually be used in a due diligence case.

The development of quality control systems to satisfy the test of due diligence will probably be one main consequence of the Food Safety Act 1990. Businesses are likely to pay greater attention to the quality of their supplies and to the quality control systems of their suppliers. If so, enforcement officers will need to do the same, and this diligence could have significant effects. Interestingly, there is a case in which the food manufacturers and distributors in question had obtained British Standard 5750 Quality Management Systems (now referred to as ISO9000 series, the European equivalent being EN29000), yet were still not successful in claiming a due diligence defence in a prosecution on a food safety matter (Anonymous, 1992d). The court, in treating a case which introduces the concept of due diligence, is trying to balance the interests of the consumer against the business. What is being considered by the court is not the whole system but rather the element that relates to the offence in question. All too often the courts lean significantly towards the consumer, thus making the claim of a due diligence defence extremely difficult.

Food Hygiene Regulations

Whereas the Food Safety Act 1990 is a relatively recent issue within the topic of food legislation, other related regulations have a much longer history. A central plank of food safety law, up to September 1995, was contained within the Food Hygiene General Regulations 1970, as amended, which applied to all food premises (Regulation, 1970, 1990d, 1991c). These regulations were reviewed and consolidated in 1995 with the implementation of the EC Directive on the Hygiene of Foodstuffs, under the DOH's copy out principle.

An examination of the 1970 regulations shows them to be non-specific, in using words such as 'sufficient', 'suitable' and 'adequate', (not dissimilar from the Directive on the Hygiene of Foodstuffs). Both the 1970 and 1995 regulations relate to premises and equipment, food handling practices, personal hygiene, construction, repair and maintenance of premises, water supply and washing facilities, waste disposal and temperature control of certain foods. There is a clear link between the 1990 Act and the 1995 regulations; a breach of these latter regulations could result in the enforcement authorities taking action.

As part of its proposals for the implementation of the EC Food Hygiene Directive, the UK government issued the Food Safety (General Food Hygiene) Regulations 1995 (Regulation, 1995a). These regulations apply equally to England, Wales and Scotland, and repeal the bulk of the existing sets of regulations. The only exceptions are those requirements relating to temperature control, which will be discussed later in this section.

The layout of the regulations follows that of the EC Food Hygiene Directive very closely. The definition of terms, such as food business and hygiene, are included in Regulation 2 and illustrate that the regulations cover both private and public businesses. In terms of application, these stipulations do not apply to those food businesses that are covered by rules made under 'vertical' directives. However, the training requirement of these regulations applies if the 'vertical' regulation contains no such training condition.

There is a general requirement in Regulation 4 that proprietors of food businesses should ensure that all food handling operations are carried out in a hygienic manner. The following regulation goes on to give details necessary to the structure of the premises (a link here being made with the schedules within the regulations).

The regulations require the identification and control of potential food hazards based on the principles set out in Schedule 2, thus introducing the principles of Hazard Analysis Critical Control Point (HACCP). Provided within the legislation is the need for food handlers suffering from certain infections to notify the appropriate local authority. In this respect, it is unchanged from the similar requirement in the existing legislation. Contravention of the regulations can incur in some cases a fine (unlimited), or imprisonment for not more than two years, or both. A final point to note is that the enforcement authorities must have due regard to any relevant Industry Guide to Good Hygiene Practice when enforcing these regulations, a topic that has already been introduced in Chapter 1.

Temperature control, while not included in the regulations just discussed, also has a long history of development in the UK. The Food Hygiene (Amendment) Regulations 1990 took effect on 1 April 1991 and specified temperature controls for certain foods (Regulation, 1990d). Further amending regulations, the Food Hygiene (Amendment) Regulations 1991, came into force on 5 July 1991(Regulation, 1991c). Similar temperature controls apply to foods in transit and to catering operations using temporary or mobile facilities, as covered in the Food Hygiene Market Stalls and Delivery Vehicles Regulations 1966 (Regulation, 1966). The amendments produced a complex set of controls for storage temperatures of prepared foods. Foods defined within the regulations were divided into categories, some of which had to be kept at 8 °C or less and some that were to be kept at 5 °C or colder. Many regarded this approach as creating a *temperature jungle.*

Further to these amendments, on 23 February 1993 the UK government announced (DOH, 1993b) its intention to review statutory temperature controls, in order to identify how they might be simplified and rationalized without compromising public health. It considered options, looking both at domestic legislation and legislation that resulted from European Community directives or international agreements. The government issued proposals on this subject for public consultation in October 1993 (DOH, 1993d), and the results of the consultation were made available in the spring of 1994. In essence, the outcome of the discussions was that the two tier temperature control system would be abandoned and a single temperature requirement of 8 °C would be introduced in September 1995. Such a temperature contrasts with France's 3 °C and the Netherlands' 7 °C. It is this inconsistency in temperature control within member states that will eventually have to be resolved on a European-wide basis. This discrepancy also means that the UK's 8 °C within the 1995 regulations may be subject to change in the medium term, although it can be argued that this anomaly should be regarded as a subsidiarity issue.

When the British government initially issued the Food Safety (General Food Hygiene) Regulations 1995, it omitted to include reference to temperature control provisions, as these were still under consideration by the European Commission (Regulation, 1995a). The standard period for the European Commission to consider these temperature control provisions expired in August 1995 and so the regulations were made on 23 August, and came into force on 15 September 1995, the same day as the Food Safety (General Food Hygiene) Regulations 1995 (Regulation, 1995a). These regulations implement paragraphs 4 and 5 of chapter 9 of the Annexe to the Food Hygiene Directive issued in June 1993, as well as containing certain national provisions relating to food temperature control (EC Commission, 1993a). The regulations are divided into four parts, with some requirements applying to England and Wales and others applying to Scotland.

The regulations, in so much as they apply to all stages of food production, except primary production and fishery products, still contain differences between the vertical or product-specific directives and the horizontal or industry-wide directives.

Food that needs to be kept chilled, because it is likely to support the growth of pathogenic micro-organisms or the formation of toxins, is required to be kept at or below 8 °C. This stipulation does not apply to mail order food, which is subject to a separate offence within these regulations. There are certain exemptions to this general requirement.

A provision can be introduced which allows for the upward variation of the standard temperature of 8 °C in appropriate circumstances. Any such variation must, however, be based on a well-founded scientific assessment of the safety of the food at the new temperature (the relevant code of practice helps define what is meant by *well-founded scientific assessment*).

Other parts of the legislation allow for chill-holding tolerance periods, and state that there are defences that relate to the tolerance periods for which food may be held outside temperature control. For instance, it is not an offence to keep food for service or on display for sale for a period of less than 4 hours at above the 8 °C temperature requirement. It is, however, not allowable for such food to be displayed on more than one occasion. Equally, if food has been transferred to a vehicle, or there has been a temporary breakdown of equipment, it is again a defence to keep food above the 8 °C temperature ceiling.

Hot holding requirements are also referred to, and the legislation notes that food that has been cooked or reheated should not be kept below 63 °C. This stipulation is in order to control the growth of pathogenic micro-organisms or the formation of toxins. There are defences which allow for downward variation of this minimum 63 °C temperature in appropriate circumstances, and for a tolerance period of 2 hours.

Regulation 10 adds a new general temperature control requirement which prohibits keeping perishable foodstuffs at temperatures that could result in a risk to health. For instance, even if food is kept at or below 8 °C, there still could be a breach of food safety legislation under this general requirement contained within Regulation 10. High risk food processes, such as sous-vide, would presumably be covered by this requirement.

Different requirements apply in Scotland and these are covered in Regulation 13–16. They re-enact, with minor and drafting modifications, the food temperature control requirements previously contained in the Food Hygiene Scotland Regulations 1959 (Regulation, 1959).

Unlike previous food temperature control regulations, these regulations do not list specific foods that should be held under temperature control conditions. The businesses themselves need to consider which food needs to be held under temperature control. There is a clear link between these regulations and the Food Safety (General Food Hygiene) Regulations 1995 and the topic of food hazard analysis (Regulation, 1995a). The temperature control requirements should be understood in the general context of the food hazard analysis requirement contained in Regulation 4 of the Food Safety (General Food Hygiene) Regulations 1995.

Labelling

Based on the Food Labelling Regulations 2002 this complex subject is summarized below. Some elements are specifically related to the catering industry. Others assist the caterer as to what specifically they are buying from suppliers.

In addition to the mainly food safety measures just mentioned, a range of additional legislation has also been introduced, or is about to be introduced, all of which has implications for the food service industry (see, Thomas, 1993 on food premises registration). Whereas such legislation is treated separately in the UK, such a division is not so clear cut within other member states.

The Ministry of Agriculture, Fisheries and Food (MAFF) issued guidelines on voluntary nutrition labelling in 1987, and revised in 1988, which take into account the Codex Alimentarius Commission's guidelines on the subject (Anonymous, 1992e), have now been overtaken by the EU Directive of 24 September 1990 on Nutrition Labelling for Foodstuffs (Morris, 1991). These changes have seen a move away from compositional standards. The complex topic of nutrition labelling became considerably clearer in 1994 with the issue by the MAFF of revised guidelines. The Directive, as adopted, applies to all foods delivered as such to the ultimate consumer and foods supplied to catering establishments. It will remain voluntary except in those cases where a nutrition claim is made. Before the Directive, only a few member states (UK, Germany, Denmark and the Netherlands) had any sort of nutrition labelling system in place and problems did arise, as identified by Saunders (1991).

A regulation entitled Food Labelling (Amendment) Regulation 1994 came into effect on 1 March 1995 (MAFF, 1993b), and provided manufacturers with a standard mandatory format for labelling. The relevance of this stipulation to the hospitality industry is that the UK government did not believe it would be appropriate to impose the full requirements on caterers, since it would be largely impractical for them to give information in the form the Directive requires. The central objective of these amendment regulations is to help consumers compare the nutritional content of different foods, and make informed choices as to their purchase. In addition, they will help industry in providing standard rules on product labelling. They will be, however, of limited relevance to non-pre-packed food sold at a catering establishment, a point identified under 37(5) of the 1984 Regulations (within Regulation 5 of the 1994 Regulations). Non-pre-packed food sold at a catering establishment does not need to carry any nutrition labelling, even if a claim is made.

Food labelling regulations date from 1984 and have often been amended in accordance with legislation at the European Union level. During 1994, MAFF issued draft regulations in order to consolidate legislation on this topic. They were implemented in 1996. The central aim of this consolidation exercise was to produce regulations that were clear and understandable. The proposals sought to move away from the term *immediate consumption*, and focus on food sold specifically in catering establishments. A considerable amount of work has also been done by the Food Advisory Committee in its published review of food labelling. Furthermore, there has been consultation by the Food Advisory Committee (FAC) on the use of graphical representations of nutritional information (MAFF, 1993c; Thomas, 1992), along with the UK government's response to the FAC on consumer research, undertaken by the National Consumer Council, on consumers' views on food labelling in catering establishments (MAFF, 1993d). A concise summary of this National Consumer Council research is contained in an article by Clarke (1993). It is likely that the trend for the future can be predicted from the USA, where compulsory labelling in some detail is required (Smith and Drandfield, 1991). Such an attitude may influence legislation within the European Union.

The Food Labelling Regulations 2002 note that if a name prescribed by law exists, it shall be used, and may be qualified by other words that make it more precise. If no name prescribed by law exists, a customary name may be used. Alternatively, if the situation is that there is neither a name prescribed by a law nor a customary name, a name sufficiently precise to inform a purchaser of the true nature of the food and to establish no confusion will be adopted. Additionally, if the purchaser could be misled without such information, the name should include an indication (a) that a food is powdered or in any other physical condition, or (b) that a food has been dried, freeze-dried, frozen, concentrated or smoked or subjected to any other treatment.

The list of ingredients should be headed or preceded by 'ingredients' (or a heading that includes the word 'ingredients') and should be listed in weight descending order at the time of their use in the preparation of the food. One particular exception to this requirement is water used as an ingredient, which should be listed in order of weight in the finished product. The name of an ingredient should be the name that would be used if the ingredient were sold as a food.

The names of the ingredients of a compound ingredient may be given either instead of the compound ingredient or in addition. One exception is that the name of the compound ingredient need not be given if the compound ingredient is less than 25% of the finished product, but in this case, any additives used and needing to be named must be listed immediately following the name of the compound ingredient. Where a food is characterized by the presence of a particular ingredient, and special emphasis is given to it on the label, there must be a declaration of the minimum percentage of the ingredient.

Durability is indicated by either the 'best before' or 'use by' label. Either of these two terms should be followed by the date (expressed in day/month or day/month/year) up to and including which the food can reasonably be expected to retain its specific properties if properly stored. Additionally, details of the storage conditions necessary for the properties to be retained until that date should be included. Either the date only or the date and storage conditions may be elsewhere on the packet if reference is made to the position after the 'use by' statement. There are various foods exempted from stating an appropriate durability indication, i.e. fresh fruit and vegetables.

For any pre-packed food that is an individual portion and is intended as a minor component to either another food or another service, only the name is required. These food items could include butter and other fat spreads, milk, cream and cheeses, jams and marmalades, mustards, sauces, tea, coffee and sugar.

Any food sold at a catering establishment which is either not pre-packed or pre-packed for direct sale, need not be marked with any of the items in the general labelling requirements discussed above. There are exceptions regarding food treated with ionizing radiation and genetically modified foods.

In terms of vending machines, when a name of a food is not visible to a purchaser, it must be given in a notice on the front of the machine or in close proximity.

Additionally, for food that is not pre-packed but for which a nutrition claim is made (whether on the machine or elsewhere), a notice giving the prescribed nutrition labelling is required.

When sold to the ultimate consumer, the required markings shall be either on the packaging or on a label attached to the packaging or on a label visible through the packaging. If sold otherwise than to the ultimate consumer, as an alternative, the details may be on relevant trade documents.

For those products that may omit certain details, they should appear on a label attached to the food or on a menu, notice, ticket or label discernible to the purchaser at the place where he or she chooses the food. Where the information is given on a menu etc., if the food contains (or may contain) irradiated ingredients this should be indicated using the words 'irradiated' or 'treated with ionizing radiation' accompanying the reference to the ingredient. In the case where irradiated dried substances normally used for seasoning are used in a catering establishment, an indication that food sold in the establishment contains (or may contain) those irradiated ingredients is sufficient.

Any marking or notice should be easy to understand, clearly legible and indelible and, when sold to the ultimate consumer, easily visible (although at a catering establishment where information is changed regularly, information can be given by temporary media, e.g. chalk on a blackboard). Such marking must not be hidden, obscured or interrupted by written or pictorial matter. When required the necessary information must appear in the same field of vision.

In terms of nutritional labelling, details must be presented together in one conspicuous place in tabular form with numbers aligned or, if there is insufficient space for this, in linear form. When required or permitted to be given, there is a prescribed order and manner of listing.

For food that is not pre-packed and is either sold to the ultimate consumer other than at a catering establishment, to the ultimate consumer from a vending machine, or in a catering establishment, prescribed nutrition labelling should give any data relevant to any nutrition claim that is made.

New regulations on food labelling, which came into force on 1 July 1998 and incorporated into the 2002 regulations, means that consumers can see on the label the actual percentage amounts of various ingredients used in foods. These changes implement new EU requirements on food labelling and became compulsory for all member states by the year 2000. The regulations:

- require the quantities of certain ingredients to be stated on the label;
- clarify the marketing rules for foods brought in from other member states or from the European Economic Area (EEA);
- emphasize that labels must use the names prescribed in EU law;
- reduce the number of single ingredient foods exempt from ingredient listing;
- require ingredients identified as 'starch' or 'modified starch' to indicate their specific vegetable origin if they are likely to contain gluten.

The UK has also taken the opportunity to make a number of other changes in order to:

- make clear that labelling exemptions for food brought into the UK from other EU or EEA states apply only if the requirements of the food labelling and other relevant directives are met;

- adjust the rules for calculating the percentage of milk fat in cream so that added ingredients, such as alcohol, are excluded;
- require foods claiming to be reduced or low energy to carry nutrition labelling.

Trade in products that do not conform to the new requirements has been prohibited from 14 February 2000.

These Regulations provide for the enforcement of Council Regulation (EC) No. 1139/98 concerning the compulsory indication, on the labelling of certain foodstuffs produced from genetically modified organisms, of particulars other than those provided for in Directive 79/112/EEC (Regulations 3 and 9). The products concerned are those which are to be delivered as such to the final consumer, having been produced in whole or in part from genetically modified soya beans or genetically modified maize (Article 1 of Regulation 1139/98 refers). The legislation allows for alternative labelling arrangements in the case of sales to the ultimate consumer by appropriate premises of food that is pre-packed for direct sale or not pre-packed, including catering establishments. These came into effect in September 1999.

The UK: a European perspective

A significant issue for the UK Catering Industry in September 1995 was the implementation of the EC Directive on the Hygiene of Foodstuffs, the regulations being brought into force 12 months later. During February of that year, the Department of Health (DOH) circulated to interested parties a major consultation document covering three main areas:

1 the Food Safety (General Food Hygiene) Regulations 1995;
2 a revision of the Food Safety Act Code of Practice No 9;
3 a draft template on the development of voluntary Industry Guides to Good Hygiene Practice (DOH, 1993d).

The implementing regulations in September of that year followed closely the EC Directive on the Hygiene of Foodstuffs, and in effect repealed the bulk of the 11 regulations in force up to 1995. A single set of general food hygiene regulations was made for England, Wales and Scotland for the first time. Provisions on food temperature controls were also implemented within these regulations, as a result of a DOH consultation exercise in October 1993.

Following the 1995 regulations, for the first time in UK catering law there is a general requirement for the training of food handlers in food hygiene. Prior to 1995, there had been much discussion over food hygiene training, and many major companies had already detailed policies on this topic. Equally, it was

Hospitality Leisure & Tourism Series

considered by these companies that food hygiene training was an important element in the defence of due diligence identified in section 21 of the Food Safety Act 1990. An indication of what is now regarded as recommended practice can be seen in the revised Code of Practice No. 9 on Food Hygiene Inspections, published in 1994 (DOH, 1992a, 1992b).

Another aspect new to UK catering law, and identified in the regulations, was the duty of food businesses to identify and control potential food hazards. Whereas such an approach is similar to Hazard Analysis and Critical Control Point (HACCP), it does not require a fully documented system. This requirement for a modified approach to HACCP led to the development of Assured Safe Catering (ASC) (HMSO, 1993) in the UK. ASC was developed within the catering working group at the Campden Food and Drink Research Association, with the cooperation of both the Department of Health and the Ministry of Agriculture, Fisheries and Food. It should be regarded as an effective response in most catering units to the requirements of the directive. ASC provides a framework for the proprietor of a catering establish- ment to assess, control and monitor hygiene standards. It involves looking at the catering operation in sequence from the selection of ingredients right through to the service of food to the customer. It identifies any hazards that need to be controlled in order for the food to be safe, and helps prevent, rather than cure, safety problems.

Whereas HACCP proceeds on an individual food basis, identifying specific critical control points, ASC identifies generic critical control points. Consideration of Schedule Two of the 1995 regulations shows an emphasis on activities crucial to food safety. This schedule requires an analysis of the potential food hazards in a food business operation. Following on from this analysis, there is a need to identify points in the operation where food hazards may occur. Critical points within the system with respect to food safety should be identified, and correct monitoring procedures should be used within the operation. Again, this topic is discussed in more detail within Code of Practice No. 9 and should be read in conjunction with the DOH's Assured Safe Catering document. In general terms, the degree of sophistication contained within the control system should be related to the size and nature of the business.

The final new aspect of the 1995 regulations was that food authorities are required to give due consideration to relevant UK or EU voluntary Industry Guides to Good Hygiene Practice. The importance of these guides is that they help in a consistent application of food safety law, irrespective of the industry sector. A template, or formula, was published by the DOH. If any UK guides are to have official government recognition, they will be subject to scrutiny from an advisory panel, comprising repre- sentatives from industry, consumers and enforcers. The panel is chaired by a senior civil servant. The DOH provided the coordination point between business sectors in the UK on this issue (now the Food Standards Agency). Otherwise, of course, this development could lead to a proliferation of documents (Joint Hospitality Industry Congress, 1994). The DOH initially took a clear responsibility on this matter by providing advice on the compilation of these guides, as well as on their aim, scope, structure, status and development procedures. As for hygiene standards, these guides introduce an element of flexibility into a wide and diverse catering industry. One important question is the status of these guides. Because of the recognition process, they can be used with confidence as a practical *vade mecum* for compliance with relevant regulations. It would always remain open to industry to display compliance with the objectives of the regulations by means other than those set out in the guides.

Germany

Background

The western part of the united Germany is divided into nine Bunderslander with the eastern Bundersland divided for geographical purposes. Two ministries have general responsibility for matters of food law enforcement: the Ministry of Health, and the Ministry of Nutrition, Agriculture and Forestry.

The principal aims of food law in Germany have been the same since the first codification in 1879: the protection of human health and the protection of the general public against misleading practices (Agra Europe, 1992).

It was in 1958 that the German food code was established within the framework of the first food legislation reform after the Second World War. The approach to food law in Germany is that it contains general prohibitions backed up with practical provisions contained within a code. The German Food Code Commission identifies criteria for evaluating the composition and properties of given foods, or food groups, and combines them to form guiding principles that, on publication, constitute the German Food Code.

Food law in Germany is a complicated network of hundreds of acts and decrees with interconnections to many other areas of legislation. The main act is the *Lebensmittel und Bedarfsgegenstandegesetz* of 15 August 1974 which covers tobacco, cosmetic products and consumer goods (Act, 1974b). This law on Foods and Commodities maintains the Food Code Commission. The foundations of this approach are expert opinions containing the views of all parties involved in the food trade. The guiding principles are published by the Federal Minister for Health, acting in agreement with other ministers, and are based on the work of a range of expert committees (Deutsches Leben-smittelbuch, 1992). The Bund für Lebensmittelrecht und Leb-ensmittelkunde (BLL) represents the food industry and works with the government in the preparation of both food law and standards. The BLL produces guidelines, definitions etc., which are accepted as self-regulatory by government.

It is the Veterinary Office within the Bundersländer which carries out the policies of the two Ministries, the head of the department being the Veterinary Doctor. The control of food safety is under the direction of veterinarians, and a significant element of their training focuses on food hygiene. Within this office, one section is devoted to Food Control (WHO, 1988).The food control section enforces all food quality, labelling, safety and hygiene legislation in all sectors of the trade, and inspection is required to be undertaken by trained personnel. If there is a danger of delay, police officers are also regarded as authorized officers in enforcing food law, a clear difference from the UK and a number of other European Countries, where police officers do not have such powers. The food control section handles all routine inspections, sampling and investigations.

A full inspection includes the enforcement of all legislation governing:

- the hygiene of food preparation, storage, display and sale areas, and personnel; and
- the safety, quality and labelling of all food and other products, and substances that come into contact with the body in daily life.

In short, this one department enforces all legislation concerning food from producer to consumer. The only aspect outside its control is the trading standards issue of weights and measures (LACOTS, 1989).

Enforcement officers are allowed to enter premises, close them down if necessary, seize, detain and dispose, inspect and sample ingredients during normal working hours. Outside these times, they are allowed to enter if there is an immediate danger to health. There is an obligation to permit entry by these officers and to cooperate in their investigations. In particular, personnel should obey the inspector's instructions to indicate the relevant rooms, equipment and apparatus, to open rooms and containers and to facilitate the taking of samples. All restaurants and similar establishments where food is prepared and sold for human consumption must be licensed (a significant distinction from the UK), by another department. However, the Veterinary Office can veto the granting of that licence. This veto can be exercised if, from the inspection of the plans and arrangements, the hygiene requirements will not be met (Wittekindt, 1991). Another aspect to the food enforcement service in Germany is that it actively uses the media if it does not gain the cooperation it requires.

Principal food legislation

A framework Act governing purity of foods and commodities is contained within the Act of 1974 (Act, 1974b), entitled An Act to Record and Clarify the Law on Trade in Foodstuffs, Tobacco Products, Cosmetics and Certain Necessities. This Act was amended in 1990, 1991 and 1992 in order to comply with EU Legislation. It now provides that any foodstuff produced and marketed legally in another member state may be imported into Germany, even if it does not meet the requirements laid down under German law.

Foodstuffs within German law are defined as substances that are intended for human consumption in an unchanged or prepared state. Equally, the coatings and casings of foodstuffs that are intended to be consumed, or might be consumed, are also regarded as foodstuffs.

The Act also encompasses additives, and defines them as substances that are added to foodstuffs to influence their characteristics or to obtain specific properties or effects. The Federal Minister of Health is empowered to include further substances within the definition of an *additive*. In this respect the Minister is supported by expert judgment and, in some cases, is required to accept the additive, if required, by the EU. The definitions are further extended by the term *necessities*, and include articles that may come into contact with foodstuffs, e.g. film wrapping. Consumers comprise not only individuals that use foodstuffs and necessities for their personal use, but also restaurants and other commercial catering outlets.

Offences under the 1974 Act with respect to foodstuffs can be considered under four areas:

- protection of health;
- additives and labelling;
- protection against deception and fraud;
- trade in necessities.

It is prohibited to produce or treat foodstuffs in such a manner that their consumption constitutes a danger to health. In this respect, the Federal Minister can make regulations to prohibit or restrict the use of certain substances, articles and processes. The Minister may also place requirements on the producer, processor or marketer of certain foodstuffs.

Focusing specifically on hygiene specifications, regulations can be issued that prevent decomposition or other disadvantageous effects on foodstuffs. Specifically, these rules cover micro-organisms, contamination, odours, temperature, treatment or pre-preparation processes. Authority for these regulations can be transferred to the county regions or Länder, thereby indicating a decentralization of power.

The general requirement in terms of additives is that in order to be allowable they should be on the permitted list. The key condition for what is permitted is taken with due reference to technological, nutritional and dietetic factors, and the protection of the consumer. Regulations are also issued with respect to the maximum quantities of additives permitted, their reactions within the product and their purity criteria. The production, treatment and marketing of additives are also controlled.

There is a requirement to use proper labelling when using additives, and the manner in which they are declared is regulated. In recent years, milk and meat substitutes have been introduced into German superstores with an application, flavour and appearance similar to *real* milk and meat products, while differing in composition. They contain animal and vegetable additives, e.g. soya bean, that can be regarded as an acknowledged substitute for meat or milk. Until 1989, no vegetable fats were permitted in dairy products. The meat regulation did not allow the production of meat products with soya bean proteins. The addition of other vegetables, such as potatoes or greens, was also not permitted.

In continuation of the *Cassis de Dijon* judgment (discussed in Chapter 1), the German regulation concerning the production of meat and milk products was annulled, the prevailing view being that the consumer could be protected by using a distinctive labelling of products. This new stipulation implied that substitutes could now be issued in Germany if produced according to the labelling requirements. The new rule does not allow substitutes to carry the name as the equivalent cheese, butter or yoghurt, since they are only allowed for the *real* products. A similar regulation still has to be established for meat products. The name *soya bean sausage* is forbidden.

Food labelling requirements are set out in the *Lebensmittel-kennzeichnungsverordnung*, as amended. A fifth amendment was debated in 1992. Recently, harmonization has been enacted in areas of EU legislation, including additives, articles in contact with foodstuffs and foods for particular nutritional uses.

A comparison in German law can be made with section 14 of the Food Safety Act 1990, in terms of nature, substance and quality. German food law creates the concept that the purchaser is entitled to buy food based on the name and description of the product. Hence, a steaklette would imply a small steak (LACOTS, 1990). Misleading presentation, designation, declaration or advertising is not permitted. It is prohibited to market foodstuffs that are unfit for human consumption or that have been adulterated. Also banned are foodstuffs whose appearance gives the impression that their properties are better than they really are. Detailed provisions are available in terms of labelling in order to protect against deception. The packaging should have specific information as to the contents, producer or whoever markets the product. The date of manufacture and shelf life should also be given, along with the required storage conditions (Bohl, 1991).

Necessities with respect to German food law include materials and articles in contact with food. Such items should not contain toxic substances that would migrate into the foodstuffs or their surfaces, except for technically unavoidable quantities that are unobjectionable from health, odour and flavour aspects. Authorization is required to use specific substances within these materials, either individually, in groups or in mixtures. Both maximum quantities and purity criteria are prescribed.

Enforcement personnel are authorized to take or demand representative samples of their choice for the purpose of examination. The sampling activities of the service are the result of a planned programme, and minimum sampling rates are stipulated by statute. Thus, enforcement practices in these respects differ from those of the UK. For a given geographical area, this requirement is based on a certain number of samples of food per 1000 of population. Further monitoring programmes are drawn up by the analyst. All sampling is programmed by laboratory staff on a quarterly basis with regard to the legal minimum samples required. All results are published, and hence available to the public at large (LACOTS, 1990).

The department or any enforcement officer can impose an administrative fine up to a certain level, as indeed can the courts. A penalty of 3 years (maximum) imprisonment, in certain circumstances, can also be handed down if a breach of the regulations is proven. Fines of up to 25,000DM can be levied. The enforcement officer has considerable discretion over what penalty can be imposed and as to who is considered responsible. In terms of the penalty procedure, the format is standardized. In addition to fines, the offender is also charged any administrative costs. Minor objections are referred to the courts. More serious matters are also referred to the courts and to the public prosecutor (Act, 1974b).

Germany: an EU perspective

The EU's directive on the hygiene of foodstuffs is not dissimilar from a 1991 proposal made by the Council Protecting Public Health (*Rat zum Schutz der öffentlichen Gesundheit*). This proposal centred on the satisfactory state of food and the observance of hygiene principles during the production, processing and issuing of food. The directive contains many elements that are already part of today's hygiene regulations in some of the Länder, and have also been components of the drafts for an uniform hygiene regulation for all the Länder (Dauer, 1991; Freidhof, 1991).

All food businesses in Germany have to exercise a quality control system in their operations in order to determine whether or not the established hygiene principles have been followed, thereby ensuring that food corresponds with the statutory requirement concerning the *satisfactory nature of food*. Businesses have to report to the authorities about their control assurance procedures. Additionally, it has been determined that the food control authorities have to regulate the businesses, and any deficiencies need to be submitted in a written report by enforcement officers, with the resulting consequences having to be followed up by the business.

The Food Hygiene Principles just mentioned apply to the whole food chain – cultivation, harvest, processing, production, packaging, distribution and retail sale of food – the central objective being the guarantee of satisfactory nature. In using the term 'food hygiene', actions are required to guarantee harmlessness, satisfactory nature and suitability of food during all steps, from cultivation and production to the final consumer. General hygiene regulations, product-specific hygiene regulations, as well as guidelines regarding the type and range of self-control, have been established within the German legislative system.

Such detailed requirements extend to the construction and equipment of the facilities where food is handled. They include sanitary facilities, the water supply, effluent and waste disposal. Finally, hygiene is regulated through the maintenance of buildings and equipment, the cleaning and disinfection of buildings, and the storage and disposal of wastage.

Every business is also required to establish a *standard cleaning and disinfection programme*. The responsibility for hygiene has to be transferred to an identified individual, who preferably controls the business and who must take responsibility for production.

France

Background

The Ministry of Economy and Finance and the Ministry of Agriculture are jointly responsible for food control services in France, covering all aspects of the food chain. Control is centrally based and the degree of local autonomy is restricted. Control by central government constitutes the essential difference between the French and UK systems of enforcement. While there are considerable advantages in having a centrally administered enforcement service, it is in practice not much better than the *home authority principle* operating in the UK. Such a devolvement of enforcement power within the UK, through the home authority principle, tends to achieve the same levels of consistency as the centrally controlled approach of the French system.

Control of food quality and hygiene in France is the responsibility of the Ministry of Agriculture. The organization of this Ministry, together with its duties and responsibilities, are contained within the decree 87.38, of February 1987. The Ministry is specifically charged with the supervision of food supplies, training and research. In effect, authority is given to the Ministry to introduce food control regulations, set standards for production, prepare and display food (Euromonitor, 1993).

Quality and safety of other foods are principally the concern of the *Direction Générale de la Concurrence de la Consommation et de la Repression des Fraudes (DGCCRF)*. Its work is mainly performed by two services of the directorate, namely:

1 the service for the prevention of fraud and control of quality; and
2 the veterinary food hygiene service.

Food of animal origin is the responsibility of the Veterinary Service, specifically with regard to hygiene and quality.

The DGCCRF at national level is organized into three main services:

1 consumer safety and quality;
2 free market competition; and
3 supervision of production and of markets.

Sub-directorates deal with more specific areas (WHO, 1988). The directorate is principally concerned with enforcing legislation relating to food quality and safety. This legislation is contained in the Act of 1 August 1905 (Act, 1905), which relates to fraud and falsification, and the Act of 21 July 1983, which concerns the safety of consumers (Act, 1983). DGCCRF responsibilities are the equivalent of the UK's Trading Standards Officers.

The Veterinary Service is a directorate of the Ministry of Agriculture and has two basic functions:

1 animal health; and
2 the hygiene of foodstuffs of animal origin.

Its general, organizational structure is similar to that of the DGCCRF (LACOTS, 1990). The service has a central directorate, with a chief and section heads, departmental inspectorates and a network of departmental veterinary laboratories coordinated by a central food hygiene laboratory. The departmental inspectorates were set up by a decree of 31 March 1967, which demarcated divisions for the veterinary inspectorate in each department (département) of the country. There are four national laboratories, one of which specializes in catering. The principal role of the service is to monitor and enforce good hygiene practices at all stages of production, processing, storage, distribution, preparation and service of high risk foods. It includes hospitality outlets and restaurants (Dehove, 1986).

The principal method of control is the inspection of premises. In setting priorities for inspection frequency, the following criteria are used:

- the inherent risk associated with a particular food or process;
- the effectiveness of food hygiene policies related to the relevant legislation;
- the size of the business, amount produced and the potential scale of the consequences in case of a control breakdown; and
- whether the products are for the domestic or export markets. (Here an assessment is made on the attitudes and capability of the operator, based on past history).

A system of registration is in operation in France which can be seen as an aid to the planning of enforcement activities. Within one month of opening for business, operators must inform the service as to the nature of the business, types of food involved, number of meals and methods of production. Once the registration process is complete, the premises are inspected and an assessment is made of their potential risk category. Matters such as design, maintenance and cleanliness of premises, equipment and fittings, personal hygiene facilities, level of management and housekeeping are all considered. Premises are thereafter inspected on a flexible basis according to their risk category. It would seem that the fundamental difference between France and the UK is that the latter relies on the Codes of Practice issued under the Food Safety Act 1990 to guide the enforcement authorities, whereas the former does not adopt such an informal approach.

Every year, in the summer, the food inspection service mounts an operation known as 'operation holiday food', that is essentially an extension of the routine hygiene and quality monitoring. Checks are made on all retail shops, including caterers and, in so doing, it is possible to establish a measure of improvement or decline in overall standards.

If products are recognized as being falsified, contaminated or toxic, the goods may be seized and, in some cases, without a court order. Officials may enter premises by day and, occasionally, by night, in order to investigate and report on any infringements of the law. Enforcement officers have the power to request a court to mandate goods that breach the legislation to be confiscated and destroyed at the cost of the sentenced person (Act, 1905).

The legal enforcement system is similar to the Scottish method, whereby infringements are formally reported to the Procurat, the equivalent of the Procurator Fiscal in Scotland, who decides whether or not to prosecute. Whereas litigation is reserved for serious cases, other routes may include advice or a written warning. Such sanctions are similar to those operating in the UK.

Where legal action is deemed necessary, the matter is referred to the legal section of either the DGCCRF or the Veterinary Service, as appropriate.

In addition to any fines incurred on conviction, the individual will be ordered to pay the costs of any court reports, samples and analysis undertaken in order to investigate the infringement.

Contravention of the 1905 Act is punishable with at least 3 months', and no longer than 2 years', imprisonment, and a fine or only one of these punishments. If the offence is considered an aggravating offence, these 'maximum' penalties can be doubled. The 1905 Act provides for the publication of judgments in newspapers, and for the same information to be displayed at the entrance to the business – not dissimilar from the UK situation. The judgment may be published in its entirety, or in extract form, with the costs being borne by the convicted person. Where such an order is made, the size and type of the notice is determined by the court. It is an offence to remove such a notice, which must be displayed for no longer than 7 days. Furthermore, the obligatory health mark required by some businesses can be withdrawn, effectively closing the premises (LACOTS, 1990). Without prejudice to the 1905 Act, infringements of the 1980 Food Hygiene Regulations can incur a fine and a second offence could lead to a sentence of between 10 days' to 2 months' imprisonment.

Principal legislation

Under the 1905 Act (1 August 1905: Fraud and Attempted Fraud), the executive is empowered by virtue of Article II (Act, 1905) to issue decrees relating to:

- inspection and analysis;
- composition, labelling and advertising; and
- cleanliness of premises and the state of health of persons working on those premises.

These powers have allowed government, as of 1999, to issue more than 100 regulations relating to food products and conditions relating to sale. Regulations may also be made by prefects and mayors concerning public order, safety and health, although they tend to be guided by the relevant ministry.

The 1905 Act makes it an offence for anyone to deceive, or attempt to deceive, a contracting party by any means or procedure, either directly or by an intermediary or third party. Regulations under this Act reduce the risk of unfair practices and protect the consumer. The DGCCRF monitors products at all stages for falsification and deception. Specifically the offences relate to:

- either the nature, type, origin, substantial qualities and composition of the product; or
- to the quantity of items or their identity; or
- to the suitability for use or their inherent risks in use.

These general offences are extended to cover *aggravating practices, falsifications with respect to contaminated foodstuffs and illegal detention*. Aggravating practices are described as those relating to goods that are dangerous to the health of human beings or animals. They also include weights and measures offences and, if convicted under this section, the penalties are doubled. Even if the falsification of foodstuffs is known to the buyer or consumer, it is still an offence to display or sell falsified, contaminated or toxic foodstuffs. This offence extends to the use of advertising or other promotional literature, points covered in section 15 of the UK's Food Safety Act 1990. If a business is found to hold falsified, contaminated or toxic foodstuffs, the proprietor is also guilty of an offence, described as *illegal detention*.

The 1983 Act deals with product safety and obliges businesses to produce reliable products and services (Act, 1983). Products and services must be sold or supplied within the normal conditions of use, or in conditions that can reasonably be foreseen to provide for a level of safety. Safety in these terms must be *as can legitimately be expected* and must not be harmful to health. It is the *Consumer Safety Commission* that issues opinions for improving risk prevention as regards product or service safety. Decrees of the Conseil d'Etat are issued after taking into consideration the views of the Consumer Safety Commission and can cover labelling and packaging, hygiene and cleanliness. Products or services that do not comply with the provisions of this Act are prohibited. Such products and services may only be put back on the market when the Minister of Consumer Affairs deems that they have conformed with current regulations (Dehove, 1986). The Minister has the option to consult with the business proprietor and, if necessary, with approved national consumer associations.

The central idea is therefore to make certain that either businesses take the necessary measures to ensure their products or services do not present any danger to consumers. A proactive, as well as reactive, approach is taken by the DGCCRF, as it is concerned with preventative measures. Inspections are carried out on a routine basis and control relies principally on sampling (LACOTS, 1990). Nine categories of qualified authorities are identified that are empowered to carry out examinations of products and services. They have a statutory right of entry to premises and must follow clear procedures at the examination stage. Results of investigations and proposals for measures to be taken should be communicated to the state representative within the département and a decision made within 15 days. The case is communicated to the relevant minister in charge. There are provisions for action in the case of serious or immediate danger to the public. The examining judge or court may, once infringements have been referred to them, order a provisional suspension of the sale of the product or service concerned. The option of appeal to a higher court is anticipated.

The principal regulation concerning food hygiene in catering establishments is contained within the decree of 26 September 1980 (Regulation, 1980). Whereas the text covers, in broad terms, the same areas as the UK's (amended) Food Hygiene General Regulations 1970 (now revoked) and the Food Hygiene General Regulations 1995 (Regulation, 1995a), it is however considerably more prescriptive.

The regulation covers catering of all types, including mobile food counters and vending machines, whether of a social or commercial character. The catering establishment has to be registered within one month of opening, a requirement that was introduced into French law some 11 years prior to similar regulations being introduced in the UK. The registration must be renewed following any change of ownership and consequent upon any significant alterations to the physical structure of the premises or any change of equipment.

The main offence contained within the regulations is that premises must not constitute a risk of rendering foodstuffs injurious to health. The regulations go on to identify various features in the hygienic design of kitchens. Such aspects include requirements with respect to floors, walls and ceilings and, in addition, the separation of certain food processes to be carried out in areas distinctly allocated for the purpose. Both hot and cold potable water needs to be provided, along with sufficient sanitary facilities for staff. Article 10 states that the establishment must have one or more refrigerators, and Article 21 identifies the relevant temperature at which food must be maintained. For most food categories the relevant temperature is +3°C, considerably lower than that required in both the UK and the Netherlands. It would seem that these regulations have created a temperature labyrinth that ranges from +2°C for fish up to +15°C for cooked pork, meat products, cheeses with rind and eggs. A similar range of temperatures is identified for frozen foods. Chapter V of the regulations covers hygiene requirements for mobile food counters, and Chapter VI is concerned with vending machines. Other requirements, such as the cleaning, washing, and disinfection of floors at least once a day, confirm the view that this is entirely prescriptive legislation. Finally, examples of this Napoleonic approach include cold dishes that must be retrieved from the refrigerator less than one hour prior to service to the customer. It would be interesting to speculate on how such legislation can be effectively enforced.

An opinion aimed at foodstuff professionals, relating to hygiene good practice guidelines, was published on 24 November 1993. According to the provisions of the 1993 directive on the hygiene of foodstuffs, the ministers in charge of Agriculture, Consumer Affairs and Health, should encourage all organizations of foodstuff professionals to establish hygiene good practice guidelines. These recommendations are approved by the French administration after obtaining the opinion of the Superior Council for French Public Hygiene. They are also presented to the National Council for Consumer Affairs. The approval of the guidelines is published in the Official Journal.

AFNOR, the French standards body, is now producing standards in the foodstuffs area. Related activities include codes of practice on food safety and the development of analysis methods. France publishes a positive list of additives which has to be approved by the Conseil Supérieur de l'Hygiène Publique de France. During the period 1991–3, EU legislation on additive use was implemented. It includes labelling rules for both the wholesale and retail trade.

France: a European perspective

Clear differences have emerged in France's approach, which takes a prescriptive stance towards legislation, and that of Germany, which relies heavily on codes of practice that have legal force. Food legislation within France is the responsibility of more than one government department, with the influence of the Veterinary Service also in evidence. With an emphasis on sampling, a reactive, rather than proactive, approach is taken.

Denmark

Background

Food legislation in Denmark has a long history. A list of approved food colours was issued by the Chief of the Copenhagen Police Force on 21 December 1836 – one of the first positive lists of food additives in the world (WHO, 1988). Other regulations extend further back in time, to the end of the sixteenth century. The first general food law was passed in 1903.

Food matters in Denmark are the responsibility of two ministries, namely the Ministry of Agriculture, and the Ministry of Health. The Danish Veterinary Service has a supervisory function regarding foodstuffs. Its particular sphere of influence relates to microbiological issues. The Consumer Agency, *Forbrugerstyrelsen*, is responsible for regulations concerning labelling, displaying, advertising prices on foodstuffs and packaging.

Ministry of Health	Ministry of Agriculture	Ministry of Fisheries
National Food Agency	Danish Veterinary Service	Plant Directorate
Foodstuffs in general	Milk and milk products	Quality control
Additives	Eggs and egg products	Fish products
Retail trade	Exports	EEC control
	Meat etc.	EEC directives
	Domestic market and EEC	

Table 2.1
Organization of food control in Denmark

The organization of food control is identified in Table 2.1 above.

The Food Act is within the purview of the Ministry of Health and the central administrative tasks are dealt with by the *National Food Agency*. Under a 1992 decree, the National Food Agency (NFA) for Foodstuffs is responsible for policy concerning the sale and marketing of foodstuffs. This policy also includes legislation aimed at protecting the consumer from health risks and misleading claims when purchasing a food product.

Whereas food control is decentralized, the NFA provides an appeal procedure against municipality decisions. Denmark has a decentralized food control system. The municipalities are responsible for enforcing regulations for the retail sale of foodstuffs and delegate all or part of their duties to local municipal food control units. Control and inspection are delegated to 278 municipal authorities which, in practice, have these duties carried out by municipal food control units. There are 32 units that undertake inspections and take samples. The inspectors are mostly veterinarians or locally trained technicians. As a rule, inspections are carried out by the local food control units. Indeed, this practice is always the case at the retail level. The units deal only with food hygiene and compositional matters, and qualified staff tend to be veterinarians (WHO, 1988). Decisions made by the local authorities against proprietors can be appealed to the National Food Agency, which has the final administrative say in a number of areas. Decisions made by the National Food Agency can, in turn, be appealed to the Ministry of Health, if the matter is of major importance.

The enforcement officers of the Food Inspection Unit within the area of the local council have a statutory right of access to food premises. The officer has the power to demand a wide range of information from the business proprietor and can request the supply of samples free of charge. Any expenses incurred can be charged to the proprietor concerned.

Food control in Denmark is financed by fees payable by the enterprises for approval, inspection and control. The fee system differs somewhat from law to law. Regarding food law, the approval fee is a one-off fee and is decided centrally. The inspection fee is determined locally on the basis of the schedule for the control activity, so that control is carried out as required. The inspection fee reflects the actual costs connected with the control of individual enterprises, so that each business knows for what it is paying. This approach encourages enterprises to improve their auto control. Thus well-run firms pay less than those requiring much control. Furthermore, the size of the inspection fee reflects the firm's efficiency in these matters. If additional control is required, the enterprises may be charged extra fees. Businesses may also be charged more for the analysis of additional samples etc.

The officer is required to provide proof of identity. Any decisions of the supervising authorities need to be communicated in writing and, if they include an order or a prohibition, a time limit for compliance will be stated. In the case of serious violations, the authority can lay down an immediate prohibition on the retail sale or food preparation in question, with a time limit attached. An appeal procedure is available to the proprietor.

The Act takes a prescriptive view of sampling, in so much as a plan for each municipality is devised. The plan contains the number of units and their functions, with a view to the effective utilization of laboratory facilities in the area. This provision ensures proper laboratory cover. Once approved by the relevant minister, it is binding on the council. It is the Minister of Environmental Protection who may make decisions on the nature and extent of the control of food and drinking water etc. to be carried out by the food inspection units. Restaurants, on written request from the appropriate authority, may be requested to supply samples free of charge if a breach of the order is suspected. If the samples are taken in connection with a routine sampling control, it is usual for a payment to be made.

The control authorities have access to all buildings, premises or means of transport where food is manufactured, stored, transported or handled. The authorities have the right to obtain any kind of information regarding, for example, production processes, raw material recipes, accounts and other material which may be of importance for control in earlier or later links of the distribution chain. In connection with approval, inspection or other control activities, the authorities have the right to collect samples, order the enterprises to have automated control, order the businesses to change production processes, prohibit sale or production, reduce the range of products, confiscate illegal foodstuffs and have them destroyed.

Regulations issued according to the provisions of this Act are punishable with a fine and/or prison sentence of up to one year.

Principal legislation

In 1973 food legislation was modernized and the various fields of legislation and ministries/authorities were clearly defined. It was decided to maintain a general law, the Food Act, which would cover the whole field, supplemented by a number of special laws on certain foodstuffs. Today, there are eight laws administered by three ministries. In 1990, a law was adopted by the Danish Parliament authorizing the government to establish the rules that were required for the implementation or application of community laws, in cases where the Food Act or the special laws did not contain adequate provisions. The foregoing laws are enabling acts, signifying that the majority of rules are found in orders issued by the relevant minister (Fredsted *et al.*, 1995).

Food products legislation is contained in a law of 1973, *Levnedsmiddelloven*, from which further decrees and orders have been derived. The laws on food production and sale are very detailed and are enforced by the inspection of outlets.

The 1973 Act applies as a minimum standard to which all foodstuffs must comply (Act, 1973). The Act itself is worded in broad terms and is merely a statement of intent, with the detail to be found in regulations made under the Act. The provisions within the Act cover the following five main areas:

- Designations of, and information about, food.
- Packing and marking of pre-packed food.
- The composition and nutritive contents of food.
- The extent to which residues of pesticides, medicaments and other contaminants may be found in food.
- The sale of food which is assumed to have been exposed to radioactivity or pollution, medical examination and other health control of persons who are occupied with the treatment of food, and general staff hygiene in the food industry.

The purpose of the Food Act is threefold:

1 To protect consumers against health risks
2 To protect consumers against deception.
3 To ensure equal conditions for the trade.

The main emphasis of the law is placed on horizontal regulation, i.e. one set of rules covering all foodstuffs.

Section 12 deals with the principle that all food sold must be fit for human consumption. The assumption here is that, if the food is to be used in the normal manner, it must not cause disease or food poisoning; otherwise, it must be deemed to be unfit. Sections 13 and 14 cover the issues of additives and contaminants, and provide for ministers to issue regulations on their nature, content and purity. In terms of the sale of food, persons who are sufferers or carriers of disease are banned from employment in the sale of food (section 19).

Section 23 deals with the principle that the consumer must not be misled with regard to the product in terms of its origin, time of manufacture, nature, quantity, composition, treatment, qualities and effects. These requirements relate very closely to sections 14 and 15 of the UK's Food Safety Act 1990. These Danish conditions contained within Part 4 of the Act go into greater detail with respect to packaging and labelling, and the information provided to the consumer – points addressed in the UK's Food Labelling Regulations.

The central part of the Act is that the production, sale or storage of foodstuffs is prohibited, unless the authorities have given their permission. Danish legislation, within section 34, provides for a system of registration or approval of retail food businesses by local councils prior to their opening. In seeking approval, the local council may issue orders or prohibitions so that the business complies with the requirements of the Act. Approval must be sought again if there have been:

- important changes in the building;
- important changes in the arrangement of the concern; and
- important changes in the production or the range of products.

Thus, an authorization is needed for premises, equipment and conditions for production before manufacture or sale can take place. The rules apply to all stages from production to retailing. All enterprises are subject to inspection by the control authorities. The local council has the option to withdraw approval if any of its requirements, particularly those relating to hygiene, are not met.

Under the 1973 Act, section 42, one duty of the National Food Agency is to advise the relevant minister, specifically the Ministry of Environmental Protection. This advice could be on toxicology and food hygiene in general, or on chemical substances and pollutants in food and drinking water.

On 9 June 1993, an Act amending the 1973 Act on Foodstuffs etc was introduced into Danish Law (Act, 1993). It allows for the relevant minister to set an annual fee, paid by businesses, to meet all or part of the costs incurred by the authorities in their supervision and inspection duties. This statutory fee can be extended to include what is described as 'any extraordinary supervision and analysis'.

The retail trade in food, including restaurants and vending machines, is subject to the provisions of Order 121, 28 March 1980. This particular Order covers retail sales, including those pertaining to the preparation and serving of food products (Order, 1980). It is within the definitions of this Order, section 3, that restaurants, vending machines and mobile food premises are specifically mentioned as coming under the terms of the legislation.

Food may not be retailed without the written authorization of the local authority. Approval is also required on the layout of an establishment. The local supervising authority has the power to state which food products and other goods may be sold and which food products may be prepared. If the details contained within the approval are not complied with or are sub-standard in any way, approval to operate can be revoked.

The Order also contains detailed provisions, within Chapters 3, 4 and 5, to ensure hygienic conditions of the premises, and in particular, the health of food handling staff. In essence, the Order specifies detailed rules to be observed so that the premises are arranged in such a way that the preparation, storage and retail sale of food products can be carried out in a proper hygienic manner. In terms of the premises, a restaurant or similar establishment shall comprise:

- A sales room, possibly with a special service area separated from the customer area by a counter.
- A food preparation room.
- A storage area.
- The necessary refrigerating and freezing facilities.
- Suitable space, possibly in the form of separate rooms for service, cleaning equipment, cleaners and disinfectants, and for empty packaging.
- An eating area and cloakroom for personnel.
- Toilet facilities for personnel.
- Toilet facilities for guests, specifically within restaurants and hospitality outlets.

The floors, walls and ceilings are to be designed so that they are of a material that is easily cleanable. Regarding doors, rooms in restaurants may not be so close to other rooms that their proximity will have a deleterious effect on food products or yield objectionable odours. Doors to preparation rooms must be smooth and washable. Rooms in restaurants are required to be adequately lit with artificial lighting, and the premises need to be effectively ventilated, for example, by means of mechanical ventilation. Any open windows are to be fitted with a fine mesh net. The requirements for fittings, equipment, machinery and containers in restaurants are contained within sections 25 and 26. They are to be of a design and material that is suitable for the purpose and easily cleanable. Unlike common practice within the UK, hardwood chopping boards are specifically allowed in Denmark.

It is the local supervising authority that decides which foods may be sold in a restaurant. The authority can also lay down requirements as to storage of the range of goods, including requirements as to the storage of refrigerated and frozen foods. It is the veterinary directorate that prepares the necessary instructions.

Responsibility, both on reception and during use of foods of a fresh and sound nature, rests with the person responsible for the enterprise, i.e. the tenant, owner or manager. Foods to be served hot should be cooked to a temperature of 75 °C throughout. The relevant chill temperature is 5 °C for heat-treated easily perishable foods. In cooling foods, the temperature interval of 65 °C to 10 °C should be achieved within 3 hours.

Chapter 7, section 45, requires all rooms within retail enterprises to be kept in good order, clean, well maintained and well ventilated. Measures must be instituted to avoid pest infestation.

Sections 43 to 51 consider the hygiene and health of personnel working within the operation. Unlike the UK, which in 1995 introduced a general requirement for food hygiene training, such a requirement has existed in Denmark with the implementation of this order. It is the veterinary directorate, in cooperation with the public health board, that issues instructions on the hygiene of personnel. There are also requirements for the notification of personnel carrying infectious diseases to inform the local supervising authority.

On 22 November 1993 the Minister of Health published three new decrees, including implementation of Bill No. 351, introducing changes in the levy and control system within the food sector (Agra Europe, 1994). They were adopted on 9 June 1993. One such decree concerns the retail sale of foodstuffs, and entered into force on 1 January 1994. The new decrees implement a simplification and rationalization of the control of foodstuffs, along with the new levy system contained within the Bill. According to the decrees, the Danish Food Agency becomes the authorizing authority, and decisions made by the Agency can be appealed to the Minister of Health. The control and application of the decrees are conferred upon the local food authority with appeal to the Food Agency (Agra Europe, 1994).

Denmark: a European perspective

During the 1990s the legislative focus was related to efforts towards creating a legal basis for the EU. Practically all new legislation in Denmark is based on the EU legislation issued by the Council of Ministers and the Commission. With the purpose of maintaining parliamentary control, and ensuring efficient national coordination, a specific decision-making procedure has been established to handle Danish participation in the EU legislative process. The main elements in this process are that:

- a number of interest groups are involved;
- the decisions are coordinated between the relevant ministries; and
- parliament is involved.

Before the Danish government can give its vote on an EU directive in a Council meeting, the government position must be approved by the standing parliamentary committee on EU questions. This condition means that the government cannot take a specific position on a directive if a majority of this committee is against it. When an EU directive has been issued, it is implemented into Danish legislation by a ministerial order.

Another aspect to consider is that, since it is rare that cases involving foodstuffs are taken to court, there are extremely few judgments. Court practice has therefore not contributed substantially to the interpretation or solution of matters of dispute. This situation has not changed since Denmark joined the EU. As far as is known, no case has been taken to a Danish court where the question of compatibility with EU law has been involved, or where there have been matters prejudicial to the European Court (Fredsted *et al.*, 1995).

One area of interest is that Denmark allows the relevant authorities to levy a charge for the official sampling of foodstuffs. Another difference is that there is a system of prior approval or licensing before a catering establishment can open, a contrast to the UK's approach in these matters. In granting prior approval, the legislation is very specific in what is required in the catering establishment.

The Netherlands

Background

The Netherlands are the largest net exporter of foodstuffs in the EU and have a wide network of quality standards. The Dutch Food Inspection Service comprises 13 regional food inspection services controlled by the Ministry of Welfare, Public Health and Culture. Each regional service serves a population of approximately one million people. Until 1986, the service was the responsibility of 16 local authorities until it was transferred to central government.

The National Institute of Public Health and Environmental Hygiene is part of the Ministry, and contributes to food control at the request of the Public Health Inspectorate for Foodstuffs and the Veterinary Public Health Inspectorate (WHO, 1988). Each individual regional service has a director, usually a chemist, who controls a laboratory and a team of food inspectors. Every laboratory has at least one specialist section, e.g. meat and meat products. Each laboratory also has a microbiological section that analyses food samples for bacterial contamination, investigates food complaints and may also specialize in the same area as the chemists.

There is a long history of legislation on foodstuffs in the Netherlands. At the end of the nineteenth century, the local authorities started to promulgate legislation to prevent the sale of suspect foodstuffs. During this period the first foodstuffs inspection department was established in 1893 in Rotterdam, followed in 1896 in Amsterdam and in 1901 in Leiden.

Compliance with the main Commodities Act is principally the responsibility of the Public Health Inspectorate (PHI), which has the objective to monitor and promote the correct observance of provisions laid down in this Act. The PHI is referred to by its traditional name – the Foodstuffs Inspection Department. Although the title suggests that inspections are carried out, the PHI has only monitoring and criminal investigative powers. These foodstuffs inspection departments have two main objectives. One is to combat fraud, in other words, to promote fair competition. The other is to protect public health.

In 1986, centralization of the then existing 16 foodstuffs inspection departments took place, and their number was reduced to 13 under the newly named Public Health Inspectorate. The consequences of this reorganization were uniformity in penalties and in examination frequency. Thus the policies regarding the investigative powers of the different departments became more attuned to each other. The activities of the PHI are mainly repressive in nature. Not all goods are systematically tested before entering the market; sometimes spot checks are done. In 1994, 165,131 companies were visited where 265,333 samples were taken, of which 14.3 per cent did not meet all requirements. The PHI issued 21,557 warnings and 9,402 (3.5 per cent) police reports were made (Lugt, 1994, 1995).

As soon as a PHI official discovers an infringement against relevant legislation, the monitoring phase ends and a criminal investigation begins. Officials with criminal investigative powers can give a warning for less serious violations instead of a full police report. Generally, a warning is accompanied by an advice, a preventative measure to forestall a violation.

The Dutch system is not strictly comparable with the UK, as it is integrated in terms of its inspectorate and analysts. Coordination is the key consideration, and the 13 regions work closely with each other. Moreover, formal links ensure that expertise and specialities are shared. The weakness in this approach is that the lines of communication are longer, and there is no direct influence by individual services on financial control and the funds available to the service.

In general, the Dutch food inspection service encounters the same food hygiene problems and scares as the UK. Hence, surveys are carried out for Listeria in cheese and salads, and foodstuffs suspected of food poisoning are investigated for Campylobacter and Salmonella. Enforcement is much easier than in the UK because limits for the quantity of bacteria in food are set out in the regulations. This situation is reflected in the number of successful prosecutions for microbiological related offences. Pathogenic micro-organisms, in quantities that may be damaging to health, must be absent from food and drink products, and specific limits are set within Article 4. For instance, the counts of *Clostridium perfringens* which can be cultivated must not be more than 100,000 organisms per cfu.

In general terms, the sampling rate is equivalent to 20 samples per 1000 head of population per year (LACOTS, 1990). The methods of examination that are laid down in order to determine whether there has been a breach of the requirements are microbiological research methods, chromatographic, organoleptic determination methods and other separation methods.

Penalties for violation of the Commodities Act are not provided in the Act itself, but in the Economic Offences Act (EOA), which contains provisions on investigation, prosecution and punishment in relation to economic crimes (Lugt, 1994). The basic assumption of this Act is that general criminal law and the law of criminal procedures are applicable to economic offences, unless the EOA determines otherwise.

Principal legislation

There is no comprehensive Act on food related issues. Food law has thus been codified in several Acts, the most frequently used being the Commodities Act. In 1919, the first Commodities Act was promulgated, with the twin objectives of serving the interests of public health and fair competition. The Act has been amended several times and the last considerable change took place in 1988 (Food and Drugs Act, 1 August 1988), principally to adapt to European legislation. The Act is applicable to all movable goods, including foodstuffs (Lugt, 1994).

Generally, the law provides that a producer is responsible for providing food of the requisite standard, and does not need prior approval, except where laid down. This provision is unlike that of Denmark, which does require permission unless exemptions are laid down (Act, 1988). Several decrees and regulations which follow on from this Act include requirements with regard to hygiene for the preparation of food products on the premises. The requirements will eventually be replaced by stipulations based on the new Food and Drugs Act (Statute Book, 1988: 360).

The Decree Preparation and Treatment of Food Products (Act, 1992) is based on the above mentioned *new* Food and Drugs Act.

This 1988 Act is in essence an enabling piece of legislation backed up by more specific regulations. The main offence with respect to food safety is contained within Article 18 of the 1988 Act, which prohibits the trade in food and drink products which, due to their inferiority, may endanger the health and safety of the consumer. This offence extends to both the preparation of products using inferior raw materials and to products which, it can reasonably be presumed, would be unsafe. Consumer protection offences are contained in Article 20, which prohibits misleading labelling, text or illustrations.

The Act (Food and Drugs Act Preparation and Treatment of Food Products 10 December 1992) aims to include in one piece of legislation all general aspects with regard to the proper preparation and treatment of food and drink products (Act, 1992). Section 1 of the Act identifies a range of general stipulations, including a number of definitions.

Article 3 provides for general matters of hygiene and makes it an offence to sell food that is contaminated, or allows organisms or toxins to multiply, to the extent that they constitute a danger to health. Another feature of this section is that there is provision for regulations to be issued with respect to premises, equipment, preparation, transport and personnel. Whereas it would be possible within this section to lay down prescriptive requirements as to premises and preparation areas, it has not been the government's intention to take this approach.

The government decided to take an essentially deregulatory stance. It called on the relevant sectors in industry in 1987 to draw up hygiene codes in which each sector indicates ways in which the food and drink products in question may be prepared hygienically. This approach, implemented during 1993, incorporates codes of practice from different industry sectors on the hygienic preparation of products.

These codes were submitted to the Advisory Committee on Aspects of the Food and Drugs Act (*Adviescommissie Warenwet* or ACWW). The codes are regarded by government and enforcement officers as a general guide to compliance with the Act, unless there is evidence to the contrary. This approach follows in broad terms Article 5 of the EC Directive on the Official Control of Foodstuffs 1993. More specifically, it is in agreement with the position taken by the EU in the Directive on the Hygiene of Foodstuffs adopted in June 1993. The preference within the Netherlands is in shifting the responsibility to industry, although if no code is issued for a sector, the government will draw up regulations in order to protect public health. As a basis, the codes draw heavily on the General Principles of Food Hygiene issued by the Codex Alimentarius Commission. Microbiological target values are required to be included within the code. Breach of such target values will probably result in legal action by the enforcement authorities. Such values relate closely to the Codex Alimentarius General Principles for the Establishment and Application of Microbiological Criteria for Foods. Different values are adopted, dependent on whether the matter is at the production or distribution stage. It is recognized that it is not entirely possible to avoid a limited increase in micro-organisms during distribution due to the intrinsic properties of the food. At the end of 1999, eight codes had been drawn up, including a hygiene code for hospitality outlets, restaurants and catering firms.

Besides delegation to ministers, the Commodities Act also contains provisions that delegate powers to *Public Industrial Organizations*. By Order in Council, the administration of a Public Industrial Organization can be obliged, or can have the competence to issue, more detailed rules, or to take other decisions. A regulation by such an organization must be approved by the Minister. Although the Advisory Committee on the Commodities Act cannot itself issue legislation on foodstuffs, it plays an important role in the field of food law, and advises ministers on proposals for legislation. The committee consists of two sections, food and non-food, each having 15 members. The influence of the ACCA in the field of food law is considerable since, despite its diverse composition, its advice is generally unanimous.

Requirements for the storage and transport of foodstuffs in 1992 took a different approach from that of other countries. Food and drink products are expected to be stored in cool conditions in order to prevent micro-biological deterioration or the growth of pathogenic bacteria. If the manufacturer has not indicated a specific storage temperature, the food must be kept at a temperature of 7°C or less. In addition, the food and drink product must carry a storage label which indicates, among other things, that the product must be consumed within a fixed number of days after purchase. Also, the packaging of products must be such that the material is separate from the product. This Act took effect in March 1993.

As with the 1992 Act just discussed, the Food Hygiene Regulations 19 February 1993 implements much of the requirements of the Directive on the Hygiene of Foodstuffs adopted in June 1993 (Regulation, 1993). It was based, to some extent, on the recommendations from the Advisory Committee on aspects of the Food and Drugs Act of 9 October 1991. Articles 1 and 2 sum up the general requirements for the hygienic design of premises engaged in the preparation of food products. Article 3 indicates that only ceilings, walls, work surfaces and equipment that are all easily cleanable shall be used. Various infections and contagious illnesses prevent persons taking part in the preparation of food, a point detailed in Article 6. This regulation took effect in March 1993.

Under the Labelling (Food) Decree 1991, any transaction of food or drink not in accordance with these regulations is prohibited. This Food and Drugs (Amendment) Decree implemented EU legislation concerning the labelling and presentation of foodstuffs for the consumer.

The Netherlands: A European Perspective

On 12 December 1994, the Commodities Act Order on the Hygiene of Foodstuffs (*Warenwetregeling Hygiene van Levensmiddlen*) was issued to implement the EC Directive on the Hygiene of Foodstuffs 1993 (Lugt, 1994, 1995). It entered into force in December 1995. Article 1 of the Dutch Order implements the definitions of hygiene and of food businesses (Article 2 Directive) by adopting the copy out principle, including no European definition of food.

An important difference between the HACCP principles contained within the directive, and the Codex guidelines for the application of the HACCP system, is that the Community principles do not contain the obligation to establish documentation concerning all procedures and records related to HACCP principles and their application. Although this record-keeping requirement had been proposed by the European Parliament (1992), it has not been included in the Directive itself. An important additional obligation for the Dutch is that Article 30 section 2 obliges businesses to keep records of their HACCP system and to make these available to supervising officials. This will require inspectors to have a capacity to monitor.

Article 5 of the directive contains provisions concerning both so-called 'national' and 'European' guides to good hygiene practice. Article 31 of the Dutch Order implements the Community provisions on national guides. Since 1987, the Dutch government has stimulated the drafting of guides to good hygiene practice. At present there are some 15 Dutch guides to good hygiene practice, many (but not all) of which contain several elements of the HACCP principles. The use of the guides raises several questions in Dutch law. A first issue concerns the way in which the guides will be viewed by the monitoring authorities. Article 32 requires the authorities to take proper account of the guides. A second question deals with the fulfilment of the HACCP requirements by the application of a hygiene guide. One issue concerns the nature of the relationship between national and European guides. Must the contents of the national guides be in accordance with the contents of the European guides?

The Directive also gives member states a great deal of freedom to decide on the organization of the national monitoring and enforcement system. In the Netherlands, the Inspectorate for

Health Protection is the main authority for food monitoring (Order, 1990).

The hygiene directive allows member states to designate their own system of penalties, whether the offence be of a criminal, civil or administrative nature. In the Netherlands, violations against food legislation come under criminal law, and the relevant authorities have similar investigative powers.

An area highlighted in the Netherlands is the use of micro-biological criteria that are written into legislation, an approach rejected by the UK government. Another feature is the organization structure of food law enforcement, in which expertise and specialities are shared between the regions of the country.

In summary, therefore, the implementation of the hygiene directive in the Dutch Commodities Act Order on the Hygiene of Foodstuffs does not cause any major difficulties. However, some Dutch interpretations could be problematic.

During 1994, the Dutch government sent a memorandum on the future of food policy in the EU to the Commission (Agra Europe, 1994). The memorandum argued for a transparent and simpler EU food policy with a preference for horizontal legislation and only limited vertical legislation. According to the Dutch government, deregulation and subsidiarity should be the leading principles, in such a way that the EU regulates the main issues clearly and with one voice, and that member states are responsible for the application and more detailed provisions. Another aspect of the memorandum is the use of instruments, regulation and directive. In the Dutch government's view, in addition to directives, regulations should be considered more often.

From the description of food law in the Netherlands and the agencies monitoring the law, it is clear that the system is highly complicated. Moreover, the ministries involved disagree on the division of powers. This lack of consensus has resulted in discussions on what form legislation should take and on the division of powers concerning the monitoring of such legislation. It is perhaps inevitable that all government institutions will be brought together into one Dutch Control Agency of Foodstuffs.

Summary

It can be seen from this chapter that the topic of food legislation is complex and will continue to evolve over the next few years. While the framework of European legislation is well established, the detail would seem to vary within individual countries. A number of differences are listed below (see Table 2.2).

The enforcement structure in member states can be categorized as either centralized or decentralized, clearly having implications for the lines of communication between government and enforcing authorities. The UK takes a deregulatory approach in enforcement and has its unique system of TSOs and EHOs. The

	UK	Germany	France	Denmark	Netherlands
Principal legislation	Food Safety Act 1990	Foodstuffs and Commodities Act 1974	Law 1st August 1905 Fraud and Attempted Fraud	Food Act etc. 6 June 1973	Food and Drugs Act 1988
Enforcement structure	Department of Health, Ministry of Agriculture, Fisheries & Food	Ministry of Health; Ministry of Nutrition, Agriculture & Forestry	Ministry of Economy & Finance; Ministry of Agriculture	Ministry of Agriculture; Ministry of Health	Ministry of Welfare, Public Health & Culture
Enforcement	Environmental Health Officers; Trading Standards Officers	Veterinary Office within each Bundersländ also Police Officers	Direction Générale de la Concurrence de la Consommation et de la Répression des Fraudes	Danish Veterinary Service; The Consumer Agency; The National Food Agency	Public Health Inspectorate veterinarians or chemists
Legal system	Legislation developed centrally, enforced locally; home authority principle	Legislation developed centrally and to some extent regionally	Controlled centrally	Legislation developed centrally, food control is decentralized. Food control financed by fees	Legislation developed centrally, enforced locally
Registration and licensing	Registration	Licensed	Registration	Prior approval/ licensing including establishment layout	No, deregulatory approach
Codes of Practice	Voluntary with no legal force	Regarded as self-regulatory and have legal force	Regarded as self-regulatory	Voluntary	Voluntary
Temperature control	+8°C	Not known	+3°C	+5°C	+7°C
Microbiological criteria	No, except in restricted food manufactured products	No	Yes	Not known	Yes

Table 2.2
Food safety: differences and similarities between five countries

Veterinary Service assumes a key role in enforcement in many member states. This difference also raises the issue of the professional qualifications of enforcement officers and the provisions for ongoing training. Another aspect is the level of financial support and commitment given by different governments to individual authorities.

Legal systems vary between member states, with Scotland being more similar to France than to England and Wales. Discretion in enforcement powers prior to a case coming to court seems to be considerably wider in mainland European countries. Equally, the enforcing powers of individual officers vary throughout Europe, particularly with respect to the penalties they can impose, which may influence a proprietor's awareness of legislation. The legal status of a range of codes of practice relating to food legislation varies from the German Food Commission to the section 40 codes of the Food Safety Act 1990, and the Industry Guides to Good Hygiene Practice contained within the EU's Directive on the Hygiene of Foodstuffs.

The registration and licensing of food businesses represent a key difference within member states. Some countries take a prescriptive view on what is required before opening a food business. Such prior approval, or a licensing approach, contrasts with the registration procedure in operation within the UK. The UK's view is that there are already sufficient powers to close businesses that pose a danger to health, and therefore licensing would be an unacceptable additional burden.

Temperature controls vary between member states and indeed, up until September 1995, vary significantly between England and Wales, and Scotland. The range is from +3°C in France to +7°C in the Netherlands to +8°C in the UK. These differences will have to be resolved on a EU-wide basis, which may see amendments to the UK's presently enforced temperature control regulations. From a food safety point of view, 3°C would seem to be the best figure. Yet the question has to be raised whether it is enforceable. Equally, food quality would suffer at that temperature, and certain open chill display cabinets would not be a suitable method of storage. It could be argued that this is a matter in which subsidiarity should apply, with the EU only getting involved with inter-EU trade.

Microbiological criteria are already written into the legislation of some European countries, an approach that follows closely the views of the Codex Alimentarius Commission. The UK is fiercely opposed to this position, not least because such criteria would have to vary between the various stages of the food chain, from the farm gate to the ultimate consumer.

The influence of the European Union's single market will mean that considerably more of the UK's legislation will originate from Brussels, and will inevitably be subject to qualified majority voting as a single market measure. It is therefore important to consider the effectiveness of an individual country's approach to food law enforcement, and whether a link can be established with trends in the number of reported food poisoning outbreaks. Effectiveness can also be considered in terms of the national resources devoted to food law enforcement and the awareness of food safety issues by catering proprietors.

The development of an internal market is a continuing process that was not complete at the end of 1992. In the course of this development, the structure of supply of the internal foodstuffs market will change, not only in terms of quantity, but also in terms of quality. It is expected that with the completion of the internal market more additives than currently allowed, for instance, in Germany, will enter the market. Furthermore, rules regarding new technologies, for example, *food irradiation*, which some countries support, others closely regulate and still others fiercely oppose, was introduced on an EU-wide basis in the year 2000. On the other hand, there are a number of improvements in food law that would not have been achieved in, for example, Germany, without the aid and impetus of the EU Commission. There are, for instance, issues of labelling, (e.g. the labelling of nutrients and of alcohol content, and the labelling regulation relating to organic products) as well as drinking-water guidelines, and various hygiene regulations regarding animal products. .

A clear distinction can be drawn between two principal types of legislated controls on the hygienic production of food. Traditionally, though only for the production of foodstuffs of animal origin, prescriptive requirements have been laid down in considerable detail to ensure that all stages are closely regulated. This situation resulted in a wealth of provisions that were not always appropriate, or necessary, in particular establishments and, to this extent, can be considered as being disproportionate or over-regulatory. Steps should be taken to eliminate such excesses where practicable. More recently, it has become acceptable to rely upon the operators of businesses, approved and monitored appropriately by the competent authority, to provide adequate hygiene controls within a framework of varying complexity, often based on critical control points – this process has already begun with the Commission's White Paper on food safety in 2000 (discussed in Chapter 1). Almost inevitably at this early stage in the development of this type of control system, member states have felt obliged to supplement their sophisticated elements with a limited number of basic obligations.

The differences between member states exist and, if harmonization of food law is to be achieved, further changes are to be expected in the years to come. The decision for the regulators is how these differences are to be resolved, which member state approach should be adopted, the method of enforcement employed and their implications for hospitality businesses and consumers.

Trends and developments in European food law

Background

Following more than 35 years of legislative activity, most national food laws have been harmonized at the EU level. Yet, at a lower level, clear differences in implementation have emerged between hospitality outlets. A gap has therefore emerged between legislative intention and operational good practice at the unit level. Such dissonance has clear implications for the provision of safe food to the customer.

This literature review has revealed that many studies, in particular *The Study of the Impact and Effectiveness of the Internal Market Programme on the Processed Foodstuffs Sector* (EC Commission, 1996), have maintained that the EU's legislative programme in the foodstuffs sector has had a generally positive impact. Even so, this book so far has highlighted a number of criticisms of the programme in terms of: unnecessarily detailed legislation, fragmentation, difficulties of adapting the legislation to innovation and problems in the day-to-day functioning of the internal market. These criticisms were given added weight in Chapter 2. When one adds these dissenting voices to recent unfortunate events, such as BSE and outbreaks of *E. coli*, together they raise doubts about the capacity of existing legislation to fulfil its public health objectives at both the EU and member state levels.

The central issue to have emerged from Chapters 1 and 2 is that, in contrast to legislation in most member states, EU food law has developed very much in an *ad hoc* fashion over time. There has been no central unifying text setting out its fundamental principles, one that clearly defines the obligations of all concerned. Views concerning vertical versus horizontal directives, regulations, the use of codes of practice and what can be described as a democratic deficit between the European Parliament and the Commission, have tended to add layers of complexity to the issue of food safety. The stance adopted over the past few years has contributed towards a piecemeal, fragmentary approach towards implementation. Chapter 2 of this book has also noted differences in food safety legislation within selected member states, for instance Scotland versus England and Wales, France, Germany amongst others. It is therefore the central objective of this chapter to consider the equivalence and effectiveness of EU food law, and also to determine whether such legislation has fulfilled its public health objectives, both at EU level and within individual member states. Equally, comments on the coherence and day-to-day functioning of food law within the hospitality industry can also be made, a discussion that is set within the overall context of this book.

The evidence suggests that across the countries investigated, there are still substantial regional variations in the market for foodstuffs and, especially between northern and Mediterranean regions, attitudes towards food safety within the hospitality sector. This situation offers a partial cultural explanation for differences in attitudes towards national legislation, although separating out national culture from other factors is clearly problematic because of the former's multi-faceted nature. In addition, more telling differences emerged in relation to outlet type and hierarchy, differences that can only be resolved with the matter as to whether to accord pre-eminence to nation state or organizational type. Against this background, it appears clear that the EU has a major role to play in promoting a clear and stable regulatory environment as the foundation for further development of this sector. In particular, the transparency and efficiency of the internal market, enshrined within the Single European Act, is important for the survival of large numbers of smaller and medium-sized independent hospitality companies which must increasingly and inevitably compete with chain operations.

One possible conclusion is, therefore, that variation between EU countries on food safety *cannot* be attributed to national culture, but that differences within hospitality firms (chain and independent), and their employees are so associated.

Studies on differences regarding attitudes towards food safety have been limited to member states of the EU, both separately and at a regional level. Investigations in the previous chapters have shown that there had been an *ad hoc* approach to research on this topic, and a number of shortcomings in the existing secondary data were identified. The first drawback was the lack of relevant, comparative information, especially concerning inspection results and food legislation in the EU and its members. This problem of comparability arises out of the different ways in which the food control services of member states operate, and the lack of common quality control standards in the laboratories and methods of analysis. While, in theory, food safety legislation is a *single market issue* contained within the Single Market Act 1987, in practice significant variation exists, particularly in the implementation of legislation between member states and, to some extent, within them (EC Commission, 1986). This point is reflected in the comments contained in Chapters 1 and 2. This dilemma is further reinforced in the difficulties the Commission has experienced in compiling the inspection results required under Article 14 of the Official Control of Foodstuffs Directive 1989 (EC Commission, 1989a). Where limited statistics are available, researchers have not reached the stage of investigating the issues surrounding the implementation of food safety policies, let alone establishing a viable framework of food safety attitudes within member states of the EU and, more specifically, the hospitality industry. Indeed, even setting aside the problems of linguistic ambiguity, the literature and information contained within the secondary data from Western Europe are limited, and fraught with difficulties of interpretation.

The essential problems encountered in the literature review (Chapters 1 and 2) were the different legal systems and the idiosyncratic enforcement of food law in EU member states. This disparity in evidence before 1989 has continued, since the Official Control of Foodstuffs Directive only harmonized, rather than standardized, the general principles of food control. In fact, the laws and regulations on foodstuffs belong to some of the oldest legislation in society, and probably explain why the statistics received from member states are difficult to compare. In elaborating this point, if one considers for instance the incidence of infringements identified in previous chapters, almost every member state has a comparable pattern of law-breaking in the fields of hygiene, additives, contaminants, composition, labelling and presentation. However, with enforcement, the prominence of hygiene may reflect how member states have placed greater emphasis on this issue. Equally, there is a problem of definition, for instance, with microbiological contamination. Differences could be explained thus: it appears that some member states include undesirable substances, such as foreign bodies, dead insects etc., in this category. Also member states use different interpretations of the basic concepts underpinning their statistics, as for instance, the nature of infringement. Sometimes legal requirements lead to an oral warning by the competent author-ities. To member states such warnings may have formal mean-ings and, consequently they are reported in the statistics. Yet, in other instances, warnings are treated in a more cavalier fashion, and hence go unrecorded.

A further weakness in the literature review is that the studies covered were too discipline-specific. Some considered cross-cultural management, while others relied on food safety law or food science. For example, sociologists investigated basic con-cepts and beliefs about cross-cultural management, but they did not extend their inquiries to subsequent attitudes and behaviour towards food safety. The fact that these studies were not interdisciplinary in nature, or lacked cross-cultural comparisons specific to food safety within the hospitality industry, raises the question of whether the result would be the same if these studies of each area of interest were combined and administered to national industry-specific subject groups.

Food legislation and policy in seven member countries

National legislation

Food and beverage facilities within the European hospitality industry can be considered a component of the broader retail catering sector, and it was evident within all the countries surveyed (United Kingdom, France, Germany, Denmark, the Netherlands, Italy and Spain) that a wide range of sub-sectors existed (Knowles, 1999).

In the review carried out in Chapter 2, it was shown that a number of government departments were responsible for food safety and that this organizational structure varied from country to country. Within the wide topic of food safety, three main areas were identified: food hygiene, composition and labelling. Here it was found that in Denmark, the Netherlands and the UK, control in the latter two categories rested with one government organiza-tion, and while responsibility for inspection was devolved by region, legislation could not be determined by region. In the UK, food hygiene matters were dealt with by a separate government organization, the Department of Health (although the whole structure of food safety enforcement changed in 1999 with the UK's Food Standards Agency). Detailed comments on the Italian situation gave information in particular on the amount and frequency of control divided by region (Knowles, 1999). The EU Directive on the Hygiene of Foodstuff June 1993 (EC Commission, 1993a), was introduced within that country's legal system during 1995. Italian food legislation is highly complex and difficult to interpret, and much has become outdated as the country's cumbersome legislative process has failed to keep up with the need for change as a member of the EU. This situation was partly a result of a post-war constitution concerned with establishing safeguards against the arbitrary abuse of power, but it has made it more difficult for Italy to implement EU legislation.

Similar complexity is found relating to Spanish food law, based on the *Codigo Alimentario*, enacted in 1967, but not coming into force until 1974. The *Codigo Alimentario* contains a description of the regulatory aims and scope of the legislation, definitions of the most fundamental concepts of food law, and a list of the persons and organizations affected by the regulations. It has been supplemented by a host of decrees, ministerial orders, product standards and sanitary regulations. The responsibility for food control is divided between central government, the *comunidades autonomas* and the local authorities. In Spain, food safety legislation is decided upon by region, although there are close similarities throughout the regions. However, with such devolvement come the problems of consistency within Spain and the directives issued by Brussels. Within that member state, food safety legislation aimed specifically at the retail catering sector is based on a 1983 decree entitled '*Vigilance, Control and Hygienic Sanitary Inspection of Collective Dining Rooms*'. This decree includes both public and private institutions and covers all aspects of the hospitality, catering and restaurant industry. Equally, it comprises those establishments serving meals and drinks during particular periods of the year. The *Ministerio De Sanidad y Consumo* deals with the inspection of food sold to the ultimate consumer. The *Ministerio de Agricultura, Pesca y Alimentacion* is responsible for food products other than those sold to the ultimate consumer (a similar distinction was found in the UK's DoH and MAFF, prior to 1999). Monitoring developments in Spanish food law is a difficult task, since there are no uniform definitions of the topics covered by the term. Food issues are regulated by a number of ministries and, unless competence can be clearly imputed to one of them, *The Committee for the Regulation of Food Matters* would intervene. This organization coordinates any action taken in this field by the different ministries. Spanish food law is made even more complicated by the fact that agriculture and public health are not exclusive competencies of the central administration, but are shared by the autonomous communities.

Hygiene inspection

The UK allocated food hygiene inspection to a second government department – the DoH – up until 1999. Yet Denmark and the Netherlands located the responsibility of food composition, food labelling and food hygiene inspection within one government department prior to 1999. In all three countries, while hygiene inspection is devolved by region, legislation remains the function of central government. Centralization is the norm in

Italy where all the major duties for decision-making in food safety and hygiene legislation are enacted by the Health Ministry in Rome. Devolution at the regional level is strictly limited to the organization, control and inspection fieldwork, as well as the evaluation of results. Italian regions cannot determine their own legislation on these matters, a situation which meant that only the operational implementation of the EU directive took place through the involvement of regional authorities. These regions use as their operational arm the *Local National Health Units*. Decree enforcement applies to the whole country, except for two provincial areas – Trento and Bolzano. Here the provincial authorities are in charge of making decisions for the enforcement of EU directives. Hence consistency within Italy as a whole has not always been achieved.

An important element of the enforcement process is sampling and, while the EU has in recent years moved away from 'end product sampling' towards preventative measures, sampling still features highly within the national legislation of the countries surveyed. While the approach of statistical sampling is not employed in either Denmark or the UK, it is prevalent in the Netherlands and Italy. However, the Netherlands do not incorporate such sampling into legislation. Instead, samples are selected on the basis of risk compared to other foodstuffs. In Denmark, the UK, the Netherlands and Italy, inspection frequency of retail catering premises is on the basis of categorizing food safety risk. Such an approach is formalized in legislation within Denmark, and it is contained within informal codes of practice or general policy in the UK and the Netherlands. Contrasts are found in Italy. The minimum frequencies and number of samples to be taken for the control of retailing catering organizations operating in Italy are as follows:

- welfare and care treatment institutions, colleges, children and infant assistance institutions, at least every 6 months;
- school, hospital and charity canteens, at least every 9 months;
- hospitalities, restaurants, snack-bar, factory canteen, small outlets such as *trattorie* and *rosticcerie*, pubs, wine bars and other similar places, at least every 12 months;
- ambulant and seasonal outlets, according to the local regional authorities.

The minimum number of samples to be taken from retail catering premises varies within Italy's regional areas. However, on a national basis there are at least 30,000 samples divided on a 50/50 ratio, between organizations operating in both the public and private sectors. According to Italian legislation, along with the general rules stated for foodstuffs, each year the following numbers of samples have to be taken for the following items used for foodstuff preparation: additives 1000; flavouring 1500; materials and objects that came in contact with food 2000. This sampling could be taken at production locations. The Italian approach contrasts with that of Spain, where managers, owners or their representatives have a responsibility to comply with every aspect of the legislation, adopting all necessary measures to maintain proper hygienic conditions. All such catering establishments in the country are obliged to have a visit book in order to record hygienic control and inspection. If the inspection visits are favourable, meaning that the establishment fulfilled all aspects determined by the legislation, a summary of the visit is written by the inspector in the visit book noting the results. If the visit is not favourable, meaning some deficiencies have been found, then the inspector can apply the sanction of a fine, or temporarily close the establishment until the next inspection, at which time the faults would be checked again. Finally, there is the option to revoke the authorization to trade, which would close the establishment. Inspection visits are made every 3 months and always summarized in the visit book. No statistical based sampling is used in Spain. Each *Comunidad Autonoma* examines all establishments every year.

European Union legislation

Not surprisingly, many, but not all, countries have seen changes to national legislation since 1993 with the adoption of the EC Official Control of Foodstuffs Directive. The clear contrast in this section was between those countries that had implemented measures before or after the directive. Whereas the Netherlands and the UK saw change to food safety enforcement practices as a result of the 1993 directive, Denmark did not, except for Article 14 returns. For instance, on 29 March 1980, Denmark introduced food safety risk assessment for catering premises, along with registration and prior approval of food premises. The recommended use of EN29000 was introduced on 9 June 1983, and the compilation of national food enforcement statistics on 20 June 1991. In the UK, the compilation of national food enforcement statistics was introduced on 1 January 1991 as a result of the directive, along with changes to temperature control in 1990/1991 (further changed in 1995), and registration of food premises in 1991. The Netherlands saw changes to temperature control in 1993, even though there was no European-wide agreement on the subject. The introduction into national legislation of the new requirements of the EC Directive on the Hygiene of Foodstuffs (EC Commission, 1993a) was not implemented until December 1995 in Denmark, and specifically Industry Guides to Good Hygiene Practice, along with food hygiene training, were introduced in the same year within the UK. The EC Directive on the Hygiene of Foodstuffs June 1993, was at March

1994 not formed in Italian law, although it was eventually introduced within that country's legislative system in 1995.

In Spain's national legislation, both differences and similarities reflect the UK's approach. Since 1983, Spanish catering establishments have needed to be authorized and registered by the competent authority. Having identified a clear difference, there were, however, many aspects of the legislation that were similar to the UK's Food Hygiene Regulations. Categories similar to the UK within Spain's legislation include premises structure, kitchen and equipment. Reference is also made to personnel in terms of cleanliness. Spanish food safety legislation before 1989 anticipated all aspects of the Official Control of Foodstuffs Directive, and so no legislative changes were made.

Food hygiene training

It is noteworthy that the UK and the Netherlands saw compulsory food hygiene training introduced in 1995, as a result of the 1993 Food Hygiene Directive. Denmark introduced such compulsory training in 1980 (28 March). While the level and content of food hygiene training in Denmark is not determined by legislation, the question of hygiene did extend to staff who did not directly handle food, a point of difference with the UK. Requirements for training in the UK are enforced by a range of codes of practice, including section 40 codes under the Food Safety Act 1990 (Act, 1990a) and Industry Guides to Good Hygiene Practice.

Licensing of retail catering premises

Another area of food legislation in which Denmark is well developed is the licensing of retail catering premises. The system was written into legislation on 6 March 1973 and the structure, fixtures, fittings and equipment of such premises were determined by legislation, rather than by non-statutory codes of practice. While the UK does not have a system of licensing, it does have one of registration. A system of licensing is also not present in the Netherlands, although there are plans to introduce a non-statutory code of practice in order to determine the structure, fixture, fittings and equipment of retail catering premises. In Spain, since 1983, there had been a requirement for catering establishments to have the appropriate authorization to trade. Such authorization could be withdrawn if breaches of the legislation occurred.

Microbiological sampling

Microbiological standards (as opposed to sampling), defined as compulsory microbiological levels laid down in statute, have existed for many years in the legislation of most countries, except for the UK (in most cases), and Denmark. However, the UK, the Netherlands, Italy and Denmark have introduced microbiological sampling of foodstuffs into legislation. In the UK, the enforcement of the microbiological safety of food does not rely on the routine examination of samples as a central feature. Before the implementation of EU directives, there were very few microbiological standards in UK food legislation, e.g. UHT milk. Microbiological criteria do have a useful role within the industry, although expressed only in terms of guidelines. The focus on this issue had been to move away from 'end product sampling' to the verification of HACCP procedures. UK food hygiene law is generally based on a preventative approach, and the implementation of the 1993 General Food Hygiene Directive was welcomed by the UK authorities as generally supporting their approach to enforcement.

Although UK legislation had introduced such a microbiological sampling requirement before 1984, it did not identify specific pathogenic organisms or legislative standards. Denmark introduced such a requirement on 1 November 1984, and identified the following four pathogenic organisms: Salmonella, *Staphylococcus aureus*, *Listeria monocytogenes* and *Bacillus cereus*. The Netherlands also introduced microbiological sampling into legislation during the period 1970–1980. Legislation in the Netherlands identified six specific pathogenic organisms, namely: Salmonella, *Campylobacter jeani*, *Staph. aureus*, *B. cereus*, *Clostridium perfringens* and *L. monocytogenes*. In March 1993, the Netherlands introduced new standards, applying at the point of sale, to foods that were to receive no further treatment before consumption. The same levels for six pathogenic micro-organisms were applied to 'ready to go foods'. Levels were set on the basis of industry-wide data on microbiological loads, covering all 'ready to eat foods' produced under hygienic conditions. The levels set, therefore, were intended to be readily achievable, rather than onerous. Foods found to exceed given levels were legally required to be withdrawn from sale. The new standards represented a considerable simplification compared with previous standards. They were introduced in the context of new temperature controls, which also came into force in March 1993. These controls allowed food businesses, in some circumstances, to vary from the required chill temperatures, provided that shelf life was also adjusted. The microbiological standards were intended to be used as benchmarks by businesses setting time/temperature combinations.

In Italy, microbiological standards have existed in food legislation for some years. The standards in this country have played a role in food safety inspection and enforcement, and a legal role in the withdrawal of unfit food. The Italian authorities seemed wedded to this approach, and have expressed concern that inspectors would not be able to secure the court's agreement to withdrawal or seizure of unfit food in the absence of such standards. They are concerned that they might not have powers to secure withdrawal of unfit foods traded from other EU member states if preventative measures were extended, and would like to see wider microbiological standards in EU legislation. Due to centralization of the responsibility for the major food safety issues at the health ministry, Italian legislation on microbiological analysis had set standards for the whole country. The analysis and controls to be executed in laboratories on samples taken during production, packaging, distribution and sale of foodstuffs are carried out, as stated by the hygiene and safety parameters contained within the legislation. The most important microbiological analysis and control contained within Italian legislation refers to the following types of organisms: Salmonella; *Staph. aureus*; enterotoxic; coliforms; total bacterial count; *E. coli*; enteropathogenic; brucellosis; *Cl. botulinum*; *Cl. perfringens*; shigella; *L. monocytogenes*; vibrio cholerae; vibrio parahaemolyticus; and *B. cereus*. According to Italian legislation, analysis is to be regarded as a microbiological control to be made on foodstuffs, especially those to be consumed raw and uncooked.

In France, there are 67 microbiological standards covering the presence of pathogenic micro-organisms in products of animal origin (decree of 21 December 1979). The decree includes standardized sampling plans and laboratory methods. French producers were required to send samples regularly (monthly or weekly), to approved laboratories, and to take action (including possible withdrawal from sale), if the results exceeded the legal criteria, a situation referred to as 'auto controlée'. Inspectors could inspect the laboratory results obtained by the business and themselves take samples. The costs of regular sampling and testing by producers are high, and so the French government during 1993 reviewed the legislation. The report of an independent advisory group proposed some simplification and took greater account of the HACCP based approach; it was published in 1993.

Germany had statutory provisions relating to the microbiological nature of milk, egg products, dietary foodstuffs and, in some federal states, ice cream. No such statutory provisions exist for other foodstuffs. Assessment schemes with guide and warning levels (which were not legally binding), had been specifically drawn up for several groups of foodstuffs not covered by statutory provisions. They are intended as guidance for assessing in-house quality control and to aid consistent, objective enforcement in individual federal states. The schemes assume good manufacturing practice and are continually adjusted to take account of new knowledge.

It is a requirement within Spanish legislation that food served should never contain any substance that represents a danger to human health. Microbiological tolerances are set for food consumed cool, warm and frozen.

Food hazard analysis

The EC Directive on the Hygiene of Foodstuffs 1993 (EC Commission, 1993a) implemented, for the first time, into the Community a general requirement to introduce the principles of Hazard Analysis Critical Control Point (HACCP). It was this requirement that prompted both the UK and the Netherlands to insert the principles of hazard analysis into legislation during 1995, a point initially developed by the DoH's publication of *Assured Safe Catering* (HMSO, 1993). In contrast, Denmark had introduced such a requirement into legislation on 28 March 1980. The control activities on Italian retail catering premises aimed at verifying the correct preparation and storage of foodstuffs. Priority was given to ready-made dishes, particularly as there might be a long time gap between production, sale and consumption. Control also extended to those items which were subject to further preparation after cooking, such as roast beef, steamed or roast meat, food that needed added sauce garnishes, salads and meat, or dishes based on egg recipes.

Temperature control

Considerable variations in temperature control can be seen in all the countries considered. The UK on 5 July 1991 introduced two categories of chill temperature – 5 °C and 8 °C – dependent on foodstuffs. The requirement was changed during 1995 to bring in a single requirement of 8 °C, with a number of qualifications and exemptions dependent on circumstances. The minimum hot-holding temperature for foods to be served hot and kept on retail catering premises in the UK was 63 °C, a requirement introduced prior to 1960 (differences still existed in Scotland). The chill temperature for perishable foods in Denmark is 5 °C and was written into legislation on 27 June 1974. The hot-holding temperature for foods to be served hot was also written into legislation in 1974 and was fixed at 65 °C. A third set of temperatures is in operation in the Netherlands; during 1993 a chill temperature of 7 °C along with a minimum hot-holding temperature of 60 °C was introduced.

The temperature control activities on Italian retail catering premises, in terms of perishables, vary according to type of foodstuff. It is as follows:

- 4 °C for perishable foodstuffs, and
- 10 °C for cooked perishable foodstuffs to be eaten cold.

Food taken from the refrigerator for cooking has to be heated to a temperature of 70 °C or above, and has to be consumed on the same day of cooking. Cook–chill or cook–freeze food has to be maintained at either 3 °C or –18 °C respectively. Cook–chill food can be kept for a maximum of 5 days. Refrigerated or frozen food that needs to be regenerated before consumption has to be defrosted and cooked within the time period of 2 hours and to a temperature of 70 °C. Its consumption has to take place within 24 hours of being processed. Self-service catering food to be consumed cool by consumers has to be placed on refrigerated plates of a temperature not above 12 °C. Food to be served warm has to be kept at a temperature of 65 °C or above.

Food control statistics

In this area, a clear disparity can be seen between the UK and the Netherlands on the one hand, and Denmark on the other. While the former two countries undertake substantially more visits than Denmark, they report significantly fewer prosecutions for food safety related offences. One reason, perhaps, for this clear difference may be the nature and structure of food safety legislation in Denmark, which would seem to be highly detailed and prescriptive. It appears that Denmark has avoided the approach taken in the UK of issuing codes of practice, a situation that introduced an element of flexibility, although possibly at the expense of consistency in the application of national legislation. Issues, such as microbiological sampling, the principles of hazard analysis and temperature control, all appear to be particularly stringent in Denmark. This severity, coupled with a detailed licensing of retail catering premises, including their nature, content and structure, would seem to make commission of a food safety offence clear-cut and less open to interpretation. Another point to note is that, particularly in the UK, enforcement authorities had the option of issuing informal warnings, which would fall short of being regarded as a prosecution.

It is perhaps surprising that only the UK openly publishes figures for the total immediate closures of catering premises for food safety reasons, contained within the Article 14 returns. In enacting the Food Safety Act 1990, the argument put forward by the UK government was that, with such a power to close premises, there was no need for the prior approval or licensing of food premises. Such an approach to food law enforcement was seen as an alternative to the more prescriptive regulatory approach taken by countries such as Denmark. It would seem that both Denmark and the Netherlands rely on penalties for food business proprietors, short of immediate closure.

No process of inspection of delivery notes and batch numbers on packaging, along with access to recipes (their composition and formulation), was found within the inspection activity reviewed, qualified only by the response from the Netherlands that inspection of documents only occurred in special cases.

The preceding discussion has illustrated some of the difficulties in charting the differences between member states, in terms of food safety practices and the dearth of food statistics published by individual countries. It has to be noted that for many years, the Commission had recognized this problem and, in consultation with member states, attempted to harmonize the way Article 14 individual returns were communicated, so that the inspection results were obtained in a comparable manner.

It is obvious from the comments presented here that caution must be used when these results are compared, not only because of the different ways in which the food control service in member states operates, but also because of the absence of common quality control standards in the laboratories and methods of analysis. While, in theory, food safety legislation is a *single market issue*, in practice, significant differences exist in the legislation between member states of the EU. This discrepancy is born out in the difficulties the Commission has experienced in compiling inspection results.

However, an indication of the results can be found from 1994 data. Results of the Official Control on Foodstuffs, community-wide, for the year 1994 were published in 1997 (COM, 1997a) and are presented in Tables 3.1, 3.2 and 3.3.

Since June 1990, a working group of experts from the member states has advised the Commission on the format of statistical returns. The format now used provides an overall view of the official control activities. The statistics comprise categories of infringement and some analysis by categories of products, including the total number of sample infringements (see Table

Table 3.1
Total number of samples, 1994

Total number of samples	1 790 146
Violative samples	153 104
Regular samples	1 637 042

Table 3.2
Distribution of samples with infringement, 1994

	No.	%
Establishments visited	2 282[817]	–
Establishments with infringements	482 206	21.12
Infringement	Violative samples	%
Microbiological contamination	56 208	36.71
Chemical contamination	21 535	14.06
Composition	23 732	15.50
Labelling and presentation	37[966]	24.79
Other	28 631	18 70

Source: COM/1997a

	General hygiene	Hygiene of personnel	Composition	Contamination other than micro	Labelling and presentation	Other	Total
Number of infringements	232 553	114 627	25 816	22 506	61 496	57 234	514 232
Percentage	45	22	5	4	12	11	

	Products	Samples with infringements	Microbiological contamination	Other contamination	Composition	Labelling and presentation	Other	Total number
1	Dairy products	22 369	8758	2497	2333	3528	2952	348 859
2	Eggs	2316	659	122	110	1301	587	22 963
3	Meat	40 860	13 878	5192	6771	9661	5141	349 778
4	Fish	10 370	2816	2275	1007	2063	1495	133 068
5	Fats	6641	793	1342	2251	380	626	76 227
6	Soups	3621	1579	696	313	716	471	43 848
7	Cereals	24 224	7256	2293	1414	2759	3291	113 339
8	Fruits	12 160	973	2013	874	1848	1709	119 933
9	Herbs	1770	153	501	252	998	256	20 571
10	Non-alcohol	5745	604	402	525	2024	1570	38 313
11	Wine	8005	9	461	2675	920	1142	69 288
12	Alcohol drinks	4680	490	346	1149	2515	462	38 481
13	Ice	10 102	5238	177	703	911	2301	71 472
14	Cocoa	1423	103	246	160	593	129	14 269
15	Confectionery	2668	201	191	406	1116	422	22 473
16	Nuts	1340	126	348	188	397	86	11 906
17	Prepared dish	18 946	8016	880	814	799	1869	105 081
18	Nutritional uses	2456	192	299	287	1205	349	20 419
19	Additives	1885	64	393	61	251	92	7447
20	Materials	4015	1855	222	775	597	266	37 623
21	Others	9011	2445	639	664	3384	3415	72 206
	TOTAL	194 607	56 208	21 535	23 732	37 966	28 631	1 737 564

Source: COM 1997a

Table 3.3
Distribution of infringements, 1994

3.3). Results of this reporting structure from 1991 and 1992 were examined during meetings with member states in a working group. This discussion was to evaluate general trends and to provide an exchange of information, with the objective to improve the control system in each member state. The communication of standardized information on food control results has required a great deal of effort from member states since they have had to adapt their reporting systems. This adaptation has not always been easy, especially when this aspect of control is executed by independent organizations or local authorities. Nevertheless, all member states now send information on the results of their official food control by using the required Commission format, and some attach comments, providing additional information that makes the results easier to understand.

With the improvements implemented, it has now been possible to draw some conclusions from the results received by the Commission, although comments cannot be made on individual member states in any great depth. For instance, those member states that returned completed forms included a percentage of the actual number of visited establishments throughout the year, as compared to the total number of outlets. The number of establishments eligible for food inspection and actually visited was more or less comparable at over 70 per cent. Furthermore, it turned out that the number of inspections on average was about twice as high as the number of visited establishments, at approximately twice a year.

So far as the incidence of infringements was concerned, almost every member state had a comparable pattern of infringements in the field of hygiene, followed by additives, contaminants, composition and, finally, labelling and presentation. This trend may reflect that member states had placed great emphasis on food hygiene.

It became clear that some apparent discrepancies could be identified, such as the number of infringements mentioned under the heading 'microbiological contamination'. This finding can be explained as follows. It appears that some member states had included undesirable substances, such as foreign bodies, dead insects etc., in this category. Also member states had used different interpretations of the basic concepts of these statistics, like, for instance, the nature of the infringement. Sometimes legal requirements had led to an oral warning by the competent authorities. To some member states such a warning had a formal meaning, and consequently was reported in the statistics. Yet, with others, this was not the case.

Enforcement of food law in the European Union is basically a matter for member states, since the Official Control of Foodstuffs Directive only harmonized the general principles of food control. The preamble to the directive identifies it as a necessity for member states to formulate their inspection programme. This requirement should be with appropriate criteria arranged within coordinative programmes at EU level, with a view to completion and operation within the internal market. Despite the long-standing traditions of food law enforcement, there is a strong and growing consensus between member states and the Commission on how to arrive at recommendations for a coordinated programme of inspections. The format agreed upon by member states and the Commission is aimed at the uniform representation of inspection results. However, despite their rather detailed structure, member states use different interpretations on concepts like infringements, inspections and sampling.

At the end of 1994, the Commission recognized these problems of interpretation and stated that it would prepare a report that would try to harmonize these concepts. Furthermore, each member state would be asked to add to the next explanatory memorandum on the statistics, in order to describe in more detail what these concepts meant. As already mentioned in the introduction, the absence of common quality control standards, both in the laboratories and methods of analysis used, gives enough reason why individual statistics are difficult to interpret. In 1993, the European Council adopted specific provisions to further approximate national legislation regarding the official control of foodstuffs (EC Commission, 1993a). Specifically, Articles 3 and 4 refer to these quality control standards, and member states had 16 months after the adoption of the directive to bring them into force. As a final comment, it is important to recognize that the results of the inspection programmes and the coordinative programmes are not yet mutually comparable. However, Table 3.4 seeks to summarize the data presented in the preceding sections of this chapter.

Contextualizing the history of EU food legislation

What is being emphasized in this chapter is that the root of the problem of food safety lies within the law rather than with individual hospitality outlets or their personnel. The arguments advanced here are for various measures that can be taken to rationalize or simplify existing EU legislation in order to address the previously discussed variances within the hospitality sector. They begin with a consideration of certain aspects of the EU's working procedures, such as the choice of legal instruments and the possibility of updating legislation in accordance with technical and scientific progress. They also consider the scope for improving the coherence of legislation through the introduction of common terms and definitions. This section concludes with a review of one main area of EU food law – hygiene – that is of particular importance to the

National legislation	With the three topics of food hygiene, composition and labelling, division of responsibility was with more than one government department. Devolvement of responsibility in implementing policy was on a regional basis. A complex situation was found in Italy and Spain where in part decisions were made on a regional basis
Hygiene inspection	Denmark and the Netherlands allocated responsibility for food inspection to one government department. Inspection in the UK was divided between two – DoH and MAFF. The situation in Italy was highly centralized. Inspection frequency was based on food safety risk, and was written very prescriptively into law
EU	Whereas the Netherlands and the UK saw change to food safety enforcement practices as a result of the 1989 Official Controls Directive, Denmark did not, except for Article 14 returns. The latter country seemed proactive in many aspects of food legislation. Spanish food safety legislation before 1989 contemplated all aspects of this Directive, and so no legislative changes were made
Inspectorate	The data from this section of the survey were incomplete as not all countries surveyed provided details regarding the size of their inspectorate. Varying criminal and administrative penalties were available to authorised officers, including – improvement, prohibition and closure notices
Training	Whereas the UK and the Netherlands saw compulsory food hygiene training introduced in 1995, as a result of the 1993 Food Hygiene Directive, Denmark had introduced such compulsory training from 28 March 1980. While the level and content of food hygiene training in Denmark was not determined by legislation, it did extend to staff who did not directly handle food, a point of difference with the UK. At the time the study was conducted, there was no requirement for food hygiene training in Spain
Licensing	Denmark had a well developed system of licensing written into legislation on 6 March 1973 and the structure, fixtures, fittings and equipment of such premises were determined by legislation, rather than by non statutory codes of practice. While the UK did not have a system of licensing, it did have one of registration. A system of licensing was also not present in the Netherlands, although there were plans to introduce a non-statutory code of practice in order to determine the structure, fixture, fittings and equipment of retail catering premises. In Spain, since 1983, there had been a requirement for catering establishments to have the appropriate authorization to trade
Microbiological Sampling	Microbiological standards (as opposed to sampling), defined as compulsory microbiological levels laid down in statute, had existed for many years in the legislation of the countries surveyed, except for the UK (in most cases) and Denmark. However, the UK, Netherlands, Italy and Denmark had introduced microbiological sampling of foodstuffs into legislation. UK legislation had introduced such a microbiological sampling requirement before 1984. Denmark had introduced such a requirement on 1 November 1984. The Netherlands had also introduced microbiological sampling into legislation during the period 1970–1980. In March 1993, the Netherlands had introduced new standards, applying at the point of sale to foods that were to receive no further treatment before consumption. In Italy, microbiological standards had existed in food legislation for some years. The standards in this country had played a role in food safety inspection and enforcement, and a legal role in the withdrawal of unfit food. In France, there were 67 microbiological standards covering the presence of pathogenic micro-organisms in products of animal origin (decree of 21 December 1979). Germany had statutory provisions relating to the microbiological nature of milk, egg products, dietary foodstuffs and, in some federal states, ice cream. No such statutory provisions existed for other foodstuffs. Within Spanish legislation, food served could never contain any substance that represented a danger to human health. Microbiological tolerances were set for food consumed cool, warm and frozen
HACCP	Following the 1993 directive, the UK and the Netherlands inserted the principles of hazard analysis into legislation during 1995. In contrast, Denmark had introduced such a requirement into legislation on the 28 March 1980. The control activities on Italian retail catering premises aimed at verifying the correct preparation and storage of foodstuffs. The survey found them wedded to end product sampling
Temperature control	Considerable variations in temperature control could be seen in all the countries surveyed – the range for chill temperatures in the countries surveyed was from 3 °C up to 10 °C.
Food statistics	Incomplete data were obtained on food hygiene statistics from the survey. Limited data were obtained from a 1997 EU publication regarding 1994 food hygiene statistics

Table 3.4
Food legislation and policy – a summary of views

hospitality industry and central to this book. All these issues are of relevance to food legislation and its implementation within the European hospitality industry.

Influences

The problems of both EU and hospitality industry food law have already been identified. Yet their effective implementation can be regarded as a consequence of a range of influences. Whereas the focus of this book so far has been directed towards the hospitality industry, the primary influence regarding food safety has evolved specifically from the realization of the internal market (EC Commission, 1986). In the future, the development of activities in the hospitality sector will also be strongly moulded by those new provisions added by the Maastricht Treaty concerning human health protection (Article, 129), consumer protection (Article, 129a) and the environment (Article 4, 130r) (see EC Commission, 1993c).

As the previous sections and chapters have shown, EU rules applicable to foodstuffs have developed from the variety of legal bases set out in the Treaty to serve different policy objectives. The legislation is also grounded on a division of responsibilities between the Commission and member states, with the situation being complex and difficult to understand. Such opacity is open to criticism since there is no coherent policy and the approach is piecemeal. The BSE crisis in the UK, which affected red meat sales in restaurants, is one example that has highlighted the need for a European food policy to mitigate the fragmentary approach of legislators.

In this context, account must be taken of the fact that, following the entry into force of the Maastricht Treaty, the Commission has acquired new responsibilities (to which reference has already been made). Additionally, in recent years, increasing attention in the hospitality industry has been paid to issues such as nutrition, health and labelling.

Rationalization

Mention has already been made of the complexity, fragmentation and incoherence of EU food law. It is argued here that there is a need for greater rationalization, specifically in terms of the formulation of a European food policy, as well as an appropriate regulatory approach.

Against the general background of the previously cited 1985 communication, it should be noted that a suggested policy change does not constitute a viable argument for wholesale deregulation or the dismantling of the system of protection that has been in place over the past 20 years. The issue being advanced, one clearly supported by the literature review, is that certain legislative provisions are unnecessarily detailed and prescriptive; they fail to take account of the development of internal control systems by the hospitality industry. Duplication of legislative provisions between vertical and horizontal rules is a case in point.

It is a truism that all developed countries, not just those in Europe, have adopted a substantial body of legislation which seeks to guarantee that food is safe, wholesome and fit for human consumption, that commercial transactions are conducted fairly and that the necessary systems of official control and inspection are put in place. In recent years, however, a new range of issues concerning foodstuffs has emerged, as a result of increasing scientific knowledge (e.g., genetically modified organisms, awareness of the links between nutrition and health), and as a consequence of the new aspirations of consumers. As work towards the implementation of the internal market has progressed, national rules have increasingly been replaced by EU legislation. Today, the vast majority of food law has been harmonized at EU level and, in many fields, the scope for unilateral initiatives by member states is severely restricted. It follows that, with this transfer of decision-making, the EU must itself develop policies that both provide for a high level of protection and meet the legitimate demands and expectations of consumers. However, at the same time, the EU must also avoid legislation that imposes unnecessary burdens on the hospitality industry, the costs of which, of course, would ultimately be passed on to customers through higher prices. In essence, the central issue in developing an appropriate policy revolves around the adopted regulatory framework.

Regulatory approach

Whereas rationalization is the key to the development of effective EU food safety law, a regulatory framework must be designed and implemented in such a way as to take full account of the fact that the primary responsibility for the production of safe and wholesome food lies with producers and the hospitality industry. Thus, whenever possible, such a framework should offer the industry flexibility to design and implement appropriate internal monitoring procedures, provided that these steps are backed up by effective official surveillance systems. Hence, the opposing issues of flexibility and control create a dilemma for legislators. Whereas in some instances specific detailed legislation may be necessary, such prescription should be kept to an absolute minimum. In other cases, it would be sufficient for regulatory requirements to be worded in terms of their objectives and intended results, rather than in terms of prescribing how those outcomes are to be achieved. Once a clear legislative framework has been established, setting out the objectives to be attained, operators can be left to implement the legislation. This implementation would be subject to the effective supervision of the authorities, using HACCP-type systems, codes of practice and other appropriate instruments.

The problem for EU legislators is that both approaches offer advantages and disadvantages. In general terms, it may be noted that, rather than favouring one approach over another in every case, it is more often a question of finding the appropriate balance between the two. A horizontal approach makes it possible to take a general overview of a particular situation and facilitates implementation, particularly for food businesses working in many sectors, including not only manufacturers, but also hospitality, in both small and large firms. A vertical approach, on the other hand, makes it possible to adjust the legislation to the needs of a specific sector, particularly in cases where a more targeted approach to legislation has been judged necessary. It also makes it possible to envisage a more integrated regulatory framework that covers all facets of a particular sector.

Since a more prescriptive stance requires legislators to identify the major risk factors and the means of managing those risks, it often makes it easier for operators to identify their obligations, and hence facilitates the duties of the authorities. In this sense, for the countries in this book, prescription results in control.

A more general approach, on the other hand, leaves the industry with greater flexibility in the implementation of legislation, and is thus likely to reduce compliance costs. It is also likely to minimize the need for frequent updating of legislation. However, it requires both hospitality businesses and the inspectorate to take a much more active role in analysing the hazards presented by different activities and in clearly ensuring that effective measures are taken to control them. Evidence from this and earlier chapters suggests that a sizeable minority of those surveyed has not adopted this proactive approach. This requirement may present particular difficulties for small businesses working in the hospitality sector (i.e. 80 per cent in the UK and 95 per cent in Italy), although the elaboration of industry-wide codes of practice may provide a partial solution to this problem.

It should also be noted that the two approaches are not necessarily mutually exclusive. Indeed, evidence from the previous chapters suggests that the industry is experiencing difficulties in adopting a general approach and, while this problematic situation does not negate such an evolving framework, stronger emphasis should be placed on training and monitoring by the authorities (Knowles, 1999). The primary data of Knowles' (1999) study showed that relatively (and surprisingly) few respondents placed a high priority on training, and that monitoring was lax in some instances (16 per cent of hospitality outlets, for instance, had not been visited by enforcement authorities in the previous

12 months). In such circumstances, it is argued that a balanced approach is necessary between detailed prescriptive legislation and a more general legislative approach.

In developing this theme of regulation, due to the sensitivity of the foodstuffs sector within hospitality, debate has occurred as to the extent to which the use of codes of practice is appropriate, either as an alternative to regulation or in order to supplement it. The problem here is the degree to which codes remain genuinely voluntary. It is noteworthy that the study by Knowles (1999) suggested that a substantial minority of his sample (i.e. on average 25–35 per cent of all respondents) were not aware of the existence of such codes and whether or not they were legally enforceable.

Another issue to recognize is that, at the member state level, there has been an increasing employment of codes of practice, a usage which brings with it the risk of new *de facto* barriers to intra-EU trade and the free movement of goods and services within the EU. In the field of food hygiene, voluntary instruments are being used to complement the existing legislation: for instance, Article 5 of the General Food Hygiene Directive (EC Commission, 1993a).

These comments about problems in implementing a regulatory approach inevitably lead to a discussion on the concept of subsidiarity. It was Article 3b of the EC Treaty which stated that in areas that do not fall within its exclusive competence, the EU shall take action, in accordance with the principle of subsidiarity, only if, and in so far as, the objectives of the proposed action cannot be sufficiently achieved by member states, and can therefore, by reason of the scale or effects of the proposed action, be better achieved by the EU. For several years, it has been the practice of the Commission to include a 'subsidiarity statement' in all new legislative proposals, in order to explain why the Commission considers that action at the EU level is necessary.

However, legislative simplification is not an easy task, particularly with an expanding membership of the EU. Provisions that are considered as over-restrictive by some member states, may be regarded as fundamentally important by others. The potential advantages of legislative simplification must be carefully balanced against the risks of reopening old controversies and of creating a long period of uncertainty for operators in, for instance, the hospitality sector. The dilemma for caterers is the difficulty of reconciling the practical concepts of simplification and subsidiarity with the maintenance of a high level of protection for the consumer. Nevertheless, if they are to be fully effective, the principles of subsidiarity and legislative simplification must be applied at the member state as well as at the EU level – situations contradicted by current available evidence (e.g. differences in temperature control within member states). Consistency in the application of this principle is important;

otherwise there will be a constant risk of fragmentation of the internal market into separate member state markets.

In keeping with the principle of subsidiarity, member states can therefore adopt more detailed legislation in order to take account of the particular situation in their own countries, a good example from this chapter being Denmark in relation to the issue of temperature control. However, in order to protect EU interests, notably the operation of the internal market, the Commission has powers to supervise the use which member states make of this possibility. In some non-harmonized areas, member states have frequently emphasized the difficulty of using mutual recognition clauses to resolve problems of free circulation.

EU working procedures

In order to be effective, consultation on food safety matters should not be limited to the technical aspects of a proposal. Such initiatives should also enable stakeholders (discussed in Chapter 1) to provide all relevant information, along with their interpretation regarding the legislative approach envisaged and the costs and benefits of the proposed measure for the hospitality industry. Adequate consultation of the socioeconomic interests affected by EU legislation, before and during the decision-making process, is the foundation of transparency and is in the long term interests of the internal market.

Although this consultation process does in part exist through the Advisory Committee on Foodstuffs, established in 1975, it is important for reasons of clarity to take steps to improve the process through, for instance, the increased use of Green Papers.

Directives versus regulations

The debate between the use of directives or regulations is particularly relevant at this juncture since the provisions of certain initiatives can be extremely detailed, and leave little or no margin for the discretion of member states in their implementation. Examples include specific EU provisions relating to materials in contact with foodstuffs. In such circumstances, the use of a regulation as an alternative to a directive may present several advantages:

- enabling the uniform application of legislation throughout the internal market;
- increasing the transparency of EU law;
- since implementing legislation by member states is not necessary, facilitating the rapid updating of EU legislation in order to take account of technical and scientific developments.

For these three reasons, it is argued that consideration should be given to greater use of regulations in appropriate cases, both in primary and in secondary EU legislation. However, legislation that is limited in scope to the harmonization of general principles and criteria, such as legislation on the Official Control of Foodstuffs, should continue to be adopted by means of a directive.

Democratic deficit

Practices and procedures within the foodstuffs industry are continually evolving and, from the points of view of innovation and competitiveness of the hospitality industry, it is important that new products should gain swift access to the European market. This environment of rapid change means that an ability to amend legislation quickly in order rapidly to take account of technical and scientific progress, is of fundamental importance. From a public health point of view, it is also important to be able to adapt legislation promptly so as to take account of any new risk factors that may emerge. However, the problem lies with a Community that does not possess the instruments that are necessary to respond to the growing pace of innovation and the ever-increasing range of scientific knowledge.

One reason for this situation is the unwillingness of the Council and Parliament to delegate to the Commission the necessary powers for the technical implementation of EU legislation. Although the Council and Parliament have entrusted significant powers to the Commission in fields such as general food hygiene, materials in contact with foodstuffs and food labelling, in other areas there has been much less delegation of authority. For example, in the realm of food additives, any amendment requires on average about 5 years to complete procedures at the EU level. This, already lengthy, period increases to 6 or 7 years, if allowance is also made for the time necessary for the adoption of national implementation measures. By contrast, in most, if not all, member states, a similar decision would be taken far more rapidly by a ministerial order, on advice from the competent national scientific advisory committee, and without the need for primary legislation. It is thus argued that the adaptation of EU legislation to innovation and technical progress in the foodstuffs sector constitutes a serious problem, which needs to be urgently addressed.

Definitional problems

Another issue to tackle in the EU foodstuffs legislation is the problem of definition. Many directives already contain a series of definitions, including those on materials and articles intended to come into contact with foodstuffs, labelling, nutrition labelling, nutrition claims, official control of foodstuffs and hygiene of foodstuffs. However, doubts have sometimes arisen as to whether these definitions apply only to those specific pieces of legislation in which they are contained, or whether they apply more generally. To remove any further doubt, these definitions should be generally applicable to all EU legislation on foodstuffs. Furthermore, although the legislation of most member states contains a definition of 'foodstuffs', the EU does not yet have its own definition. The benefit of an EU definition is that it would ensure that all such legislation on foodstuffs would apply to the same products and substances in all member states.

A further question concerns the application of the definition of primary food production, which may be intended either for human consumption or for industrial use (e.g. potatoes, which may be consumed as food, or used for the production of industrial starch and chemicals, both of which may be used as food additives or for other industrial purposes). Their inclusion within the scope of the definition would mean that producers would have to fulfil all the relevant obligations arising under EU food legislation, which may be inappropriately restrictive. However, it is obviously necessary to ensure that all substances used in food meet the requirements of EU legislation.

Furthermore, the concept of 'placing on the market' is employed several times in EU food legislation, without actually being defined. Although a definition of marketing is included in the veterinary hygiene directives, its use is not entirely suitable for the purposes of foodstuffs legislation since it excludes retail sale. Other definitions of placing on the market are included in Directive 90/220/EEC (EC Commission, 1990b) on the deliberate release of genetically modified organisms into the environment, but these definitions are not entirely appropriate to the foodstuffs sector.

Having considered various procedural and definitional issues, the next section of this concluding chapter advances arguments on a matter of specific relevance to the hospitality industry – that of food hygiene.

Food hygiene

EU legislation on food hygiene and the hospitality industry is an area that raises difficult questions for simplification and rationalization within the Community. For instance, foodstuffs of animal origin are covered by a series of 11 vertical directives establishing specific conditions of hygiene for the categories concerned: fresh meat, poultry meat, meat products, minced meat and meat preparations, rabbit, farmed and wild game, fish, shellfish, eggs and egg products, milk and milk products, and other products such as frogs legs, snails and honey. These directives set out specific regulatory requirements for various features of these products, while using a HACCP based approach for other aspects.

Alternatively, for foodstuffs not covered by these specific provisions, it is the General Directive on the Hygiene of Foodstuffs that applies (EC Commission, 1993a). This directive adopts a more generalized approach to hazard management, based on the application of HACCP principles and the development of voluntary codes of good hygiene practice.

The co-existence of these two approaches opens the door to numerous criticisms of inconsistency and incoherence. Thus, Article 1 (2) of the General Hygiene Directive requires the Commission to establish a relationship between specific hygiene rules and those of the General Directive and, if necessary, to make proposals.

As a first step in this process, the Commission launched a large-scale consultation exercise on the inter-relationship between the vertical veterinary hygiene rules, which apply to foodstuffs of animal origin. To this end, the Commission prepared a guide to certain rules governing the production, marketing and importation of products of animal origin intended for human consumption. The guide envisaged the consolidation of the provisions of 14 separate directives relating to animal and public health into a single text that would also cover the conditions of imports from third countries. Certain common principles, such as HACCP, would be extended to cover all the directives, and a number of unnecessarily detailed provisions and contradictions in the texts would be eliminated.

Additionally, the Commission has launched a consultation exercise on the possibilities for simplification of the rules, with the following areas being investigated:

- the role of voluntary instruments, such as standards or codes of practice in veterinary hygiene;
- temperature control requirements;
- the need and appropriateness of derogations (allowances) for small and medium-sized enterprises;
- the international dimension of veterinary hygiene rules;
- the role of self-control by manufacturers and the role of the public authorities;
- authorization procedures and procedures for the approval of establishments;
- conformity marking.

Further questions have also been raised concerning the inclusion in hygiene legislation of quality or labelling provisions that are not directly related to food hygiene.

Once the relationship between the specific vertical hygiene directives has been clarified, consideration must be given to the association between them and the general directive on food hygiene. In this context, it would appear appropriate to give priority to ensuring that there is a coherent and consistent body of legislation relating to food hygiene. This goal can best be achieved by the application of HACCP principles and by limiting detailed prescriptive provisions to cases where they are considered essential. Nevertheless, it should be noted that there is some flexibility in the manner whereby HACCP principles are conceived and applied in present legislation, a point explored in earlier chapters.

Under the General Hygiene Directive, it was not considered necessary to lay down formal HACCP requirements regarding verification and documentation, a situation that may be considered a significant weakness. Each food business is left with the flexibility to decide what requirements are necessary, subject to the supervision of the competent authority, thus leaving an element of discretion. By contrast, because of the nature of the foodstuffs concerned, the basic principles for 'own checks', set out in the veterinary hygiene directives, include detailed rules on keeping written records for presentation to the competent authority. This example illustrates flexibility in the design and implementation of food hygiene regulations in order to ensure the maintenance of a high level of protection, while keeping the regulatory burden for a business to a minimum. The search for consistency and coherence between the two approaches has therefore not been successful. At the end of the day there is no uniform system.

Weaknesses are therefore emerging in this twin track approach, since to be effective, any system of food hygiene legislation must cover the entire food chain, from primary production to the point of consumption. The General Food Hygiene Directive covers all stages of food production and distribution *after* primary agricultural production. There is no general community legislation covering the hygiene of products of non-animal origin at the primary agricultural production stage. In the case of foodstuffs of animal origin, the primary production stage is covered by the veterinary hygiene rules. These directives cover all phases from primary production to distribution. However, retail sale in general is excluded from the scope of the veterinary hygiene rules, and the General Hygiene Directive therefore applies. The result of all this confusion is a lack of coherence and consistency.

Developing trends in the EU

Protecting the consumer

In the previous section, the discussion centred on the legislative approach adopted in EU food law, and specific attention was paid to food hygiene. Yet, an equally important issue is that of consumer protection. Contained within Article 100a (3), Article 129 and Article 129a of the Treaty, there are varying requirements for the Commission to address this public health matter (EC Commission, 1986). It is suggested that the establishment of a proper EU food policy that gives pride of place to consumer protection and health is an important step towards satisfying these Treaty obligations. In this spirit, the EU must provide itself with the necessary means of action, by identifying two imperatives:

1 A closer involvement of Parliament in the decision-making process (to this end the Commission should make more use of Article 100a, qualified majority voting).
2 The need to give the EU greater powers in the field of health.

As far as food safety is concerned, there can be no scope for compromise. The Treaty requires the Commission to take as its basic position a high level of protection in its proposals, in order to ensure that public health requirements are fully integrated into its policies. This level of protection must be kept under constant review and, where necessary, it must be adjusted to take account of new information, or of a re-evaluation of existing information. This section shows how these objectives are integrated, success-fully or otherwise, into the EU's policies for the management of the internal market.

Integration

In principle, consultation with independent scientific experts is the best means of guaranteeing objectivity and consistency of hazard analysis during the preparation of rules relating to public health. However, to be totally effective, the process of risk assessment must cover the entire food chain. A number of scientific committees have responsibilities that relate to the foodstuffs sector (discussed in earlier chapters). In order to be effective, an integrated approach to risk assessment may require consultation with several of these committees. However, while the involvement of several committees is necessary, their coor-dination is essential in order to avoid repeated evaluation of the same risk or unnecessary duplication of effort. Furthermore, the regrouping of all Scientific Committees under the same Commis-sion Directorate-General would ensure a greater synergy and a better coordination of their work.

On the other hand, it is important to note the limits of the role of the Scientific Committees. At the EU level, a clear distinction should be drawn between the concepts of risk assessment and risk management. According to definitions that are under consideration by the Codex Alimentarius, risk assessment is a scientifically based process consisting of the identification and characterization of hazards, the assessment of exposure and the measurement of risk. Risk management, by contrast, is the process of weighing policy alternatives in the light of the results of risk assessment and, if required, selecting and implementing appropriate control options, including regulatory measures. Clearly, such a distinction can lead to conflict as evidenced by the UK's, now defunct, 'beef on the bone' regulations. Whereas the task of risk assessment may be delegated to scientific advisory bodies, the task of risk management remains the responsibility of the regulatory authorities and, at the EU level, of the Council, Commission and European Parliament.

Particular difficulties may arise in those cases where, because of scientific uncertainty or an absence of data, the Scientific Committees are unable to undertake a comprehensive risk assessment. In such cases, in accordance with the obligation to provide a high level of protection, it would appear necessary to take a conservative approach to risk management through the application of the precautionary principle. To enable the scientific cooperation process to operate effectively, each member state is required to designate a single authority that is responsible for cooperation with the Commission and the distribution of work to the appropriate institute.

The management of food safety tasks at the state level is the responsibility of the coordinating institute. The Commission undertakes the overall management of the scientific cooperation process. As a final point, it is important to recognize the complementary nature of the scientific cooperation process and the function of the Scientific Committee on Food (SCF). In the area of risk assessment, the role of scientific cooperation is to collect and collate the best information available to member states on a particular problem and to evaluate risk.

Safe and wholesome food

Another aspect of consumer protection is that existing EU legislation imposes a series of obligations on food producers in order to ensure that foodstuffs meet certain required conditions. However, certain member states are more specific. Besides adopting existing EU legislation, they have also introduced into their domestic legislation an obligation of food safety, meaning that only food that is safe, wholesome and fit for human consumption can be placed on the market. Any food business selling a food that does not meet these standards is liable to a criminal or administrative penalty. It is important to emphasize that such a condition of 'safety and wholesomeness' constitutes an obligation owed by food businesses directly to the competent authorities. It is thus totally separate from the question of the liability of *producers* to *consumers* for defective products.

Although EU food legislation sets out a series of obligations on food businesses, except for the general Product Safety Directive, it does not currently contain a legal obligation that *only food that is safe, wholesome and fit for human consumption should be placed on the market*. Individual directives approach the question in different ways. For instance, there is an explicit requirement in some vertical hygiene directives for certain products to be fit for human consumption. Yet the General Hygiene Directive only states that the 'preparation, processing, manufacturing, packaging, storing, transportation, handling and offering for sale or supply of foodstuffs shall be carried out in a hygienic way' (EC Commission, 1993a).

In contrast to food legislation, Article 3 (1) Directive 92/59/EEC regarding general product safety imposes on manufacturers the obligation to place only safe products on the market (EC Commission, 1992b). However, doubts have been expressed as to whether the concept of product safety, which is laid down by this directive, is or is not different from the requirement that foodstuffs should be safe, wholesome and fit for human consumption. For example, food may be adulterated with substances that do not of themselves present a health risk, and would not make the foodstuff unsafe within the meaning of Directive 92/59/EEC (EC Commission, 1992b). Nevertheless, such foodstuffs would not normally be considered as fit for human consumption. The introduction of a general obligation of food safety and wholesomeness (in addition to product safety) would thus serve to reinforce the overall level of consumer protection within the EU, by encouraging all food businesses to introduce their own internal safety and supervisory procedures.

Such a new obligation of food safety may also help simplify overall EU food legislation, since it would avoid the need for more specific regulations in areas where general provisions would be sufficient. However, it would also be necessary to ensure that the introduction of a new obligation of safety and wholesomeness did not result in the creation of barriers to trade within the internal market. Thus, all measures should be compatible with the principles of the internal market and, in particular, with the Treaty rules on the free movement of goods.

To be effective, any new general obligation of food safety and wholesomeness should, in principle, apply to the whole food chain, from primary production to the final sale of the foodstuff to the consumer. It must also take account of the fact that interactions between producers, manufacturers and distributors are becoming increasingly complex.

Such a new development should result in greater joint responsibility throughout the food chain, rather than dispersed individual responsibilities. Each link in the food chain should adopt the necessary measures to ensure food safety within the context of its own specific activities, applying HACCP-type principles and other similar instruments. Where a food product is found to be not up to standard, the liability of each link in the chain should be reviewed according to whether it has properly fulfilled its own specific responsibilities. For example, it would appear wrong in principle to hold food retailers liable for the presence of an excessive quantity of food additives in a canned product over which they have no control. However, where cooked sliced cold meats are found to be microbiologically contaminated at the point of sale, further investigation would be required to determine whether or not the contamination has arisen as a result of poor hygiene during manufacture, a failure to respect the cold chain during distribution, or poor handling and storage at the point of sale. This discussion is closely related to the next section on due diligence.

Due diligence

This situation on product liability raises the question of so-called 'due diligence' defence. When a food company markets a foodstuff that does not conform to the safety requirements prescribed by EU or national law, that business may be liable to criminal or administrative penalties under the law of the member state concerned. However, in some member states, e.g. the UK, the firm is not liable if it can demonstrate that it has taken all the steps that could reasonably be expected of it in order to ensure that the food meets legal requirements (due diligence and all reasonable precautions). Thus, compliance with the due diligence obligation constitutes an absolute means of defence in any subsequent judicial or administrative procedure. In other member states, however, an operator would still be liable, although the fact that a company had exercised due diligence would be taken into account, in order to reduce the severity of the penalties imposed.

It is therefore argued here that a general obligation to insert food safety requirements into EU legislation should be accompanied by the introduction of a 'due diligence' defence. The question of 'due diligence' defence should also be considered in connection with the possibility of extending the scope of the obligation of safety to primary production.

Product liability

In recent years, increasing demands have been heard, in particular from consumer organizations, for the inclusion of unprocessed primary agricultural production within the scope of the Product Liability Directive. These demands have escalated as a result of the BSE crisis in the UK and in other mainland European countries.

In principle, the inclusion of unprocessed primary agricultural production within the scope of the Product Liability Directive should constitute an important step in the protection of consumers under EU legislation. Nevertheless, it must not be thought that such an extension would automatically constitute a solution to all the problems that may arise. Article 4 of the directive stipulates that an injured person shall be required to prove the damage, the defect and the causal relationship between the defect and the damage. Experience has shown that it is very difficult to trace the precise source of outbreaks of food-borne disease. The longer the period between exposure to the contaminated foodstuff and the onset of symptoms, the greater this problem becomes. In the specific case of BSE, even if a link were proved with the new variant of Creutzfeldt Jakob disease, the associated lengthy incubation period means that it is virtually impossible to prove that a particular product is responsible for the damage caused.

A further question concerns the problem of tracing the origin of a foodstuff from the point of sale to the consumer and back to the point of production. The EU has recently adopted measures to ensure the traceability of products of bovine origin back to the point of production, and it has been suggested that these rules might be extended to other products of animal origin. Consideration is also needed as to whether further rules on traceability should be laid down in legally binding instruments, or whether these would be better covered on a voluntary basis.

In these circumstances, it would appear that the extension of the scope of the Product Liability Directive to cover unprocessed primary agricultural production should not be considered as an alternative to the development of appropriate product safety rules and effective official control systems, but as an additional measure in its own right.

Consumer concerns

Taken together, these protection issues focus on the concerns of consumers. The principal aim of EU food law until now has been to ensure the free circulation of foodstuffs within the EU, largely through harmonized food legislation. By contrast, EU food law has not dealt, to any great extent, either with nutritional issues or with finding ways of meeting the needs of consumers. For instance, consumers have become more and more worried about the methods through which their foods are produced. Increasingly, customers wish to ensure that the foods they eat are yielded in a manner that is environmentally friendly and meets the welfare needs of farm animals. Recent events, in particular, fears about the possible transmission of BSE to humans, have highlighted concerns that certain production methods may also have an impact on food safety. Other issues relevant to consumers have focused on the ethical and environmental impacts of new scientific developments, such as genetically modified organisms (GMOs) in foodstuffs and the application of cloning techniques.

EU legislation already contains many provisions that are intended to address these concerns. Nevertheless, they raise two important questions of direct relevance to food law: the safety issue and the matter of consumer information.

As far as food safety is concerned, there is no scope for compromise. The previous sections of this chapter have described how risk assessment and risk management techniques are integrated into the EU's policies for the foodstuffs sector. The maintenance of a high level of protection implies that it would not, however, be appropriate to authorize unsafe foods or food production methods subject to a labelling requirement. If they are not safe, they simply cannot be permitted.

As regards labelling, at present, Directive 79/112/EEC only requires information on processes or treatments to be provided on food labels in cases where the omission of such information is likely to create confusion in the mind of the consumer, for example, where products are powdered, freeze-dried, deep-frozen, concentrated or smoked (EC Commission, 1979). In addition, irradiated foodstuffs must always be labelled. However, EU legislation does not require the labelling of production methods or processes that do not have an impact on the food characteristics of the finished product. It is high time that it should, and some believe that this requirement should be extended to restaurant menus and wayside food stalls!

In general, experience suggests that, where there is a genuine consumer demand for more information about certain characteristics of a foodstuff, this demand will frequently be met by producers and distributors on a voluntary basis, for example, through labelling, telephone information lines or the Internet. It is therefore important for new EU measures to encourage the development of such voluntary initiatives. Moreover, in certain cases, such as the recent beef-labelling scheme, further mandatory measures may be appropriate.

Implementation

Now that the harmonization of national foodstuffs legislation has largely been completed, it is necessary to ensure that the internal market operates effectively in order to provide the benefits anticipated for both the hospitality industry and consumers.

The need to ensure efficient management of the internal market has been recognized by the Sutherland Report of October 1992 ('The Internal Market after 1992: Meeting the Challenge') and by the European Council (EC Commission, 1992a). A series of

Commission communications to the Council has also emphasized the need for efficient operation of the internal market:

- Management of the Mutual Recognition of National Rules after 1992 (COM (93) 669 final, 15 December 1993).
- Development of Administrative Cooperation for the Implementation and Application of EU Legislation in the Framework of the Internal Market (COM (94) 29 final, 16 February 1994).
- Making the most of the Internal Market (COM (93) 632 final, 22 December 1993).
- The Action Plan for the Internal Market (COM (97) 184).

More recently, the Internal Market Council has adopted a series of resolutions which is intended to ensure that the rules governing the operation of the internal market are as simple and straightforward as possible. While the possibilities for the simplification of EU food law have been considered already in this chapter, the following comments deal with current arrangements for ensuring the effective implementation of EU legislation within the internal market.

Functioning

In order to ensure the proper functioning of the internal market, it is clearly necessary to monitor the adoption of EU directives by member states and to verify that the rules are applied correctly. Besides the incorporation of EU legislation, it is common practice for the authorities in member states to issue implementing instructions or guidelines for enforcement officials. Such guidelines are intended to ensure that the legislation is applied uniformly throughout the member states concerned, and to resolve practical implementation problems. Nevertheless, such guidelines may cause difficulties for management of the internal market when even member states adopt different interpretations of the legislation, with the result that provisions are not applied uniformly throughout the internal market. It is important, therefore, that transparency be maintained at EU level and that these differences be resolved wherever there is divergence.

For several years the Commission has followed the informal working practice of submitting questions concerning the implementation of EU legislation to the standing committees. The ultimate responsibility for the interpretation of EU law lies with the Court of Justice.

According to the Treaty, responsibility for control and enforcement of EU rules primarily rests with the competent authorities of the member states. The main role of the EU in the field of control is not to replace the enforcement activities of the latter, but to control the manner in which they are implementing the relevant legislation in their countries. A central element of this control process is the Official Control of Foodstuffs Directive 1989 (EC Commission, 1989a).

Control

The Official Control of Foodstuffs Directive 1989 lays down general principles for foodstuffs. The objective of the directive is to facilitate the operation of the internal market by establishing mutual confidence between individual country inspectors, thereby removing the need to repeat controls for products produced in other member states. Nevertheless, it should be emphasized that the official inspectorates of member states have limited resources and cannot examine every single batch of each product on a market, where the consumption of foodstuffs is evaluated at some 500,000 million ECU. Moreover, systematic official inspections would not be appropriate, in view of the quality and safety control procedures developed by the industry in recent years.

For this reason, official inspections in all industrialized countries are increasingly focusing on the suitability and reliability of companies' own internal control procedures for meeting product conformity objectives. This situation means that public resources are used more efficiently, since inspection authorities can concentrate their efforts on those companies whose activities give grounds for concern, and reduce the frequency of official inspections of those firms that have introduced reliable and suitable control systems.

It would therefore seem appropriate, if a safety obligation is to be imposed on food companies, to include in EU provisions a general requirement that the official inspectorates should determine the intensity and frequency of inspections, not only in accordance with the level of risk presented by foodstuffs and the operations concerned, but also as a function of the suitability and reliability of internal procedures introduced by companies for ensuring and verifying that foodstuffs conform to the required standards. Applying this principle would bring the general provisions on the inspection of foodstuffs into line with Article 8 of the General Directive on the Hygiene of Foodstuffs (EC Commission, 1993a), which states that all food premises should be inspected at a frequency which has regard to the risk associated with the premises. In addition, due account should be taken, in the operation of the control systems, of new tools which are being developed by the industry, such as indicators of freshness, which may be used to indicate whether or not there has been a break in the cold chain during the distribution of a product.

Finally, concerns have been expressed about the lack of transparency of certain aspects of food inspection and control activities, and the lack of consumer access to the work of the inspection systems. In its Communication on the role of sanctions in the implementation of EU legislation in the field of the internal market, the Commission concluded that the penalties laid down by member states for the infringement of internal market legislation should be equivalent to the sanctions set out in the corresponding provisions of member state legislation – effective, proportionate and dissuasive. These general principles were endorsed by the Internal Market Council in its resolution of 6 June 1996. It would therefore appear necessary that these principles should be introduced into EU food legislation.

In sectors that have not been harmonized at EU level, the jurisprudence of the Court of Justice provides a basis for ensuring the free movement of foodstuffs. In its interpretative communications, the Commission has presented its understanding of the principles concerning the free movement of foodstuffs in the light of the case law of the court. For example, in its 1989 Communication on the Free Movement of Foodstuffs within the EU, the Commission set out its interpretation of the rules applicable in the absence of EU legislation. Member states are required to admit to their territory foodstuffs lawfully produced and marketed in other member states. The importation and marketing of such foodstuffs may be restricted, in the absence of harmonized rules at EU level, only where such a measure can be demonstrated to be necessary in order to satisfy mandatory requirements (public health, protection of consumers, fairness of commercial transactions and environmental protection), that are:

- proportionate to the desired objective, and
- the means of achieving that objective which least hinders trade.

In these communications, the Commission also described the major specific problems that concerned the free movement of foodstuffs, namely:

- trade description (i.e. the name under which imported foodstuffs can be sold), and
- the presence of additives in foodstuffs.

Subsequently, the major problems described in the communications appear to have been largely resolved, either as a result of the harmonization of legislation or as a result of developments in the case law of the court.

From 1 January 1997, the Commission has had available an important new mechanism for the management of the internal market. In accordance with the provisions of the Decision of the European Parliament and the Council, establishing a procedure for mutual information on individual country measures deviating from the principle of the free movement of goods within the EU, member states are required to inform the Commission of any measure which impedes the free circulation of products that are legally produced or marketed in another member state. The progressive implementation of this new procedure provides the Commission with a much more accurate overview of the true situation within the internal market, thereby enabling it to take appropriate remedial action where necessary. These developments have several consequences for EU activities in the food sector:

1 The growing requirement to provide scientific justification for its measures at the international level.
2 The importance of taking account of the international dimension of its scientific assessment work.
3 The need to ensure that new measures adopted by its major trading partners are also in accordance with their international obligations.
4 The ability to play a full role during the negotiations within the Codex Alimentarius and other fora that lead to the adoption and acceptance of international standards.

Concluding remarks

The central message coming out of this study is that the realization of food safety legislation within the context of the internal market, whilst laudable, has encountered, and will continue to meet with, difficulties in its effective implementation. In considering specifically food safety within the European hospitality industry, there has been a move away from prescription to generalized principles contained within the relevant legislation. Yet, with such flexibility, differences have emerged in interpretation, all at the expense of the single market, free of trade barriers. Additionally, attitudinal differences have appeared at the unit level within the countries considered (Knowles, 1999).

The size of the EU inevitably means that more emphasis regarding food safety procedures will be placed on shifting responsibility to hospitality proprietors and also on appropriate monitoring by authorities. However, because of the nature and structure of the European hospitality industry, in terms of chain and independent units, and its transient workforce, the evidence suggests that a substantial minority is still not ready to assume these responsibilities. Such a situation may result in a twin-track approach to legislation, where the *desire* may be for a horizontal approach, while the practice reflects a return to prescription. A legislative body in 'two minds' will call into question the idealism of the Single European Act 1986 as it applies specifically to food (EC Commission, 1986).

This and earlier chapters have led to the conclusion that a choice lies between food safety initiatives that are 'wide yet shallow' or 'narrow and deeper' in their content. Differences in attitudes towards food safety have emerged. Additionally, legislation has been shown to vary within the EU. Such differences are probably a result of the piecemeal nature of implementing EU food safety laws and the historical development of food safety within individual member states. Evaluative labels such as *good food* and *good wine* will inevitably vary inside an institution as diverse as the EU. Such food safety problems will only begin to be resolved once the EU takes the important step of establishing a European-wide food safety policy (expected 2002–2003), expands the administrative food safety structure at the Commission and places greater emphasis on training, education and effective monitoring and control mechanisms. It is only with the development of such a policy and its effective coordination that the EU will avoid the legislative fragmentation that currently exists within the European hospitality industry.

PART 2

The Practical Application of Food Safety

An introduction to food microbiology

Prevalence of food poisoning

There has been much concern in recent years over the dramatic increase in food poisoning incidents reported to the government agencies that monitor trends in illness. Analysis of the figures provided by the UK's Public Health Laboratory Service (PHLS) shows a rise in a number of infections since 1982. The significant increase in food poisoning infections between 1982 and 1990 has been attributed to one type of Salmonella (usually associated with poultry and possibly fresh eggs). Greater public awareness of food poisoning may also be a factor in the continuing increase in the number of cases notified.

For instance, the incidence of salmonellosis in England and Wales reached its highest level ever in 1999, when over 32,000 cases were reported. The 12.5 per cent increase in laboratory confirmed cases between 1996 and 1997 represented a sharp upturn after a period of relative stability since the early 1990s. Most strains are closely associated with eggs and poultry. Looking to recent published data for 1999, 15 per cent more laboratory confirmed Campylobacter infections were reported in the first 49 weeks of 1999 than in the same period of 1998. Cumulative totals for the first 49 weeks of 1998 for *Escherichia coli* O157 was 873 compared to the previous year of 948.

The rationale of Article 14 of the Official Control of Foodstuffs Directive 1989 is that it attempted to introduce a level playing-field in enforcement procedures with respect to food safety and recognized that, through enforcement, food safety standards can be maintained at an acceptable level throughout the EU. These controls extended to other materials which come into contact with foodstuffs, and aimed to prevent health risks, protect consumers' interests and ensure fair trade. Under this directive there is a community-wide programme, agreed each year by the Standing Committee on Foodstuffs, to look at specific issues. Even with the aim of standardization, the directive allows member states a certain degree of freedom as to the practical means of carrying out inspections. It therefore does not prescribe which system is best suited for a particular situation in each member state, thus explaining why differences still exist between countries.

As mentioned, one key element of the directive is Article 14, the contents of which oblige member states to draw up forward programmes that govern the nature and frequency of food safety inspections. This information is required to be sent to the Commission, along with all necessary information on the previous year's inspection programmes. The statistics, which represent these inspection results, should provide a general impression of the state of affairs of official food control in the EU. Such an approach serves as a source of useful information for both the Commission and the competent authorities of the member states in helping to establish mutual confidence in the functioning of the internal market.

Details of the inspection statistics for the UK for 1999 as required by Article 14 of the Directive on the Official Control of Foodstuffs were released by the Ministry of Agriculture, Fisheries and Food (MAFF) during 2000. The data were submitted to MAFF by all 527 food enforcement authorities active in 1999 and cover the period January to December 1999. Some of the main findings are as follows.

- Having been constant at between 615,000 and 620,000, the number of establishments subject to inspection fell. The number of prosecutions dropped again, continuing the trend of the previous 5 years. The conviction rate of 84 per cent is in line with previous years.
- The data show a further decline in the use of the improvement notice, which also continues the trend of the past 5 years. The number of written warnings has also dropped slightly but is in line with previous years.
- The data reflect a decline in prosecutions, with drops in all the main categories. The information provided shows a further slight drop in the number of formal samples. The number of unsatisfactory samples declined slightly but the resulting

number of prosecutions dropped by about one-third. Overall, this represents a prosecution rate of about 1.1 per cent.

As well as causing physical discomfort, food poisoning can be expensive to the affected person, can cost industry money through sickness absence, can be expensive to treat and can have severe results (outlined below) for the business that made or sold the food. The costs to caterers will include:

(a) loss of business from closure and decline in product confidence;
(b) costs of renovation, cleaning and replacement of equipment;
(c) costs of legal action;
(d) increased insurance premiums;
(e) costs of promotion of company or business;
(f) salary costs of additional or replacement staff.

Food poisoning can also cause death. An outbreak of food poisoning associated with the *E. coli* O157 bacteria was responsible for over 15 deaths in Scotland in November 1996. Outbreaks of food poisoning are becoming increasingly common and can be attributed to a variety of different foodstuffs, besides meat.

Faults in food preparation which led to over a thousand outbreaks of food poisoning in England and Wales are summarized below. An outbreak is usually associated with several of these factors rather than just one. Most faults involve improper temperature control in cooking and storage. Common contributory factors to food poisoning for all bacteria are the preparation of food too far in advance with storage at the wrong temperature.

Categories of food poisoning

Chemical food poisoning

This occurs when food is contaminated by chemicals:

- during growth of the food, e.g. pesticides;
- during its preparation, e.g. disinfectants;
- during storage, e.g. substances incorporated in the storage vessel.

Chemical contamination may taint food or cause mild to very severe illness. For example, the odours from phenols, often used in disinfectants, may make food unpalatable and could cause illness if consumed. This type of poisoning can result from carelessness in the kitchen. Detergents, disinfectants and pesticides are often bought in bulk or in concentrated solution and need to be diluted and decanted into smaller containers for everyday use. Even when care is taken, spillages and leakage are possible. It is therefore important to keep dangerous substances including detergents, disinfectants and pesticides away from food, to label containers and never to use empty chemical containers for food storage.

Several metals which may be found in cooking utensils are poisonous if ingested in sufficient quantities. The risk is particularly high when these metals are in contact with very acidic foods such as fruit or fruit juices. This is why foods should never be left in open cans as the contents may erode the can's lacquer lining and render the food poisonous. Care should be taken to avoid prolonged contact between acidic foods and equipment containing the metals.

Natural poisons (toxins)

These occur in a wide variety of plants (e.g. raw beans), mushrooms, toadstools, fish and shellfish. This is discussed later in this chapter.

Types of bacteria

These are by far the most commonly reported causes of food poisoning are discussed below in detail. The nature of bacteria is discussed later in this chapter.

The genus **Campylobacter** covers a diverse range of species. Two of the main species are *C. jejuni* and *C. coli*. These two species are responsible for most infections that occur, which are generally referred to as *C. enteritis*. Campylobacter is the most common cause of food poisoning; over 43,000 cases were reported in 1999, which is just over half of all reported food poisoning cases in England and Wales. Infants and young adults have the greatest incidence of the infection. There is also a seasonal trend, the highest incidence occurring in spring/early summer.

The incubation period is usually 2–5 days.

The symptoms are fever, malaise and diarrhoea. Blood and mucus may also be present in stools.

Symptoms in most people last 1–11 days; however, the symptoms may last for several weeks.

Campylobacter is found in the intestines of many animals, such as cattle and sheep. It is frequently associated with undercooked poultry, and from cross-contamination of other food. Barbecue and fondue cooking methods carry an increased risk of infection. Infection has also been attributed to the contamination of milk by birds that peck through the tops of milk bottles.

Campylobacter more readily survives at chill temperatures such as on/in chilled chicken. It can also be transferred to foods via hands and utensils.

Most strains of *Escherichia coli* are harmless bacteria inhabiting human intestines. However, a number of strains can cause illness. *E. coli* O157 is a particularly severe strain responsible for several outbreaks and deaths. At the end of 1996 there were 633 reported cases and 16 deaths.

The incubation period depends on the strain. *E. coli* O157 has an incubation period of 1–7 days. Toxins are released causing the symptoms.

The symptoms are mainly diarrhoea and abdominal pain, although more serious illnesses such as kidney failure can occur with strain O157.

Length of illness is variable and is linked with the type and strain responsible.

E. coli is found in animals and may be spread by undercooked or cross-contaminated meat, unpasteurised milk or other ready-to-eat foods. A person can be infected in the following ways:

- through the faecal–oral route;
- through contaminated water'
- from person to person.

The different bacteria of the genus **Salmonella** (generically referred to here as salmonellae) are one of the common causes of food poisoning in this country; over 29,000 cases were reported in 1998. Symptoms can be severe and they cause approximately 50 deaths each year. The young, the elderly and people with existing illnesses are most at risk.

The incubation period is usually 12–72 hours. Salmonella bacteria enter the small intestine where they multiply and release a toxin resulting in illness.

The symptoms are mainly diarrhoea, vomiting and fever accompanied by headache. In 1–2% of reported cases a more serious generalized infection occurs.

Symptoms in most people last 1–10 days, however some people can be ill for much longer. Even after recovery a person can have Salmonella bacteria in his or her stools (faeces) for long periods.

Salmonellae are found in the intestines of many animals, including cattle, pigs and poultry. In the kitchen salmonellae are found in raw foods, particularly meats and poultry, unpasteurised milk and eggs. Other raw foods including vegetables and spices have occasionally been found to be contaminated. A person can be infected in the following ways.

- From contaminated raw foods if not properly cooked. (In the laboratory temperatures above 65 °C throughout food will kill salmonellae.)
- Salmonellae from raw foods may contaminate work surfaces, utensils and hands. When this occurs the bacteria can be

transferred to other foods which touch those surfaces. If already cooked, such foods become a severe risk if kept in the temperature danger zone (8–63 °C) for a long period.

- Insects and vermin can introduce or spread salmonellae around the kitchen.

About 1000 cases of **Clostridium perfringens** infection are reported each year, making this a common type of food poisoning, although illness is usually short in duration. Clostridia grow in anaerobic conditions (without oxygen) but heat-resistant spores are formed when growth conditions are unfavourable, i.e. when exposed to air or if there is lack of moisture.

The incubation period is 8–22 hours (usually 12–18 hours). When bacteria reach the intestine they form spores and at the same time release a toxin which causes illness.

The symptoms are diarrhoea and marked abdominal pains (rarely vomiting), which generally last no more than 12–48 hours.

Cl. perfringens can often be found in the intestines of animals (including humans) and spores can be found in the soil. It enters the kitchen in raw meats and on raw vegetables, particularly when coated with soil. Flies are often contaminated with Clostridia bacteria.

Spores that survive cooking germinate in the food and the bacteria will multiply rapidly given ideal conditions. Foods cooked slowly at low temperatures and then stored warm are particularly at risk. Such high risk foods include stews, gravies, pies and large meat joints.

Staphylococcal food poisoning is less common than it used to be and is characterized by a short incubation period and a relatively quick recovery. The bacteria produce a toxin which is more resistant to heat than the bacterium itself.

The incubation period is 1–7 hours (usually 2–6 hours).

Large numbers of bacteria produce a toxin in the food before it is eaten. As the toxin irritates the stomach and is already present in the food when eaten, the onset of illness is rapid.

The symptoms are severe vomiting sometimes followed by collapse; occasionally diarrhoea and abdominal cramps. Dehydration can also occur. This usually lasts for 6–24 hours.

The bacteria are frequently found in the nose, the throat and on the skin of healthy people and are also found in septic cuts, spots and boils on the skin.

They enter the kitchen via food handlers directly touching food and by sneezing or coughing etc. over food. Contamination also occurs by contact with cuts not covered by a proper waterproof dressing and by food handlers touching septic spots then touching food.

The bacteria will grow on salty foods and foods which have been cooked and are then eaten cold or only given minimal reheating (e.g. cold meats or puddings such as trifles). A toxin is released into the food as the bacteria multiply and may be present even after the bacteria have been killed.

The **Bacillus** bacteria, especially *Bacillus cereus*, are increasingly being reported as agents of food poisoning. Growing cells produce toxins in food and illness is characterized by a relatively short incubation period and recovery usually within 24 hours. Two types of illness occur. Either a very short incubation period of 1–5 hours due to toxin in the food acting on the stomach, or a longer incubation period of 9–18 hours due to a toxin which acts on the small intestine.

The short incubation illness causes mainly vomiting while the longer incubation illness invariably leads to diarrhoea. The duration of the illness is usually 6–24 hours.

B. cereus spores are common in the environment and are often found on cereals, particularly rice, and in spices. They may also be present in powdered cereal products such as cornflour.

The spores will survive many cooking processes. If food is cooled too slowly or stored at temperatures in the danger zone the spores germinate and the bacteria multiply rapidly producing the toxins; rice dishes are typically associated with this type of food poisoning. Prolonged warm storage of cooked cereals, especially rice, should therefore be avoided.

The 'vomiting' toxin is produced in the food and is heat-resistant; the 'diarrhoea' toxin is destroyed by cooking.

Listeria infections do not usually occur in healthy adults, but pregnant women and the elderly are particularly at risk.

Flu-like symptoms may occur, with occasional diarrhoea. However many symptoms are severe and include meningitis or septicaemia.

Listeria is found in animals, and especially in soft cheese and milk. *Listeria monocytogenes* can grow in refrigeration temperatures meaning normal cooling of food does not guarantee freedom.

In addition to the common agents of food poisoning already described, a rare but very serious type of food poisoning which affects the nervous system is caused by ***Clostridium botulinum***. This bacterium produces a toxin which can be fatal in severe cases and surviving cases may take many months to recover. (The toxin, however, is destroyed by cooking.) The bacteria do not require air to grow and produce heat-resistant spores, so faulty canned, bottled or vacuum packed foods are at special risk. Any such product with evidence of gas inside (e.g. blown cans) should be discarded immediately.

Bacteria and their characteristics

Bacteria are self-contained, single-celled organisms, so small that they can only be seen through a microscope. They are found everywhere – in soil, air, water, on people, animals and food – so even an apparently clean kitchen surface could have many millions of bacteria on it. Bacteria are measured in micrometres and therefore they are only visible in large numbers, i.e. slime on the surface of food, or with the use of a powerful microscope. To understand why good food hygiene standards are necessary it is important to understand how bacteria grow and how to prevent them growing.

Bacteria are a diverse group of organisms, and only a few thousand types (species) of bacteria are pathogenic, i.e. causing disease in humans. An even smaller number cause food poisoning or are transmitted via contaminated food.

Of those bacteria which are not harmful, there are some whose properties can be used to a positive advantage in the:

- production of some essential vitamins in the human body;
- manufacture of cheese and yoghurt;
- fermentation of certain foods and drinks;
- production of antibiotics and other medicines.

On the negative side, however, bacteria may cause two types of food spoilage:

- a deterioration in the food's appearance, smell, taste or texture (e.g. fermentation) which, whilst not necessarily dangerous, discourages consumption;
- a non-apparent but dangerous deterioration in the food.

In addition, storage conditions that lead to a deterioration in the appearance of food are also likely to require immediate attention.

Appearance

In the laboratory, bacteria are first differentiated by their shape. Those which are most commonly associated with food-borne illness may be spherical (cocci), e.g. streptococci; rod shaped (bacilli), e.g. salmonellae; or curved rods (vibrios). These may grow individually, in clumps or in chains.

Spores

With minor exceptions, only two bacterial genera, Bacillus and Clostridium, are able to form spores capable of surviving adverse conditions. Temperatures achieved during normal cooking may destroy most bacteria, yet any spores present will probably survive. Furthermore, as the food cools down spores may germinate and reproduce. Very high temperatures, in excess of 100°C are often required for long periods to ensure their destruction, hence the canning of low acid foods is based on the destruction of *Clostridium botulinum* spores at 121°C for 3 minutes.

Toxins

It is possible that bacteria could release poisons known as toxins and in extreme cases those produced by *Clostridium botulinum* can cause death. There are a number of types of toxin production. One example is exotoxins – highly toxic proteins produced by bacteria, quite often produced in food and occasionally heat-resistant.

Identification

The process of identifying bacteria is complex, although in simple terms it commences by spreading the bacterial mixture onto the surface of a culture medium. Selective media, atmosphere and temperature are critical in promoting or precluding growth of specific bacteria. During incubation, the bacteria grow to create colonies; their shape, size and colour will aid identification. One technique of identification is the bacteria's reaction to staining.

Bacteria can be divided into two groups, Gram-positive and Gram-negative, dependent on whether or not they retain a violet/iodine dye after treatment. Additionally, the use of microscopes allows observation of staining reactions. Other more sophisticated techniques are available in the investigative process.

Multiplication

Bacteria grow by absorbing nutrients from their immediate environment and multiply by simply dividing in two; in the right conditions these processes can be remarkably quick. For instance, 1000 bacteria could become 1 million in less than 2 hours and may cause food poisoning. Bacteria can usually be killed by heating or by chemicals such as chlorine and strong detergents. However, some bacteria, including a few species that cause food poisoning, form very resilient spores when conditions for growth become unfavourable. These spores may be able to survive attack by chemicals and even boiling for 3–4 hours. When conditions again become favourable for growth, the spores germinate and the bacteria begin to multiply. If such spores are present in a food that has been cooked they can pose a threat if the food is then stored at room temperature for more than a few hours.

Factors influencing multiplication

Most bacteria are aerobes, that is, they need air to survive. Some, however, including a few species which cause food poisoning, grow and multiply in the absence of air; these are known as anaerobes. Many modern foods are packaged deliberately to exclude air (e.g. canned and vacuum packed food) and are processed in ways that destroy aerobic and anaerobic bacteria and thus are normally very safe. Serious problems can occur if even a minute hole is made in the packaging; bacteria can enter and spoil the food or the contents can be contaminated with bacterial species able to cause serious forms of food poisoning, e.g. *Clostridium botulinum*. The main requirements for bacteria to grow are:

- food
- nutrients
- pH
- moisture
- temperature
- time
- oxygen
- competition.

Food

Bacteria will grow and multiply in a wide variety of foodstuffs, particularly those rich in protein. Thus meat, poultry and meat products, dairy products and egg products provide ideal food for bacteria. It is important to note that even small amounts of these foods, if trapped in cracks or joints on working surfaces, can provide nutrients for large numbers of bacteria and therefore act as a source of contamination. This is why the need for regular, thorough cleaning of working surfaces is given so much emphasis. Obviously, it will be easier to keep surfaces clean if they are made of materials such as stainless steel or polypropylene which do not crack or pit easily and joints are kept to a minimum. This is also the reason why wooden chopping boards are not appropriate in kitchens.

Nutrients

A related issue to food is one of nutrients, as bacteria require carbon, hydrogen, oxygen and nitrogen along with other elements, all dissolved in water, before they can enter the bacterium. Most bacteria obtain the basic elements from sugar, amino acids, fats and minerals and favour high protein foods such as milk, eggs, meat and fish. Foods with high sugar or salt content are unsuitable for growth of most bacteria.

pH

On a scale of 0 to 14, acid foods have a pH value less than 7 and alkaline foods above 7, while 7 is neutral. Bacterial growth tends to progress best at pH 7 and least in high acidic foods.

Moisture ❋ ❋ ❋

Many foods, e.g. raw meats, contain enough moisture to enable bacteria to grow. In some foods the amount of water available to bacteria is deliberately limited so as to prevent growth. Thus, food may be dehydrated, e.g. dried milk powder, dried fruit and vegetables; preserved in a high concentration of sugar, e.g. jams; or preserved in salt, e.g. salt meat. These methods reduce the availability of water to the bacterial cells, which cannot then survive. It is important to note that dried food, such as milk powder, once reconstituted by adding water, becomes an ideal growth medium for bacteria and should either be used immediately or be refrigerated until needed.

Temperature ❋ ❋ ❋

Bacteria will grow and multiply at temperatures between 8°C and 63°C. This temperature band is known as the **danger zone**. The majority of the pathogenic bacteria (which cause food-borne illness) grow most quickly at body temperature (37°C). If the temperature rises above this, bacteria will multiply more slowly and begin to die. Bacteria will normally be killed if boiled for more than 2 minutes although many which cause human illness will die at the lower pasteurization temperature of 63°C. However, those bacteria which can make spores (e.g. *Clostridium perfringens*) may survive boiling for prolonged periods. At temperatures below 37°C the rate at which bacteria multiply will also gradually decrease, until below 4°C many types will cease growth completely. Some spoilage bacteria and some human pathogens will, however, continue to grow at refrigerator temperatures (below 8°C). In frozen food any bacteria present will be preserved (but not killed), even though they do not grow. These bacteria will only become a problem if the food is thawed or warmed up, until at room temperature any bacteria present will start to multiply again. It is therefore recommended that frozen foods are thoroughly defrosted in a designated refrigerator, defrost cabinet or temperature controlled area. If the centre of a joint of meat remains frozen prior to cooking, the meat may not reach a high enough centre temperature to kill bacteria during cooking.

Once cooked, food should be either:

- kept above 63°C until served, or
- cooled quickly (but not in a refrigerator) prior to chilled storage and service.

Time ❋ ❋ ❋

The length of time food is kept in warm conditions is of vital importance. Cooked food can be an ideal growth medium for bacteria. Emphasis should therefore always be given to limiting the time food is kept at temperatures in the danger zone (between 8 °C and 63 °C). This is because in ideal conditions bacteria can multiply every 20–30 minutes, allowing dangerous levels to be reached in a few hours.

Oxygen

Some bacteria require oxygen to grow (aerobes) and others can grow in the absence of oxygen (anaerobes). Oxygen is normally present in food unless it has a high water content and has been boiled or is vacuum packed.

Competition

If there are many different bacteria present in food, they will compete and, unless present in high numbers, will usually die.

Moulds and other fungi

Moulds belong to the kingdom of the fungi, a completely separate group of higher organisms that exist alongside the plant and animal kingdoms. Fungi exhibit very varied forms and have complex structures. They range in size from the microscopic, single-celled yeast to the macroscopic puffball. Other examples of fungi include rusts, smuts, mildew, mushrooms and toadstools.

Fungi lack chlorophyll with which to synthesize organic molecules from sunlight (photosynthesis) and so, like animals, must derive energy and the food they need for metabolism from pre-synthesized organic molecules. They feed on dead organic matter (saprophytes) or are parasites on animals, plants or other fungi.

In breaking down dead organic material fungi help continue the cycle of nutrients through ecosystems. In addition, most vascular plants could not grow without the existence of the symbiotic fungi, or mycorrhizae, that inhabit their roots and help in the uptake of essential nutrients.

Most fungi, including moulds such as mucor, derive their rigidity by forming 'tubes' made from a substance called chitin (a polysaccharide also found in the exoskeletons of arthropods), whilst others utilize cellulose as the structural component, as do green plants.

Fungi reproduce and disperse themselves by producing spores; a habit they share with the non-flowering plants like mosses and ferns. The systems used for spore production and dispersal are amongst the most interesting features of the biology of fungi.

The spore-forming structure may be simple or very elaborate. The term mushroom, for instance, is given to the large fruiting body of certain fungi and consists of an upright stem surmounted by an umbrella-like cap. On the underside of the cap spore-forming gills radiate outward from the central stem. The mushroom is designed both to protect spores from rain splash, increase the surface area for spore production and to release the spores into turbulent air so dispersing them over a wide area. Once the spore has settled it will germinate if conditions are favourable. A system of branching threads called the mycelium results, each branch of which is called a hypha.

In other fungi the fruiting body is very tiny or microscopic. In some, spore-like structures (conidia) are produced externally on the tips of specialized branches. Others, such as the familiar pin-moulds, produce aerial hyphae from which small structures called sporangia are formed that contain the spores.

Moulds are of great economic importance. Some can be parasites of food crops causing a number of significant plant diseases whilst others are responsible for the spoilage of fruit and vegetables both in storage and in the field. Grey mould on the strawberry, brown rot of apple, potato blight and potato wart disease are all of current importance. Ergot (a fungal disease of rye and other cereals and responsible for the madness known as St Anthony's Fire) has become less significant with the introduction of modern milling methods.

Fungi are perhaps less important than bacteria and viruses in causing disease in man and other animals but those that do occur can be difficult to treat because they do not respond to many antibiotics. Examples of fungal infections in man include ringworm, athlete's foot and other fungal skin complaints such as dermatophytosis. Moulds may grow on walls and other surfaces in poorly ventilated rooms and can be indicative of poor housing generally. The tiny spores can be inhaled deep into the lungs giving rise to a number of serious respiratory ailments such as aspergillosis.

Moulds and fungi are important in the food industry. Yeasts for instance are very versatile. In the presence of oxygen they produce carbon dioxide which is used as a raising agent in bread making. Without oxygen, the yeast's ability to ferment sugar into alcohol is used in the manufacture of beer and wine. In some cheeses, like Stilton and Brie, the formation of mould is encouraged in order to add flavour and help ripen the cheese.

Fungi are an important food in their own right, and some, such as the truffle, are considered great delicacies. Many of the edible mushrooms belong to the genus Agaricus. There are eight types of edible mushroom grown commercially.

Many moulds have the ability to produce chemicals that are toxic to bacteria. This has been of great medical importance and numerous drugs such as penicillin and other antibiotics have been (and continue to be) developed.

Factors influencing the growth of mould

For the caterer to control the proliferation of mould both on food and within the catering environment it is necessary to have an understanding of the factors that influence mould growth. The food source, temperature, pH, oxygen, moisture and the mould's own by-products of metabolism are all influencing factors.

Nutritional needs of fungi

Moulds and other fungi require an organic source of carbon such as sugar. Many can utilize starch and cellulose. They also require a source of nitrogen (usually in the form of an amino acid or an amide) and various inorganic ions. All are usually abundant in food used for human consumption.

Temperature

Although values vary somewhat from species to species most fungi will not grow readily below temperatures in the range of 2–5°C. There are moulds, however, such as *Cladosporium herbarum*, which can grow below freezing point and may cause problems in refrigeration equipment.

pH

Moulds will tolerate a broad range of pH from the quite acidic (pH 3) to the fairly alkaline (pH 9). It is worth noting that a food source which is acidic enough to prevent the growth of bacteria may nevertheless allow certain moulds and fungi to flourish.

Oxygen

All fungi are able to grow aerobically (in the presence of oxygen) but some, like the yeasts, are able to grow anaerobically as well. Those fungi that require oxygen may nevertheless grow happily at very low oxygen concentrations.

Moisture

In common with all living organisms, moulds and fungi require a source of water in order to live and grow. The developing fungal mycelium must either be in a watery solution or in an environment where the humidity of the air is approaching 100 per cent. Fungi are, however, able to survive extended periods with very little water by forming spores (sporulation).

By-products of metabolism ◦ ◦ ◦

The by-products of fungal metabolism will themselves act to reduce growth. This self-limiting factor can be seen in the fermentation of sugar by yeast during the wine-making process. Here it is the increasing concentration of the alcohol (partly coupled with the corresponding reduction in sugar) which inhibits the further multiplication of yeast cells.

The significance of moulds and other fungi to the caterer

Apart from those instances where moulds are used in food manufacture, the presence of mould on food is considered undesirable. Moulds will frequently determine the shelf life of a particular food and often reduce it considerably. They can, however, be useful in providing an early warning of food that is out of condition. Mould can often been seen and can impart an unpleasant taste or smell to food. Moulds are often the first to colonize certain types of food and their growth may competitively exclude other organisms (like bacteria), some of which may be more harmful.

As well as colonizing food, moulds will also grow on damp walls and wet, unsealed woodwork in the catering environment. Most significantly the mould *Aspergillius niger* is responsible for the black discoloration of damp food equipment such as cutting boards and piping bags.

Legal considerations ◦ ◦ ◦

The presence of mould on food may render it 'not of the substance or quality demanded by the purchaser' (Food Safety Act 1990, s.14). Alternatively, mouldy food may not comply with food safety requirements by virtue of it being 'unfit for human consumption' or 'so contaminated that it would not be reasonable to expect it to be used for human consumption in that state' (Food Safety Act 1990, ss.8(1), 8(2b) and 8(2c)). Food equipment visibly contaminated with mould would be considered dirty and contravene the Food Safety (General Food Hygiene) Regulations 1995. Similarly, mould on walls would be contrary to provisions within the same regulations which require a food premises to be clean.

As well as the generality of the above requirements, the prevention of mould within food premises is referred to specifically in the Schedule to the regulations. The layout, design, construction and size of food premises shall be such as to protect against the formation of condensation or undesirable mould on surfaces (Chapter I). Moreover, in those rooms where foodstuffs are prepared, treated or processed, ceilings and overhead fixtures must be designed, constructed and finished to prevent the accumulation of dirt and reduce condensation, the growth of undesirable moulds and the shedding of particles (Chapter II).

Wild mushrooms ⊛ ⊛ ⊛

It has become quite fashionable for restaurants and now supermarkets to sell wild mushrooms. As well as having a detrimental effect in terms of conservation and ecology, picking wild mushrooms can be dangerous if species are misidentified. Certain wild mushrooms and toadstools are extremely poisonous containing a number of harmful chemicals called mycotoxins. Depending on the type of mushroom eaten, death may result in 20–90 per cent of cases and every year a small number of people still die from eating them. A few species contain toxins that are so potent that death may result from eating just a single specimen. Sometimes symptoms are not apparent until after the toxin has passed beyond the stomach, by which time effective treatment can be problematic. Fungi such as *Amanita phalloides* (the Death Cap) are responsible for what can be a prolonged death due to liver and kidney failure.

Contamination with mould ⊛ ⊛ ⊛

People may also be poisoned by inadvertently eating food that has been contaminated with a fungus. Members of the genus Aspergillus can sometimes be found on foods such as peanuts and cereal grains grown and stored in damp conditions. They can produce harmful toxins (aflotoxin) which, as well as being potent carcinogens, can cause liver and kidney failure.

Yeasts ⊛ ⊛ ⊛

Yeasts are microscopic, unicellular fungi that grow best in the presence of oxygen, although fermentative types grow slowly anaerobically. Yeasts are tolerant to many adverse conditions and traditional preservation methods such as increasing a food's pH, or increasing its osmotic potential by salting or adding sugar, may not be sufficient to control their growth. Jam, fruit juice, honey, meat and wines are all susceptible to spoilage by yeast, especially if stored at temperatures between 25 and 30°C. Yeasts are used in the manufacture of foods such as bread, beer and vinegar.

Prevention and control ⊛ ⊛ ⊛

The significance of mould to the caterer should not be underestimated. Moulds commonly affect bread and other bakery products but can also be found on all manner of other foods and surfaces within kitchens. Cooking will kill moulds and mould spores but subsequent contamination is difficult or impossible to avoid. Control is therefore largely restricted to the prevention of mould growth and the use of food within specified time limits. The manufacturers' recommendations should always be followed.

Adequate stock rotation is imperative if moulds are to be prevented from establishing themselves on certain foods. Best before and use by dates should always be followed. Foods that have been decanted into other containers should bear an indication as to their shelf life taken from the original packaging. As well as using food quickly, an important factor affecting shelf life is the prevention of cross-contamination. New food should therefore never be placed on top of old food or in contact with it.

The trend towards foods that contain fewer preservatives has increased the need for refrigeration as a means of reducing mould growth during storage. Some, previously shelf-stable, foods (i.e. bottled sauces) are now required to be refrigerated after being opened so as to maintain quality and maximize shelf life. Under the Food Labelling Regulations 2002 as amended, any special storage instructions must be printed on the product label.

Moulds favour damp and humid conditions. Special attention should be paid to keeping dry foods dry and this is best achieved by providing a separate, cool and well-ventilated store, well away from the humid conditions which exist in most kitchens. Fluctuating temperatures will increase the chances of surface condensation on food, creating a microclimate in which moulds can thrive. Typically, moulds will favour the hidden surface beneath a food where conditions are moist and air movement is restricted. Containers holding dry foods should be airtight to prevent the entry of moist air whilst foods wrapped in cellophane should be kept cool to prevent the condensation. Equipment that is designed to come into contact with food and which may be susceptible to the growth of fungi should also be kept dry. Piping bags and vinyl cutting boards can be stored in racks designed to allow air to freely circulate between and around them.

Effective control can sometimes be achieved by removing oxygen from the food surface or by maintaining a near oxygen-free environment around the food, for example, vacuum-packaging. However, the mishandling of vacuum packs may result in punctures that render the packaging ineffective. Storing foods like tomato puree under oil reduces oxygen levels and helps to prevent mould spores from coming into contact with the food.

Toxins

Food poisoning organisms can affect people in two ways:

- First, they may enter the body in the food and then cause a reaction either by invading the tissues of the intestine or by producing waste products which are poisonous.
- Second, they may produce poisons (toxins) in the food itself; it is the ingestion of these compounds by the victim that causes illness.

There are also some organisms, such as several of the species in the genus Bacillus, which fall into both categories. In addition, there is always the risk of ingesting poisons (such as pesticide residues on plants) which are in no way related to micro-organisms.

Clostridium perfringens

This organism (formerly know as *Clostridium welchii*) produces a toxin in the intestine. The organism is common in both animal excreta and soil and is found in a wide range of foods, including raw meat and poultry. It is an anaerobe (growing only in the absence of oxygen), which produces spores that can not only survive cooking but are stimulated to develop by the cooking process. The organisms multiply rapidly in foods stored at incorrect temperatures (they are capable of dividing every 12 minutes at body temperature) but there is little growth below 10 °C. Cooked meats, pies, stews and gravies are common sources of infection with this organism. Little toxin is formed in the food, but if the organisms are swallowed they produce a toxin in the intestine. Abdominal pain, diarrhoea and nausea occur from 6 to 24 hours after eating contaminated food and may last for up to 48 hours. Rapid cooling of cooked foods and storage at suitably low temperatures (+4 °C) should effectively prevent any infection.

Escherichia coli

Most forms of *Escherichia coli* are native, harmless inhabitants of the gastrointestinal tract. Enterotoxigenic forms of the bacterium (ETEC) produce a heat-stable toxin in the intestine. Such organisms may reach food from food handlers due to poor personal hygiene or enter cooked foods by cross-contamination from raw items. The organisms themselves are readily killed by cooking. *E. coli* is a particularly common cause of traveller's diarrhoea. Good hygienic practices and proper food storage should prevent the development of infections associated with these organisms.

Another form of *E. coli* which produces toxins is Verocytotoxin *Escherichia coli* (VTEC), also known as *E. coli* O157, which is responsible for an outbreak in the United States of America in 1992, where 501 cases of *E. coli* and 3 deaths were reported, and were attributed to the eating of undercooked hamburgers. A very large outbreak with some 11,000 cases occurred in Japan in the summer of 1996 and was linked to the consumption of school meals, although the exact source was never identified. *E. coli* was also responsible for the outbreak in Scotland at the end of 1996.

Campylobacter and Salmonella · · ·

Heat-labile enterotoxins can occur from Campylobacter and Salmonella. The symptom most commonly caused by the toxin is diarrhoea, but unlike *E. coli* the toxin itself is not the major cause of food poisoning and the toxin is only a limited part of the infection.

Staphylococcal toxin · · ·

Staphylococci are very common and can be isolated not only from animals but also (and in the kitchen most importantly) from man. Several species of staphylococci are found on the human skin, but the only species associated with food poisoning is *Staphylococcus aureus*. This species is found on the hands, in the nostrils and in boils, cuts and other lesions such as whitlows (an infection near the nail). The main source of *Staph. aureus* food poisoning is from the poor personal hygiene of the staff who prepare food. Prepared foods such as creams, custards and trifles are the common vehicles of infection, together with cold meats and poultry.

Staphylococci are remarkably resistant to both salt and sugar and so are able to survive and grow in many cured or preserved products (such as ham). The toxin is produced as the organisms grow, and although the organisms themselves may be destroyed by normal cooking, the toxin is heat-stable (it can survive boiling for up to 30 minutes). As the toxin is produced in the food – that is to say it is taken into the body 'pre-prepared' and acts on the stomach lining – the onset of symptoms is rapid, often occurring in less than two hours. Severe vomiting, diarrhoea, abdominal pain and cramps occur. The recovery period (usually 6–24 hours) is generally rapid. Careful personal hygiene and proper low temperature storage of foods (+4 °C) will prevent problems occurring.

Botulinum toxin · · ·

Clostridium botulinum is another anaerobic organism. Common in the environment, it is fortunately rarely found in foods; fortunate as the toxin it produces is one of the most poisonous substances known to man. When heated during cooking, spores of the organism germinate. As the bacteria grow and divide a toxin is produced. The ingestion of this toxin is followed within 24 hours by fatigue, headache and dizziness, then disturbance of vision and loss of speech. Death can occur due to paralysis of the respiratory system. If the patient survives – and the mortality rate can be high – convalescence can take months.

The spores of the organism are very resistant to heat and readily survive boiling. The toxin itself is heat-sensitive but may be protected by the material of the food itself. Improperly preserved foods are usually responsible for food poisoning outbreaks. For example, in a large outbreak in the UK, a hazelnut purée used as an additive for yoghurt was the source of the toxin. During manufacture the purée was heated in the can to kill bacteria, however this process was quite inadequate to kill *Cl. botulinum* and some cans were heavily contaminated. 'Blown' cans, i.e. cans that have become deformed by the production of gas in the can by the multiplying bacteria, must be suspected as containing *Cl. botulinum*. If there is any suspicion of 'blowing', a can must not be used.

Bacillus cereus

Bacillus cereus can produce toxins either in the food or in the intestine. It is an aerobic (growing only in the presence of oxygen), spore-forming bacterium frequently found in dried food such as cereals and rice. As is the case with *Cl. perfringens*, the spores can survive cooking. If the food is subsequently stored under conditions that are too warm the bacteria can multiply and produce a toxin. *B. cereus* can in fact produce two toxins, one causing an illness similar to staphylococcal food poisoning with a short incubation period and symptoms of acute vomiting, the other producing a diarrhoeal illness.

The toxin producing the vomiting form of the infection is very heat-resistant and is produced in the food. It can survive pressure cooking for one and half hours and frying for short periods. The second toxin, that causing the diarrhoeal syndrome, is much less stable and is produced in the intestine – the amount of toxin depends to some extent on the number of bacteria ingested. It is destroyed by heat and probably cannot survive the acids in the stomach.

Bacillus cereus poisoning has, in the past, been particularly associated with Indian and Chinese restaurants where large batches of rice may be cooked and then used up over several days, being reheated as necessary. If the rice is not stored at a sufficiently low temperature the organisms may grow and produce a toxin that is not destroyed when the rice is reheated.

As with the prevention of *Cl. perfringens* food poisoning, rapid cooling and correct cold storage can prevent the problem.

Other toxins

The most important toxin associated with fish is 'scombrotoxin'. This is, in fact, a compound called histamine which is produced by bacteria growing on fish such as tuna and mackerel (particularly smoked mackerel). The symptoms include vomiting, facial flushing, dizziness, nausea and headache. The toxin is very heat-stable and canned fish may be contaminated.

Seven incidences of scombrotoxin food poisoning associated with eating tuna steaks imported from Sri Lanka were reported in the UK during October and November 1996. Approximately 40 incidences of suspected scombrotoxin food poisoning occur each year.

In general this type of food poisoning is beyond the control of the cook if canned materials are used as it is not apparent that the fish has been contaminated. The use of fresh or frozen fish together with proper temperature controls in the kitchen can minimize the risks.

Both fish and shellfish can become toxic to humans if they have fed on toxic algae. The symptoms of this type of poisoning can include numbness of the lips, fingertips and tongue shortly after eating, followed by nausea, vomiting and diarrhoea. Convulsions and death may follow in rare cases. This type of poisoning from fish is called 'ciguatera' poisoning; although rarely found in fish in the UK, fish from the Caribbean may occasionally be contaminated.

Algal toxins in shellfish produce a form of poisoning known as paralytic shellfish poisoning (PSP). In addition, some shellfish (such as whelks) may contain natural toxins. There is no simple method of judging if seafood is contaminated but such forms of poisoning from seafood are rare. Caterers must rely on information from the monitoring of algal blooms in the seas around Britain in areas where seafood is gathered.

A range of other toxic substances can occur in foods. A number of species of fungi are poisonous and the careless use of wild fungi in the diet has caused numerous cases of poisoning. Fungi growing in stored foods are also capable of producing poisons.

Many species of plants are poisonous (e.g. deadly nightshade) but in addition some parts of otherwise edible plants are poisonous. The leaves of rhubarb contain toxic amounts of oxalic acid and apricot stones contain a substance which can break down in the body to produce cyanide. Red kidney beans and haricot beans are an occasional cause of food poisoning. These beans, which are used in chilli con carne and in salads, contain a toxin which can cause acute vomiting and diarrhoea. The toxin is completely destroyed by adequate cooking, for example by boiling beans for at least 15 minutes.

Viruses

Viruses are much smaller and much less complex in structure than bacteria. Unlike bacteria, viruses do not multiply or produce toxins in food. They need to invade living cells to replicate themselves but some are able to survive outside these cells when conditions are favourable.

The two viral illnesses of importance that may be transmitted through food are hepatitis A and viral gastroenteritis. In recent years there has been a notable increase in the number of reports relating to food-borne incidents of both diseases.

Viruses are usually transferred directly from person to person; on occasion certain viruses may also be transmitted through foods. It is only viruses that are infectious when ingested that are of importance in relation to food or water, i.e. those that spread by the faecal–oral route.

Viruses are preserved by refrigeration and freezing (the very conditions chosen for the prevention of bacterial and fungal spoilage of foods) but are killed by normal cooking processes. They are sensitive to ultra-violet irradiation and chemical disinfection, chlorine-based compounds being the most effective. Viruses that infect via the intestinal tract, such as hepatitis A and gastroenteritis viruses, are resistant to acidic conditions and may survive in, for example, foods preserved in vinegar. Viruses may also survive in foods containing high levels of sugar or foods preserved in alcohol.

Hepatitis

Hepatitis is an inflammation of the liver. The disease is most readily recognized when a person becomes jaundiced (evidenced by yellowish skin and eyes). Other symptoms include nausea and general malaise. Illness may last several weeks but fatalities are rare. Once infected, a person is immune from further infection for life.

Hepatitis A

Hepatitis A is a notifiable disease. The proportion of cases caused by eating contaminated food is unknown, but may be estimated at less than 10% of all hepatitis A cases. The incubation period is 2–6 weeks. It is therefore difficult to identify a food-borne source of infection unless there is a very well-defined outbreak. The association of hepatitis A with contaminated foods is certainly under-recognized. However, with currently available technology it is not feasible to detect viruses in food even in the unlikely event of suspected food items being available for microbiological testing.

Hepatitis E

A newly recognized form of hepatitis, called hepatitis E, has been implicated in some large-scale water-borne outbreaks in under-developed countries. There exists, therefore, the potential for contamination of shellfish imported from, for example, the Far East.

Viral gastroenteritis ⊛ ⊛ ⊛

Several different viruses cause gastroenteritis. These viruses are usually transmitted from person to person via the faecal–oral route and outbreaks frequently occur in both community and institutional environments. One type of virus, a small round structured virus (SRSV), has been particularly linked with the food-borne transmission of gastroenteritis. The most famous SRSV is the Norwalk virus, and hence SRSVs are often referred to as 'Norwalk-like' or 'Norwalk group' viruses.

Food-borne viral gastroenteritis tends to mimic bacterial food poisoning, but there are characteristic features which suggest the cause of illness may be viral rather than bacterial. Symptoms frequently include both vomiting and diarrhoea. The incubation period is somewhat longer than for most food poisoning organisms, with a peak around 30 hours (range 15–60 hours); secondary cases may occur through person-to-person spread. Although overt symptoms rarely last more than one or two days, people may feel debilitated for up to 2 weeks. The economic implications are thus considerable. However, gastroenteritis is usually considered a minor illness and most people are unlikely to consult their doctor so the extent of the problem is unknown. Unlike hepatitis A, immunity to SRSVs is not long lasting and as there are also several different types of SRSV, people may be subject to repeated attacks during their lifetime.

Viral contamination of food

Food can be contaminated with viruses in two ways:

- Contamination may occur at source if food within its growing area comes into contact with, for example, sewage pollution. This is known as primary contamination.
- Food may be contaminated by infected food handlers during preparation. This is secondary contamination.

Shellfish ⊛ ⊛ ⊛

The most striking evidence that viruses may be transmitted through food has come from outbreaks of viral illness associated with molluscan shellfish. Most illnesses associated with molluscs are in fact viral rather than bacterial. Some reported outbreaks have involved several hundred people.

It is bivalve molluscs (oysters, clams, mussels and cockles) harvested from shallow estuarine and inshore waters that cause problems since such waters are liable to sewage pollution. Bivalves feed by filtering particulate matter, including potentially harmful bacteria and viruses, out of the large volumes of water passing over their gills. While the viruses that affect humans do not multiply in shellfish, they can accumulate in sufficient numbers to ultimately cause human illness.

Some shellfish, such as cockles, are subject to a brief heat treatment before sale, but more prolonged cooking renders shellfish meat tough and unpalatable. The Ministry of Agriculture, Fisheries and Food (MAFF) has made recommendations to the shellfish industry suggesting that the internal temperature of shellfish meat should reach 85 °C to 90 °C and be maintained for 1½ minutes. Although such conditions kill hepatitis A virus, the conditions necessary to render gastroenteritis viruses inactive are not known, as they cannot be cultured in the laboratory. Nevertheless, since the implementation of the MAFF recommendations in early 1988, there have been no major reports of viral illness arising from heat-treated molluscs.

Oysters that are to be consumed raw cannot, of course, be subjected to heat treatment. Producers normally cleanse oysters in tanks containing clean water for 48 hours. It is expected that harmful micro-organisms will be washed out by the oysters' natural feeding processes. While the cleansing procedure is effective in removing bacterial contamination, it does not necessarily remove viruses; raw oysters continue to be associated with illness. Until a safe supply can be guaranteed, the consumption of raw oysters remains risky.

Fruit and vegetables

Another potential source of primary viral contamination is the application of polluted water and sewage sludge to fruit and vegetable crops during irrigation and fertilization. Soft fruits, such as raspberries, have been implicated in some outbreaks of hepatitis A. Salad items are frequently implicated in outbreaks and may have been primarily contaminated, but more usually contamination is believed to have occurred during preparation.

Secondary contamination

Food may be contaminated from infected food handlers in the same way as bacterial contamination occurs. Viral contamination is largely associated with cold food items that require considerable handling during preparation, such as sandwiches and salads. Viruses are spread to foods and working surfaces through faecal contamination of hands, and vomiting.

Although viruses do not multiply in food or on work surfaces, both hepatitis A and gastroenteritis viruses are believed to be highly infectious in very low doses such as might survive at secondarily contaminated sites.

Food handlers with symptoms of gastroenteritis should be excluded from work. Staff should be instructed that even if their symptoms are very minor, they should not attend work. It is not clear how long people remain infectious but present evidence suggests that it is reasonable to allow return to work 48 hours after symptoms cease. For hepatitis A, the main infectious period precedes its symptoms so exclusion of infectious personnel is unfortunately impossible. By the time there is clinical recovery virus excretion has ended. In some cases, there may be a need for immunoglobulin vaccination of potentially exposed food handlers.

Preventing the spread of viral infections through foods depends on scrupulous attention to normal hygienic practices, including frequent handwashing and strict separation of raw and cooked foods. Salad items, fruit and raw vegetables should be thoroughly washed. In the kitchen, uncooked shellfish should be regarded in the same way as uncooked meat, i.e. as potential vehicles of food poisoning micro-organisms. Viral gastroenteritis may be very sudden in onset and commence with projectile vomiting. Viruses will be spread over a wide area in aerosol droplets. If vomiting occurs in a food preparation area, work surfaces, door handles and toilet areas could be contaminated and all areas affected must be thoroughly disinfected. Chlorine-based disinfectants are most effective for viral decontamination. Contamination of uncovered food is likely to have occurred and it will be necessary to dispose of all food items.

Viruses are not only spread by vomiting, but are also excreted in faeces. In the event of any worker exhibiting symptoms there should be a reinforcement of handwashing procedures. Even extremely low levels of viral contamination are able to cause illness, so direct handling of food should be kept to a minimum. Wearing gloves may reduce the risk of faecally contaminated fingers coming into contact with food, but will not prevent the transfer of viruses from contaminated work surfaces to food.

Cross-contamination

Cross-contamination is a common term for the way in which harmful food-borne bacteria (pathogens) are passed on to humans. Indeed, for some bacteria, such as Campylobacter, it may well be one of the most important ways. There are three types of contamination:

- bacteria, moulds or toxins
- foreign bodies, including insects
- chemicals, including pesticides and detergents.

Raw meat and poultry are the food items most likely to carry pathogens and therefore to act as sources of organisms for cross-contamination. Surveys of fresh chickens have shown that up to 70 per cent may carry salmonellae or campylobacters. Although red meat is less likely to carry such pathogens it cannot be assumed to be free of contaminants. The wisest course is to assume that all raw meats and raw fish are contaminated and to treat them accordingly.

Staff handling food can be a source of cross-contamination as hands are never free of bacteria and so the importance of regular handwashing can never be overstressed, as indeed cannot all other aspects of personal hygiene.

Cross-contamination can occur via insects (flies/cockroaches), but most commonly occurs via knives, chopping boards or other pieces of kitchen equipment. The presence of such foreign bodies as glass or rodent droppings should be regarded with great concern and it represents a breakdown in hygiene policies and procedures.

A third area of cross-contamination is chemicals, particularly those used for cleaning purposes. Such detergents should be appropriate for the purpose and in no circumstances be allowed to taint the food. They should be properly labelled and stored. An additional area is the increasing use of pesticides which may be found on the surface of some foods, hence the need for proper washing prior to preparation.

Vehicles and routes

There are four main vehicles in cross-contamination:

- hands
- cloths and equipment
- hand contact surfaces
- food contact surfaces.

There are two main routes by which cross-contamination can occur:

- directly from one food item to another
- indirectly, via a vector, e.g. human hands, flies.

As part of the training process, staff should be aware of both these vehicles and routes in order to prevent food poisoning and to apply appropriate controls. Prevention depends on either eradicating the sources of contamination or establishing barriers between them, the vehicles and routes.

The routes of contamination can be complex and surprising. For example, an outbreak of Campylobacter enteritis occurred in 1984 in a catering college in the south of England. Initial interviews with patients suggested that the vehicle of infection might be chicken but some of the patients were vegetarians who had eaten only salads. Further investigation showed that salad had been included in all the menus but salads are not common vectors of this disease. Investigations were undertaken in the kitchens of the college and the route of cross-contamination was finally discovered to be the cloths which the trainee chefs were carrying at their waists. They had prepared New York dressed (ungutted) poultry prior to the preparation of the salads and had been in the habit of wiping their knives on these cloths. The knives and chopping boards had been carefully washed between each food type but the organisms were on the cloths and contaminated the knives when they were wiped.

Any food which is to be eaten raw (such as salad) or which has been cooked and is subsequently to be eaten cold or with only brief warming must be assumed to be at risk of being contaminated and should be treated accordingly.

Cross-contamination can be prevented by a few common-sense rules but constant vigilance is necessary to prevent lapses which can lead to outbreaks of food poisoning. A likely site for direct cross-contamination is the refrigerator or chill room. Ideally, cooked and uncooked foods (or foods that are to be eaten raw such as salads) should not be stored in the same area, but if they are then raw meat must be:

- covered with a suitable wrapping
- stored in a deep pan to prevent spillage of juices
- stored below cooked foods or salads.

Another example was an outbreak of salmonellosis that occurred in a factory canteen. Although no food was available for laboratory testing, investigations showed that the infection had reached the patients in custard pies. These of course had been cooked and no evidence could be found that there was any problem with the cooking. However, subsequent investigations of kitchen practice showed that the pies had been stored in a refrigerator on shelves below some chickens which had been thawing out. Juices from the chickens had dripped onto the pies, contaminating them with salmonellae.

Even simply storing raw and cooked foods next to each other can lead to contamination. Care must be taken in the kitchen and also in food display cabinets to ensure that such items are correctly and adequately separated.

Control

The following guidelines should be observed in order to control this problem of cross-contamination:

- Institute appropriate checks on suppliers and their method of food delivery.
- Clearly separate unfit food, chemicals and refuse away from stored food.
- Maintain a pest control programme.

- Separate preparation areas should be used to prepare different types of food products – the same areas or surfaces should not be used for raw meat and cooked items or salads.
- Thaw foods in an area separate from other foods.
- Cool foods in an area prior to refrigeration.
- Colour coding of plastic knife handles and polypropylene chopping boards should be used to differentiate those used for raw and cooked items; use plastic chopping boards as it is impossible to thoroughly clean and decontaminate wooden chopping boards.
- Regular handwashing by food handlers must be ensured to minimize the risk of transfer of bacteria on the fingers; handwashing is particularly necessary after handling raw foods, after using the toilet, and between different tasks in the kitchen.
- Hand-drying facilities should include paper towels in preference to hot air driers – if roller towels are used they should be of the type which presents a clean area of towel for each user (the roller towel – a loop of towelling hanging from a roller – can cause cross-contamination and should be avoided whenever possible).
- Taps on hand basins in kitchen areas should be of the elbow or preferably of the knee or foot operated type to prevent re-contamination of hands after washing.
- Wash-hand basins in kitchens should never be used for the preparation of food items or for the washing of equipment, e.g. knives or chopping boards.
- Food slicers must be separate for raw and cooked items as they can act as important vehicles of cross-contamination, particularly as they are difficult and time-consuming to clean.
- Protective clothing (aprons, overalls) should be changed after handling raw meats if subsequent preparation of cooked items or salads is required (always remember that some apparently cooked foods are in fact raw, for example, salamis are fermented meats, not cooked meats and should not be sliced on the same slicer as raw meats being prepared for cooking, but should be sliced after foods such as corned beef which is cooked in manufacture).
- Institute hygiene procedures to control visitors to and management of the food preparation area.

Prevention ● ● ●

Prevention of cross-contamination centres around the principles of the Hazard Analysis Critical Control Point system (HACCP) (see Chapters 9 and 10). However, with respect to this section the key theme to be identified in terms of prevention is the training of staff during induction, reinforcement during the year and formalized refresher seminars (see Chapter 8). Whilst it is for management in consultation with staff to establish appropriate design, structure, layout and maintenance of food rooms along with the right equipment, personal hygiene, including protective clothing, is the responsibility of all operational staff. Additionally, cleaning procedures and pest control need to be established.

Bacteriological standards

Background

Bacteriological standards are primarily used in food production but may also be an important consideration for caterers. There is no legal requirement for caterers to test their products for microbiological safety. The Food Safety Act 1990 does, of course, place a responsibility on caterers for the food they sell and checks must be made on these food products. The decision as to whether the checks should include independent, microbiological testing depends on a consideration of all the following factors.

1 The size and resources of the business. In general, the larger the business and the greater the volume of food passing through that business, the greater is the need for more thorough checking.
2 The nature of the supplied produce. The level of checking should be related to the risk associated with an individual food product. For example, processed and prepared products bought in from suppliers which are sold for cold consumption have a greater potential to cause illness than supplied products served hot.
3 The level of checking by suppliers. Reputable suppliers of processed and prepared foods should test their foods for microbiological safety. Caterers must have, at the very least, a good knowledge of their suppliers' quality control systems, including microbiological testing. The decision to undertake further independent testing rests on whether it is reasonable in the circumstances to rely on these suppliers' checks.

All of the above factors are likely to be considered by a court if a serious problem occurs and a caterer plans to make use of the defence of 'due diligence' under the Food Safety Act 1990.

The reasons why microbiological testing, and therefore bacteriological standards, are important relate to the two most important objectives in the production of food:

(a) the control of contamination by food poisoning organisms or their toxins; and
(b) the control of contamination by organisms that will spoil food during storage and distribution.

Specifications or limits are therefore set on the numbers of these organisms within a particular food item. They are designed to provide safe food with an acceptable shelf life to the end user or consumer. They must take into account the type of raw materials involved, the process and handling procedures used so that these standards are consistently achievable by the producer. For example, bacteriological standards are set for cheeses taking into account the bacteria produced as a part of their manufacturing process.

Specifications for food products

Appropriate microbiological methods must be chosen and specified if the results of repeated testing are to be comparable and therefore of value. Measurement of microbiological standards must be undertaken by a specialist.

Microbiological specifications should include standards for food poisoning organisms (e.g. Salmonella spores) and food spoilage organisms (e.g. yeasts and moulds). Within food producing premises, the following categories may be used when adopting a microbiological specification.

- **Target:** That level of micro-organisms which:
  (a) assures the safety of the consumer;
  (b) guarantees the integrity of the food during storage and distribution;
  (c) is achieved when every phase of the manufacturing process is working at maximum efficiency.

This target level provides the ultimate goal given existing production methods. However, developments in processing methods may mean that these targets can continue to be improved.

- **Acceptable:** That level of micro-organisms which:
  (a) assures the safety of the consumer;
  (b) guarantees the integrity of the product during storage and distribution;
  (c) is achieved under normal manufacturing conditions, including breakdowns and stoppages.
- **Unacceptable:** That level of micro-organisms which indicates some fault or failure in the manufacturing process and/or unacceptable handling practices. Products containing unacceptable levels of micro-organisms could constitute a health risk to the consumer. As a result, these products must be isolated at the relevant point of production pending further tests to determine the level and type of micro-organism present. If the product has already been despatched it must be withdrawn or recalled. Determination of the type of organism

present will assist in tracing the source of the original contamination, e.g. contaminated raw materials.

The advantages of microbiological standards include the following.

1 Targets provide a monitor to ensure good standards of hygiene and food handling in both food production areas and during service of food to the consumer.
2 They ensure levels of micro-organisms are such that food poisoning will not occur.
3 They also ensure that the levels of micro-organisms in the food products are such that they will not cause spoilage during the food's shelf life, thereby reducing wastage.

Maintenance of standards

The numbers of micro-organisms in food can be kept to a minimum by the use of good hygienic working practices, including adequate managerial and financial support in all aspects. The following procedures should be adhered to:

1 The separation of cooked and raw food at all times – including storage and distribution. Utensils and work surfaces must not be used for the preparation of both cooked and raw food. Colour coding is a useful way reliably to separate cooked and raw food equipment, utensils etc.
2 Raw poultry must be completely isolated from all other food products as poultry meat naturally contains food poisoning organisms, notably Salmonella bacteria. Poultry must therefore be fully cooked to ensure that these organisms are destroyed.
3 Equipment must be carefully selected to allow easy and thorough cleaning. Wood is not suitable as it presents a risk of microbial contamination. Any damaged or defective equipment must be replaced or repaired immediately.
4 Refrigeration units must be able to maintain foods at temperatures at or below 8°C to inhibit bacterial multiplication. They must be regularly serviced to ensure correct and efficient operation.
5 All equipment and utensils must be thoroughly cleaned and, where necessary, disinfected after use.
6 All workers must maintain high standards of personal hygiene including frequent handwashing, especially after handling raw meat or poultry and after visiting the toilet. Clean protective clothing should always be worn.
7 Unfit food, waste food and general kitchen refuse should be removed immediately from kitchen areas to avoid any contamination of food in preparation.

8 Food handling by staff should be kept to an absolute minimum. Tongs, plates etc. should be used rather than hands.

9 The building should be properly sealed to prevent the entry of pests, e.g. rodents, birds and insects. These pests spread bacteria and increase wastage.

10 Time temperature exposures must be observed; the time between removal from the refrigerator and cooking as well as the time between cooking and eating or refrigeration must be as short as possible.

Microbiological criteria for foods

Background

Specialist laboratories can test food or other samples for microbiological contamination. This section describes the use of routine testing in practical situations and how to interpret the results.

In theory, it would be wonderful to have a simple, cheap and reliable test for the safety of food. All food could be checked before it was sold to make sure that it was safe. In practice, it is much less simple. Bacteria like *E. coli* are dangerous in very small numbers and to detect them is like 'finding a needle in a haystack'. The tests are slow and relatively expensive. What is more, any system of end product testing has a major drawback. What do you do if the result is unsatisfactory? The only option is to reprocess the food or throw it away, both of which are expensive.

So, for practical purposes, control of food production should never rely upon end product testing. Instead, there should be effective process controls at all relevant preparation steps based on a thorough hazard analysis, a system that is discussed in Chapter 9. Once that is in place, some businesses find that a limited programme of microbiological testing provides useful validation that the principles of Hazard Analysis Critical Control Points (HACCP) are working effectively.

The costs of testing can be high, and in many cases, the costs of transport of samples to the lab can equal the cost of testing. So it is rarely cost-effective to have a routine programme of testing in small catering outlets that produce food in small batches. However, operations involved in larger batch production, for example central production units, may be more likely to benefit from a sampling programme. In addition to a routine sampling programme, food may be tested following complaints, or by EHOs as part of their normal surveillance programme.

Tests do not have to be confined to food samples. It is possible to test food contact surfaces, worktops, cutting boards or other equipment to check for contamination. These tests are often

An introduction to food microbiology

known as 'cleaning swabs' because the surface is sampled using a cotton wool swab to check cleaning. They may be especially valuable as the tool to monitor effective disinfection in an HACCP plan. Once again, the drawback may be the speed of the test. If a result is not received before the equipment is used again then it is not much use, and conventional test methods often need a day or two to produce results. More rapid methods are now becoming available for this type of application. These tests and their interpretation need to be fine-tuned to a specific operation following the equipment suppliers' instructions and/or expert advice. The rest of this section will deal only with food sampling.

There are many types of micro-organisms that are significant in food. Bacteria are by far the most important and the criteria described below are confined to bacteria. Specialist laboratories will be able to test and give advice on other micro-organisms such as yeasts and moulds, parasites and viruses. The foodborne viruses are especially difficult with very few labs worldwide able to detect SRSV (small round structured viruses sometimes known as Norwalk viruses) in food.

Deciding exactly what the results mean can often be troublesome and the source of much argument. The precision and reproducibility of many micro tests are variable. Then there may be discussion about the significance of certain organisms or their significance in certain foods. The issue may come down to numbers. For some organisms, low levels of contamination are almost inevitable whilst higher levels may be dangerous. But where exactly should the line be drawn? Furthermore, contamination in a batch of food can be variable if not erratic. What does the result of one sample indicate about the whole batch? If a good result is received from one sample in a batch, is the whole batch good? If bad, how much of the batch must be condemned?

Also, levels of bacteria keep changing during the life of chilled foods. Low levels of bacteria may be expected on a food that has just been produced, but higher levels will be found at the end of several days' shelf life even if it is kept under good hygienic conditions. So in many cases it is important to relate the microbiological criteria to the point at which the food is sampled.

For many situations, the question of interpretation of the results is now easier because we have national guidelines from the UK's Public Health Laboratory Service (PHLS).

Types of microbiological criteria and their legal status

There are three types of microbiological criteria, each of which has a different purpose and different status.

Microbiological standards ◦ ◦ ◦

Standards are legal requirements included in regulations. Historically, these have been very popular in many parts of Europe and other parts of the world, but much less so in the UK. A few standards are included in current EU directives and regulations but these generally apply to situations early in the food chain. There are very few if any microbiological standards that apply to small retailers or caterers. The General Food Hygiene Directive 93/43/EEC has a provision that could allow the EU to establish micro standards for foods at the retail or catering level. There is no indication that it intends to use this power in the near future.

Small businesses involved in the production of dairy products, the harvest or primary processing of live molluscan shellfish (oysters, cockles, mussels and so on), producing minced meat or similar products, or bottling of water may find that they are subject to microbiological standards.

Microbiological specifications ◦ ◦ ◦

Specifications form part of a buying agreement between two parties. Businesses may wish to include microbiological criteria in buying specifications. Or they may find that their customers impose specifications on them. The detail of the specification is a matter for agreement between the two parties. They do not have to be based on any other standards or criteria. Once businesses have signed a supply contract, it will be legally binding. A buyer may reject a consignment if any part of the contract, including a microbiological specification, is not met.

Microbiological guidelines ◦ ◦ ◦

Guidelines are criteria that are not prescribed directly in regulations or specifications. Guidelines may still have legal significance. The Food Safety Act 1990 and its regulations have a number of provisions that imply microbiological quality or safety. It is very likely that the results of microbiological tests will be produced in court to support these charges. For example, section 8 offences that food is 'unfit for consumption' or 'so contaminated that it would be unreasonable to expect it to be used for human consumption in that state' or under section 14, 'not of the nature or substance or quality demanded by the purchaser'.

The network of Public Health Laboratory Service (PHLS) laboratories around England and Wales is commonly used by enforcement officers for microbiological examination of food. To promote consistency and a common approach between labs PHLS produced guidelines for ready-to-eat foods. These were revised in 1996. These guidelines are likely to be regarded by the courts as the most authoritative microbiological criteria. They would be supported by the examiner in court appearing as an expert witness.

Different ready-to-eat foods will have different levels of contamination depending upon their ingredients, how they were processed, and how much handling they have received.

The guidelines cover both total bacteria counts (aerobic plate count) and pathogens and class the results under four headings from 'satisfactory' to 'potentially hazardous'. They stop short of classifying any food as 'unacceptable, potentially hazardous' solely on the basis of total count. Explanatory notes state: 'Prosecution based solely on high aerobic plate counts in the absence of other criteria of unacceptability is unlikely to be successful.' Guidelines also cover a third group known as 'Indicator organisms'. These are not necessarily pathogens in their own right, but are likely to indicate that the food has been subject to contamination or inadequate processing.

Aerobic plate counts are not applicable to certain fermented foods, salami, soft cheese and live yoghurt. Acceptability is based on appearance, smell, texture and the level or absence of pathogens.

Procedures for sampling and analysis

Samples must be handled carefully if the results are to be meaningful and this is especially true of samples for microbiological tests. If the food is contaminated during sampling, or allowed to deteriorate before being tested, the result will not be representative of the food offered for sale. A code of practice (No. 7) made under section 40 of the Food Safety Act 1990 outlines the procedures that enforcement officers should follow during sampling for analysis or examination. Officers must have regard for section 40 codes. The Food Safety (Sampling and Qualifications) Regulations 1990 also ensure that tests are conducted by properly trained examiners. EHOs have the power under the Food Safety Act to enter premises (s.32) and to take samples (s.29) for analysis (chemical composition) or examination (microbiology). To obstruct the officer may be an offence under section 33. If EHOs take 'informal' samples they may choose to use different procedures, but the results of samples that have not followed Code of Practice No. 7 (whether deliberately or accidentally) may not be used as the basis for legal proceedings.

Businesses that are arranging for their own samples to be tested should follow similar procedures to those in the code. This will ensure that results are meaningful, and will underpin their evidential value if they have to be used in court. If an EHO is taking samples from a business, especially if they may be used in legal proceedings, the business would be advised to observe the way in which the samples are handled. Any evidence that the sampling officer did not follow the correct procedures may be valuable later. The following are the key points from Code of Practice No. 7:

- Officers should follow the code for all micro samples (para. 3).
- Samples must be taken by qualified officers specifically trained in sampling techniques (para. 7).
- Officers may 'take' or 'buy' the samples at their discretion – they should give a receipt if asked for one (para. 8).
- Micro samples do not have to be divided into three – this procedure only applies to samples for analysis (para. 24).
- The size of the sample may be important – too small and the analyst may be unable to analyse it (para. 25).
- Samples must not be contaminated or subjected to conditions that may allow growth or cause death of micro-organisms (para. 26).
- Sampling instruments and containers must be sterile (para. 27).
- Samples must be properly sealed and labelled to include date and time of sampling (para. 27).
- Samples must be transported in conditions to prevent any change in microbial numbers – frozen foods must be kept frozen, and chilled between 0°C and 5°C (para. 28).
- Samples must be taken to the examiner as quickly as possible, preferably within 2 hours and within 4 hours maximum (para. 29).
- The code details information to be recorded about the sample (para. 30).
- If the sampling officer has evidence that an offence has been committed under the Food Safety Act 1990, he or she must notify the manufacturer as soon as possible (para. 31).

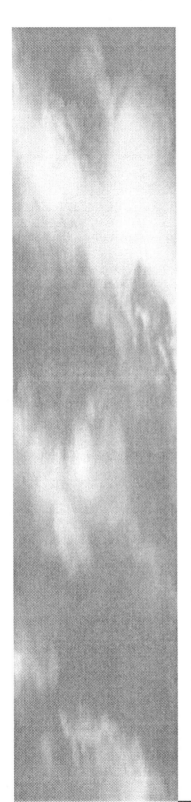

CHAPTER 5

Supply and storage of food

Supplier auditing

Often a food business will rely on a supplier's reputation, but just what does it mean to be a reputable supplier and how does one measure a company's reputation? Can one company, by definition, be more reputable than another? It is important to be able to determine at first hand whether a particular supplier can be relied upon to produce a commodity of acceptable quality and one that is safe.

Without having addressed these issues, any food hazard analysis or hazard analysis critical control points (HACCP) plan which relies upon the use of 'the reputable supplier' may be called into question (see Chapter 9). To be confident in one's suppliers is to know (as far as it is reasonably possible) that they are capable of supplying a commodity that is within the parameters acceptable to a food business. It is inadvisable to rely solely on hearsay or the proclamations of a company that has an obvious vested interest.

The confidence a food business can place in a supplier might be regarded as having a monetary value since it has implications as to whether that business can raise a successful 'due diligence defence' in the event of legal action by a food authority or trading standards officer (see Chapter 10). Customers themselves are becoming increasingly litigious and the loss in confidence in a food business's product or brand name can be disastrous. Consequently, it can be worth a company investing in the time, energy and money it takes to audit a main supplier, or the supplier of a critical ingredient, in order to show that such confidence has been well placed.

The sale of food which is unfit or which does not conform to food safety requirements or which is not of the nature, substance or quality demanded by the purchaser is an absolute offence. All that is required of a prosecuting authority is to prove that the food was in such a condition at the time of sale and that a 'sale' was made. With the passing of the Food Safety Act 1990 the new defence of 'due diligence' was introduced. This was designed to redress what some saw as the imbalance of the absolute offence by providing the proprietor with a statutory defence. The onus was now on the proprietor to prove, in their defence, that they 'took all reasonable precautions and exercised all due diligence to avoid the commission of the offence by himself or by a person under his control'.

In establishing the 'due diligence defence' the burden of proof is 'on the balance of probabilities' and is a lesser burden of proof than 'beyond reasonable doubt', which any prosecuting body must establish. Despite this, it seems that 'due diligence' is becoming harder to prove and Magistrates' Courts are becoming increasingly hard line. 'All reasonable precautions' and 'all due diligence' means just that, if a proprietor should forget a reasonable precaution and/or be careless in its implementation the defence will almost certainly fail.

The auditing of a main supplier is a perfectly reasonable measure and therefore almost certainly necessary if a due diligence defence is to be proved.

Defining the supplier audit

An audit is 'a documented activity performed to verify, by examination and evaluation of objective evidence, the effectiveness of an organization'. It therefore follows that to obtain meaningful results the audit should be structured. It is also necessary to measure the organization against a known standard in order that non-conformities can be identified and rectified. Such standards might be the standards you have set for your own business or one that embraces good manufacturing practice (GMP). The International Standards Organization (ISO) 9000 series provides such a framework and is a standard to which many companies aspire.

The award to an organization by an accredited certification body of ISO9000 status recognizes that the organization has demonstrated the means whereby it can achieve the level of quality it has set out to achieve. However, just because a supplier has achieved ISO9000 status or equivalent does not necessarily mean it is going to meet the needs of a particular company. It simply says that organization has achieved what it set out to. The goals of the supplier and that of the company being supplied may be entirely different. One company may accept one stone in every ten thousand bags of their raisins whilst the other might expect none.

Choosing the suppliers to audit

It is perhaps unrealistic (and possibly unnecessary) to audit every supplier in detail. Exactly how much time and effort can be placed in this activity will largely depend on the resources available to a business and the degree of risk involved. At some stage an assessment will have to be made of each of the suppliers and their audits placed in order of priority. Such a decision could be based on those suppliers who supply a critical ingredient, i.e. an ingredient or packaging, the quality of which will be critical to the safety of the food produced. The possibility of broken glass in a glass jar used to contain a food is such an example.

An auditing team should be established and the need for any shortfall in the knowledge of team members ascertained and additional training sought.

Before ever visiting the site, the proprietor should begin by asking the supplier some simple questions, such as the following:

- Do they have a quality statement backed by a quality assurance system?
- How is their system organized?
- How is quality assurance implemented?
- Is it organized in such a way as adequately to meet the needs of the food business being supplied?
- Who has overall control and what authority do they have within the structure of the company to rectify non-conformities as they arise?
- How many complaints do they have in a year?
- How are these followed up?
- What system do they have for tracing product through their organization?
- Do they subscribe to external and/or internal audits?
- Are the results of these audits available for scrutiny?

Enquiring proprietors should not confine themselves to quality assurance issues but ask questions as to how the company ensures the safety of food as well. Some examples follow:

- Do they have a HACCP plan?
- Has the company correctly identified all the critical control points?

- Are the controls they have in place at each critical point adequate to eliminate the hazards or reduce them to acceptable levels?
- How do they monitor these critical points effectively?
- Is their system documented, audited and reviewed?

It should be possible to see the Environmental Health Officer's most recent report. What hazard rating was assigned to the supplier? Any 'reputable company' would make copies of these documents available.

Visiting the supplier

The food proprietor will by now have a clear understanding of their supplier's operation and will not be bamboozled into accepting a simple guided tour of the factory floor.

An appointment will have to be made, at least initially, with the supplier since it is imperative that the right people are present during the auditing process. These should comprise those senior members of staff who are in authority and might include the managing director and the quality control manager.

Agreement should first be sought as to the standard to which the premises is to be inspected. If the quality assurance and HACCP plans have proved acceptable to a food company then the appropriate standard might be that which the supplier has set for themselves (i.e. are they doing what they say they should be doing?). Alternatively, the supplier might be audited against the standards of the auditing company or that of good manufacturing practice.

An opinion might already have been formed as to the adequacy of a supplier's systems. Now is the time to ask questions of the management and staff in order to iron out any perceived deficiencies.

Inspecting the premises

Rarely will there be enough time to inspect and audit the whole organization. Inevitably, reasoned choices will have to be made as to which areas are more important in terms of risk or more representative of the company's ability as a whole.

The inspection will be conducted to the agreed standard and might make use of the checklists already devised. For larger operations it may be necessary to arrange for several members of a company to inspect at one time with the work appropriately allocated.

The inspection should be detailed and precise. The auditing company should have a clear idea of the areas they want to inspect. Representatives of the supplier will be there to accompany the auditors. It is not their role to guide the auditors to places they want them to see. Questions can be asked of the lowliest of workers since it is what they understand of the objectives of the organization that so often determines whether systems are being implemented as they should. The use of open questions will test a person's understanding whilst closed questions (those requiring Yes and No answers) offer the best chance for objective scoring. The auditor should use all their senses and be ready to depart from the checklist if the need arises. It is often the things that are not there which are as telling as the things that are.

Closing the audit

The inspection over, the audit is closed by the auditors conveying their findings to the organization concerned. This may either be done verbally at the time or by way of a written report later. It is politic to allow time for senior managers to analyse the results of the audit and devise ways of dealing with the non-conformities that will have been unearthed. A further meeting may have to be arranged at a later date to allow both parties to air their views. Timescales should be agreed upon and urgent items given priority.

If the supplier operates to a high standard there will almost certainly be areas from which the auditing company can learn. There is no harm in discussing these areas since both organizations are links in a chain that leads to the final consumer. Ironically, the supplier may be just as interested in what the auditing company does with the raw ingredients they supply.

The auditing team is in a position to feed the results of the audit back to its organization and any improvements can be considered in the next HACCP or quality review.

Recording and scoring

Whatever the result of the audit it will almost certainly be necessary to keep a record in order to help establish a due diligence defence, should the need arise. It may be possible to summarize the results on a record sheet along with any more detailed findings. Some companies employ a scoring system, which may help in giving an overall impression of how well a supplier is achieving its stated objectives. Such empirical measures also offer a means whereby weak areas within a company can be readily identified or whether one supplier is chosen over another.

The certain knowledge gained by first hand experience of the workings of an organization is of real value in terms of proving the defence of due diligence. No longer is relying on a company's reputation an option, since such terms, without empirical evidence to back them, are generally worthless. A structured

Hospitality, Leisure & Tourism Series

audit of an organization offers a means whereby such evidence can be gleaned. The feedback from an audit can be beneficial to all parties concerned.

Deliveries

Effective delivery and receiving practices are fundamental to food quality and safety in any catering operation. The Food Safety (General Food Hygiene) Regulations 1995 place a requirement on suppliers, where necessary, to use vehicles or containers that are capable of holding foodstuffs at appropriate temperatures and to have some method of monitoring such temperatures. The requirement under the same legislation for the control of those steps critical to food safety means that proper control measures for the checking and receipt of food deliveries is of some importance.

Temperature control

The legal controls (see below) on the temperature requirements for delivery vehicles apply to certain chilled foods and frozen products. There is no requirement under any relevant legislation for delivery vehicles to be refrigerated. The controls merely state maximum temperatures at which food is to be delivered. These temperatures may be maintained by refrigerated vehicles or by using insulated boxes with dry ice packs or eutectic inserts placed at the top of the box (cold air falls). Insulated boxes are likely to be more appropriate where caterers are collecting chilled foods from a cash and carry using their own transport. If the journey time is very short (i.e. less than 30 minutes) and the food is unlikely to rise above the specified temperature before delivery, then no specific precautions need to be taken. If the journey is long enough to cause a temperature rise or takes place during warm weather, then the use of an insulated box is recommended.

Chilled foods ◦ ◦ ◦

There are legal controls on the maximum delivery temperature for certain chilled foods covered by the Food Safety (Temperature Control) Regulations 1995. The controls apply only to those foods that are likely to support the growth of pathogenic micro-organisms or the formation of toxins.

The maximum temperature allowed for the delivery of these foods, in England and Wales, is 8°C. In Scotland there is no specific maximum temperature, the foods simply have to be kept cool. The law does allow for slight upward variation in food temperature that may take place during unloading. However, such increases in temperature must be consistent with food safety and may require some justification. In practice it is preferable that such food, once delivered, is placed into chilled storage without delay.

Frozen foods

There are no legal controls on the delivery temperatures for frozen food unless it is labelled 'quick-frozen'. The Quick-frozen Foodstuffs Regulations 1990 specify a delivery temperature for quick-frozen food, i.e. no warmer than –15°C. All other frozen food should ideally be delivered at a temperature of –18°C (certainly no warmer than –12). It should then immediately be transferred to frozen storage.

Dry foods

Dry food products including flour, raw vegetables, tinned foods etc. can be delivered at ambient temperatures (15–25°C).

Hot foods

Hot food deliveries must be organized so that the food remains above 63°C unless it will be served within 2 hours of the completion of preparation.

The supplier

As part of the supplier nomination process, a prospective supplier should be checked as follows:

- How will the food be delivered (ambient, chilled or frozen) and in what type of transport?
- What time will the food be delivered?
- What area of the building will the food be delivered to?
- What packing will the food be delivered in (vacuum packed, heat sealed, boxed etc.)?

It is recommended that before a supplier is nominated, a product specification and supplier specification are drawn up as follows.

- **Quality:** The specification of the product to exact detail including weights and thicknesses.
- **Delivery**, including:
  (a) type of packaging;
  (b) despatch and delivery temperatures;
  (c) delivery times and procedures.
- **Returns:** A return policy on which both supplier and customer agree.

- **Documentation:** The delivery documentation that is required, such as the delivery note, invoice and who is designated to sign for the produce.

These specifications will then go towards making the purchasing system for the establishment and will form the basis for purchase specifications and delivery.

Checking deliveries

Delivery areas should be equipped with scales so that weights may be checked against the specification, order and delivery note. A probe thermometer should be available so that temperatures may be checked on chilled and frozen deliveries. Goods should be checked for signs of visible damage and codes inspected.

Analysis and due diligence ◦ ◦ ◦

A designated person must be responsible for the receipt of all deliveries. Suppliers must be aware of the arrangement and know when that person is available. It is important that the designated person is aware of the following:

- legal requirements on the temperatures of certain foods;
- temperature measurement using a digital probe thermometer;
- notices of food products withdrawn from sale through a trade withdrawal, food hazard warning or emergency control order.

Unattended food ◦ ◦ ◦

Under no circumstances must food be left unattended in the delivery area. This practice could lead to serious consequences:

- chilled or frozen foods may stay at ambient temperatures for prolonged periods;
- food may be left on the floor and be open to the risk of contamination;
- food may be short delivered by the supplier with no opportunity of obtaining a credit;
- food may be subject to tampering or theft.

Receiving and storage

Once food has been accepted it should be unpacked and placed in suitable storage without delay.

Fruits and vegetables must be removed from packing cases before they are stored and placed in clean, hygienic storage containers. This ensures:

- products are retained in prime condition;
- packing cases/cardboard are not placed in food storage areas;
- more efficient storage and effective use of available space;
- food is covered and protected from contamination.

There are a number of companies that manufacture lidded Perspex boxes for this purpose.

Chilled food should immediately be placed into chilled storage, again after removing any unnecessary packaging. Meat delivered vacuum-packed should be placed directly into chilled storage. Other meat should be removed from its packaging and placed in hygienic trays or containers in chilled storage.

Frozen food should be placed straight into freezer storage once any unnecessary packaging has been removed. Under no circumstances should any food that has been allowed to thaw be re-frozen.

Dry goods should be placed off the floor into clean, dry and well ventilated storage immediately.

Storage

Adequate food storage facilities are necessary in any food business in order to ensure that minor fluctuations in supply do not adversely affect sales and/or production. Furthermore the bulk purchase of foodstuffs will generally be a cheaper alternative to purchasing small quantities. It is important, however, to ensure that perishable foodstuffs are not stored in large quantities but are purchased on a regular basis and stored for short periods of time only.

Storage facilities must be designed and used in such a way that foodstuffs are protected from contamination, deterioration and damage. Contamination can be caused by:

- micro-organisms, e.g. Salmonella;
- chemicals, e.g. bleach;
- physical objects, e.g. staples from packaging materials.

Deterioration can occur if spoilage organisms are allowed to grow causing chemical changes within the food. Damage can be caused either by pests, e.g. rodents, or by incorrect storage procedures leading to damage to packaging. Foodstuffs could also be tainted by stronger smelling foods if incorrectly stored.

Failure to apply sound storage principles can at the very least lead to early decomposition of foodstuffs with the consequent reduction in shelf life. More serious problems could occur if food poisoning organisms were allowed to multiply to dangerous levels during storage.

Storage conditions must therefore ensure that foodstuffs are maintained at as high a quality, both nutritionally and bacteriologically, as possible. This can only be achieved by ensuring that correct systems of storage and rotation are applied, that temperature and ventilation are ideal, and that foodstuffs are stored in properly constructed containers. These principles apply to all types of food storage, i.e. refrigerators, freezers, cold rooms, dry food rooms, vegetable stores and cellars.

Safe food storage and adequate stock rotation are enhanced through the use of properly thought out systems and associated equipment.

Various packaging materials and containers are available for food storage, all of which should:

- prevent bacteriological, chemical and physical contamination;
- retain quality and nutritional value;
- prolong shelf life.

Under the Materials and Articles in Contact with Food Regulations 1987 (as amended), Regulation 4, it is an offence to sell, import or use materials and articles which may come into contact with food, which bring about any unacceptable change in the food's nature, substance or quality. All containers holding, for example, cleaning chemicals should be clearly labelled as such and safely discarded after use.

Manufacturers use a variety of materials such as laminates, plastics and tins for packaging food products. Once foodstuffs have been delivered a caterer should remove external packaging wherever possible. This achieves two functions.

1 The food can be inspected.
2 Some containers used for delivery could insulate products if placed in a refrigerator, e.g. cardboard boxes. The effect of temperature control on that product would then be lost.

A caterer should rewrap or cover foodstuffs prior to placing in storage. Gastronorm containers with lids are ideal for this purpose although silver foil and film wrap can be used to cover most foodstuffs and therefore protect them. Film wrap should not be used to cover high fat foods (e.g. cheese) and must not be allowed to come into actual contact with any foodstuff during cooking, reheating or defrosting in a microwave oven.

Storage systems refer to the use of equipment that protects food, allows for easy inspection, and enables it to be safely transported from the store to the site of use. There are five basic systems currently in use: mobile racks, slotted trays, bins, mobile silos and pallets.

1 **Mobile racks**. These are sets of stainless steel shelves which are mounted on wheels. The shelves are usually supported by an adjustable mount, allowing changes to be made in the shelf spacing to enable larger/smaller items to be stored. Inspection of stores and cleaning is made easy by the fact that the shelves may be pulled out allowing all-round access.

2 **Slotted trays**. These are trays made from high density plastic and are frequently used by bakeries. The trays have slots allowing them to be stored in stacks. When in use for high risk foodstuffs, i.e. those which will readily support bacterial growth and will not receive any further cooking, then the tray closest to the floor should generally be left empty to help avoid contamination from the floor. The trays are useful for additional storage as they can be dismantled and stored in 'nests' when not in use, thus saving space.

3 **Bins**. These are generally used for storage of dry goods in bulk, e.g. flour, rice. They are normally plastic or metal in order to protect food from damage by pests. The bin can be relatively easily transported from dry stores to point of use. Bins are always preferable to allowing food to remain in sacks and bags as the product inside the bag can only be inspected after opening. If opened bags are then put in storage, spillages and attack by pests are common.

4 **Mobile silos**. These are similar to bins but are much larger. The foodstuffs stored inside are discharged into a gravity-fed hopper.

5 **Pallets**. These are generally used when large quantities of bulk goods are to be stored. The pallets can be transported with a fork-lift truck or hand-operated pallet trucks. Pallets used in food premises should not be made from wood to ensure cleaning is effective.

Use of any or several of these systems can help in stock rotation.

Stock rotation

A clearly defined system of stock rotation is vital to ensure that older foodstuffs are always used first. The first stage in any stock rotation system is a delivery checklist. This list should check the following:

- The integrity of the packaging.
- The temperature of the product at the time of despatch and on delivery, particularly if it is a chilled or frozen product.
- The best before or use by date coding.
- Any manufacturer's instructions.
- The weight of the product.

Once the delivery checklist has been completed, the product should be placed directly into the relevant storage area. The stock must then be correctly rotated.

Stock rotation applies to all types of foodstuffs, although checks on stock levels will have to be more frequent when dealing with perishable foodstuffs. With all foodstuffs the golden rule must always be 'first in first out'.

Stock that remains undisturbed for long periods of time will encourage rodent and insect infestations, so it is important to occasionally check products that do not deteriorate quickly, e.g. canned products. Stock rotation will also aid the maintenance of correct stock levels in order that an unpopular foodstuff is not re-ordered.

Stock rotation systems are greatly aided if systems of coding are used. The Food Labelling Regulations 1996 (as amended) require food products which are delivered to catering establishments (and consumers) to carry a date code except for certain exemptions as follows:

- Fresh fruit and vegetables (including potatoes but not including sprouting seeds, legume sprouts and similar products) which have not been peeled or cut into pieces.
- Wine, liqueur wine, sparkling wine, aromatized wine and any similar drink obtained from fruit other than grapes and any drink made from grapes or grape musts and coming within codes 2206 00 91, 2206 00 93 and 2206 00 99 of the Combined Nomenclature.
- Any drink with an alcoholic strength by volume of 10% or more.
- Any soft drink, fruit juice or fruit nectar or alcoholic drink, sold in a container containing more than 5 litres and intended for supply to catering establishments.
- Flour confectionery and bread, which are normally consumed within 24 hours of their preparation.
- Vinegar.
- Cooking and table salts.
- Solid sugar and products consisting almost solely of flavoured or coloured sugars.
- Chewing gums or similar products.
- Edible ices in individual portions.

The words 'use by' followed by a date and an indication of recommended storage conditions must appear on all supplied food products which are susceptible to bacterial spoilage. The use by date can be expressed as a day and a month, or a day, a month and a year. For products with longer expected shelf lives, the words 'best before' followed by a day, a month and a year or 'best before end' followed by only a month and a year should appear. These date coding regulations do not apply to:

- deep-frozen food;
- cheese which is intended to ripen completely or partially in its packaging; and
- any food with an expected shelf life of more than 18 months.

In order to ensure that rotation is carried out when products do not have a manufacturer's date code, it is advisable for retailers and caterers to devise one of their own. Whatever system is used, it must identify the delivery date or production date. For example, the product can be labelled with a handwritten date. Alternatively a system of colour coding may be used, with a different colour allocated to different days of the week. Obviously this system can only be used for perishable products that will be in stock for less than one week.

Under the Food Labelling Regulations 1996 (as amended), it is an offence to:

1 sell any food after its use by date;
2 alter any use by or best before coding from the original.

While it is not an offence to sell food beyond its best before date, it cannot be recommended. An Environmental Health Officer would undoubtedly recommend legal action if out of code stock was found to contravene food hygiene legislation.

Adequate systems and stock rotation alone cannot ensure the integrity of food products. Correct temperature control and adequate ventilation are also of vital importance.

Cold-holding

The simplest method of extending the shelf life of perishable foods such as dairy products, poultry, meat, fish and fruit is to reduce their stored temperature, thus reducing the rate of multiplication of spoilage bacteria. To ensure the safe storage of food items it is necessary to balance the following.

1 The initial quality of the food. Will cold-holding in a chill room, refrigerator or freezer adversely affect a food product's taste, colour and texture? Some fruits and vegetables will suffer physiological damage if stored at refrigerated temperatures.
2 The food's service requirement. Given the existing facilities, equipment and requirements, what is the period of time between preparation/cooking and serving for each food product and can it be reduced?
3 The food's storage life. What is the shelf life for food products at refrigerator and freezer temperatures, which assures both safety and quality?

Commercial refrigerators and chill rooms should store chilled food at between −1 and +4 °C, temperatures that delay rather than prevent food spoilage.

Storage temperatures ※ ※ ※

Storage temperatures are subject to the provisions of the Food Safety (Temperature Control) Regulations 1995. These regulations refer only to those foods that are capable of supporting the growth of pathogenic micro-organisms or the formation of toxins, and do not give lists of specific foods to which they apply, as was the case with previous legislation. As a general rule, it may be inferred that the regulations apply to the following types of foods:

- Soft or semi-hard cheeses ripened by moulds and/or bacteria.
- Dairy-based desserts, e.g. fromage frais, mousses, crème caramels, and others with a pH of above 4.5.
- Cooked products containing meat, fish, eggs, cheese, pulses, cereals or vegetables.
- Ready-to-eat foods, such as sandwiches, containing any of the above.
- Smoked or cured fish.
- Smoked or cured ready-to-eat meat which is not ambient shelf-stable.
- Prepared vegetables, vegetable salads and mayonnaise.
- Uncooked or partly cooked pastry and dough products such as pizzas, pasta and ready-to-bake meat pies and sausage rolls.

The general requirement in England and Wales, is that these foods are subject to a maximum chill storage temperature of 8 °C. In Scotland such foods simply have to be kept cool.

Many other foods are kept chilled for purely quality reasons, such as milk and fats. If temperature control is not needed to prevent the growth of pathogens in such foods, then the legislation does not apply to them. However, in practice, it is easier to ensure that all foods that require chill storage, for whatever reason, are subject to the same temperature control regime.

The legislation recognizes that there may be unavoidable reasons for temporary increases in the temperature of food, for example following equipment breakdown, or defrosting or transferring foods to or from a vehicle. Generally, such a rise of not more than 2 °C for not more than 2 hours will not result in a breach of the Regulations. Time limited periods outside temperature control are also permitted for foods that should be kept cold where the food is required for service or display.

Different foods should ideally be stored at different temperatures in separate units. Food products may be divided into three general temperature storage categories according to their relative safety and spoilage characteristics.

1 Foods that are susceptible to rapid spoilage and therefore tend to have a short shelf life (i.e. less than a week).
2 Foods that do not possess any inherent preservative properties and therefore rely on chilling as the major means of preservation.
3 Foods that have some inherent preservative properties and therefore do not rely entirely on chill storage for their preservation.

Where separate refrigeration is not possible, higher risk foods should be placed near to (without obstructing) the cooling unit (generally the coldest part of a refrigerator) in preference to foods of lower risk. Note: The warmest part of a refrigerator will be on the top shelf at the front.

Unlike meat and fish, fruits and vegetables require adequate ventilation during chilled storage to prevent condensation and the growth of mould. The ability of fruits and vegetables to withstand chilled storage depends on their species, country of origin and maturity. The late varieties of most species store best at refrigeration temperatures. Vacuum packed produce has a longer storage life than conventionally packed produce. Apples and pears require perforated packaging to allow ventilation and avoid fermentation.

The sensitivity of some fruits and vegetables to chilled storage temperatures will require separate storage conditions for different types of produce if chilled storage life is to be maximized.

Refrigeration equipment must have the capacity to maintain correct food temperatures at maximum production and storage demands. To ensure operating efficiency, it is important not to position the refrigerator cabinet near to heating units, high intensity lights or in direct sunlight. Large motors are best positioned outside the kitchen area if possible, as they collect dust and generate heat. Even at maximum load capacity, air should be able to circulate around and below stored food. It is important not to exceed the manufacturer's load capacities or store food directly in front of the cooling unit.

Temperature variations

The frequency and length of time the refrigerator door is open should be minimized. Temperature variations can be controlled more effectively in fan-assisted units which ensure a constant circulation of chilled air, although such systems will increase the rate of drying of unwrapped food. Do not place hot food directly into the refrigeration units. This will cause:

Hospitality, Leisure & Tourism Series

- an increase in the air temperature of the refrigeration unit;
- condensation and water drippage;
- ice build-up on the cooling unit.

The design of units must aid the maintenance of temperature control and thus assist in the safety of their stored produce. Door seals, for example, should be regularly checked and it is advisable for chill room doors to be self-closing and protected by air locks or air curtains.

It is important to maintain as constant a temperatures as possible throughout the storage period. This is particularly important for meat and fish and also for the fruits and vegetables that are best stored at temperatures close to 0 °C. Fluctuations in temperature can cause condensation or moisture on the stored products which may promote the growth of micro-organisms.

Temperature monitoring

The Food Safety (Temperature Control) Regulations 1995 specify temperatures at which foods are to be stored, not temperatures at which equipment is set to operate. Monitoring will be assisted if refrigerators are equipped with temperature-indicating devices such as front-mounted gauges, interior thermometers, colour-change stripes and thermograph charts which give a continuous paper record of temperature over a period of time. However, it can be misleading to rely continually on automatic indicators. Any monitoring system should include the requirement for manual readings using a digital probe thermometer and those readings should be recorded. Periodic testing of the stored produce should also be undertaken, including destructive testing.

Cross-contamination

It is important to store cooked food in a separate cabinet or storage facility to raw food. If this is not possible, store cooked food above raw food on separate, marked shelving. This prevents cross-contamination resulting from dripping, most usually associated with raw meat, poultry or fish.

Any liquids stored in shallow trays should be placed on a lower shelf in case of spillage.

Additionally, cover all unpackaged food. This will reduce the dangers of cross-contamination as well as preventing drying out and absorption of odours. Plastic film wrapping with a 'cling' property should not be used as a wrapping for high fat foods such as cheese; lidded containers are a suitable alternative.

Ventilation

Ventilation may be necessary for fruits, vegetables and foods with a strong flavour such as cheese, but is not usually required for meat and fish.

Cleaning

Any spillages should be cleaned up immediately. On a weekly basis, all units should be cleaned with a solution of bicarbonate of soda or a surface sanitizer. Prior to weekly cleaning, stored produce should be removed and placed in another refrigeration unit if available. Alternatively, the chilled produce can be stored temporarily at ambient temperatures if the cleaning task is completed with speed and efficiency (i.e. not more than 30 minutes).

Storage life

It is important to stress that the chilled storage lives of food products will depend on the following factors:

- the product's country of origin;
- the product's quality and maturity prior to chilled storage;
- type and condition of packaging;
- manufacturing treatments;
- transport conditions.

Storage lives will be significantly reduced if the refrigeration equipment used at any stage is unable to maintain consistent temperatures.

It should be noted that the storage life quoted for chill storage of fresh food products relates to the total storage life from harvest, slaughter or capture and assumes that the foodstuff has been constantly kept at the requisite temperature throughout all stages of processing, distribution and storage. Hence the storage life available to a caterer will be much shorter.

In the case of fresh fish, the Sea Fish Industry Authority recommends that it is not kept more than one night in a caterer's chill store to ensure that customers enjoy a quality product.

With all fresh foodstuffs the aim should be to keep the product for as short a time as possible.

Storage practice

The guidelines for refrigeration regarding ambient temperatures, air circulation, temperature variations, temperature monitoring and cleaning are equally important for freezer units. The following points should also be noted.

Frozen food should be delivered in a vehicle capable of maintaining a temperature colder than −15°C. When delivered, the temperature of the food products should not be warmer than

−12 °C. The despatch note should bear the temperature of the food on loading and should be recorded with the delivery temperature. Once delivery is accepted, the food should be stored in a deep freeze as soon as possible. In no circumstances should it be left at ambient temperature awaiting storage for more than 15 minutes.

The Food Labelling Regulations 2002 require frozen foods to carry the words 'best before' followed by a day, a month and a year, or 'best before end' followed by only a month and a year.

Under Regulation 44 of the Food Labelling Regulations 1996 it is an offence to alter any 'use by' or 'best before' coding from its original. The freezing of any produce exhibiting a 'use by' date is therefore not recommended.

It is an offence to sell any food after the date shown in the 'use by' date relating to it. The recommendations for stock rotation for refrigerated foods are the same as for frozen produce.

All food products should be tightly wrapped in plastic film for frozen storage, to limit ingress of oxygen which causes rancidity to develop. Unwrapped or loosely wrapped food will also be liable to incur freezer burn.

Refreezing of food is generally not to be recommended as it will invariably cause a reduction in the quality of the product while the risk of contamination increases with the length of time stored unfrozen. Hygiene problems increase greatly if the food is stored unrefrigerated, i.e. above 8 °C prior to freezing.

In the event of a freezer breakdown or power failure it may not be necessary to destroy all the affected stored produce. When frozen food thaws out bacteria in the food will recommence growth. If the majority of the food remains frozen, its outer layers are likely to be at temperatures below 8 °C and bacterial growth will be at a relatively slow rate. Such foods should be transferred to a refrigerator or chill room and used within 48 hours or, if refrozen, used as soon as possible. In each case a discretional judgment has to be made based on the temperature gain, the time period, the type of food and the individual condition of the stored produce. However, if the food has thawed at an unknown temperature it should not be used.

If other freezer units are not available and food cannot be transferred, the affected freezer should be insulated by ensuring the door remains shut. Any produce not completely thawed but considered unsuitable for refreezing should be cooked thoroughly and used immediately.

Temperature control and measurement

Food begins to decompose as soon as it is taken from the plant, the ground or the animal. The rate of decomposition is related to how quickly spoilage bacteria grow and multiply. Temperature control can be used to slow down the rate of multiplication and therefore prolong the life of the product.

More importantly, temperature can be used to control the growth of harmful bacteria (pathogens). The majority of pathogens will multiply between the danger zone temperature band of 8 °C and 63 °C. Below 8 °C the majority of these pathogens will remain relatively dormant; some may be able to grow, notably *Listeria monocytogenes*, but the rate of growth will be extremely slow. Adequate rotation of stock to ensure that products do not remain in storage for long periods of time should control this pathogen.

Tinned products will not normally require temperature control, as the high temperatures used in the majority of canning manufacture will ensure the destruction of spoilage organisms, pathogens and spores. Without extremely high temperatures, spores could survive canning and then germinate to form new bacteria on cooling. The only type of canned product that does require storage in controlled conditions is one that has only been heated to pasteurization temperatures, i.e. 63–71 °C. At these temperatures spores will not have been destroyed and could potentially grow and contaminate the product. Cans of this nature will usually be labelled to that effect.

All food products, with the possible exception of dried food (flour, rice, gravy mix) require controlled temperatures. Strict temperature control is particularly important for poultry, fish, shellfish and high risk foods.

Temperature measurement

Caterers are responsible for controlling the temperature of designated foods from the moment of transfer to their premises to the moment a customer is served with the final product.

In order to maintain high standards of food temperature hygiene for customers and to demonstrate to Environmental Health Officers that these responsibilities have been discharged, caterers will not only need to measure temperatures, but also keep regular records of the measurements at the various critical stages of the food service operation. The records will need to contain enough detail to ensure that different batches of food are separately identifiable. By making and keeping detailed records caterers will be able to use them as part of a 'due diligence' system.

There are two categories of temperature measurement that are applicable in every catering organization:

- the measurement of the temperature of the food itself; and
- the measurement of the air temperature where the food is stored.

The Food Safety (Temperature Control) Regulations 1995 relate to the temperature of the food itself, not the air temperature of the storage unit. Automatic temperature monitoring equipment must therefore be supplemented with food temperature readings using a thermometer.

Thermometers

To measure the temperature of food, the use of a digital thermometer (often referred to as a 'probe thermometer') with a measuring range from –30°C to at least +100°C and a system accuracy of ±0.5°C is recommended. The thermometer should display results with a resolution of 0.1°C and provide an indication whenever the battery needs replacing.

The thermometer should be equipped with a food quality stainless steel probe that is long enough to measure the centre temperatures of food products and that can be cleaned and sterilized. The probe needs to be strong enough to penetrate dense materials and have a handle large enough to prevent fingers being scalded when hot food is being tested. To prevent cross-contamination risks between cooked and raw foods either separate thermometers or a thermometer with colour coded, interchangeable probes should be used.

Thermometers must be checked for accuracy on a regular basis. A check can be performed against a wet ice mixture. The ice should be broken up into small pieces and placed in a container and wetted with water. The probe should be placed in the mixture and agitated and the temperature taken after 3 minutes when stabilized. This should give a reading of 0°C.

Making a measurement

When taking temperature measurements with a thermometer the following guidelines should be adopted.

1 Check that the thermometer is working correctly and that the battery low symbol is not showing. Fit a new battery if required.
2 Ensure that the probe is clean and sterilized. Use anti-bactericidal wipes or leave to soak in a food quality sterilizing solution. Read the instructions carefully and always allow enough time for the sterilizers to work.
3 Insert the sterile probe into the centre of the food. The tip of the probe must be inserted at least 25 mm into the food to give an accurate reading. Allow sufficient time for the reading to stabilize – up to 30 seconds in a wet substance and 2 or 3 minutes in dry granular products. (These times can be reduced by pre-cooling or pre-heating the probe, as appropriate.)

4 Conduct experiments on the particular products used to establish these times. Remember to keep a record of the measurements and to clean the probe after use.

Measurement points

The critical points at which food temperatures must be measured will vary from organization to organization. The list below highlights some of the more usual control points.

- **Deliveries**. Without knowing the temperature on receipt, a supplier's problem may also be the caterer's problem. This is the 'front line' of defence against receipt of temperature abused products:
  (a) chilled products (raw meat and poultry, shellfish, dairy products etc.) should be delivered at 5°C (maximum 8°C);
  (b) frozen products should arrive at –18°C (maximum –12°C);
  (c) dry products can be delivered at ambient temperatures.
- **Microwave oven**. After microwaving, measure the temperature in a number of places to ensure the food is fully defrosted or properly cooked to a centre temperature of 75°C, as appropriate.
- **Cooking**. Check that food has reached a centre temperature of at least 75°C to ensure harmful bacteria have been destroyed.
- **Cooling after cooking**. Cool the cooked food to below 8°C (or lower as appropriate) as quickly as possible. Check the temperature before placing the food in refrigerated or freezer storage.
- **Reheating food**. After reheating, measure the temperature in a number of places to ensure that all the food has reached 75°C. In Scotland, food must be reheated to a temperature of not less than 82°C, see regulation 14 of the Food Safety (Temperature Control) Regulations 1995.
- **Hot-holding**. Hot food must be kept at a minimum of 63°C before serving.

By adopting a planned sequence of temperature measurements the performance of equipment and recipes can be cross-checked and the checks form part of the daily routine. For example, measuring the temperature of food before reheating as well as after reheating and cross-checking with the storage temperature of the refrigerator.

Measuring storage temperatures

To measure the temperatures of refrigerators, hot or cold display cabinets or other storage areas a range of measuring equipment can be used. Measurement devices should be positioned to measure the air temperature and should be accurate to ±1°C. As with hand-held thermometers, they must have their accuracy checked on a regular basis.

Equipment ranges from simple fixed liquid in glass or bi-metallic thermometers through to brightly illuminated panel meters, continuous analogue or digital recorders that also automatically keep records. Thermometers should be fixed in position so that the readings are clearly visible each time access is made to the storage equipment.

Alternatively the digital thermometer used for measuring food temperatures can also measure air temperatures using the correct type of probe. To ensure consistency of measurement and to eliminate the problem of poor speed of response in refrigerators and freezers (still air is a very good insulator), probes can be permanently fixed in place and the display instrument can be connected to them when the measurement is taken.

Records should be kept of the temperatures of all temperature-controlled storage units. Automatic recording of the temperature of food storage areas or equipment has many attractions since it ensures that records are kept and that temperatures are monitored even when the premises are unattended. However, they are not a 'fit and forget' solution. The records must be regularly checked so that if a problem has occurred the correct remedial action can be implemented.

There is a wide choice of automatic monitoring equipment. It ranges from single channel circular chart recorders, through multi-channel 'strip' chart recorders to multi-channel digital printers or computers.

Both the circular and strip chart recorders monitor continuously and present their results in graph form that requires interpretation by the user. Digital recorders measure at predetermined intervals (at least once every 10 minutes) and highlight when a particular measurement has exceeded a preset limit. They can also give warning of such an event so that action can be taken immediately. The more sophisticated systems can be linked to the telephone system to relay the warning if the premises are unattended.

Air temperature measurement in storage equipment

The air temperatures of storage equipment should be regularly monitored on a manual basis (even if automatic recording equipment is fitted) and those temperatures recorded.

Caterers may use any of three basic types of chilled display unit. In the **forced air** type, cooled air is blown across the food by use of a fan. **Gravity cool** units use a similar system without the fan, thus relying on natural convection for their cooling effect. **Dole wells** cool by direct contact with a cold surface. Some units will use a combination of systems, e.g. gravity cool units will often also have a direct contact base.

The effectiveness of all of these units can be increased by remembering the following points:

- When using a direct contact unit (dole well) always use a food container with a flat base. The greater the surface area of the container in contact with the base, the greater the cooling effect will be. Containers with a rim around the base will trap an insulating layer of still air between the container and the unit.
- Always pre-cool food and then place it in a pre-cooled container before loading any of these units.
- Always keep the height of food displayed to a minimum. The temperature in all these units increases with the height above the base of the well.

Check and record the air temperatures with a thermometer at two points. In a settled condition temperature differences should vary between +3 °C and +5 °C. There should be no restriction of air flow.

These units have virtually no air flow and so air temperature measurement is inappropriate. Monitoring may be achieved by direct measurement of food temperature. The measurement should be taken in the top of the food displayed at the greatest height from the base.

As with display units, service cabinet refrigerators can be equipped with a number of refrigeration systems. With forced air cabinets, air temperature monitoring is appropriate and readings should be taken at the coolest and warmest points. The other types of unit rely on air circulation by gravity and convection and are very sensitive to door openings and have long temperature recovery times. They are essentially domestic refrigerators and may not all be capable of keeping food at the required temperature in commercial kitchens. Air temperature measurement is not therefore appropriate.

It is important that the thermostat is on and set at the appropriate level with the door closed. It is also particularly important to check that there is no obstruction to air flow by overstocking and blockage of gangways or evaporator air ducts.

Dial thermometer probes in chilled rooms are usually located near the doors to ensure that higher rather than lower temperatures are taken.

Air temperatures should be taken at the return air duct, near to the door, at the ceiling centre and the base of the chill room. The temperature gradient from floor to ceiling and door to evaporator should not exceed 5 °C.

A **food simulant** is a substance that has similar thermal properties to food. It is permanently kept in the storage equipment and its temperature can be periodically recorded as an alternative to taking air or food temperatures. Food simulants may have a temperature sensor permanently embedded in them or simply have a probe inserted into them periodically. Commercially produced products are now becoming available; alternatively a table jelly tablet can be used.

Food simulants should be placed near the warmest position in storage equipment. In service cabinets this is usually to one side of the front of the top shelf. In display cabinets they should be placed towards the front of the cabinet.

Where air measurement is difficult and a food simulant is not available, between-pack temperature readings may be taken. A flat-sided probe is held between two packs of food. This probe should be pre-cooled in the cabinet or chill room before taking the measurement. The readings obtained using this method are likely to be higher than the actual temperature of the food due to the insulation effects of the packaging. A 2°C tolerance should be allowed, i.e. the reading obtained is likely to be 2°C above the food temperature.

Transportation of food

Transport of food on a large scale during the course of a catering business only applies to certain specialized operations such as cook-chill production or event catering. Many other caterers will often transport smaller quantities of food from time to time, for example by collecting from a cash and carry or other supplier or by offering a home delivery service. Transport may also take place around premises within which a caterer is operating, such as moving food from a kitchen to wards in a hospital.

The transport of food offers many opportunities for the contamination and spoilage of foodstuffs. These can occur if the food is carried in dirty receptacles, or is inadequately packaged, or in damaged packaging, or is not subjected to any appropriate temperature controls. Where suppliers deliver to a catering outlet, legal compliance is the responsibility of the supplier. Where a caterer collects from a supplier, or otherwise moves food around, the responsibility rests on the caterer.

The hygiene requirements relating to the transport of food are laid down in Chapter IV of Schedule 1 to the Food Safety (General Food Hygiene) Regulations 1995. The requirements of this chapter apply to the construction, maintenance and cleanliness of conveyances/containers used for transport and the prevention of contamination and maintenance of adequate temperature control of food during transport.

Construction and maintenance

All conveyances and/or containers used for transporting food must be kept clean and maintained in good repair and condition in order to protect foodstuffs from risk of contamination and, if necessary, designed and constructed to allow adequate cleaning and/or disinfection. This requirement relates to any vehicle used for transporting food and also containers, which may include trolleys, bags, boxes, trays and crates. The type of vehicle/container used must reflect the risk associated with the food being transported. Vehicles used for transporting high-risk, open foods must be fully enclosed and capable of being thoroughly cleaned and disinfected. Family cars/estates should not be used to transport high-risk foods, but are suitable only for those which are fully enclosed or wrapped and require no temperature control, e.g. canned foods, biscuits, soft drinks etc. Similarly, containers should be constructed of materials suitable for the foods intended to be carried, i.e. a wooden crate used to transport raw vegetables to an outside event would not be suitable for transporting high-risk, open foods. High-risk foods should be transported in containers made from material such as plastic or metal, which is easy to clean, and where significant amounts of such food are carried, purpose-made containers should be used.

Protection from contamination

Receptacles in vehicles and/or containers must not be used for transporting anything other than foodstuffs where this may cause contamination, and where food and non-foodstuffs are carried at the same time, there must be effective separation of products in order to prevent contamination. Similarly, where different foodstuffs are carried these must not be allowed to contaminate each other. These requirements mean that food must be segregated from anything that may contaminate it by adequate separation, wrapping and/or packing and that there is no risk of spillage or contact that may contaminate food. These precautions apply not only for carrying chemicals that may taint or are toxic, but also where, for example, raw meat and poultry are being carried along with cooked food.

Open foods should be carried in enclosed vehicles and/or covered containers. These must protect against dust or debris from the vehicles or containers falling into the food and against dirt and fumes from traffic contaminating the food.

If vehicles and/or containers have been used for the transport of non-food items or for different foods, there must be effective cleaning between loads to avoid the possibility of cross-contamination. The more contaminated the previous load and the more high-risk the next, the more effective the cleaning must be. Where high-risk, ready-to-eat foods are to be carried, the cleaning should include disinfection.

Transportation and temperature control ⁂ ⁂ ⁂

Where necessary, vehicles and/or containers must be capable of maintaining foods at appropriate temperatures and be designed to allow those temperatures to be monitored. This requirement will apply to the transport of both hot and cold foods that fall within the requirements of the Food Safety (Temperature Control) Regulations 1995, that is, those foods likely to support the growth of pathogens or the formation of toxins. In general, this means that the transport arrangements must ensure that such foods are maintained either at 8 °C or below, or at 63 °C or above. The method of meeting this requirement will depend on the duration of the journey and how many times the vehicle/container is opened during the journey. For some journeys, using insulated vehicles or containers will be sufficient, but for long or multi-drop journeys, mechanical or cryogenic chilling will be required.

Transport of chilled food can take place in insulated boxes or trolleys with eutectic plates or gel packs. The food must itself be properly chilled before being placed in such containers, which ideally should themselves be pre-chilled by being placed open in a cold room or refrigerated. The chilled eutectic plate or gel pack should then be placed above the food and the container closed. A similar system, using a heated eutectic plate may be used for short-term transport of hot food.

Where purpose-built vehicles are used for the transport of food, they should be fitted with a means of monitoring food temperature, either directly or indirectly by monitoring air temperature within the vehicle. This temperature should be displayed in the cab so that it is visible to the driver. Where high-risk foods such as chilled meals are being transported, some form of recording system that constantly monitors temperature during transport should be provided. Hand-held probes may be an acceptable alternative for simple journeys involving few drops. The simplest method of checking temperature within an insulated container is to measure the food temperature when it is loaded into the container and again at the end of the journey.

CHAPTER 6

Food preparation and service

Preparation of food

Food preparation represents an integral stage in the processing of raw materials to produce a quality finished food product for consumption. All food produced must be safe, wholesome, nutritious and palatable.

The preparation process requires consideration of a number of critical areas:

- Personal hygiene.
- Cleanliness of food contact surfaces and equipment.
- Structure of surfaces and equipment.
- Cross-contamination.
- Raw materials.
- Food processing:
  (a) ingredient preparation
  (b) ingredient processing
  (c) product holding.
- Waste disposal and cleaning.

Personal hygiene

All staff handling food must be in a good state of health and any illnesses preventing the food handler from safely processing food must be reported before any duties are commenced.

Any cuts or abrasions should be adequately covered with a blue (for easy identification) waterproof plaster. Hands and finger-nails must be washed thoroughly in a suitable wash-hand basin (not a food preparation sink) before work begins and frequently during the course of work, especially between handling raw and cooked foods. Hot and cold water or water at a suitably controlled temperature should be provided, along with soap, nailbrush and hand-drying facilities. Suitable and sufficient protective clothing and headwear should always be available and must be light in colour, clean and preferably without pockets on the outside.

Jewellery should be removed, as it can harbour harmful bacteria. Stones from rings and winders from watches also pose a potential foreign body risk. Employers should provide a secure place away from the food preparation area for these items.

Cleanliness of food contact surfaces and equipment

All surfaces and equipment coming into contact with food must be thoroughly cleaned. Surfaces should be cleaned down with a solution of detergent sanitizer prior to use. The cleaning compound used must be approved by the manufacturer for use in association with food and should only be used at its recommended dilution. Attention must be paid during any cleaning process to the hidden and awkward areas of any equipment that may harbour dirt and bacteria. Congealed food debris provides a medium for bacterial growth and represents a potential foreign body risk.

Chapter V of the Food Safety (General Food Hygiene) Regulations 1995 requires that any article, fittings or equipment which food does or is likely to come into contact with is kept clean and is constructed in a way and made of such materials and is kept in such repair and condition to minimize any risk of contamination of food and, with the exception of non-returnable containers and packaging, is such as to enable thorough cleaning, and where necessary disinfection. It should also be installed so as to allow adequate cleaning of the surrounding area. A comprehensive cleaning schedule should be in operation for all food preparation areas and equipment. Reactive cleaning (e.g. wiping up food spillages) must also take place as appropriate.

Structure of surfaces and equipment

Equipment in contact with food must not only be clean but also of food grade quality. Surfaces and equipment are of food grade quality if they are free from crevices, cracks or corners in which dust or other debris may collect, impervious to water and can be easily and thoroughly cleaned.

There is an extensive range of plastics manufactured but not all are suitable for use with food. The plasticizer components of certain non-food grade products can pass from the plastic into the food. Similarly, certain metals may rust and flake and this corrosion can contaminate the food. Wood represents a porous material that cannot be easily cleaned. Wood should not therefore be used as a preparation surface or in the construction of food utensils. Stainless steel of high quality represents the ideal food preparation surface. Many items of equipment and utensils used to process and handle food are now available in stainless steel. Polypropylene chopping boards are recommended for certain stages of ingredient preparation as sharp knives will score and possibly slip if cutting directly onto stainless steel.

A colour-coded system for equipment, e.g. chopping boards, knives, could be utilized to reduce the risk of cross-contamination.

Cross-contamination

Cross-contamination involves the transfer of bacteria from raw to cooked food or from a dirty to a clean area. The transfer of any such food poisoning bacteria may give rise to food poisoning. The design of the food preparation area should be such that there is a continuous linear workflow that will ensure the physical and practical separation of clean and dirty areas and processes. Food being prepared should only travel in one direction and should not be passed from a clean area back to a dirty area.

Where kitchen size renders separate preparation areas for raw and cooked foods impractical then there must always be a thorough clean down and sanitizing procedure of all surfaces and equipment between handling these two types of food. The avoidance of cross-contamination risks will require separate utensils for handling of the same product in its raw and cooked stages. Utensils used to baste a raw chicken before placing it in the oven must not be the same utensils used ultimately to test whether the chicken is cooked and to remove the cooked bird from the roasting tin. Staff must wash their hands between handling raw and cooked items to prevent the transfer of bacteria.

Raw materials

The quality of the raw materials used as components of a food product will have a direct relation to the ultimate quality of the food produced. It is therefore important to specify high quality ingredients when arranging contracts with food suppliers. The specification may incorporate reference to bacterial quality. Ingredient quality will no doubt feature as a control point in any hazard analysis and critical control point analysis. Food delivered must be:

(a) fresh;
(b) appropriately sealed/packed;
(c) at the right temperature;
(d) showing no signs of physical contamination or damage.

Bacteriological quality cannot be so easily determined and a microbiological analysis may be required.

Food processing

Ingredient preparation

All ingredients should be checked visually for quality and fitness upon removal from their respective storage areas. Different foods will require different preparation processes but certain requirements are standard.

1 All fresh fruit and vegetables should be thoroughly washed to remove soil, bacteria, pesticide/insecticide residues and other physical contaminants. Tap water treated with sodium hypochlorite to provide a solution of 60–80 ppm sodium hypochlorite should effectively reduce the bacterial count on such food. Food should be washed in a sink designated only for that purpose and should never be washed or drained in the wash-hand basin.

2 Frozen food, unless specified otherwise in the manufacturer's processing instructions, should be thoroughly defrosted prior to cooking. This is particularly important in respect of large joints of meat or poultry where the outside of the food may appear defrosted whilst the inside still contains ice crystals. Thorough defrosting is required so that the heat employed in cooking can penetrate the product and ensure all vegetative bacteria are killed.

3 Dried foods should be checked for any signs of insect infestation, i.e. stored product insects such as Pharaoh's ants. Date codes on the top of all packets should be checked to ensure that any product has not exceeded its shelf life.

Ingredient processing

Food poisoning bacteria can double in number every 10–20 minutes when conditions are favourable. It is important to restrict their growth by controlling one or more of the following factors:

- Time.
- Temperature.
- Food.
- Moisture.

It is obviously impractical in the course of ingredient processing to restrict the available food but the other three factors can be controlled.

Time ◦ ◦ ◦

Bacteria present in food require time in order to be able to grow and multiply. A chef should therefore ensure that protein food in the course of preparation is held for as short a time as possible at ambient temperature. This is particularly important where the preparation process may involve several stages separated by a period of time. Partly prepared food should be placed under correct temperature control pending further processing and only removed from temperature controlled storage when required. Unacceptable delays in the processing of food should be avoided with staff being encouraged to complete one task before progressing to another.

Temperature ◦ ◦ ◦

The danger zone for bacterial growth is between 8 °C and 63 °C. Food should therefore be kept outside this temperature zone as far as possible. The presence of the food within this zone during the course of its preparation should be as short as possible. Correct temperature control in accordance with the requirements of the Food Safety (Temperature Control) Regulations 1995, is either above 63 °C, or below 8 °C (for England and Wales only), depending on the food. There is no specified chill-holding temperature for Scotland, however the hazard analysis requirements of the Food Safety (General Food Hygiene) Regulations 1995 apply to Scotland and operators could be asked to justify the temperatures at which foods are held. These temperature control criteria apply not just to the partially completed dish but throughout all the production stages.

It is advisable to make temperature checks on the food during the course of the preparation stages. This information can be incorporated into a production sheet which follows the food from its raw material stage through its processing to the ultimate finished dish. Any probe thermometers used to test food temperatures must be thoroughly clean and sanitized between uses or else a cross-contamination risk is created. The operating temperatures of refrigeration and freezer units should also be checked to ensure that the equipment is operating satisfactorily and in such a manner as to enable the food to be safely stored outside the danger zone. A malfunctioning refrigerator or bain-marie could provide conditions akin to an incubator.

The temperature of the kitchen should be kept as low as possible since extremes of heat will result in a food temperature entering the danger zone. Natural or mechanical extraction of heat and moisture produced in the kitchen is required.

Moisture ❋ ❋ ❋

Dried food does not provide a suitable medium for bacterial growth. Where moisture in the form of water or milk is added to dry ingredients then conditions suitable for bacterial growth are established. Time and temperature requirements must of course also be met. Reconstituted dried food must be placed under correct temperature control. The relative humidity of dry food stores and kitchens is important as high humidity levels can provide a source of moisture which could encourage bacterial growth.

Product holding ❋ ❋ ❋

Prepared foods awaiting cooking must be stored under refrigeration. High-risk foods (i.e. protein foods that will undergo no further cooking) must be stored separately from other foods. If practical, separate refrigerators should be provided for low and high-risk items. Where cost or space constraints render this impractical, the refrigerator should be organized so that cooked products and products undergoing no further processing are positioned towards the top of the refrigerator whilst raw meats/poultry are stored in the base of the refrigerator. This minimizes the cross-contamination risk.

Hot food should not be placed directly into the refrigerator but should be allowed an initial cooling period not exceeding 90 minutes, preferably utilizing a blast chiller. Hot food placed directly into the refrigerator will only serve to raise the temperature of the foods already stored there and will also create condensation problems. All stored prepared food must be suitably covered to prevent it becoming contaminated and must be stored at the correct temperature.

Food should be handled as little as possible and, where practical, clean tongs or other utensils should be used in preference to hands. Prepared foods should only be tasted to determine correct seasoning levels etc. by using a clean spoon. After each use the spoon should be thoroughly cleaned.

Waste disposal and cleaning ❋ ❋ ❋

All waste food and packaging arising from the preparation process must be properly disposed of. Food may be processed through an on-site waste disposal unit which will discharge ultimately to the drainage system. Waste food must not be permitted to accumulate as its presence encourages insect pests and vermin, introducing a further contamination risk. The minimum amount of waste only should be stored within the food room and waste bins regularly emptied with their contents being transferred to the main refuse storage area external to the building. All waste bins both inside and outside the kitchen should be fitted with close fitting lids. Waste bins provided within the kitchen should preferably be foot operated.

Cooking

Food that is cooked fresh and eaten while hot should not be the cause of food-borne illness. Cooking will destroy most of the bacteria associated with food poisoning that are present on food in its raw state. Toxins that survive cooking or bacteria that form heat-resistant spores will remain inactive if cooked food is kept at a minimum of 63°C until served or cooled for refrigerated storage. Temperature maintenance during the cooking process is therefore an important aspect of food hygiene and food safety; if carried out improperly, cooking has the potential of rendering food hazardous to its consumer.

Overcooking will cause food products to be unpalatable, risk burning or other irreversible spoilage and reduce the food's quality and nutritional value. Culinary skills must balance the two extremes of overcooking and undercooking.

Undercooking remains one of the major factors contributing to outbreaks of food poisoning. The reasons for undercooked food include:

- inadequate thawing of frozen food;
- excessive thickness or quantity of food to be cooked;
- culinary craft requirements and customer preferences;
- failure or malfunction of cooking equipment;
- inadequate processing of ingredients introduced during the cooking process;
- cooking technique, i.e. slow cooking;
- human factors: haste, lack of understanding, bad planning.

Temperature and time are two of the major factors controlling the growth of harmful bacteria (pathogens). Pathogenic growth is severely restricted at temperatures below 8°C and above 63°C. Most pathogens are destroyed if boiled for more than 2 minutes; however, those bacteria able to make heat-resistant spores (e.g. *Clostridium perfringens*) and some toxins may survive boiling for prolonged periods.

In the correct conditions bacteria can multiply very quickly. Food products should therefore be held at danger zone temperatures (8–63°C) for as short a time period as possible.

For safe food, the cooking process should raise a food's centre temperature to 75°C.

Hazards from specific cooking methods

Most types of modern cooking equipment such as forced-air convection ovens, steam ovens, steam jacketed boiling pans, tilting kettles, bratt pans, pressure cookers and deep fryers present no potential cooking hazard in normal use and proper operation. There is, however, a greater risk from some other cooking methods, which are detailed below.

Conventional ovens

A conventional oven distributes heat from its source throughout the cooking chamber by the natural circulation of heat (convection). While the temperature across a shelf is likely to be constant, the base shelf could be up to 30 °C cooler than the top shelf of the oven chamber.

Temperature variations within the oven are affected by the age of the appliance and the degree of service maintenance received, as well as the bulk and number of products to be cooked simultaneously. An old or inadequately maintained oven could display temperature settings or indicators that do not represent the actual cooking temperature in the oven compartment. Such a defect may not necessarily be apparent in the food's appearance, therefore it is important to check:

(a) the actual temperature of the oven in comparison to its temperature setting (by arranging a regular calibration check in servicing contracts);
(b) the centre temperature of food products immediately after cooking and/or prior to service (on an occasional basis).

The fan in a forced-air convection oven recirculates air in the oven compartment and will assist in ensuring a consistently even temperature throughout the chamber, thus eliminating some of the problems of a conventional oven.

Slow cooking

Electrical slow cookers typically consist of a glazed earthenware dish and lid, with an aluminium outer casing. Slow cooking can assist with service requirements and will give a tenderness to meats, which by any other cooking method would remain of an unsuitable texture and quality. Cooking food at low temperatures for a long period of time will not compromise the safety of food if the following points are noted:

1 Use only a purpose-designed vessel such as an electric casserole or commercially available slow cooker.
2 Follow the manufacturer/supplier's instructions accurately, ensuring that food quantity is not exceeded and that the recommended minimum cooking time is completed.
3 Test the final temperature. Although cooking is carried out at lower temperatures than usual, slow cookers are still designed

to attain an eventual minimum temperature of 63 °C through the bulk of the food.

4 Red kidney beans should be boiled for 15 minutes before addition to any slow cooking process.

5 Ensure food is served immediately upon completion of the cooking process.

6 Any food left over should not be retained for subsequent use.

Microwave ovens

The dangers with microwaves relate to undercooking because of:

- poor heat penetration due to unsuitable containers or excessively dense foods;
- inadequate power output;
- microwave energy does not brown food, resulting in a lack of visual indication of cooking efficiency;
- uneven cooking.

Boiling top cooking

During the preparation of large volumes of liquids such as stocks, gravy, soups etc. it is important to maintain an even distribution of heat. A bubbling surface gives no indication of the presence of cold spots. It is vital that these cold spots are eliminated. This can be accomplished by the following methods:

1 Cook as small a volume as possible. Split the bulk into smaller pans if necessary. Do not cook more than 25 litres in bulk.

2 Use wide low pans but with the boiling top burner, plate or ring equal to the diameter of the base of the pan.

3 Keep lids on the pans.

4 Stir the bulk frequently, at least every 10 minutes.

5 Ensure the stirring implement is not placed in a potentially hazardous position between stirring. Do not place on the floor or a soiled area of a work bench. Lay it on a plate near the cooker or if practicable, across the lid of the pan in such a way that the handle is not exposed to heat or causes an obstruction to passers by.

Caterers should also be aware of an alternative method of cooking fluids in bulk, e.g. the use of jacketed kettles, tilting kettles or bratt pans.

Stock pots

The boiling pot or stock pot traditionally remains on the burner throughout the whole day, with various items added to the stock during the cooking period.

Modern kitchens and refurbished units are rarely designed to accommodate a stock pot boiler but in existing kitchens it may still be an established and significant component of the caterer's craft.

If use is made of a stock pot, the following precautions (in addition to those listed for 'boiling top cooking' above) should be taken:

- All contents should be discarded daily.
- Uncooked meat products or unwashed vegetables etc. should not be added as this may introduce contaminants into the liquid.

Hazards associated with specific foods

Meat ◦ ◦ ◦

As heat penetrates slowly into meat the hazards from inadequate cooking are more likely to occur with larger joints. Precautionary measures include:

- limiting the size of any joint to 3 kg (6.5 lb) pre-cooked weight if possible;
- measuring the temperature of the centre of the joint with a probe thermometer, to ensure a minimum temperature of 75 °C.

Most meat served rare is deep muscle meat and provided it has been correctly handled, is unlikely to contain significant levels of harmful organisms. Although the centre temperature during rare cooking will not reach 75 °C, it is likely to reach pasteurization temperature of 63 °C. This temperature will invariably render prime cuts safe to eat and also satisfies the legal requirements.

The only meats that should be served rare are prime cuts of beef and lamb. Boned and rolled joints should not be served rare as surface contaminants may be turned into the centre of the joint during preparation, greatly increasing the bacterial count and thus increasing the need for thorough cooking to 75 °C.

Poultry ◦ ◦ ◦

All raw poultry should be regarded as hazardous, through contamination by salmonellae in particular. It is therefore important that poultry is never undercooked. Heat penetration into the body cavity should ensure a centre temperature of 75 °C.

The traditional and reliable indicator of adequate cooking is the point when the juices of the cooked bird run clear, check this by inserting a skewer or knife into the deep joint between the leg and the body.

Commercial and practical considerations are such that it is often necessary to cook birds of large bulk. The weight of a large bird should not be increased by stuffing the cavity; stuffing should be cooked separately. If possible the bulk of the bird should be reduced by boning and rolling the fresh bird. Boning and rolling a 9 kg (20 lb) turkey, for example, will produce two 3 kg (7 lb) leg–breast joints. Alternatively, frozen pre-cooked turkey, whole or breast, will reduce the potential hazards if correctly stored and defrosted prior to serving.

Game

Game that is hung prior to cooking for extended periods (e.g. pheasant, grouse and hare) must be thoroughly cooked before serving due to the increased risk of contamination associated with this process.

The presence of lead shot in game is unlikely to give rise to an offence under s.14 as it can reasonably be expected to be present within the meat.

Frozen food

Some frozen foods, e.g. vegetables, burgers, fish fingers, chops, thin cut steaks, can be safely cooked directly from frozen.

Problems are experienced in the cooking of frozen meat joints and poultry, which must be defrosted thoroughly before cooking. Tests are always advised using a temperature probe and/or a visual test for clear juices in the body cavity and joints.

Red kidney beans

A naturally occurring toxin is found in red kidney beans, which can cause illness if the beans are eaten raw or undercooked. If processed and canned red kidney beans are not used, the raw beans should be boiled for 15 minutes before serving and before their addition to any other dish, e.g. stock pot, casserole, vegetarian burger.

Shepherds pie, pastry meat pies etc.

Two stages of cooking are required, one to cook the filling and one to bake off the topping. Potential hazards are introduced due to the extra cooling and reheating period.

The following precautionary measures should be noted:

- Cook the filling from the fresh raw product. Previously cooked food or 'leftovers' should not be used.
- Where practicable, cook on the day of requirement. If this cannot be achieved, ensure correct rapid cooling and refrigeration are carried out.

- Minimize the pie thickness. No more than a 10 cm thickness is recommended. The oven temperature must be sufficient to penetrate adequately into the filling as well as to cook off the topping.
- In the case of meat pies, a pre-formed and cooked pastry top can be placed on the cooked pie filling. This is particularly advantageous in the serving of individual 'convenience' baked pies.

Cook–chill and cook–freeze

Caterers basically use one or more of five different systems in the production of food for consumption by their consumers. These are:

- Cook-serve.
- Cook-warm hold.
- Convenience/fast food catering.
- Cook–chill.
- Cook–freeze.

Cook–chill and cook–freeze systems are methods of preparing food in advance of need thus allowing the separation of food preparation and service and the rationalization of the catering process. Both systems are widely used for the manufacture of meat, fish, vegetable and dessert items for both catering and home use.

Ideally, caterers would use the cook-serve option but this can be resource-hungry in terms of staff and facilities and can be impracticable in many mass-catering operations. Here, caterers have traditionally utilized a cook-warm hold system but this can cause quality deterioration in the food and lead to problems in maintaining adequate temperatures. New methods involving the optimization of resources, both equipment and personnel, have evolved leading to the greater use of convenience products in fast food catering and the more system-based approach of cook–chill or cook–freeze in larger catering operations.

Principles

Cook–chill catering involves processes that were, until fairly recently, regarded as inherently unsafe, that is cooking food, keeping it and then reheating for service. The development of effective refrigeration equipment, particularly blast chillers, allowed the introduction of a safe system that depend upon a number of characteristics of bacteria to prevent food poisoning.

The method of food preservation in many cook–chill foods is low temperature. Pathogenic bacteria will not grow at temperatures below 3 °C and the activity of many spoilage organisms is also severely curtailed at this temperature. The growth of all bacteria has a lag phase, a period when no growth occurs, when in a new environment as would occur following cross-contamination. This period normally lasts for several hours. Cook–chill therefore depends upon cooking foods to at least pasteurization temperature, to ensure that most pathogens are killed, and then rapidly reducing the temperature of the food to 3°C or below within the lag phase period. This is followed by strict temperature control during the storage period to maintain the safety of the product.

Chilling, as used in cook–chill catering, should not be confused with refrigerated storage as practised by most caterers. Cook–chill relies on equipment capable of removing heat from food in a rapid and controlled way. The rate of chilling is dependent on a number of factors. Factors independent of the food being chilled include:

- the nature of the chilling medium (air, nitrogen, carbon dioxide, water);
- the temperature of the chilling medium;
- the circulation of the chilling medium;
- the shape of the food container;
- the depth of food in the container;
- the head space in the container;
- whether or not the container is lidded.

Factors dependent on the food being chilled include:

- its heat conductivity and heat capacity;
- its density;
- its initial temperature;
- its bulk and volume;
- its moisture content.

Some of these factors can have significant effects upon chilling rates. For example, unlidded containers chill about 15 per cent more quickly than lidded ones, although gas chilled systems such as air and nitrogen do tend to dry out unlidded foods. Similarly, a head space reduction from 20 mm to 10 mm will also give a 15 per cent saving in chilling time, but remember to cut down the head space by using a shallower container rather than by increasing the depth of the food.

Method

Strict personal and equipment hygiene must be maintained; ideally separate equipment and staff will be used in the pre- and post-cooking areas, especially in large-scale operations.

Cook–chill systems can be broken down into the following stages:

1 Cook the food to ensure pasteurization. This means ensuring that the food reaches a core temperature for at least 2 minutes.
2 Portion, or tray out the food into containers for chilling within 30 minutes of the end of cooking. The depth of food in trays should not exceed 50 mm and joints of meat should not exceed 2.5 kg in weight.
3 Place the food into a blast chiller and chill to 3 °C or below within 90 minutes. Meat and poultry joints should reach 3 °C within 150 minutes.
4 Place in refrigerated storage at between 0 and 3 °C.
5 Transport/distribute at between 0 and 3 °C.
6 Reheat to a temperature of at least 70 °C for 2 minutes and commence serving within 15 minutes of the end of the reheating process.

The recommended maximum life for cook–chill catering foods is 5 days, including the days of production and consumption. If, during storage, the temperature of the food rises to above 5 °C, but below 10 °C, the food must be consumed within 12 hours. If the temperature of the food rises above 10 °C, it must not be consumed but should be discarded. If any food is not consumed after reheating, it must be discarded. Because of the strict temperature requirements on food storage, refrigeration used must be specifically designed for chilled food storage, normally having an operating range between 0 and 2 °C, and preferably fitted with automatic temperature monitoring and recording and an alarm.

Guidance on cook–freeze systems is very similar except that the chilling stage is replaced by freezing to –5 °C within 90 minutes and subsequently reaching a storage temperature of –18 °C or below. Storage and/or distribution temperatures of –18 °C or below should be maintained until the reheating stage. Some caterers use a cook–freeze-thaw-reheat system; in these cases the thawing stage in particular requires careful monitoring to ensure that product temperature does not rise excessively.

Monitoring

Any cook–chill operation will have been subject to a food safety assessment based on HACCP principles, and although not a strict legal requirement, such a system should be documented when it covers such a high-risk operation. The following monitoring and recording should be completed, whether a full-scale cook–chill system is being operated or a caterer is using cook–chill as a supplement to a conventional system.

(a) The name of the food and the production date.
(b) The time of the end of the cooking process and the core temperature of the food.

(c) The time the food entered the chiller.
(d) The time the food left the chiller and the core temperature of the food.
(e) The temperature of the storage refrigerator.
(f) The core temperature of the food at the end of reheating.

During storage, the container should be labelled with the name of the food and either the production or use by date to ensure correct stock rotation. The records above will establish that the food was pasteurized (b), was portioned within 30 minutes (c–b), was chilled within 90 minutes (d–c), was chilled to the correct temperature (d), was stored at the correct temperature (e) and was repasteurized on reheating (f). Similar records should be kept when operating a cook–freeze system.

Other systems

Apart from the system described above, the only other cook–chill system of importance is sous-vide. The difference here is that food is vacuum-packed and then cooked, chilled, stored and often reheated still in the packaging. This system is much more popular on the Continent than it is here. It is not suitable for all types of food, e.g. pastry, but because the food is sealed during cooking it is said that it retains its flavour and moisture. It is usual for food to be cooked for longer periods and at lower temperatures than in conventional cooking so control of the cooking process is critical to ensure pasteurization. A claimed advantage of the system is an increase in storage life – between 21 and 42 days at 0 to 3°C. However, as the system produces anaerobic conditions, suitable for the growth of clostridial bacteria, strict temperature control of stored products below 3°C is critical.

Many caterers will use brought-in chilled and frozen cooked products. These are not usually the result of a cook–chill system as described above but are a manufactured product produced according to similar food safety considerations. As such, the manufacturer's instructions relating to shelf-life, storage temperatures and reheating instructions should be followed. In particular, stock rotation can be a problem, especially where best before or use by dates are only printed on the outer packaging and not on individual products. In these cases, dates should be transferred onto individual items if they are not being stored in the original outer container.

Cooling

Bacteria which are harmful to humans do not constitute a risk if food is kept hot (above 63°C) or stored cold (below 8°C) for a limited period. Between these temperatures is the danger zone where bacteria can multiply most rapidly. To minimize bacterial multiplication and hence the risk of contamination, it is important to cool hot foods (and to heat cold foods) rapidly through this zone. Risks can of course be eliminated if preparation is planned so that food is served hot on completion of the cooking process.

Cooling food without the benefit of blast chilling equipment can compromise the safety of the cooling food unless there is a full understanding of the functions and capabilities of the different refrigeration systems. Cooling (or chilling) and freezing facilities are designed to remove large quantities of heat from the food by reducing its temperature. Holding and storage facilities are designed to do no more than maintain the food at its required final temperature. Both the environmental conditions and the refrigeration capacities differ considerably between 'heat removal' and 'temperature maintenance' systems and neither should be used for the wrong purpose.

'Heat removal' systems (e.g. blast chillers, blast freezers) operate at air velocities which are too high for storage and problems of food drying will occur if they are used for this purpose.

'Temperature maintenance' systems (e.g. refrigerators or chill rooms) usually have only sufficient capacity to cope with small heat inputs such as occasional door openings. Attempts to cool substantial quantities of food in a refrigerator will raise the air temperature to the detriment of both the existing stored produce and performance of the refrigerator itself.

Factors affecting cooling times

The time taken to lower the temperature of any food item from its cooked temperature to a safe storage temperature will depend not only on the methods used but the following factors.

Thickness and surface area

Cooling times are lower for foods if their thickness is small and surface area large. Thus sausages will cool quicker than meatballs of the same weight; portions of meat will cool quicker than complete joints. As food has poor thermal conductivity (it loses and gains heat relatively slowly), the thickness of food products is likely to be the principal factor controlling cooling time.

Packaging

Tight wrapping will have little effect on cooling times but if wrapping is loose it will extend cooling times considerably due to the insulating effect of the entrapped air. Unwrapped food will cool more quickly but it is likely to dry very rapidly if the air velocity passing over the food is high. Food must therefore be wrapped tightly before being placed in, for example, a blast chiller or blast freezer.

Silver foil will retain the heat within food by trapping in insulating air and also by reducing radiation losses, thus increasing cooling times.

Temperature ◦ ◦ ◦

The greater the difference between the temperature of the food and the refrigerated air, the faster the rate of cooling.

Air velocity ◦ ◦ ◦

The higher the velocity of the air cooling the food, the faster the rate of cooling.

Cooling is therefore optimized in systems where food is tightly wrapped, placed in a good air flow, with a maximum air/food temperature difference. This contrasts with storage that requires little air/food temperature difference and low air velocity particularly if the food is unwrapped (as in a delicatessen display).

Cooling methods

Blast chilling ◦ ◦ ◦

A blast chiller is a piece of equipment purpose-made for the rapid cooling of food items. The temperature of the air and the speed it is passed over the cooling food depends much on the design of the individual blast chiller, although on average most catering units are able to chill food products from 70°C to 3°C within 90 minutes.

In the light of the Food Safety (Temperature Control) Regulations 1995 and the importance of temperature control for food safety, blast chillers should be considered as a high priority for all caterers who regularly cool food as part of their service requirements.

Temperature control ◦ ◦ ◦

- Cooked food products should not usually be placed in blast chilling units until the surface temperature of the food has cooled to 70°C. Food above 70°C is not at risk and can significantly increase the unit's ambient temperature if placed in a chiller.
- In the same way as an oven is pre-heated, a blast chiller should be switched on in advance of use enabling the chamber to reach the required cooling temperature.

- Blast chillers should be equipped with food thermometer probes which give a digital display of the food temperature during the chilling process. The cycle can also be controlled by programming the chiller to the probe temperature. The measurement of temperature should, as with all temperature controlled equipment, combine manual recording with automatic (in-built) recorders.
- The temperature of the food at the end of the chill cycle and prior to refrigerated storage should be 3 °C in all cases.

Food handling

Liquids placed in the chiller should be limited to 10 cm in depth. Packs of solid food or joints of meat should be limited in weight to 2.5 kg (6 lb) and in thickness to 10 cm where practicable. Standard culinary, gastronorm or purpose-designed lidded containers may be used, avoiding any large air gaps between the food surface and the lid which will increase cooling times substantially.

Large meat joints and poultry

It is easier from a safety perspective to portion whole joints or large poultry prior to cooking or within 30 minutes of the completion of cooking. The manufacturer's guidance with regard to chilling times (which should be provided) must be closely followed. For specialized chilling of large bulk items it may be necessary to lower the temperature of the blast chiller to a value that just avoids surface freezing. If cooling rare meats, a blast chiller only should be used. In the absence of a blast chiller, cold rare meat should not be served.

Maintenance

Any condensate on the inner lining of the chamber should be removed before the blast chiller is switched on. Following the chilling process, the chamber should be thoroughly cleaned, taking care to remove any spillages.

Cryogenic chilling

Cryogenic chilling systems rapidly cool food using liquid nitrogen or liquid carbon dioxide. Cooling times can be reduced by over 50 per cent in comparison to conventional blast chilling but the units are relatively expensive, require large outside coolant facilities and should only be considered for catering operations that regularly chill large quantities of food.

Ambient (room temperature) cooling ◦ ◦ ◦

Small bulk food items and liquids can be cooled at room temperature but the risks of contamination can be considerable. It is inevitable that the temperature and humidity in a working kitchen will be relatively high, therefore it is important to ensure a suitable area in the kitchen or store room is available, away from food preparation surfaces, for cooling small amounts of food or liquid. Ideally a safe cooling area such as a larder with a lower ambient temperature should be chosen. Food contamination risks and cooling times will be reduced if the following points are considered.

1 Cook food thoroughly. For bacteriological safety, solid food should be brought to 75 °C and liquids boiled for 10 minutes.
2 Transfer viscous liquids such as gravy, stews, casseroles etc. to shallow wide containers on completion of cooking. The thickness of the fluid should not exceed 10 cm.
3 Cook solid food in portions if possible. This will increase the surface area of the food and reduce its thickness, so reducing cooling times. It will also limit any unnecessary handling of cooked products.
4 Cover all food to be cooled with a tight wrapping to prevent contamination from flies, dust etc.
5 Food items should only be left to cool at ambient temperatures for 90–120 minutes maximum.
6 Transfer the food to refrigerated storage.

Chill rooms ◦ ◦ ◦

Chill rooms store foods that tend to deteriorate at room temperature and, because of food quantities or service requirements, are unsuited to 'reach-in' refrigerators. They can operate at any temperature between 0 and 10 °C depending on the type of food requiring storage. Provided they are designed and used correctly, chill rooms will allow food to be cooled more rapidly and safely than cooling at room temperature prior to serving or further cold storage. When considering the safe cooling of food products in chill rooms, it is important to note the following.

- Chill rooms should not be used for any substantial cooling unless they have been specifically designed to do so. To function as a cooling unit, chill rooms must have sufficient refrigeration capacity to extract the increased heat load.
- The cooling of food items must not increase the storage temperature of other foods in the chill room. Regular temperature checks should be made using a manual probe thermometer and these readings recorded.
- Shelving should be of a solid construction, light in weight and allow easy cleaning. Open mesh shelving will facilitate the

circulation of chilled air around the food thus reducing cooling times.
- Cooked food should be stored separately or above raw food on individually marked racks to avoid cross-contamination. It is recommended that no food products be stored less than 48 cm from the ground.
- Chill rooms should be regularly cleaned with a mild, odourless disinfectant.

Refrigerated storage after cooling

Food should be immediately transferred to a refrigerator or chill room following completion of the cooling period in a blast chiller etc.; it is useful if the blast chiller incorporates a warning sound to signal completion of this period, ensuring immediate transfer.

The difficulties associated with refrigerated storage following cooling without a blast chiller can be considerable if the quantities involved are large. The requirements of the product (fast cooling and early storage) cannot in theory be met by a temperature maintenance unit such as a refrigerator. In practice, a 4.5 kg (10 lb) ham joint at 55 °C introduced into a large, efficient and correctly loaded chill room, should not raise the temperature of the chill room or its existing produce. There is, however, no simple formula to calculate temperatures at which cooling produce can be safely placed in refrigerators or chill rooms.

Catering operations without blast chilling equipment must regularly test and monitor the temperatures of different food types and quantities as well as the surrounding air temperature, from the completion of cooking to refrigerated storage. The ultimate aim is to cool food as quickly as possible from 75 °C to below 8 °C.

Defrosting

Correct defrosting is an essential food safety step in many catering operations. Whilst many foods are specifically prepared for caterers to cook or reheat directly from the frozen state, most raw frozen meats and poultry must be carefully thawed under controlled conditions before further preparation or cooking.

There are two hazards that may directly arise if food is not defrosted in a careful and controlled manner. As a failure at this stage in a catering operation may not be rectified at a later stage, especially with regard to the cooking of poultry, it must be regarded as being critical to food safety and thus a critical control point.

Pathogenic bacteria that may be present in, for example, raw frozen poultry may survive a subsequent cooking process if the poultry is not completely thawed before cooking commences. If it is still partially frozen when cooking commences, heat energy will be used in thawing out the frozen core rather than cooking the meat. This may lead to the situation that the surface may be cooked or even burnt whilst the centre remains relatively undercooked and contains viable pathogens.

Should meat become too warm as a result of the process, there will be the opportunity for the growth of bacteria, especially on the surface. This could result in the opportunity for spoilage of food and the presence of excessive numbers of pathogens. The defrosting process should ensure that the temperature of the food only rises sufficiently for the food to thaw whilst still remaining below that required for bacterial growth.

An indirect hazard associated with the process is that liquid from thawing raw meats and poultry is a potential source of cross-contamination to other foods and so the location of the defrosting process should be physically separate from other foods, particularly those that are ready-to-eat.

Factors affecting defrosting times

The time taken to raise the temperature of any food product from its frozen state to a temperature suitable for preparation, storage or cooking will depend not only on the methods used but also the following factors.

Thickness and surface area ◦ ◦ ◦

Defrosting times are shorter for foods if their thickness is small and surface area large. Defrosting will therefore be quicker if, for example, poultry is frozen in portions, rather than as a whole bird. Food products of much smaller thickness, e.g. vegetables, will defrost quickly and should not require defrosting prior to cooking.

Packaging ◦ ◦ ◦

Tight or vacuum packaging will have little effect on thawing times; loose plastic wrapping (enclosing an insulating layer of air) will increase thawing times. Defrosting food that is unwrapped will lead to initial surface wetting followed by drying and discoloration.

Silver foil will also trap in insulating air and reduce heat radiation, thus increasing defrosting times.

Temperature ◦ ◦ ◦

The greater the difference between the temperature of the food prior to defrosting and the ambient temperature, the faster the rate of defrosting. Surface cooking or burning could result, of course, if the temperature is too high (similar problems can occur with incorrect defrosting in a microwave oven).

Air velocity ◦ ◦ ◦

The higher the air velocity of the defrosting medium, the faster the rate of defrosting. Moving air and water will defrost frozen produce faster than air or water that cannot circulate.

Methods of defrosting

Refrigeration ◦ ◦ ◦

Refrigeration temperatures (1–4 °C) provide a controlled environment for the defrosting of food products. The rate of thawing will be slower than defrosting at ambient (room) temperatures as there will be only a small difference between the refrigeration temperature and the surface temperature of the food as it starts to defrost. Despite these time problems, the growth of pathogens on the food's surface is severely limited and the bacteriological safety of the product will be generally assured.

When defrosting food in a refrigerator or chill-room, note the following:

- **Bulk:** Limit the weight of food products to 3 kg (6.5 lb). Separate individual food items that are frozen together as early as possible to reduce their combined bulk and increase the surface area.
- **Air circulation:** A refrigerator fitted with a fan will speed up defrosting times provided the defrosting food is not crowded or packed together within the unit.
- **Cross-contamination:** Store defrosting food away from cooked or prepared items to reduce the risks of cross-contamination. Defrosting meat or poultry should ideally be stored in a separate refrigerator or section of a refrigerator. Liquid from thawing, uncooked poultry or meat products contains harmful bacteria and will contaminate any surface it touches. All equipment in contact with defrosting poultry or joints of meat will require thorough cleaning after each use.
- **Containers:** Place the products to be defrosted in a container large enough and of sufficient depth to contain the food and any defrosting liquids. The depth of the container should not, however, be sufficient to trap an insulating layer of air around the defrosting food product. When defrosting high risk foods place the container at the bottom of the unit to prevent cross-contamination from drip.

Ambient (room) temperature ◦ ◦ ◦

Food will defrost faster at ambient room temperature (up to 25–30 °C) than at refrigerated storage temperatures. As the ambient temperature range falls within the bacteriological danger zone, much closer controls are required to prevent unacceptable levels of bacteriological growth during the defrosting process; bacteria will multiply rapidly on a food's surface if the temperature of its outer layers rises at any time above 8°C. To increase the control during defrosting it is necessary to bring the defrosting temperature closer to refrigeration temperatures. A cool larder at 10–15°C will provide a balance between defrosting food in a refrigerator or chill room (bacteriologically safe but slow and possibly uneconomical with space) and defrosting at room temperatures (comparatively fast but carrying a higher risk of dangerous contamination). The precautions regarding cross-contamination and containers for refrigerators should also be applied in ambient or cool conditions.

Cold running water

The defrosting times of food products in cold running water depend on the bulk of the products as well as the rate of flow of the water, the temperature of the water and the size of the sink. Defrosting times are obviously quickest for small weight products in a large sink with fast flowing water.

Defrosting in cold water does have a number of disadvantages.

- **Speed:** Defrosting times using flowing water can, under certain circumstances, be slower than defrosting in air, e.g. when defrosting small chickens.
- **Water usage:** A very modest flow of water from a cold tap running overnight (14 hours) would result in the use of 840 litres of water. On premises where water thawing is regularly used and water use is metered, charges for water could therefore be considerable.
- **Cross-contamination:** When defrosting meat (in particular poultry) the potential for cross-contamination is considerable. Sink water will quickly become contaminated with bacteria from meat and poultry and splashing may distribute these bacteria around the kitchen. With poultry, bacteria from the cavity of the bird may be washed onto the skin, further increasing the risk of contamination.

Food products should not be immersed in still water as a method of defrosting. Still water will quickly form a static insulating layer around the product (considerably slowing the rate of defrosting) and could create a serious contamination risk. Warm water should never be used for defrosting as this will almost certainly lead to unacceptable levels of bacterial growth.

Microwave ovens ⁕ ⁕ ⁕

The majority of commercial microwave ovens have a defrost facility where the energy is pulsed on and off during the total time setting. Cooked and raw frozen food may be defrosted in the same way but not at the same time. However, microwave ovens should not be used to entirely defrost these foods as the microwave energy is likely to cook the food's outer layers before the centre has been fully defrosted.

- Use the defrost setting only. A higher power will not speed up the process and could cause the food irrevocable damage.
- Arrange the food evenly and in a shallow layer on the rack or plate. This aids even defrosting.
- With chops or chicken portions, place the thick areas of the food towards the outside of the dish and thinner areas towards the centre.
- All visible ice crystals should be brushed off or removed as ice is reflective to microwaves.
- When defrosting meat or fish particularly, inspect the areas around the bones. Bone is reflective to microwaves and therefore the meat attached to it is likely to defrost at a slower rate.
- Pierce plastic pouches and boil-in-bag products.
- Split up frozen packs of food into individual items as soon as possible.
- Break up and stir liquids, casseroles etc. at least twice during the defrosting time to distribute the heat evenly.
- Food should stand or rest (for varying periods of time depending on the food product) after or between bursts of defrosting, allowing the heat to equalize from the outer layers through to the centre.
- Cover all foods during the standing time before cooking or transferring to refrigerated storage.

It is important that during the defrosting time the food does not begin to cook. If there is any danger of this occurring, any defrosted parts of the food should be removed or shielded using a small piece of aluminium foil. The foil should be wrapped shiny side out over thinner, smaller or fatty areas of food but must not be allowed to come into contact with the inside surfaces of the oven.

Rapid thaw cabinets ⁕ ⁕ ⁕

Purpose-made cabinets are commercially available for rapid defrosting of frozen foods. Rapid thaw cabinets pulse air at approximately 15–20 °C around their contents. The controlled temperature environment inside the cabinet combined with air circulation provides the fastest yet safest practical method of defrosting.

Unless the process is continually monitored, products of substantially different weights (and therefore substantially different defrosting times) should not be placed in cabinets at the same time. If the product when manually tested has not reached a centre temperature of −1 °C, it will require further defrosting before cooking or refrigerated storage.

The major disadvantage of a rapid thaw cabinet is its cost; unless defrosting is required by a food business on a regular basis, it could be difficult to justify the expense.

Large bulk products

The principles for thawing large bulk products, e.g. large turkeys and prime meat cuts, are the same as for smaller bulk products. However, with service time constraints and limitations on refrigerator/chill room space, it may not be practicable to thaw large bulk products under refrigerated conditions. Products over 3 kg (6.5 lb) should therefore be defrosted in a cool larder (10–15 °C) rather than at the higher ambient temperatures (25–30 °C), which could result in excessive surface bacterial growth. In these circumstances, where portioning is not possible, extra care is needed to ensure products are both thoroughly thawed before cooking and thoroughly cooked before serving.

With meat and poultry in particular, it is important to ensure food items are thoroughly defrosted. The following should be observed:

- On completion of defrosting, the flesh should be pliable.
- In the case of poultry, there should be a complete absence of crystals in the body cavity. Any giblets should be removed during the cycle as soon as physically possible.
- Test the food's temperature with a needle probe thermometer. The probe should pass into the food with no differential resistance at or near the centre.
- The temperature of all parts should not be lower than −1 °C prior to cooking or refrigerated storage.

Display of foods

Foods are put on display for sale in a wide range of catering premises, for example in buffet operations, carveries, sweet trolleys and salad displays. The foods involved are invariably high risk and can be either partially or completely self-service. This would suggest that display can be regarded as a critical step in many businesses and so must be effectively controlled.

Hazards associated with display

Uncontrolled displays of hot or cold high risk foods can give rise to problems of bacterial growth and/or bacterial contamination. Since the next step following display will be consumption of the food, display must be regarded as a critical control point, there being no further opportunity to rectify anything that may have gone wrong at this stage.

Prevention of bacterial growth can be assured by either limiting the time for which food is displayed to less than that needed for a significant increase in bacterial numbers or by keeping the food at temperatures either above or below those necessary to allow growth to take place.

Prevention of bacterial contamination depends on control of the environment in which the food is displayed and can be affected by factors such as equipment hygiene, choice of serving utensils, for self-service operations, and screening of displayed foods.

Time/temperature controls

Time or temperature controls to limit bacterial growth are closely inter-related, as recognized in the Food Safety (Temperature Control) Regulations 1995. If food is likely to support the growth of pathogens or the formation of toxins, then, generally, it must be kept below 8°C or above 63°C. However, these regulations make allowances for certain catering practices and provide exemptions allowing for the time-limited display of foods outside of temperature control. It is important to appreciate, however, that these allowances are written as a defence to the general duty to keep food under temperature control and the burden of proof to show that the defence has been met falls upon the caterer.

It is important to note that only one period of display outside temperature control, of up to 4 hours for cold food or 2 hours for hot, is allowed. If a dish of food is put on display at ambient temperature for a period of one hour, it cannot subsequently be put out for another 3 hour period at the next service but must be kept refrigerated until sold.

When relying on time-limited, non-temperature controlled display, some system of demonstrating that the time limits have not been exceeded may be required. These could be the use of a label to show when the food went on display. In some situations, such as workplace restaurants where the service period lasts for less than 4 hours, that may be enough in itself to show that the requirement has been met.

A safer option to control bacterial growth is by use of temperature control. This may involve either hot- or cold-holding. In either case, the limitations of the equipment used to maintain temperature control must be understood. It is important to appreciate that both hot- and cold-holding display equipment are only designed to maintain the temperature of food that is already either hot or cold. Bains-marie, hot cupboards and heat lamps are not designed to heat food, but simply to keep hot food hot. Similarly, dole wells and refrigerated cabinets will not cool warm food, they will only maintain the temperature of cold food.

Most commercially available hot-holding equipment will satisfactorily maintain hot temperatures. A potential problem with such displays is where the food on display was intentionally below 63°C when placed on display. Examples include rare beef and hollandaise sauce. In these instances the cooking process will have left the temperature below 63°C and the hot-holding equipment is unlikely to be able to raise the temperature sufficiently to comply with the legislation. Under these circumstances, use will have to be made of the time-limited exemption and the food either heated to above 63°C or chilled to 8°C or below or discarded at the end of 2 hours.

Many cold displays are not particularly effective at holding food at or below 8°C. Many rely on contact between a refrigerated plate and the base of the dish in which the food is displayed. Others use ice, which again relies on contact with the dish. More effective are those systems that use blown, refrigerated air. Where cold-holding equipment is used, reliance on it to guarantee food safety should only be given where it is known that temperatures will be maintained. This means that food temperatures must be taken over a period of time to demonstrate that the equipment is satisfactory. If in any doubt about the effectiveness of equipment, any food displayed in it should also be time-limited.

Some useful points to consider in managing food displays are as follows:

- Ensure that all display unit channels and fans are kept clear of debris, utensils etc. to help maintain operating temperatures.
- If the equipment relies on contact to chill, do not place cloths etc. between it and food dishes. This will simply insulate the food from the equipment and prevent any meaningful temperature control.
- Pre-chill containers for cold displays and pre-heat containers for hot displays.
- Where possible, place foods on display in small quantities. Replenish displays as food is sold but do not top up bulk containers as this may mean food at the bottom of the container could remain on display for too long or may be subject to temperature abuse.
- Make regular temperature checks of displayed foods.

- It may be possible to use some items for display purposes only, and to retain the bulk for sale under controlled conditions, e.g. in a refrigerator. The display items can then be discarded at the end of service.

Prevention of contamination ● ● ●

Bacterial contamination of displayed food can arise from a variety of sources. Most catering outlets will only display ready-to-eat food but some may display raw and cooked in the same cabinet. For example, many kebab restaurants display raw kebabs. These should not be displayed in the same cabinet as ready-to-eat items such as salads. Hygiene of the display equipment is also important. Regular cleaning of such equipment should be a feature of the cleaning schedule.

Displays using self-service could be contaminated by the customer. A potential route of such contamination is the utensil used for service. The handle should not come into contact with food. One way of avoiding this is to ensure that handles are longer than the diameter of the food dish so that the utensil cannot fall into the dish and so contaminate the food. Some protection from bacterial contamination from customers may be afforded by the use of sneeze screens, but this type of protection is more likely to assist in the prevention of physical contamination from dirt, dust and other debris.

Screening ● ● ●

Food that has been placed on display will be open to the risk of cross-contamination if it is not properly screened from sources of contamination. Cross-contamination is the process whereby pathogenic bacteria are transferred from a source to a high risk food. The common sources of bacteria are raw food, people, dirt and dust, and pests. Adequate cleaning procedures should eliminate pests from any display area. Raw foods can be kept separate from cooked in any display cabinet. Food must, however, be screened to prevent contamination by people or by dirt and dust.

The best type of screen for a fixed display unit is one that totally encloses the food. This type of screen does not allow any self-service, and can only be used practically in a retail situation. When a closed unit is not practical, e.g. on a salad bar, a sneeze screen should be affixed directly above the food on display. It must be remembered, however, that customers may still contaminate foods by touching them. Time and temperature controls must also be applied.

CHAPTER 7

Premises, cleaning, health and safety

Design and construction of food premises

Well-designed and constructed food premises are important factors in achieving high standards of food hygiene practices. However, few operators of food businesses have the opportunity to design entirely new premises and, very often, it is a matter of converting existing premises which may or may not have previously been used for food preparation. Another difficulty is that it is easy to underestimate the volume of business to the extent that the food preparation areas come under pressure from being too small and as the business expands, this can result in extra space being sought from food storage, preparation and production areas, subsequently giving rise to serious hygiene problems. Any sacrificing of preparation and storage areas should therefore be resisted.

Unless appropriate in-house resources are available, operators are well advised to engage design and construction specialists with a knowledge of food hygiene requirements. Additionally, the involvement and advice of the local environmental health officer at both the outline and detailed planning stage is essential.

Hospitality food preparation and beverage facilities broadly fall into three groups.

1 Multiple choice of restaurants and bars along with banqueting areas. This requires a main kitchen near stores with satellite kitchens adjacent to banqueting rooms.
2 One or two restaurants and function rooms on the same floor. A main kitchen generally serves the restaurants and function rooms direct.
3 Minimal food service provided. Reliance may be on vending facilities.

Food production is invariably organized into one or more systems that enable the operations to be rationalized. Catering systems allow labour and equipment to be more effectively used and provide control over food and energy costs, hygiene and quality. Kitchen and storage areas used should be based on the number of seats or covers in the restaurants or banquet halls served. As a general principle, a linear workflow should be incorporated into the kitchen design taking into consideration the following eight issues.

1 Working conditions should avoid cross-contamination and the various preparation processes (e.g. raw and cooked foods) should be kept separate.
2 Workflow should progress from raw ingredients to finished product with distances in the kitchen minimized.
3 Facilities for personal hygiene should be incorporated.
4 Temperature control should be adequate.
5 Ease of cleaning should be facilitated.
6 Pest control should be adequate.
7 Drainage facilities should be incorporated within the kitchen, in refuge collection points and in the area where food materials are delivered.
8 Provision for staff welfare should be made.

Overall design considerations

Planning

In planning for a new food business it is important to assess accurately, as far as possible, the likely volume of trade so that a proper balance is made in the allocation of space. There is no point in planning a restaurant with a seating capacity for 200 customers if the kitchen is only suitable for the preparation of 50 meals at any one time. To some extent the balance between the various areas will be determined by the type of catering involved. The restaurant that takes advantage of convenience foods where there is minimum preparation and handling will require a smaller kitchen area than one that prepares all the food from the raw ingredients. If food premises are being planned, the appropriate space allocation can only be achieved by a thorough

examination of the entire operation, ensuring that adequate s̶
is allotted not only for the processes involved but also for th
necessary equipment.

Certain basic guidelines apply when designing new premises or converting existing ones. The Food Safety (General Food Hygiene) Regulations 1995 set out the general requirements that food premises should:

- be kept clean and properly maintained;
- enable proper cleaning and/or disinfection to be carried out;
- protect against:
  (a) the shedding of particles into food
  (b) the accumulation of dirt
  (c) contact with toxic materials
  (d) the formation of moulds or condensation etc.
- encourage good food hygiene practices and the avoidance of cross-contamination;
- be free of pests.

It is also important to ensure that:

- adequate space is provided in all the food handling and associated areas for equipment;
- adequate space is provided to ensure that the various processes can be carried out safely;
- adequate space is provided to enable frequent and routine cleaning to be carried out.

The calculation of the amount of space required for the kitchen and ancillary areas is very complex, being dependent on a mixture of influencing factors, including the following.

- The volume of meals served.
- The time over which the meals will be served.
- The size of the menu.
- The complexity of individual menu items.
- The style of service, e.g. counter/plate/guéridon.
- The mix of fresh and convenience food production.
- The number, type and size of dining facilities served by the kitchen (e.g. restaurants, floors).
- The type of cooking methods to be used.
- The structural features of the building.
- The cost of floor space in the planned facility.

After a consideration of the equipment that can be shared and therefore located centrally, it will be apparent that a basic amount of equipment is needed in all situations, regardless of the size of the facilities. Following this analysis, space allocation will be influenced by the number of customers to be served per hour and

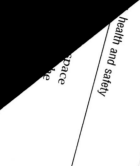

the factors listed above. Consideration must also be given to the following:

- The required refrigeration and dry stores capacities.
- Waste storage and disposal – wet and dry.
- Access for delivery vehicles.
- Any local environmental considerations, e.g. air pollution, smells, flood risks.
- The provision of staff changing and other facilities.

Kitchens and related food preparation areas also require critical design attention, as their mechanical, electrical and plumbing systems must be fully integrated within the layout of the kitchen equipment. In addition, the design of the kitchen (usually the largest single back-of-house area) is a major factor influencing labour costs; distances should be as short as possible, related activities should be located close together, and layouts should be flexible. The planning and design aspects of kitchens will require the coordinated attention of a variety of specialized kitchen and engineering consultants.

Wherever possible, the architect should attempt to locate the receiving area, food storage, kitchen and all outlets on a single floor. If this is not possible, the designer must assess the relative merits of alternative groupings of service and public functions.

Kitchen design

Food preparation areas should be planned to allow a work flow, whereby food is processed through the premises from the point of delivery to the point of sale or service with the minimum obstruction. The various processes should be separated as far as possible and food intended for sale should not cross paths with waste food or refuse. Wherever possible there should be separated clean and dirty sides, thereby minimizing the risk of cross-contamination and reducing wasteful journeys by staff which are inefficient and not cost-effective.

Both the design and construction of different parts of the food premises may vary depending on the food or food process involved. A vegetable preparation area, for example, will mean that there are quantities of water being used to wash vegetables, therefore adequate facilities for the washing and for drainage should be provided. Other processes such as pastry preparation involve a dry activity, although one should remember that flour is likely to be released into the atmosphere which can create a cleaning problem.

But whatever the process or whatever the premises there are basic guidelines that should be applied and these will not only make for easier working conditions but will also satisfy any requirements of the food hygiene legislation. In determining the design and construction of premises one should have regard to the implications of subsequently introducing 'food hazard analysis' and 'risk assessment' programmes.

The food service consultant should propose a preliminary design after the food preparation area space has been allocated. If the major planning criteria are met, the overall design can be greatly simplified and duplication of equipment eliminated.

Food preparation areas

There is no doubt that the proper design and layout of the preparation area can make a major contribution to ensuring good food hygiene and effective management. It is also true that staff generally respond to good working conditions by taking more of a pride in themselves and in what they are doing.

Surfaces ◦ ◦ ◦

All food contact surfaces should be smooth, impervious to water and easy to clean. Indentations, cracks, holes, crevices etc. in a surface must be avoided and can harbour bacteria causing potentially dangerous food contamination.

Any material that may chemically react with food (such as copper and zinc) or which is otherwise toxic should not be used in the construction of any food contact surfaces. Worktop areas should be adequate in size for the preparation process so that the food handler has all the necessary food and utensils near to hand. Inadequate sized worktops can introduce both hygiene and safety problems, not least because food and equipment can fall onto the floor.

As a general rule, most food preparation surfaces should be of good quality stainless steel. An inferior alternative is a plastic laminate veneer finish but this is not as durable as stainless steel. Wood in whatever condition should not be used as it is absorbent, damages easily and cannot be readily cleaned.

Floors ◦ ◦ ◦

Chapter II of the Food Safety (General Food Hygiene) Regulations 1995 requires that the floors should:

- be maintained in sound condition;
- be easy to clean, and where necessary disinfect;
- be of materials that are non-toxic, impervious, non-absorbent and washable, unless the proprietor of the food business can satisfy the food authority that other materials used are appropriate;
- allow adequate surface drainage, where appropriate.

Good practice suggests that they should not be slippery or in any way dangerous. They should be constructed on a firm base, whilst the choice of finish will usually depend on the type of food business. In a kitchen, for example, quarry tiles, or a granolithic finish are best because they are hard wearing, will withstand grease and water and can be easily cleaned. In certain circumstances a granolithic finish may be vulnerable to acids and some oils.

Floors in storerooms or retail areas may be similarly surfaced although industrial sheet linoleum or vinyl, secured by a suitable adhesive may be acceptable. Seamless joints should be used and the floor covering firmly fixed to the under surface. Wooden floors are not acceptable as dirt can collect in cracks and joints even if they have been sealed. There is a risk of harbourage for insects and rodents in the voids behind the surface of suspended wooden floors, or even some types of solid floors.

Concrete floors are not suitable in most food rooms because the surface can break down and cause dust. Although surfaces can be sealed, concrete is not advisable where there is heavy wear, besides which it can be vulnerable to attack by acids, alkalis, fats and oils. In certain circumstances the application of a polyurethane seal will provide some protection. Granolithic concrete is a more acceptable variation.

Various types of composition floors are available which incorporate the strength of concrete/cement whilst overcoming some of the disadvantages, by adding bituminous or mastic compounds. The main disadvantage of these is that they tend not to withstand heavy use by trolley wheels and sharp footwear.

A commendable development in recent years has been in connection with epoxy resin flooring, and though more expensive than many traditional coverings, it has the advantages of being hard wearing and resistant to a range of materials/chemicals and it can be trowelled to eliminate joints.

Where quantities of water are likely to find their way onto the floor or in areas where a wet cleaning process is preferred, then adequate drainage should be provided, either to a central gulley or by way of channels. In either case the floor should be properly laid to avoid pooling, and drainage channels should be laid to an acceptable incline. Grids and grease traps should be provided to filter out material that might obstruct the drainage system and full access should be provided to permit proper cleaning. Where grids are provided, they should not be made inaccessible through being under or behind equipment. Lighter metals are preferable to cast iron to enable more ready access although care is necessary to ensure that these are sufficiently strong not to bend under foot pressure.

The use of absorbent material such as newspaper, cardboard, sawdust or sawdust substitute on floors is not acceptable as these can become a harbourage for bacteria and in any case hamper the effective cleaning of the floor surface. The installation of a non-slip surface is recommended wherever slippery conditions are encountered.

Walls

Chapter II of the Food Safety (General Food Hygiene) Regulations 1995 requires wall surfaces to be maintained in a sound condition. They must be easy to clean and, where necessary, disinfect. This requires the use of impervious, non-absorbent, washable and non-toxic materials and a smooth surface up to a height appropriate for the operations, unless the proprietor of the food business can satisfy the food authority that other materials used are appropriate.

Good practice suggests that glazed tiles, stainless steel, PVC or polypropylene sheets or cladding provide the most suitable surfaces for food rooms, although tiles should not be used near to sources of heat such as cookers which may cause them to crack. It is important with any surface covering to ensure that it is firmly attached to the wall in order to eliminate hidden voids that can become a harbourage for insect pests.

In kitchens and other food preparation areas the most vulnerable parts are those up to approximately 1.5 m and it may be necessary to tile or clad up to that height. The legal requirement is for walls to be treated to a height appropriate to the operation being carried out in that area. Wall areas where there are likely to be special problems, for example near cookers or where they are likely to be knocked by work tools or other equipment, should be covered with seamless metal sheeting.

Tiles should be laid evenly on a sound base and the jointing compound should be mixed with an appropriate sealant to prevent absorption. Alternatively, an epoxy grouting may be used. Other areas may be covered with laminated sheeting or gloss painted but care should be taken with sheeting to ensure that no voids are created behind it that can provide a harbourage for pests.

The choice of wall covering is important, not only from an aesthetic point of view but also with regard to creating safe working conditions. Light colours show up dirt better, besides which they make the best use of available light. The use of metal edging strips around doorways is a sensible precaution against accidental damage by trolleys etc. Plastic or metal crash rails can also be fitted to walls to prevent impact damage. Walls should be as clear of obstruction as possible to enable easy cleaning. The pinning or taping up of posters should be discouraged.

It is good practice to cove walls and floors to eliminate corners where dirt can accumulate and to enable ease of cleaning.

Wall surfaces in retail shops, storerooms and other less vulnerable areas may not need the level of attention required in the food preparation areas of a commercial kitchen, although one should again apply the rule of using smooth and impervious finishes that are in good condition and easy to clean. The use of gloss paint may be extended, for example, particularly where the walls are unlikely to be exposed either to damage or extremes of temperature. Wallpaper should not be used in food preparation areas although there are some washable varieties which may be used in certain circumstances in dry areas such as retail shops.

Pipework and ducting should be chased into the wall or floor or constructed tight to the ceiling enabling an effective seal to be made preventing rodents and insects passing from one room to another. Horizontal pipework collects dust and dirt and frequently results in condensation. This causes dripping which can contaminate any uncovered food beneath. Both to prevent contamination and insulate against heat loss or frost, pipework may be insulated, but the insulation must be firmly fixed around the pipework or ducting to avoid fragmentation. Pipework should not be boxed in as the enclosed area can provide a harbourage for rodents and insect pests.

Ceilings

Chapter II of the Food Safety (General Food Hygiene) Regulations 1995 requires ceilings and overhead fixtures to be designed, constructed and finished to prevent the accumulation of dirt and reduce condensation, the growth of undesirable moulds and the shedding of particles. The choice of materials for ceilings needs special attention because they may be exposed to extremes of temperature, fumes and steam. At the same time they are not normally readily accessible for cleaning. They should be smooth and capable of being easily cleaned, although they also need to be partially absorbent so as to minimize the risk of condensation that may result in droplets falling onto the food, thereby causing contamination. Effective ventilation will also reduce this risk.

The most suitable material is plasterboard sheeting where the joints have been properly made to prevent harbourage by dirt, and once finished with a skim coat of plaster and decorated it can be wiped over to remove concentrations of dirt.

Gloss finishes should be avoided and it is recommended that ceilings, whether suspended or mainframe, should be insulated to reduce the risk of condensation.

Ceilings should be neither too high nor too low, and, subject to any building control considerations, a recommended height for an average sized kitchen is 3–3.5 Suspended ceilings should be avoided where possible because they can provide a harbourage for pests and may be difficult to clean. If a suspended ceiling is installed then ready access to the space behind should be provided.

Windows

Chapter II of the Food Safety (General Food Hygiene) Regulations 1995 requires windows and other openings to be constructed to prevent the accumulation of dirt. Those that can be opened to the outside environment should be fitted with insect-proof screens which can be easily removed for cleaning. Where open windows would result in contamination of foodstuffs, windows must remain closed and fixed during production.

Doors

Chapter II of the Food Safety (General Food Hygiene) Regulations 1995 requires doors to be easy to clean and, where necessary, to disinfect. This will require the use of smooth and non-absorbent surfaces, unless the proprietor of the food business can satisfy the food authority that other materials used are appropriate.

Equipment

Given acceptable premises the choice of equipment will have an important influence on food hygiene standards.

Kitchen equipment should be designed to incorporate the minimum number of areas which may be difficult to clean, on both the equipment's external and internal surfaces. Cleaning is made easier if equipment is movable (i.e. on castors) allowing access to the unit's rear and side surfaces as well as wall/floor junctions. However, food preparation tables should be firmly affixed to the floor – even if castors are lockable, they are still likely to move making the surface unsuitable for safe cutting or chopping during food preparation.

It is important to ensure that the equipment used on catering premises has been specifically designed for commercial use; this point is particularly important for the safety of food in temperature control equipment for cooking, cooling or cold-holding. This is important because if equipment is not maintained in an acceptable condition then it may become difficult to clean and can become a harbourage for dirt and bacteria apart from any health and safety implications.

Equipment must be designed to enable it to be easily cleaned and where it needs to be dismantled to ensure the constituent parts can be effectively cleaned, then it is preferable to select a design where this can be achieved easily and safely. If the dismantling operation takes a long time then it is likely that the cleaning operation will be neglected. The Food Safety (General Food Hygiene) Regulations 1995 set out clearly the requirement for equipment to be constructed and be of such materials and maintained so as to minimize any risk of contamination of the food.

To satisfy these regulations, equipment must be of such design that:

- there are no hidden areas where food debris can accumulate and
- it can be routinely cleaned.

In effect, the legislation stipulates, with few exceptions, that equipment must be made from materials that are smooth, impervious and capable of being readily cleaned. This is a golden rule in any food business and one that can be applied very often both to the choice of equipment and to the construction of the premises.

Wood should not be used where open food is prepared or stored as in its natural state it is absorbent and cannot be readily cleaned. Wood might be used, for example, albeit as a less acceptable alternative, for shelving in a dry store, but it would need to be effectively sealed to prevent any absorption and to enable cleaning to be carried out. Most sealants are not impact resistant so if wooden shelves are to be used for the storage of, say, canned goods, then it is better to provide a more durable, laminated surface whilst at the same time ensuring that the underside and edges are sealed.

In summary, the kitchen planner should endeavour to meet the following objectives.

- Detailed planning with proper consideration given to space allocation for each of the work processes and items of equipment.
- A straight-line flow of food from the storage to the serving area.
- Minimizing the distance between the kitchen serving area and restaurant seating area.
- Arranging compact work centres.
- Secondary storage areas located near each workstation, as required.
- Shared facilities positioned centrally.
- Consideration of sanitation and employee safety.
- A minimum of heat-generating equipment.
- An efficient use of all utilities.

In addition to standards for ventilation, lighting, extraction systems and finishes, the detailed plan for food service areas must include the following features:

- Automatic fire protection systems should be provided throughout the food service areas, especially over cooking equipment.
- Depressed floor slabs (to accommodate floor insulation) for refrigerated storage to ensure the finished floor is even with the kitchen floor.

- Walk-in refrigerators and freezers grouped together to share common walls and compressors. Compressor systems are best located away from storage areas.
- The service dish drop-off area positioned immediately inside doors from each restaurant, feeding a single dishwashing area.
- Security at the kitchen service bar.
- Aisles at a minimum width of 1.1 m.
- Equipment set on concrete curbs.
- The space for the dining room cashier positioned near to waiter circulation.

Health and safety at work

Health and safety at work is covered by a large body of legislation. The main statute covering health and safety at work is the Health and Safety at Work etc. Act 1974 (HSWA). This Act sets out general duties, powers of inspectors, administration of health and safety law, liability of directors etc. Over the years, many regulations have been made under the Act covering different areas of occupational health and safety. The main health and safety legislation that applies to catering and the food and drinks industry is described below.

The Health and Safety Executive (HSE) compiles statistics for different sectors. In the food and drink industries, the HSE reported the following:

- Of the major injuries reported between 1994 and 1997:
    33 per cent were caused by slips;
    17 per cent were caused by falling from a height;
    12 per cent were caused by accidents with machinery.
- Of the 'over three day' injuries reported between 1994 and 1997:
    31 per cent were caused by manual handling;
    22 per cent were caused by slips;
    15 per cent were cause by being struck by moving objects, e.g. knives.

Section 2 of the Health and Safety at Work etc. Act 1974 puts a duty of care on employers to ensure the health and safety of their employees while they are at work. Section 2 specifies areas that employers must pay particular attention to, as follows:

- providing and maintaining safe plant and safe systems of work;
- making arrangements for safety in relation to the use, handling, storage and transport of articles and substances;
- providing information, instruction, training and supervision, as necessary;

- maintaining places of work in a safe condition that are controlled by the employer, including safe means of access and exit;
- providing and maintaining a safe working environment, including suitable welfare facilities.

Section 3 of HSWA extends this duty of care to state that employers must conduct their undertaking in a way that does not expose non-employees, such as visitors, to the site or neighbours, to risks to their health and safety.

Section 7 of HSWA puts duties on employees to:

- take reasonable care of their own health and safety and that of anyone else who may be affected by their acts or omissions at work;
- cooperate with their employer, or anyone else, in relation to complying with health and safety legislation.

Section 8 of HSWA makes it an offence intentionally or recklessly to interfere with, or misuse, anything provided in the interests of health, safety or welfare.

Management

The Management of Health and Safety at Work Regulations 1992 (Management Regulations) impose a legal duty on employers to carry out general risk assessments for all their work activities. In some cases, more detailed risk assessments may be required by other health and safety legislation. For example, where a general risk assessment identifies potential risks from a manual handling task, a detailed assessment must be carried out under the Manual Handling Operations Regulations 1992 (see Manual Handling below).

Under the Management Regulations, employers must carry out a risk assessment for their employees and self-employed people must carry out a risk assessment for themselves. The risk assessment should be carried out by a competent person and should:

- correctly identify all reasonably foreseeable, significant risks;
- allow the assessor to decide what appropriate action needs to be taken, and what the priorities should be;
- be appropriate for the type of activity;
- remain valid for a reasonable time;
- reflect what employers may reasonably practicably be expected to know about the risks associated with their undertaking.

The time and effort put into an assessment should be broadly proportional to the degree of risk. Risk assessments must be reviewed and updated where necessary, e.g. if a new piece of equipment is introduced. Employers of five or more employees must record the significant findings of the assessment, together with details of any group of employees found to be especially at risk. It is not necessary to record the risk assessment if the risk is clearly so small as to be insignificant.

The person who carries out the risk assessment should be competent, i.e. understand the workplace, have the ability to make sound judgements, and have knowledge of the best practicable means to reduce the risks identified. Competency does not require a particular level of qualification but may be defined as a combination of knowledge, skills, experience and personal qualities, including the ability to recognize the extent and limitation of one's own competence. There are a number of basic steps in assessing risk, as identified below.

1 Identify component parts of the undertaking. For example, this may be done by area (e.g. food preparation area) cooking area, chill cabinet, dishwashing area, dining area, rest areas, etc.
2 Identify all jobs in each area, including who carries them out, how regular they are carried out, the equipment and methods used, the level of competence required, existing control measures, experience of accidents or ill health in the past.
3 Identify the hazards associated with each activity, e.g. chopping vegetables would give rise to exposure to sharp instruments, standing for long periods, possible use of machinery, possible manual handling of heavy bags or boxes, etc.
4 Assess the risk. The hazard is the potential source of harm, e.g. being cut by a knife, and the risk is the likelihood of the harm occurring and how severe it is. For example, if a young, untrained person uses a sharp knife, the risk may be assessed to be likely (that they will cut themselves) with the potential of being harmful (deep cuts). This risk would be considered substantial. On the other hand, if an experienced chef is using the same knife, the risk may be assessed to be unlikely but still harmful. In this case, the risk would be considered moderate.
5 Define and implement control measures. A risk assessment will not improve health and safety unless it results in the necessary control measures being identified and implemented.

The Management Regulations contain a number of provisions relating to temporary workers. These are as follows.

• **Risk assessment**. Employers must carry out an assessment of the health and safety risks associated with their operation. The risk assessment should identify who is at risk, and should include consideration of temporary workers where they may be affected by the employer's undertaking. Temporary workers may only be present occasionally, and may not be there when the risk assessment is carried out. However, the person who makes the assessment should identify the areas where temporary workers are occasionally employed and assess the level of risk they are likely to encounter.

- **Information for employees**. Employers must provide employees with comprehensible and relevant information. The employees who must be given this information include temporary workers and those on fixed duration contracts. The information that must be provided is as follows:
  - (a) the risks identified by the risk assessment;
  - (b) the measures taken to control these risks and protect their health and safety;
  - (c) the action they should take in the event of an emergency;
  - (d) the identity of the competent person;
  - (e) the risks notified to the employer by the employer of other employees working on-site.

- **Cooperation and coordination**. Where the employees of more than one employer share a workplace, the employers must cooperate and coordinate health and safety measures to ensure the health and safety of everyone on-site. The employers must inform each other of any health and safety risks that arise from their work activities. Temporary workers, whether they are employed by another person or are self-employed, create a shared workplace for the purposes of this regulation.

- **Working on other premises**. Employers must provide comprehensible information on the risks and control measures that are relevant to the employees of others, such as temporary workers, who are working on, or visiting, their premises. This information must include details of the arrangements for emergency situations.

- **Temporary workers**. Employers must provide temporary workers, and those on a fixed term contract, with comprehensible information on what qualifications and skills they must have in order to carry out their work safely. Employers must also provide temporary workers etc. with details of any health surveillance they are required to have for the work they will be carrying out. If the temporary worker has an employer or an employment agency, the host employer must provide the worker's employer or agency with this information. The worker's employer must then inform the worker of the requirements.

The arrangements required for fire safety for individual premises, including training, are set out by the fire certificate, issued under the Fire Precautions Act 1971. As temporary workers are unfamiliar with the premises and procedures, they should be provided with fire safety training when they first arrive on-site. Such training should include the following:

- the action they should take if they discover a fire;
- how to raise the alarm;
- the procedures for evacuating the building safely;
- the location of fire fighting equipment and how to use it;
- the location of fire escape routes.

The Management Regulations were amended by the Management of Health and Safety at Work (Amendment) Regulations 1994, which added requirements relating to new and expectant mothers. Employers must assess the risks that new and expectant mothers may be exposed to while at work, for example lifting heavy boxes may pose a significant risk to a pregnant woman. Where a risk to their health and safety is identified, the employer must:

- try to eliminate the risk;
- remove the woman from the risk if it is not possible to eliminate it, e.g. by changing her work or suspending her on full pay if there is no suitable, alternative work;
- inform the woman of the risk, explain the action that will be taken to control the risk and provide her with suitable training.

The main risks to new and expectant mothers can be classified as follows:

1 Physical agents, such as:
   (a) manual handling of heavy or awkward loads;
   (b) vibration and noise;
   (c) extreme temperatures, such as working in a chiller;
   (d) work where the woman has to adopt awkward postures;
   (e) work involving standing for long periods of time.
2 Chemical agents, such as:
   (a) mercury;
   (b) lead;
   (c) dangerous chemicals that are absorbed through the skin, e.g. some ant killers;
   (d) carbon monoxide.
3 Biological agents, such as blood-borne diseases (see Hazardous Substances below).

Training

Most health and safety legislation requires employers to provide their staff with suitable health and safety training, including HSWA, the Control of Substances Hazardous to Health Regulations 1999, the Manual Handling Operations Regulations 1992, the Provision and Use of Work Equipment Regulations 1998 etc.

The Management Regulations require employers to provide training to employees:

- on recruitment;
- when they change their job or their responsibilities within the organization;
- when new equipment or new technology is introduced, or when existing equipment is significantly modified;
- when the system of work changes.

Training must be reinforced by supervision in order to make sure that the staff are putting what they have been taught into practice. Training and supervision are particularly important in food businesses. There is often a high turnover of staff, employment of temporary workers and a variety of dangerous equipment used in the workplace. Food hygiene training is also important in food businesses and often it will be combined with health and safety training.

Whenever a new person starts work, even if they will only be there for a short time, they must be given induction training so that they know how to do their job efficiently, hygienically and safely. Induction training should be given on the first day of work and should be followed by close supervision and encouragement of the worker to ask questions, until the supervisor is confident that the worker is competent. In terms of health and safety, induction training should include the following aspects.

- Practical demonstrations of how to use equipment, how to clean it safety, how to use the safety features and why it is important to use them.
- Making clear what equipment the worker is not allowed to use.
- An explanation of the risks in the workplace and how they are controlled.
- Emphasizing the importance of reporting any problems and who to report them to.
- Explanation and demonstration of safety procedures, e.g. explaining that it is important for spills to be cleaned immediately and showing the new worker where to find the mop.
- Explanation and demonstration of emergency procedures, including isolating faulty equipment from the power supply and procedures in the case of a fire.

Once a new employee is familiar with the job and their supervisor is confident that the worker is able to carry out their job safely, the employee will require training in certain situations only. For example, it may become apparent that they are carrying out some aspect of their job incorrectly, e.g. the supervisor may notice them cleaning a dangerous machine without unplugging it first. In this case, it would be necessary for the supervisor to repeat the training and emphasize how important it is to follow procedures.

Existing staff will also need training if any aspect of their job changes. For example, if a new piece of equipment is introduced, it is necessary to demonstrate to them how to use and clean it safely. Where possible, all staff who will be using new equipment should be present when it is installed, so that the supplier can show them how to use it and answer any questions. In particular, supervisors should be present when new equipment is being introduced.

Training must be backed up by supervision. Supervisors not only need to know about the practical health and safety measures in the workplace but may also need training in how to enforce safety rules and how to manage people effectively. For example, they should know how to handle a situation where they become aware that one of their staff is ignoring procedures or what to do if workers complain that one of their tasks is unsafe.

Supervisors' workloads should be organized so that they have enough time to provide induction training for new staff, check their progress, check that all staff are complying with the procedures and provide further guidance where necessary.

Hazards

Hazardous substances

Compared to some types of business, such as heavy industry, the risk from hazardous chemicals in food businesses is relatively small. However, hazardous substances will inevitably be present in all businesses, so the risks must still be evaluated and controlled.

The main law that applies to all employers who have substances present in their workplace is the Control of Substances Hazardous to Health Regulations 1999 (COSHH). COSHH was originally introduced ten years ago, but has been amended and replaced a number of times. However, the basic requirements for employers remain and can be summarized as follows.

1 Employers must carry out a risk assessment of all hazardous substances that employees may be exposed to while at work. A written record of this assessment must be kept.
2 Where the risk assessment identifies a risk to employees' health, employers must make sure that exposure to the relevant hazardous substances are controlled by:
   (a) preventing exposure, e.g. eliminating the chemical from the workplace by using a less hazardous product to do the same job;

(b) controlling exposure, e.g. reducing the length of time the employee is exposed to the chemical;

(c) providing personal protective equipment to protect the employee from exposure (this option should be a last resort), e.g. providing rubber gloves for employees who wash dishes so that their hands are not regularly exposed to detergents.

3 Employers must make sure that employees use, and know how to use properly, equipment provided to protect them from exposure to hazardous substances.

4 Employers must maintain equipment provided to control exposure to hazardous substances, including carrying out checks, inspections, repair and replacement where necessary.

5 Employers must monitor employees' exposure to hazardous substances, where appropriate.

6 Employers must provide employees with relevant health surveillance, where appropriate.

7 Employers must provide employees with training and instruction in relation to working with hazardous substances.

The main type of hazardous substances found in food businesses are cleaning materials, including bleaches, detergents, surface cleaners etc. COSHH came into force in 1989, so in theory a COSHH assessment should already have been carried out for the chemicals used in the business. The assessment needs to be updated if a new chemical or product is introduced. If a written COSHH assessment has not been carried out, the person responsible for health and safety must make sure it is done as soon as possible, and that the other requirements of COSHH are met.

Whether starting a COSHH assessment from scratch or extending an existing one to include a new chemical product, the main source of information on the hazardous properties of the substance is the label on the container. Suppliers of hazardous substances must also provide detailed information on a safety data sheet that must be provided with the substance. In the case of retail sale, the safety data sheet does not necessarily have to be provided at the point of sale, but employers requiring more information should contact the supplier or manufacturer to request a safety data sheet.

While assessing the risk associated with a hazardous substance, not only the obvious means of exposure, i.e. how it is normally used, should be considered, but also increased or unusual means of exposure, such as spillage. Remember that the health effects can either be gradual due to exposure over a period of time, e.g. dermatitis caused by regular exposure to detergents, or immediate, e.g. burns caused by exposure to corrosive products.

It is very important to keep substances in their labelled containers, rather than decanting them into other containers, as this could lead to the substance being mistaken for another substance, e.g. used incorrectly or accidentally swallowed if mistaken for a drink. It is also important not to mix cleaning products as they may react together to form corrosive or toxic gases.

Blood-borne diseases

In recent years, attention has been given to the risks of contracting blood-borne diseases while at work. HIV, which leads to acquired immune deficiency syndrome (AIDS), has been the subject of media hype since the 1980s. In some cases, workers may be worried that they could catch HIV at work through normal contact with infected people. Whilst it is necessary to protect workers from blood-borne diseases, it is also important to make workers aware of which situations will put them at risk and which situations will not. Hepatitis B and C are also transmitted by blood and body fluids, have no cure and are currently carried by a higher percentage of the population than HIV. Precautions in the workplace should aim to prevent all three diseases.

HIV gradually destroys the body's immune system, so that the affected person will be unable to resist diseases, such as pneumonia, which will eventually cause death. Hepatitis B may cause the liver to swell and cause liver damage. Only about 1 per cent of people die from the initial infection, although around 10 per cent will carry the virus for the rest of their lives. Hepatitis C may cause short-term or long-term liver disease and liver cancer. Around 90 per cent of those infected with hepatitis C will carry the disease for the rest of their lives.

In food preparation businesses, there are situations where workers may be exposed to infected blood. Catering staff work with sharp objects, such as knives, and they may accidentally come into contact with sharp objects, such as broken glass. If a member of staff, or anyone else on the premises, cuts themselves the blood should be treated as if it were infected. Procedures should be in place to deal with blood spills safely and staff should know what to do if they cut themselves.

In premises where members of the public are present, e.g. restaurants, there may be a greater risk of coming into contact with infected needles, e.g. when handling rubbish bins in the toilets.

There is a fair amount of misinformation on how HIV is transmitted because it is such a sensitive issue. There is no evidence that it can be transmitted by contact such as shaking hands or handling dirty dishes and glasses that may have traces of saliva on them. The virus cannot survive for long outside the human body. Hepatitis B is much hardier and can survive in a dried state on surfaces at room temperature for at least a week. It may also be carried in saliva, unlike HIV.

Precautions for blood-borne disease ▣ ▣ ▣

There are a number of precautions that should be taken to reduce the risk of contracting a blood-borne disease at work. These are as follows.

- Procedures for the safe cleaning up of blood spills should be in place and all employees should be aware of them. Procedures should include isolating the area until it has been cleared, having designated, trained people cleaning up the spill, wearing disposal gloves and other suitable personal protective equipment to clean the spill and the safe disposal of contaminated clothes and other waste.
- Allow the use of syringes at the workplace only for medical conditions (employees using syringes at the workplace for any reason other than for treatment of a medical condition may be subject to disciplinary action).
- First-aiders should be trained in how to avoid contracting blood-borne diseases when treating injured people. They should be provided with suitable personal protective equipment, including protection for mouth-to-mouth resuscitation.
- Anyone handling rubbish bags, especially those in public areas, should be trained in how to do so safely, for example:
- (a) do not reach into bags or press down on them with bare hands;
  (b) hold rubbish bags by the top, away from the body;
  (c) do not use a hand underneath the bag to support it.
- Ensure that all cuts and abrasions are suitably protected by wound dressings whilst at work, particularly in areas of food preparation.

Electricity ▣ ▣ ▣

Electrical safety in the workplace is governed by the Electricity at Work Regulations 1989. These Regulations basically require employers to make sure all electrical systems and equipment are safe and to provide safe systems of work for activities involving electricity. One of the key requirements is for electrical systems, including electrical equipment, to be maintained in safe working order. This involves regular checks, although the frequency would depend on the type of system or equipment, the frequency of use, the level of risk etc.

The regulations require that all electrical work must be carried out by someone who is competent for the task. In many cases, such as installing, servicing and maintaining electrical equipment, the person will have to be a qualified electrician. Where applicable, electricians must make sure their work complies with the Institute of Electrical Engineers (IEE) Wiring Regulations.

Electricity gives rise to a risk of shock (which can be lethal at the standard mains voltage of 240 V) and burns. There is also a risk of fire caused by system overloading or electrical faults. Use of electricity in food preparation areas generally presents a greater risk than, for example, in an office, because of the presence of other factors, such as water, heat, constant use of equipment etc.

In order to identify the level of risk of electrical equipment and other systems used, an assessment should be carried out. The person who makes the assessment should be competent in terms of having the knowledge and experience of electrical systems to be able to judge whether they are safe and how often they should be tested.

Electrical equipment

Many items of electrical equipment in food preparation areas will be connected to the mains supply by a permanent cable. These should be installed, regularly maintained and repaired by a qualified electrician. All fixed equipment with a permanent cable should have an isolator to disconnect it from the electrical supply for cleaning, repair, in an emergency etc. It may be necessary to label isolators to make it clear which item of equipment it is connected to.

Portable equipment, such as kettles and small food mixers, have a cable with a plug which can be connected to the mains supply. In a commercial catering environment, domestic standard plugs and sockets are unlikely to be adequate, so industrial type plugs and sockets which comply with BS 4343 should be used. Where the plug has to be connected to the equipment cable, this must be done by a competent person and a fuse which is suitable for the equipment must be fitted. The cable should be protected at both the plug and the equipment ends by suitable cord or cable grips. There should be enough sockets provided at places where the equipment is used to avoid the need for extension leads or multiple socket adaptors. Extension leads tend to trail across work areas, creating a trip hazard and the risk of damage to the cable resulting in electrical shock. Multiple socket adaptors can lead to overloading the system, increasing the risk of fire.

Regular checks of all electrical systems should be carried out. The frequency and level of test depends on a number of factors, for example cables on equipment used every day should be checked by a competent person at least once a week.

Training and electricity

Training is essential for anyone who may come into contact with electricity. For example, staff who use electrical equipment should know:

- how to use it safely;
- to ensure it does not come into contact with water;
- to avoid trailing cables;
- to prevent cables coming into contact with heat and hot surfaces;
- what to check before they use it, e.g. that the plug is not cracked, the cable is not loose or damaged etc.;
- not to use damaged equipment or to try to repair it themselves;
- whom to report it to if they discover that the equipment is damaged.

Gas

Gas is a fuel commonly used in food businesses for cooking and heating. Gas is usually either piped through the mains or, in the case of liquefied petroleum gas (LPG), supplied in fixed or portable tanks and cylinders. The use of gas creates a risk of fire or explosion if gas accumulates in the air and is then ignited. The other main hazard is that incomplete combustion of gas produces carbon monoxide, which deprives the body of oxygen if present in sufficient quantities, sometimes with fatal results.

All gas appliances must be installed by a competent person, i.e. someone registered with the Council for Registered Gas Installers (CORGI), as required by the Gas Safety (Installation and Use) Regulations 1998. The person with responsibility for health and safety within the food business should check that anyone who installs a gas appliance is registered with CORGI. This should involve asking to see a copy of their registration or contacting CORGI to get confirmation, rather than taking the installer's word for it.

When choosing a position for installing a gas appliance, bear in mind that the appliance should be well lit and the location should be as draught-free as possible. Sufficient ventilation is essential to avoid the production of carbon monoxide, and this may be provided either naturally or mechanically.

Gas maintenance

As with installation, maintenance and repair of gas appliances must be carried out by a competent person, i.e. registered with CORGI. Regular servicing is essential – the manufacturers' instructions should give guidance on how frequently servicing should be carried out. As a guide, the 1998 Regulations require landlords of domestic premises to have gas appliances checked by a CORGI-registered gas engineer at least once a year.

Whenever servicing or repairs of gas appliances are carried out, a written record should be kept. This will not only help to prove a safe system of work is being provided, but is also useful as a memory aid. To assist in an efficient management system, a written schedule of servicing may be useful, listing all gas appliances used on the premises, the date of their next service and some means of noting that the work was carried out. It is also useful to record any faults found and remedial action taken.

Gas training

It is important to provide staff with suitable training on gas safety. This should include instruction in the following areas.

- The hazards associated with gas, including the symptoms of carbon monoxide poisoning.
- The safe way of lighting gas appliances and other gas safety measures they must take.
- What to do if they smell gas.
- The importance of reporting faults in gas appliances and whom to report them to.
- Where gas shut off valves are, both for the mains and for individual appliances.
- What actions may only be taken by a competent person, e.g. relighting appliances after mains gas has been switched off.
- How to handle and store LPG cylinders safely.
- The procedure for changing LPG cylinders.

Manual handling

The Manual Handling Operations Regulations 1992 require employers to eliminate the need for hazardous manual handling operations, wherever reasonably practicable. For example, when there is a delivery of supplies that includes heavy loads, it is best (where possible) for the delivery person to carry the load to the place where it will be used. This avoids a catering worker having to move it later.

For hazardous manual handling operations that are not reasonably practicable to avoid, the employer must carry out a thorough assessment and introduce risk prevention and control measures. The assessment must be carried out by someone who is competent to do so, and must be recorded. The assessment should look at the whole operation. There are a number of factors that should be considered, as follows.

1 The task, for example:
   (a) how the load is lifted and the distance that it is lifted, e.g. from floor level or waist level;
   (b) how it is carried;
   (c) the distance travelled when moving it;
   (d) how it is lowered and the distance that it is lowered;

(e) whether it is necessary to adopt an awkward posture to carry it;

(f) the time restraints put on the worker, e.g. whether they are likely to have to rush the task.

2 The load, for example:

(a) the weight of the load;

(b) the shape of the load, e.g. a box with handles is easier to carry than a sack of potatoes with no handles;

(c) the stability of the load, e.g. the awkwardness and instability of a load of dirty dishes is likely to present more of a problem than the weight;

(d) the nature of the load, e.g. if the load contains a boiling liquid, the risk is increased.

3 The working environment, for example:

(a) the amount of space available;

(b) the floor surface and any obstacles along the route travelled, including steps, areas where the floor may be wet, and uneven floors;

(c) the level of lighting along the route;

(d) the temperature and humidity, e.g. high temperatures will speed up fatigue and sweaty hands can cause problems with grip.

4 The individual, for example:

(a) the strength needed for the task;

(b) factors that increase risk, such as pregnancy, a history of back problems, recent surgery.

Once the risks have been identified by the assessment, risk reduction measures may be needed to protect the workers' health and safety. Risk reduction measures will not necessarily cost much money, if any. For example, in some cases it will be possible simply to split one heavy load into several lighter ones. It may be appropriate to designate certain stronger members of staff to be responsible for lifting heavier loads. Reducing the distance travelled may also be possible, e.g. by storing the heaviest items nearer to the food preparation area.

In other cases, it will be necessary to provide handling aids, such as electric or manual hoists, sack barrows or other suitable trolleys to reduce the risks.

In all cases, staff should receive information, instruction and training, including:

- the principles of kinetic lifting;
- a safe system of work;
- how to use risk reduction methods provided.

Work equipment

The Provision and Use of Work Equipment Regulations 1998 (PUWER) relate to the safety of all work equipment, including machinery, knives, ovens etc. The basic requirements of PUWER are as follows.

- Employers must ensure that work equipment provided is suitable for its intended purpose.
- Employers must ensure that work equipment is well maintained, so that it remains in efficient working order and good repair.
- If work equipment gives rise to a specific risk, employers must ensure that it is only used, repaired and maintained by designated employees.
- Employers must provide suitable health and safety information, instruction and training to anyone using work equipment and their supervisors.
- Employers must ensure work equipment that they provide complies with relevant product standards.
- Employers must ensure that dangerous parts of machines are guarded, or if this is not reasonably practicable, some other means is provided to prevent anyone coming into contact with dangerous parts.
- Employers must take appropriate measures to protect people against:
  (a) being struck by something either falling from or being ejected from the work equipment;
  (b) parts of the work equipment rupturing or disintegrating;
  (c) work equipment catching fire or overheating;
  (d) accidental or premature release of anything produced by, used by or stored in the work equipment, e.g. hot fat from a fryer;
  (e) accidental explosion of the work equipment.
- Employers must take measures to prevent people coming into contact with extremely hot or cold surfaces.
- Employers must ensure that work equipment is provided with suitable start, stop and emergency controls.
- Employers must ensure that work equipment controls are located in a safe place and are marked so that they are easy to identify.

When first purchasing machines for food preparation, managers should make sure they comply with the relevant European safety standards. One way of doing this is to check that it is 'CE' marked, which indicates that it has been manufactured to the required standard.

An area of particular risk is maintenance and cleaning of machinery. Machines in food preparation areas usually have to be cleaned frequently, for food hygiene purposes. Cleaning may involve exposing dangerous parts of the machine, so anyone carrying out the process must be trained and wear any personal protective equipment that is appropriate to carry out the task safely. The machinery should be disconnected from the power supply during cleaning and maintenance.

The workplace

The working environment in food preparation areas is fairly unusual, when compared with a typical office or industrial workplace. There are extremes of temperature (from the heat from cooking equipment to the cold of chill cabinets), usually maximum use of space with a lot of movement of people and various levels of lighting, often with an absence of natural light.

The main health and safety law that covers the working environment is the Workplace (Health, Safety and Welfare) Regulations 1992 (the Workplace Regulations), which apply to almost all workplaces, including kitchens and other food preparation areas.

Temperature ◦ ◦ ◦

The Workplace Regulations state that the temperature in areas where people work must be 'reasonable'. Although there is no statutory maximum or minimum, the Approved Code of Practice advises that the temperature should be at least 16 °C, or at least 13 °C in areas where the occupants are carrying out strenuous work.

Food preparation generally involves heat and water, so the working environment in food preparation areas is likely to be hot and humid. There is not much that can be done to avoid the use of heat, but the comfort of workers can be improved by making sure there is adequate ventilation of the area. Although extractor fans are one way of ventilating the area, on their own these may not provide enough ventilation, so extra extractor or circulation fans may be needed. Of course, if the area has windows, natural ventilation will generally improve the situation.

The Workplace Regulations require that workrooms must have thermometers provided, to allow the temperature to be checked.

The low temperatures in chillers and cold stores also put workers' health and safety at risk, although it is not practicable to maintain a 'reasonable' temperature in these areas. The time spent in these areas should be reduced as far as possible. If necessary, protective clothing should be provided and there should be precautions in place to prevent anyone from getting locked in.

Lighting ◦ ◦ ◦

The Workplace Regulations state that employers must provide suitable and sufficient lighting in all work areas. Where it is reasonably practicable, this should be by means of natural light.

The various tasks in food preparation areas require different levels of lighting. For example, more light is needed for chopping vegetables than for retrieving a box of food. HSE publication HS(G)55 Health and Safety in Kitchens and Food Preparation Areas recommends the following lighting levels for catering departments:

- areas where food is prepared or cut – 540 lux;
- kitchens – 300 lux;
- passageways and storage areas – 150 lux.

Lights should be positioned to try to get the most consistent level of light possible, with the aim of avoiding glare and shadows. Employers should make sure that light does not reflect off surfaces in the food preparation area, causing glare.

Space

The Workplace Regulations require that there must be enough space in workrooms to avoid overcrowding. The amount and positioning of equipment, furniture, work surfaces and other objects in the Approved Code of Practice recommends a minimum area of 11 m per person, calculated by measuring the volume of the room and dividing that figure by the number of people who normally work in it.

The layout of food preparation areas is crucial to avoid overcrowding, especially as maximum use of space is made in kitchens and there are many items of equipment. Space is particularly important where people are using knives or working with hot pots, etc.

In areas where there is a lot of activity, there should be enough space to stop people from bumping into each other. In order to prevent accidents, separate doors into the dining area should be marked 'In' and 'Out'. If there is only one door, it should have a suitable window, so that staff can see each other approaching the door.

Confined spaces

Under the Confined Spaces Regulations 1997 the employer or self-employed person is required to assess the risks relating to people entering and working within confined spaces. Confined spaces are enclosed spaces that could give rise to a reasonably foreseeable risk of injury. The cellars of licensed premises in which dispense gases are used or stored will almost certainly fall within the scope of this definition.

Welfare facilities ❀ ❀ ❀

The Workplace Regulations cover the provision of welfare facilities in the workplace.

Employers must provide toilets that are:

- adequately ventilated;
- adequately lit;
- kept clean and in an orderly condition;
- separate for men and women, unless the toilet is in a separate room with a door that is lockable from the inside;
- connected to a suitable drainage system;
- provided with means for flushing water;
- provided with toilet paper in a holder;
- provided with somewhere to hang coats;
- provided with a means of sanitary dressing disposal, if they are used by female workers.

The minimum number of toilets that must be provided is one toilet for 1 to 5 workers, two toilets for 6 to 25 workers, three toilets for 26 to 50 workers, four toilets for 51 to 75 workers and five toilets for 76 to 100 workers.

Although this is not specified in the Workplace Regulations, toilets used by food preparation staff should have a notice reminding people to wash their hands.

Washing facilities must be provided that:

- are in the immediate vicinity of toilets and changing rooms;
- have a clean supply of hot and cold (or warm) water, which should be running;
- have a clean supply of soap or other means of cleaning;
- have a clean supply of towels or other means of drying;
- are adequately ventilated and lit;
- are kept clean and orderly;
- are separate for men and women, unless the washing facilities are in a room intended for use by one person at a time and which is lockable from the inside (this does not apply for facilities intended for washing the hands, forearms and face only).

The minimum number of washing units that must be provided are the same number of washing units for the same number of workers as given for toilets above.

There must be a wholesome supply of drinking water with vessels to drink it from. However, it goes without saying that this will be available in a food preparation area.

There must be accommodation for workers to store their personal clothing not worn at work and their work clothing that they do not take home. This is relevant to many food businesses, as workers will generally wear uniforms or other overalls for hygiene reasons while at work. Clothing accommodation must be secure and in a suitable location. Facilities for drying wet clothes should be provided, where reasonably practicable.

If it is not possible for workers to change their clothes in a work room, e.g. for reasons of propriety, separate changing facilities must be provided that have somewhere to sit and are separate for men and women.

Employers must provide rest facilities that are easy to access and are suitable and sufficient, including rest facilities for pregnant women and nursing mothers. In many food premises, it is acceptable for a rest area to be provided in a workroom, rather than having a separate rest room. However, workers should not be excessively disturbed during rest periods if the rest area is in a rest room. The rest facilities provided must allow for the protection of non-smokers from the discomfort of tobacco smoke and must contain enough tables and seats for the workers.

There must be eating facilities where workers can get a hot drink and if hot food is not easily available, there must be facilities for workers to heat their own food. Again, this is not likely to be a problem for workers in a food preparation area.

Safety signs

The Health and Safety (Safety Signs and Signals) Regulations 1996 impose a duty for safety signs to be displayed. Basically, if a safety sign is identified as being necessary by the risk assessment (carried out to comply with the Management Regulations), the 1996 Regulations cover the detailed requirements. However, safety signs should only be used to protect people's health and safety if all other appropriate safety measures have been taken, but the risks cannot be adequately reduced without them.

The term 'safety sign' is relatively broad and basically means a sign that covers a specific situation, object or activity and gives information or instructions relating to health and safety. The information and instructions may be provided by means of:

- a signboard;
- a safety colour;
- an illuminated sign;
- an acoustic signal;
- a verbal communication;
- a hand signal.

Prohibition signs are round with white background and red border and diagonal cross bar, and with a black pictogram. The sign means that something must not be done, for example in a dining room, a non-smoking area would be marked with a 'No smoking' sign.

Warning signs are triangular with a yellow background, and with a black pictogram. This sign warns of a particular hazard or danger, for example a wet floor that is in the process of being cleaned may be marked with a mobile sign to warn that the area is slippery.

Mandatory signs are round with a blue background, and white pictogram. These signs state what specific behaviour or action is expected, or what protective equipment must be worn, for example in an area where heavy boxes are moved, there may be a sign reminding staff to wear protective footwear.

Emergency escape or first aid signs are square or rectangular, with white pictogram on green background. These signs indicate safe conditions, such as indicating the location of first aid equipment or emergency routes.

Fire-fighting signs are square or rectangular, with a white pictogram on a red background. These signs identify and show the location of fire-fighting equipment, for example in a kitchen there would be a sign next to a fire extinguisher to help draw attention to it if it is needed in an emergency.

An example of an acoustic signal is a fire alarm or a beeping from a food delivery truck while it is reversing. Hand signals and verbal signals may occasionally be used in food preparation business, for example while directing a delivery driver into a space.

Safety signs will become ineffective if they are not maintained. The type and frequency of maintenance will depend on the safety sign and its environment. Maintenance may include:

- regularly cleaning signboards;
- checking illuminated signs and replacement of bulbs where necessary;
- testing acoustic signals.

Where safety signs need electricity to work, e.g. illuminated signs and acoustic signals, a back-up supply of power may be needed in case the main power supply fails in an emergency.

In many cases, the meaning of safety signs is easy to understand. However, remember that some employees, particularly new recruits and young people, may not be familiar with all the safety signs used on the site. Explanations of safety signs should be given during induction training and employees should be told what could happen if they ignore the safety signs.

The 1996 Regulations contain detailed requirements for the colour and design of safety signs. The regulations require safety signs to include a pictogram, so a sign giving only a text instruction is not acceptable, if the sign is needed to protect health and safety. In most cases, it is best to buy safety signs from a reputable dealer whose signs comply with BS5378.

Personal protective equipment (PPE)

Risk assessments carried out under the Management Regulations, COSHH, etc. will identify the level of risk and what methods are suitable for their control. The control measures may include the provision of PPE, where necessary.

PPE should only be provided where other control measures determined by the risk assessment provide inadequate protection, i.e. it should only be considered as a last resort or as an interim measure to reduce the risk while other measures are put into place. The reasons for this include:

- PPE only protects the user, other people nearby are not protected from the risks.
- PPE is only effective if it is worn and used properly, i.e. anyone who forgets (or otherwise fails) to use PPE is not afforded protection.
- The person wearing the PPE may have a false sense of security and take more risks.
- PPE may be awkward or cumbersome to wear, e.g. protective gloves often reduce hand dexterity, and give rise to additional health and safety risks.
- PPE has to be well maintained in order to remain effective, i.e. any defects will increase risks to the worker.

Where employers identify the need to provide PPE, they must comply with the Personal Protective Equipment Regulations at Work 1992 (PPE Regulations). These cover all PPE provided to protect workers against risks to their health and safety. They do not apply for equipment and clothing provided for other reasons, such as overalls provided to kitchen workers for food hygiene purposes.

Employers must assess any PPE that they plan to provide to make sure it is suitable, i.e.:

- it is appropriate to the risk it is intended to protect against;
- it is manufactured to an approved standard (in many cases, this means that it must be 'CE' marked);
- it is suitable for the individual who will be using it and for the job for which it is intended;
- it will not create additional risk, as far as reasonably practicable.

Once the PPE has been provided by the employer, it must be stored correctly and regularly maintained. Maintenance will involve regular checks and repair or replacement as necessary. The PPE Regulations require employees to report any lost or defective item of PPE to their employer as soon as possible.

Employers are required by the PPE Regulations to give employees suitable information, instruction and training on any PPE provided. This should include:

- the reason why the PPE has been provided;
- how to use it properly;
- the risks that it will protect against;
- their responsibilities in terms of maintenance, e.g. correct storage, reporting defects.

Employers only have to provide their employees with PPE. Self-employed people are responsible for providing their own PPE.

There are various risks commonly found in food preparation areas that are likely to warrant the provision of PPE. The risk of burns from ovens, hot pans, hot service equipment etc. will mean protective gloves or oven clothes are needed. Work in cold rooms for any length of time will require the provision of protective clothing to prevent frostbite, particularly protective gloves and footwear.

Hazardous chemicals used in the area, such as detergents and bleaches used in cleaning, may cause chemical burns or dermatitis. Protective gloves may be needed if non-hazardous cleaning materials cannot be used.

Another example of PPE that may be needed is a protective gauntlet when the job involves extensive use of sharp knives, as in meat cutting. Other sharp objects, such as broken glass in waste, may mean that protective gloves are needed.

Housekeeping

Poor housekeeping in any workplace creates hazards to employees. In the food and catering business, the hazards are particularly relevant because there are likely to be dangerous machinery, sharp edges and equipment, and extremely hot liquids. It is also likely that, at least during busy periods, there will be many staff rushing around under pressure in a relatively small area.

The hazards associated with housekeeping include slips, trips, spills and falling objects. Slips and trips may be caused by wet floors or tripping over obstacles. Spills of hot liquids and dropping heavy or sharp objects may also result from tripping over, or bumping into, obstructions.

The Workplace Regulations cover the following aspects of housekeeping.

- Floors, walls and ceilings of all indoor workplaces must be capable of being cleaned.
- Workplace furniture, furnishings and fittings must be kept clean.
- Waste materials must not accumulate in the workplace, except in suitable receptacles.

- Floors of traffic routes (which include areas where people circulate) must not be slippery and must be free from obstacles, substances and articles which may cause a person to slip or trip.
- Measures must be taken to prevent risks from falling objects, e.g. safe storage of objects on high shelves.

In practice, food businesses are likely to have strict cleaning procedures for the purposes of food hygiene. Cleaning procedures should be extended from food hygiene to cover risks to health and safety, e.g. spills of liquids should be cleaned immediately to avoid the risk of slipping. It is important to make sure that the cleaning operation itself does not create a risk to health and safety, e.g. by putting up a portable warning sign to alert people to wet floors that have just been cleaned.

Waste receptacles should be provided which prevent spills or leaks. These receptacles should be emptied before they are so full that waste may overspill, and any receptacles containing waste food etc. should be emptied at least daily. The receptacles themselves should be cleaned daily.

Storage of equipment and objects should be designed and used to prevent health and safety risks. For example, knives should be stored in such a way that their blades do not present a risk and boxes and tins of food should be stored out of the way so that they do not create a trip hazard.

Staff should be trained in good housekeeping measures, including:

- cleaning methods and frequencies;
- spillage procedures;
- correct use of storage systems;
- waste disposal procedures.

Accidents

Accident reporting

The Reporting of Injuries, Diseases and Dangerous Occurrences Regulations 1995 (RIDDOR) require accidents at work to be reported if they result in one of the following.

- An injury which renders an employee incapable of carrying out their normal work for more than three days, including days when they would not be at work, e.g. weekends and bank holidays.
- A major injury to an employee.
- A fatality to an employee or a non-employee.
- An injury to a non-employee which requires that person to be taken immediately to the hospital for treatment.

If the accident has to be reported under RIDDOR, there are certain required timescales. All fatal and major injury accidents must be reported immediately by the quickest possible means, usually the telephone. It is therefore important to have the telephone number for the enforcing authority ready to hand at all times. All reportable accidents, including those resulting in over-three-day injuries, must be reported. The responsible person should make sure they have the relevant forms available before an accident happens.

Accidents must be reported to the relevant enforcing authority. In the case of most food businesses, the relevant authority is the environmental health department of the local authority. For food and drink manufacturing and processing, the relevant authority is the Health and Safety Executive.

Responsible person

In most cases, the employer of the injured person is responsible for reporting accidents. This duty should be delegated to a responsible person, such as the safety officer or catering manager. For non-employees, the person responsible for reporting the accident is as follows:

- For workers on the premises who are employed by someone else, e.g. some temporary workers, their employer is responsible.
- For self-employed people, the person in control of the premises where they were injured is responsible.
- For people who are not at work, such as members of the public, the person in control of the premises is responsible.

Record keeping

The responsible person must keep records of all accidents reported, e.g. photocopies of all accident report forms submitted.

In addition to the accidents reportable under RIDDOR, if ten or more people are employed at any one time, employers must record all injuries in an accident book, as required under the Social Security (Claims and Payments) Regulations 1979. This is regardless of how minor the injury appears, including minor burns and cuts.

Accident reports must be kept for at least three years, i.e. RIDDOR records and accident books.

First aid

Under the Health and Safety (First Aid) Regulations 1981, employers must provide adequate first aid equipment and facilities for employees in case they become injured or ill while at work. Employers should carry out an assessment to decide what first aid provision is adequate for their particular circumstances. The guidance suggests that such an assessment should consider the following:

- The hazards and risks associated with the work, e.g. the level of risk would be higher in a food preparation area where dangerous machines are in use.
- The size and nature of the workforce, e.g. the number of employees, employment of young persons, frequent turnover of staff.
- Accident statistics and trends for the organization.
- The distribution of the workforce, e.g. whether they are all in one kitchen or working in several kitchens spread out over a large workplace.
- Accessibility to external emergency facilities and services, e.g. a food preparation area near (or in) a hospital with an emergency department would have much faster access to medical help than one in a remote, rural setting.
- The arrangements between employers where work premises are shared by different employers.
- Arrangements for covering planned and unplanned absences of trained first-aiders.
- Trainees.

Under the 1981 Regulations, employers must provide an adequate and appropriate number of suitable persons (with specific regard to the particular workplace) to render first aid to ill or injured employees at work. A suitable person is a qualified first-aider, i.e. someone who holds a current first aid certificate issued under a training course approved by the HSE.

Sometimes qualified first-aiders are not required, i.e. where they are absent in temporary and exceptional circumstances. In these situations, an appointed person is required to take charge of any situation where an ill or injured employee requires medical attention.

Appointed persons must not give first aid, except emergency first aid if they have been suitably trained. Their main role is to take control of the situation and summon medical help, e.g. phone for an ambulance. For work in food preparation areas, appointed persons should be given basic training in:

- emergency actions;
- cardiopulmonary resuscitation;
- treatment of burns and scalds;
- control of bleeding and treatment of wounds;
- treatment of unconscious casualties.

Hospitality, Leisure & Tourism Series

It is not acceptable to provide an appointed person as a full time alternative for a trained and qualified first-aider. The only exception is where the assessment for determining first aid provision justifies an appointed person instead of a qualified first-aider.

The speed of treatment is a crucial factor in the severity of burns and scalds. There should, therefore, be a sign in food preparation areas giving clear, easy-to-understand instructions on what action to take if someone is scalded or burnt. Employees should understand that if a colleague is scalded or burnt, they should follow the instructions as soon as possible, rather than waiting for the appointed person or a first-aider to turn up.

The guidance on the 1981 Regulations sets out the minimum contents of first aid boxes:

- A general guidance leaflet on first aid.
- 20 individually wrapped sterile adhesive dressings (assorted sizes) appropriate for the work environment (detectable dressings should be available for food preparation areas).
  2 sterile eye pads.
  4 individually wrapped triangular bandages (preferably sterile).
  6 safety pins.
  6 medium-sized individually wrapped sterile unmedicated wound dressings (approx. 12cm).
  2 large sterile individually wrapped unmedicated wound dressings (approx. 18 cm).
  1 pair of disposable gloves.

The recommended marking for first aid boxes is a white cross on a green background.

Health and safety policy

Section 2 of HSWA requires anyone who employs five or more people to have a written health and safety policy. The policy should include the following.

1 General statement: This should be endorsed and signed by the top manager, i.e. the person who is ultimately responsible for health and safety, e.g. the Managing Director. It should be a statement of:
  - the organization's commitment to the health and safety of its staff and others who may be affected by its activities;
  - the organization's intention to comply with all its legal obligations in terms of health and safety.
2 Organization: This should outline how the business is organized, in terms of line management and allocation of health and safety tasks. For example, it should make it clear to whom staff should report safety problems.

3 Arrangements: This will be the largest part of the policy and should set out the details of what arrangements have been made for health and safety. This section should cover the arrangements for different areas and risks, such as equipment safety, welfare, electricity, personal protective equipment, emergency procedures, accident reporting, first aid, house-keeping etc. It should also cover the following:

- risk assessment;
- training;
- cooperating with the employer and other employees;
- safety inspections;
- safety representatives and safety committees;
- procurement procedures;
- policy review.

Cleaning and disinfection

It is vital to keep all parts of food premises clean. The critical areas will be those that come into direct contact with food. These will include work surfaces, food equipment (including knives and other utensils), food containers and the hands of staff. These surfaces should be disinfected as well as cleaned. But even surfaces that do not come into contact with food must be cleaned regularly. A build-up of food debris in any part of the food premises will attract pests that may spread contamination. Performing hazard analysis should indicate the preparation steps where contamination may occur and where effective cleaning and disinfection is necessary. In addition there is a broad requirement in Schedule 1, Chapter I, of the Food Safety (General Food Hygiene) Regulations 1995 to keep food premises clean.

To be effective, cleaning and disinfection must be planned. The plan should outline all areas or equipment which must be cleaned and how frequently. Detailed schedules for every area should indicate how the job must be done.

Basic principles

Effective cleaning usually requires three elements: heat, chemical detergents and physical work. All of these need to be properly controlled to have the right effect. For example, detergents must be used at the right strength, water at the right temperature and changed frequently as it cools or becomes dirty. A cleaning schedule should always include the temperature of water, the detergent concentration and the actual method of cleaning together with equipment to be used.

Disinfection involves removing microbiological contamination. It is not the same as cleaning. Normally, surfaces must be clean before they can be disinfected but surfaces that look clean may still be contaminated with micro-organisms. The most common methods of disinfection in food premises are heat and chemicals. The chemicals that kill micro-organisms are different to the detergents that remove dirt. However, they are sometimes combined in a single product, usually called a detergent-sanitizer.

Typical disinfectants used in food premises are chlorine-based (bleach) or chemicals known as QACs (quaternary ammonium compounds). Iodine-based disinfectants are used occasionally, for example in glass-wash machines. Many other disinfectants are available but are unsuitable for food use for one reason or another. For example, many products have a strong odour that would taint food, whilst products like alcohol would present a fire hazard.

Like detergents, these chemicals will only work effectively in the right conditions. The dosage must be carefully controlled (especially for chlorine-based products) and the contact time will be important. Disinfectants will not act instantly, especially if contamination is heavy. Again these factors should be covered in cleaning schedules.

An important point to remember is that disinfectants work badly in the presence of dirt. This is especially true of chlorine-based disinfectants. A surface may be both heavily soiled and heavily contaminated, for example if it has been used to prepare raw chicken. It is no good applying disinfectant until the surface has been cleaned. The most effective disinfection follows a two-stage process. First clean, then disinfect. Even if a combined detergent/sanitizer is used, you should treat it as a two-stage process if there is heavy soil: first to remove the dirt and then, using a fresh clean solution, to disinfect. Expecting these products to work miracles in heavily soiled conditions will simply result in poor disinfection and contamination of food that comes into contact with it. The stages of cleaning and disinfection should be detailed in the cleaning schedule.

Heat is also used to disinfect equipment in food premises, for example in spray wash machines. Hot water or hot air 'knife sterilizers' are commonly used in meat cutting premises. Other tools such as steels, forks or tongs may also be sterilized in the same equipment and they are now finding their way into other food premises and kitchens. If heat is used for sterilization then precise temperature control is necessary. For knife sterilizers, water temperatures above 80°C are recommended.

'Cleansability'

The nature of the equipment or surface to be cleaned will also affect cleaning. Throughout Schedule 1 of the Food Safety (General Food Hygiene) Regulations 1995 are requirements that premises and equipment must be cleanable. This means several things.

1 The structural materials must be suitable. Normally that requires smooth, impervious and durable finishes. Light colours are recommended to make it easier to see if they are clean.
2 The design and construction is key. Structures that have sharp angles or voids will be difficult to clean. Coved junctions, recessed fittings and smooth joints will make it easier.
3 Access for cleaning. Equipment should not be fixed in such a way that it is impossible to clean behind or beneath. Equipment or even food should not be stored in a way that restricts proper cleaning.
4 Maintenance of the premises and equipment. No matter how good equipment is when first installed, steps must be taken to keep it in that condition.

The first three of these are prerequisites in the design and construction of the premises. If these are not done well in the first place, cleaning will always be difficult. Maintenance should follow a routine plan in the same way as cleaning.

The regulations also require that equipment must be capable of being disinfected 'where necessary'. This has been taken to mean food contact surfaces, especially surfaces that contact ready-to-eat foods. Equipment that would not satisfy this requirement would include untreated wood and wooden cutting boards.

Cleaning of hands of food handlers is an important measure in controlling food contamination. Premises must have an adequate number of hand-wash stations that should be kept stocked with detergent, warm water and facilities for drying. Cleaning of staff uniforms also plays a part in hygiene control and proper arrangements should be made. It would not be considered acceptable for staff who handle high-risk foods to travel to work in their protective clothing or to be responsible for laundering it at their home.

It should be accepted that chemical disinfection is more difficult to control and monitor than other critical process controls, for example heat treatment or cooking. Where possible other controls should be used in addition to cleaning and disinfection. For example, instead of using the same equipment or work areas for raw and cooked food and relying upon effective disinfection in between, it is much better to use separate areas or separate equipment. Colour coding is helpful to identify what belongs where.

Planned cleaning

Effective cleaning must be planned and the correct resources provided. This will include sufficient human resources. The only effective method is for cleaning to follow detailed schedules. The main components of a typical schedule will be as follows:

- identify the area or equipment to be cleaned;
- when it must be cleaned;
- the task to be done (for example 'cleaning AND disinfection');
- the cleaning chemicals and equipment to be used;
- safety precautions needed with those chemicals;
- who does the job;
- preparation of the equipment or area for cleaning down, for example precise details of how much it should be stripped down;
- the cleaning method (including the contact time for disinfectants);
- the standard expected (monitoring criteria if possible);
- reassembly methods or other conditions before the area/equipment can be put back into use;
- who supervises the job.

Many reputable chemical suppliers will provide help with cleaning schedules so that their products are used correctly to obtain the best results. There are several ways in which the cleaning plans and schedules may be presented, but it is essential that the plan ensures that all equipment and all parts of the premises are cleaned with the appropriate frequency, and that the schedule for each item or area describes exactly how the job should be done.

As mentioned earlier, direct food contact surfaces are the most critical areas for effective cleaning and disinfection. But other areas are also important even though they may be less obvious or more difficult to access. For example:

- wall surfaces beneath and behind sinks;
- floors beneath low equipment such as ovens, bains-marie, cabinet fridges or shelving;
- internal parts of dishwashers;
- gaps between cooking ranges;
- behind and beneath surface mounted pipework;
- service lifts or dumb waiters;
- the underside of tables and shelving;
- rubber seals on drinks dispensers, milk machines and so on;
- rubber seals on fridge doors;
- can-opener blades and stands;
- blade guards and sharpeners on slicing machines;
- drains and drain covers;
- drawers, door handles, door push plates, switches and any other surface that may be regularly touched by hand.

Cleaning schedules

The following systematic approach to producing cleaning plans and schedules is recommended.

- **Stage 1:** Draw up a list of the equipment or areas to be cleaned. It may be useful to list these according to the frequency of cleaning and also cross-reference the specific cleaning schedule or task card.
- **Stage 2:** Produce a cleaning schedule or task card for every area or piece of equipment in the list.
- **Stage 3:** All weekly, daily or 'after every use' task cards should be incorporated in this schedule. Every week, some tasks that are only required monthly or even less often should also be assigned to that week's schedule so that every task is completed in rotation. Thus there is a work schedule for the week.
- **Stage 4:** The week's work schedule should then be assigned to particular members of staff according to their duty rota.
- **Stage 5:** Managers or supervisors must monitor all cleaning tasks to ensure that work is being done to the schedule and to the required standard. Cleaning schedules are often designed to act also as record cards. Staff may sign-off that a task is completed and supervisors may note that the work has been checked. Records should be kept.

Monitoring

For surfaces and equipment that come into direct contact with ready-to-eat food, control of contamination will inevitably be a critical control point from a hazard analysis. This means that there must be appropriate controls (an effective cleaning and disinfection schedule) but also that there must be monitoring to ensure that controls are followed on a routine basis. In a few operations disinfection may be monitored by swabs or other assays, but for most, the best monitoring tool is close supervision by management.

The same is true of all cleaning tasks whether or not they are critical control points. Management should assess cleaning standards as a matter of routine. This is important so that any equipment or work area that is not up to standard may be put right immediately. But it will also ensure that the general ethos of the operation is to maintain the best standards of cleaning.

The following points should be borne in mind to maintain an effective system.

- Any defects in cleaning standards may indicate shortcomings in the cleaning schedule.
- Do not be afraid to amend the schedule in the light of experience.
- Ensure that any defects noted during EHO visits are rectified.
- Similarly, any defects noted by any other hygiene audit.
- The chef or kitchen manager must allocate tasks and check standards throughout the working day.

- In addition, a regular visit by another level of management would give even better control of standards. In larger operations there may be a designated quality manager who conducts structured audits of standards. It is important that the quality manager has the right authority or lines of reporting to get action taken when it is needed.

It is valuable to keep records to show that cleaning tasks have been done and that supervisors have checked that they were done properly. There are three reasons why they may be helpful:

- to show that there is active monitoring of critical control points;
- to demonstrate due diligence if the defence is ever needed in the event of prosecution;
- at a more practical level, to allow management to track the improvement or decline in standards over a period of time.

Cleaning equipment can itself become a source of contamination unless it is kept in good condition. Poor cleaning methods can also spread contamination around the premises or allow it to develop.

Pest control

Pest control is a vital part of any company's hygiene programme, especially where food is manufactured, packed, prepared or served. Flies, mice, cockroaches, Pharaoh's ants and rats can easily carry many organisms; these organisms could lead to illness for the consumer and loss of production and reputation by the caterer. One fly may carry up to two million bacteria, which it may transfer from waste matter and filth to food. One mouse sheds an average of 70 droppings every day, urinates frequently to mark its territory and therefore will contaminate all areas in which it is present. Cockroaches carry a considerable array of disease organisms in their gut and on their feet and bodies. Four or five people die each year from Weil's disease contracted from water or other material polluted by rat urine. Most 'foreign body' complaints of contaminated food relate to pest infestation.

Owners and occupiers of property and premises still have a legal duty under the Prevention of Damage By Pests Act 1949 and the Food Safety (General Food Hygiene) Regulations 1995 to keep their premises free from infestation. Under the Food Safety (General Food Hygiene) Regulations 1995, Chapter I, the layout and design of food premises shall permit protection against external sources of contamination such as pests. Chapter IV states that conveyances and containers used for transporting foodstuffs shall be designed and maintained so as to prevent contamination.

Under Chapter VI, refuse stores must be designed and managed so as to protect against pests. Finally, Chapter IX of the Regulations states that adequate procedures must be in place to ensure pests are controlled with regard to all food that is handled, stored, packaged, displayed and transported. In some cases, local authorities have the power to close food premises that are infested by rodents or insect pests. In addition, all pesticides and their method of application must comply with the requirements of the Control of Substances Hazardous to Health Regulations 1999 (COSHH) and the Control of Pesticides Regulations 1986.

Why pest problems occur

The conditions found in a hospitality, restaurant or canteen kitchen are particularly attractive to pests. A wide variety of insects, mites and a few bird species enter catering premises for the following reasons.

- **Food:** Even in small quantities food enables pests to survive and multiply. An adult Brown Rat eats only 28 g (one ounce) of food per day; an adult house mouse can exist on as little as 3 g (1/10 ounce) a day and the minute biscuit beetle only consumes several milligrams of food daily. Many small moths and beetles can maintain life on the wide range of foods and general debris that can be spilt and inadvertently built up in warehouses. The presence of mites living within bulk food can render it unfit for consumption.
- **Warmth:** Pests of all types are attracted to buildings that offer even a limited amount of warmth and shelter from chill outdoor conditions. A few degrees increase in temperature inside helps to provide conditions in which breeding is enhanced, particularly for pests such as cockroaches, ants, textile pests and stored product insects.
- **Shelter:** Almost every building provides a variety of harbour-ages for pests. Contrary to common opinion, it is newer buildings, with suspended ceilings, panelled walls, service ducts and enclosed electrical trunking, which are more likely to create a pest risk than older buildings without such features, unless practical pest-proofing is properly considered at the design stage.

The problems caused by pests

Pests are prohibited by legislation, cause expensive deterioration, spread dangerous contamination and can destroy the reputation of any catering establishment or food manufacturer. Most pests cause detectable damage. Rats and mice seek hard and often inedible materials to gnaw in order to wear down their incisor teeth, which grow throughout their life. Damage therefore can occur to the structure of the premises, furnishings, fabrics, decorations, power cables, as well as all types of cartons or packaging. Pigeons and starlings can damage the outside of buildings and their nests can block guttering and downpipes.

Under the Food Safety Act 1990, penalties for unhygienic food premises can be up to £2,000 on each charge or conviction in a magistrates' court, and local authorities can immediately close premises if there is an imminent threat to health. The penalty for the sale or possession of pest-damaged or contaminated food can be up to £20,000. A four-star hospitality operation in Scarborough was fined £15,000 plus costs of £1,835 in 1998 for having cockroach infested kitchens.

Penalties in the Crown Court can be unlimited fines and up to 2 years in prison and the person responsible can be banned from running a food business.

- A Birmingham supermarket was fined £7500 for cockroach infestation.
- A Rugby restaurant was fined £8500 for flies in the kitchen.
- A London superstore was fined £9500 for harbouring mice, cockroaches, flies and wasps.
- A Norfolk pub was fined £2000 for selling fly-infested chicken.
- A Shropshire pub was fined £4000 for mice on the premises.

These are typical examples of recent prosecutions.

Many pests are vectors of disease. Mice leave 60–80 droppings a day, and innumerable urine droplets wherever they travel. Similarly, rat urine frequently supports the bacteria that cause Weil's disease (*Leptospira icterohaemorrhagiae*) which enter the body via cuts and abrasions of the skin or via the mucous membranes lining the nose, mouth or eyes.

Rodent droppings contain pathogens that are easily transmitted onto the surfaces over which the animals run, often at night. These pathogens include those responsible for food poisoning. In similar ways, flies, cockroaches and indoor ants transmit disease, fouling and tainting everything they touch with vomit excretory deposits. Over 40 disease-causing organisms have been isolated from cockroaches inside buildings, and flies have been implicated in epidemics of cholera, dysentery and a wide range of other illnesses. Mites can cause dermatitis in food handlers and birds may spread respiratory infections from their droppings.

Pests distress most people and few will tolerate the presence or evidence of rodents or insects, especially on food premises. The nuisance of wasps, garden ants, fleas and other pests can lose business, customers and staff. Having pests is bad for public relations. Loss of business from closure of premises or damage resulting from bad publicity because of prosecution for infestation can be considerable.

Three lines of pest control

Integrated Pest Management (IPM) requires all aspects of building design, maintenance, waste disposal, hygiene, cleaning and reporting to be combined to eliminate infestation, but there are three essential components.

Keep pests out (as far as possible) by making sure the structure of the building is sound, with no broken air bricks, gaps under doors or around windows and no piles of rubbish or weeds against the outside walls. Have nylon bristle strip or mastic filler as appropriate, applied to horizontal and vertical gaps and cracks to stop rodents and insects getting through. Strip curtain doors can minimize the risk of birds and flying insects getting into warehouses and despatch bays. Opening windows should be fitted with insect screens.

Restriction means denying pests food or harbourage wherever possible, both inside and around the immediate external areas. Prevention methods include scrupulous cleaning, prompt efficient waste disposal, sealing gaps where pipes, service ducts or conveyor belts pass through interior walls, proper stock rotation and correct storage of commodities. All incoming foods should be inspected for signs of infestation and isolated from production or sales areas until cleared.

If basic preventative measures have failed to eliminate pest problems, chemical pesticides may be required. As pesticide residues on or close to stored food products are perceived to pose almost as great a risk to food safety as the pests themselves, the use of pesticides must be strictly controlled and must meet the requirements of the Control of Pesticides Regulations 1986 and the Control of Substances Hazardous to Health Regulations 1994.

Record keeping

Prosecutions under the Food Safety (General Food Hygiene) Regulations 1995 are far less likely if proper up-to-date records are kept to show that all practical means are undertaken to prevent any breach of the law. This includes records provided by contractors as part of a continuous process to meet the defence of due diligence if any problem arises, or indeed to prevent any problem developing.

Efficient record keeping depends upon close liaison between named responsible individuals in both clients' and contractors' organizations. Regular reports and action points must be presented and confirmation of work carried out must be provided by the appropriate authority.

In complex premises, work in progress charts and visual aids may supplement the paper and computer records, and relevant training sessions may be held for staff, especially production, storekeeping and cleaning staff, on their part in contributing to IPM.

Whether pest control is undertaken in-house, or by a local authority or by a specialist contractor, it is important that an accurate record of all visits is kept and the minimum required is a pest book maintained on the premises under the control of management. The following information should be included:

1 The results of the initial survey.
2 The works carried out as a result of the survey.
3 The degree of infestation found and the type of pest involved.
4 Details of each treatment carried out and the pesticides used.
5 The recommendations made by the contractor on each visit and the action taken.
6 A record of any special or emergency visits made by the contractor.
7 Records of all reported sightings by staff of pests on the premises.

All this information should be included in the book and signed by the contractor and a representative of management. It should be established whether the pest control contractor would carry out any minor works of rodent proofing or repair as it might affect rodent or pest infestation, and any such works that are carried out should be included in the record.

Food safety matters relating to personnel

Training

The Food Safety (General Food Hygiene) Regulations 1995 introduced, for the first time, a legal requirement in respect of training. Chapter X of the Regulations states that the proprietor of a food business must ensure that food handlers engaged in the food business are supervised and instructed and/or trained in food hygiene matters commensurate with their work activities.

In addition to this specific legal requirement, these regulations require the implementation of a food hazard analysis system as detailed in Regulation 4(3). The significance of this in relation to food safety training is that it is necessary to implement and monitor the controls identified. Of major importance here is communication of the system to staff at all levels, to ensure that food handlers are aware of their responsibilities. Training therefore plays an important part in this process.

Investigation of food poisoning outbreaks and the questioning of food handlers about bad practices observed during an inspection by an enforcement officer often reveals a lack of awareness in respect of basic food hygiene and the need for care and attention whilst handling foods. This is especially true of staff, but also of food business management.

By providing staff with a comprehensive hygiene training programme, the food business should be able to achieve the following benefits:

- Satisfied customers.
- Good reputation and therefore increased business.
- Increased shelf-life of products.
- Compliance with legislative requirements.
- Good working conditions, higher staff morale and lower staff turnover.

The possible risks from poor standards of food hygiene, due to inadequate training of food handlers, include:

- Food poisoning outbreaks, potentially resulting in serious illness or even death.
- Legal action and a risk of closure.
- Fines and costs of legal action.
- Loss of business and reputation from bad publicity.
- Food contamination.
- Pest infestation.
- Wasted food due to spoilage/infestation.
- Increased cost of production/cost of alternative production.
- Lower staff morale and higher staff turnover.

Applying the legislation: key definitions

The Food Safety (General Food Hygiene) Regulations 1995, Chapter X, state that the proprietor of a food business must ensure that food handlers engaged in the food business are supervised and instructed and/or trained in food hygiene matters commensurate with their work activities. Key elements of this requirement are as follows.

Food business ◦ ◦ ◦

The legal requirement applies to all food businesses, as defined in the Regulations, i.e. any undertaking, whether profit-making or not, and whether public or private, which carries out any or all of the following activities: preparation, processing, manufacturing, packaging, storing, transportation, distribution, handling or offering for sale or supply, of food. The Regulations exclude primary production from their scope. Primary production is defined as including harvesting, slaughter and milking. Once the action of harvesting vegetables has been completed, for example when the vegetables are being placed on a trailer for transportation out of the field, the Regulations will apply.

Proprietor ◦ ◦ ◦

The proprietor in relation to a food business means the person by whom that business is carried on (s.53 of the Food Safety Act 1990). This can be either a manager or owner of the food business depending on the precise relationship between the person concerned and their level of involvement in the food business.

Regulation 7(c) and the application of section 20 of the Food Safety Act 1990 (offences due to the fault of another person) would also allow enforcement action to be considered against managers with relevant responsibilities where the proprietor is not responsible for commission of an offence.

Food handler ◦ ◦ ◦

Although 'food handler' is not actually defined in the 1995 Regulations, according to the guidance issued by the Department of Health in August 1995, a food handler is a person who handles food in the course of his or her work as part of his or her duties. In the Industry Guide to Good Hygiene Practice: Catering Guide a food handler is defined as any person involved in a food business who handles or prepares food whether open (unwrapped) or packaged (food includes ice and drinks).

These two definitions clearly exclude, for example, general catering assistants who are responsible for washing equipment, removal of rubbish etc., and who do not come into contact with food. However, their actions can expose food to hazards, for example by not thoroughly cleaning equipment. The Industry Guide recognizes the need for such staff to be trained, stating that, as a matter of good practice, staff who are not food handlers may also require instruction, training or supervision – this would cover cleaners, catering assistants etc.

Moreover, senior supervisors and managers who do not actually handle food, but who have a direct influence on the hygienic operation of the business should also receive training as a matter of good practice. They should have training in food hygiene appropriate to their job and their level of responsibility.

Supervision ◦ ◦ ◦

All staff should be supervised, dependent upon the competence and experience of the individual food handler. Where an operation employs only one or two people, supervision may not be practicable. In such cases, training must be sufficient to allow work to be unsupervised.

A greater degree of supervision may be needed in the following cases:

- for new staff awaiting formal training;
- for agency or temporary staff;
- for staff handling high-risk foods;
- for less experienced staff.

Instruction ∗ ∗ ∗

Instruction is likely to require a person, especially a new member of staff, to be made aware initially and where appropriate, routinely of what needs to be done and the methods and systems employed by the business. Usually this would be referred to as 'induction'.

Instruction can be supported by the issue of a staff handbook or simple instructional card, and by the use of appropriate adhesive signs and notices, for example 'Raw Food Only' and 'Now Wash Your Hands'.

In some circumstances, instruction with intensive supervision can substitute for training, for example, where there is a high turnover of staff. Instruction may also be followed up by more formal training at a later date to reduce the level of supervision required. Staff who, as part of their duties, handle high-risk open foods, are likely to require both instruction and training.

Training ∗ ∗ ∗

Training implies that the recipient will have a greater level of understanding at the end of the process than if they were simply provided with instruction. The level of training that a food authority can expect in respect of persons handling high-risk open foods is the equivalent of training contained in the basic or certificate food hygiene course accredited by the following bodies:

- The Chartered Institute of Environmental Health (CIEH).
- The Royal Institute of Public Health and Hygiene (RIPHH).
- The Royal Environmental Health Institute of Scotland (REHIS).
- The Society of Food Hygiene Technology (SOFHT).

It is acceptable to deliver in-house training but it is useful to be able to demonstrate the contents of such courses to EHOs. In-house training may be able to provide an equivalent level of training, even if the training is not accredited by such organizations. 'Equivalent' in this context means equivalent in training standard – course content must also be appropriate.

Commensurate with work activities * * *

Commensurate with work activities means that training must relate to the actual job of the individuals. The training/instructional needs should relate to the actual job of the individual. It will also need to relate to the type of food that they handle, staff handling high-risk food needing more training/instruction than those who handle low-risk foods.

When planning and delivering training, the following should be taken into account:

- The nature of the food.
- How operators handle food.
- Critical control points.
- The need for formal training.
- Keeping training up to date.

Employees' duties relating to training * * *

It is the duty of the proprietor of the food business to ensure that food handlers are trained. Once provided with sufficient knowledge and training, food handlers must put those principles and skills into practice because they also have responsibilities which are clearly defined in the regulations.

Enforcement

Guidance for enforcement officers on the standards required to meet legal requirement is provided in Code of Practice No. 9: Food Hygiene Inspections (revised 1997 and 2000) issued under section 40 of the Food Safety Act 1990. The code gives food authorities advice on the frequency and nature of inspections carried out to assess the hygiene of premises and the approach needed to enforce the 1995 hygiene regulations. Section L of the Code of Practice No. 9 relates to the enforcement of the training requirement. All food businesses must use guidance from the Code of Practice, which outlines the requirements for training and supervision of food handlers.

Training requirements should be assessed by each food business as part of their food hazard analysis system. Where there is a satisfactory food hazard analysis system it should not be necessary for authorized officers to assess the effectiveness of training by discussion with staff, other than to confirm the effectiveness of the system.

Where the authorized officer identifies food hygiene concerns that relate to deficiencies in the level of food hygiene awareness, they should be discussed with the proprietor. In giving any advice or guidance on training, the food authority should not imply that any particular course or examination provided by any training organization is a mandatory requirement.

The service of an improvement notice for training will usually necessitate the proprietor being denied use of that authority's food hygiene courses.

Officers must also give due consideration to Industry Guides and advice issued by Central Government Departments or by the Local Authority Co-ordinating Body on Food and Trading Standards (LACOTS).

In assessing whether the level and content of any training provided meets the legal requirements, the food authority should consider the relative risks arising from the operation.

The Industry Guide to Good Hygiene Practice: Catering Guide gives advice to catering businesses on how to comply with the various requirements of the 1995 Regulations, as well as providing advice on good practice. This is an official guide to the Regulations that has been developed in accordance with Article 5 of the EU Directive on the Hygiene of Foodstuffs. Whilst the guide has no legal force, food authorities must give it due consideration. The information given in this guide is relevant to all catering premises including:

- restaurants
- hotels
- health services
- social services
- transport catering.

As already stated earlier in this section, the document defines a food handler as any person involved in a food business who handles or prepares food whether open (unwrapped) or packaged. The document also goes on to suggest that lower level training may also be applicable to cleaners and other support staff.

The guide provides a model system for implementing the training requirement of Chapter X of the Food Safety (General Food Hygiene) Regulations 1995 and in summary covers the following:

- Categories of food handler.
- Stages of training and levels of formal training.
- Content of training.
- Arrangements for existing staff, new employees and agency staff.

In providing guidance to compliance and good practice advice, the Industry Guide provides a matrix, providing three stages of training for three categories of food handlers. The categories of staff are summarized in Table 8.1.

The three stages of training, as described in the Industry Guide, are outlined below.

Category	Activities	Likely job titles
A	Handle low-risk or wrapped food only	Waiter/waitress, barperson, counter staff, cellarman, delivery staff
B	Food handlers, who prepare and handle open, high-risk foods	Commis chef, cook, catering supervisor, kitchen assistant, barperson (with responsibility for food preparation)
C	Managers or supervisors who handle any type of food	Unit manager/supervisor, chef manager, bar/pub manager, chef, general manager, owner/operator of home catering or mobile catering business

Table 8.1
Staff categories and activities

Stage 1: 'The Essentials of Food Hygiene'

In order to comply with the Regulations, a food handler must receive written or oral instruction in 'The Essentials of Food Hygiene', an outline of which is given below.

The Essentials of Food Hygiene

1 Keep yourself clean and wear clean clothing.
2 Wash your hands thoroughly before starting work and after each break, before handling food, waste or raw foods, and after using the toilet or blowing your nose.
3 Before starting work you must inform your supervisor if you have any skin, nose, throat, stomach or bowel trouble or an infected wound. If you do not do this you are breaking the law.
4 Cover cuts and sores with a waterproof, high-visibility dressing.
5 Avoid unnecessary handling of food.
6 Never smoke, eat or drink in a food room, or cough/sneeze over food.
7 Anything you see which is wrong should be reported to your supervisor.
8 Food should not be prepared too far in advance of service.
9 Perishable food should either be kept refrigerated or piping hot.
10 It is imperative that the preparation of raw and cooked food are kept strictly separate.

11 Reheated food must get piping hot.
12 All equipment and surfaces should be kept clean.
13 Follow any food safety instructions either on food packaging or from your supervisor.

The guide states that the above points can be adapted to suit each business to ensure relevance, which should prompt the proprietor to ask, 'who requires the training?'

Every food handler must receive written or oral instruction in The Essentials of Food Hygiene before starting work for the first time. The guide also advises that it would be good practice to give this information to all other staff employed in the business. Also, any visitors to the premises should be instructed in those points which relate to personal hygiene.

Stage 2: 'Hygiene Awareness Instruction' ⁕ ⁕ ⁕

The following is an outline of Hygiene Awareness Instruction, which aims to enable the employee to develop a knowledge of the basic principles of food hygiene. The topics covered should be appropriate to the job of the individual and may include some or all of the following.

1 The organization's policy, i.e. how priority is given to food hygiene.
2 Germs and the potential to cause illness.
3 Personal health and hygiene, i.e. smoking, illness reporting etc.
4 Cross-contamination, how it is caused, and how to prevent it.
5 Food storage.
6 Waste disposal, cleaning and disinfection.
7 Foreign body contamination.
8 Awareness of pests.
9 Any control or monitoring points that have been identified.

All food handlers in categories A, B and C must receive this stage of training, preferably at induction, but at least within four weeks of starting employment. Part-time employees should be trained within eight weeks. The duration and depth of training will depend on the particular individual's job, and the risk involved. This training will form a module of Stage 3 training (see below).

Stage 3: 'Formal Training' ⁕ ⁕ ⁕

Formal training at three levels is described below.

Level 1

The overall aim is to develop a level of understanding of the basic principles of food hygiene. The course would last approximately 6 hours and the content is outlined below.

1 Food poisoning micro-organisms, and their types and sources.
2 Simple microbiology, e.g. toxins, spores, growth and death.
3 Premises and equipment.
4 Common food hazards.
5 Personal hygiene.
6 Preventing food contamination.
7 Food poisoning – its symptoms and causes.
8 Cleaning and disinfection.
9 Legal obligations.
10 Pest control.
11 Effective temperature control of food, e.g. storage, thawing, reheating and cooking.

It is category B and C food handlers who must be trained to Level 1 of the Formal Training. This should take place within 3 months of employment, or as soon as possible thereafter.

Levels 2 and 3

More advanced training courses will deal with food hygiene in more detail and cover management and systems. Level 2 will typically involve courses of 12–24 hours' duration. Level 3 will involve courses of 24–40 hours' duration.

It would be good practice for category C food handlers to receive training up to Levels 2 and 3 as their responsibilities increase. The Industry Guide recommends that employees are assessed or tested after formal training to ensure their understanding.

Food hygiene training does not have to be conducted as a separate exercise to vocational courses, as many vocational courses will include food hygiene training. Food handlers do not have to take additional hygiene training if their vocational training (e.g. NVQ or SVQ) has provided hygiene training to the appropriate level.

Particular needs of other groups of staff

Existing employees should be instructed and/or trained to the appropriate level as soon as is practicable.

Where an organization uses agency staff, it should liaise with the employment agency to determine responsibilities for the training and/or instruction of the individuals, and the provision of necessary documentary evidence. Where such evidence is not available then the proprietor should assume that they are not trained and deploy or supervise them accordingly.

The training programme

The practicalities of devising a food safety programme revolve around five key stages.

Stage 1: Food safety training policy ⁕ ⁕ ⁕

Whilst such a policy is not a legal requirement, it does give guidance to the firm in the implementation of procedures and establishes a useful framework. The food safety training policy should consist of:

- Statement of intent (the policy's general aims).
- Objectives (specifically stated required outcomes).
- The organization and arrangements for ensuring the policy is put into place.

Stage 2: Identifying training needs ⁕ ⁕ ⁕

After producing the food safety training policy, the next stage is to identify the training that is needed.

Job description

All food handlers should be provided with a comprehensive job description setting out their duties and clearly defining their hygiene responsibilities and the level and frequency of training necessary to fulfil these.

Staff selection

Once job descriptions are established, staff should be selected, where possible, to fit the post and training standards. Advertisements should state clearly the level of skills and qualifications required for the post so that both management and applicant time is not wasted. In certain areas of the country it may not be possible to appoint staff with the necessary experience and qualifications and in such circumstances these shortfalls will indicate specific training needs. Where appropriate during the interview, applicants should be tested on their knowledge of recent food hygiene legislation and any changes in established practice.

New employees may claim that they have already been trained. If they cannot produce documentation to support this, it is appropriate to assume that they have not been trained.

Training needs

For each food handler the job description and training profile for the post will establish the level of instruction/training necessary to meet the 'commensurate with work activities' requirement. For new staff, the selection process will establish their current level of training, any shortfalls and thereby their future training needs. For all new members of staff, The Essentials of Food Hygiene should be provided before starting work for the first time, followed as soon as is practicable, but within the recommended timescales in the Industry Guide, by the Hygiene Awareness Instruction. Whilst new recruits may have held a similar post with their previous employers, it should not be assumed that they followed all the same practices and procedures (e.g. colour coding, cleaning procedures and materials etc.).

With respect to existing staff, it will be necessary to ensure that full details are available of their training both within the organization and prior to joining so as to determine their training shortfalls or needs.

Statement of training needs

The training needs identified from the survey of existing staff and newly appointed staff should be utilized to prepare a statement of training needs. The statement should not be limited to necessary hygiene training but should reflect the total training needs of the position (e.g. job training, development needs, supervisory/management training, special skills). Consideration must also be given to the length of time that has passed following training and any need for refresher training.

The 'statement of training needs' record can also be utilized to develop a budget statement in respect of future training costs. Each section of individual identified training can be costed, with the total cost reflecting the necessary budget.

Planning food safety training

After the training policy has been written and the training needs identified, the next stage is to plan the training. The training needs must be prioritized and costed to allow adequate resources to be made available. A training plan is a detailed statement of the training that will be implemented and will cover a specified period. A typical plan will cover the following.

1 Details of all training requirements, by job classification and the number of employees involved.
2 Details of the standard to be achieved, e.g. examination.
3 Details of the person(s) responsible for organizing and monitoring the training.

4 Details of the training strategy to be used, e.g. internal or external, on-the-job.
5 Details of who will provide the training, e.g. supervisor or external consultant.
6 How much the training will cost.
7 The duration of the training, e.g. one day, 3 hours etc.
8 When the training will take place and the target date for completion.

The plan should be regularly reviewed and updated, particularly when fundamental business changes are made that may have an impact on training requirements.

Stage 3: Delivery of training ⁂

Delivery of training will involve the consideration of three issues:

1 The method of presentation: on-the-job or off-the-job.
2 Location, timing and duration of training.
3 The trainer: in house or external.

Method of presentation

Before organizing any in-house training session it is important to examine the following.

- Staff nominated for the course should be interviewed by management and advised of the purpose of the session. Any concerns the nominee may have should be answered. Such a procedure will assist in breaking down any barrier there may be to training or identifying any matters that concern the candidate, e.g. the examination.
- Ensure that the trainer is suitably qualified and experienced.
- Ensure that adequate support material (e.g. video, slides, overheads) is to be utilized.
- Where possible, try to incorporate practical demonstrations (studies show the highest level of information retention by participants is when trainees hear, see and do, whilst the lowest response is when they hear only).
- Ensure that the training room is suitable, well ventilated, warm and with balanced lighting. The chairs and any tables should be arranged to ensure that all participants have a clear and unobstructed view of the trainer and any support equipment such as a screen.
- Ensure that all equipment is in place and in good working order. A few minutes explaining the operation of the equipment to a new trainer or invited speaker can save some very embarrassing problems part way through a lecture.

- Where appropriate, arrange for tea, coffee and refreshment breaks and if provided, ensure that they arrive on time with adequate cups etc. Clear instructions should be given to prevent a session being interrupted by a tea trolley being wheeled into the training room.
- Ensure that the participants are welcomed on arrival.

Videos, slides, films and hygiene games are all useful support material for training sessions. The material selected must be both interesting and relevant. Videos, slides and films permit information to be assimilated in a mentally non-taxing and informal way and can usually be employed to reinforce matters that have previously been the subject of theoretical study. Hygiene games provide the potential for group interaction that may assist in the breakdown of any barriers to communication. Overhead transparencies projected onto a clearly visible screen enable the participants to view and, if they wish, write down the salient points. Participants should not be required to copy all the information displayed as their concentration of the oral explanation may be severely affected.

Handouts or booklets are a particularly useful tool to reinforce matters that formed the subject of previous discussion or an overhead transparency presentation. They ensure that the participant, if unclear about a specific point, has a reference to the correct information subsequent to the course. They will also provide a useful revision aid for any examination to follow.

Demonstrations are particularly useful in relation to food hygiene as the subject matter is very practical in nature. Plate cultures of bacteria can usefully demonstrate bacteria nature, occurrence and growth.

The timing of training is crucial to success and must be carried out at the most appropriate time for the trainee. Food safety induction training needs to start before the food handler starts work and then more detail can be provided in the days that follow. The time of day that training is provided will also influence its effectiveness and this must be considered. If staff start work early in the morning and have to attend a training course late in the afternoon they are unlikely to learn much as they will be tired. Similarly, staff who work night shifts are unlikely to be able to concentrate on courses during the day. The timing of training must be planned with consideration to shift patterns and hours of work.

In terms of duration, a course that is too long will lose the attention of delegates and one that is too short does not allow enough time to present all the relevant information using the best method or to test that learning has been achieved. Food safety courses should be divided into sections of a suitable duration.

The location of training will have an effect on its success. Food safety training should take place in a clean, quiet room that is away from work activity. Comfortable seating needs to be provided and tables or desks if delegates need to write. There should be enough space for any activities and suitable equipment and domestic facilities should be available, for example toilets and refreshments.

Although the use of the above support material will be beneficial, it must be stressed that any trainer must have the following qualities in order for any training session to be successful:

- An ability to communicate effectively and concisely at all levels, avoiding a monotonous delivery.
- A high level of competence in the subject matter and an ability to accept valid criticism or correction and to respond to participants' questions.
- Good organizational skills.
- Empathy with the group and its component individuals.
- Creativity in respect of teaching methods.
- Absence of annoying mannerisms.
- Interest in and enthusiasm about the subject so as to generate the same in the participants.
- A smart appearance and suitable dress.

Stage 4. Training specific groups

There are six groups of staff that can be identified as requiring training. New starters to the catering organization need to be trained, with the level and content being appropriate to the individual, i.e. school leavers as opposed to those with work experience. The areas that should be covered with this group are:

- Job-specific food safety risks (knowledge) and controls (skills).
- Details of company hygiene policy and its relevance to the job.
- How the employee's job affects food safety in other areas.

The second group, food handlers, must be trained commensurate with their work activities. Those who only handle low risk packaged food will not need as much training as those who handle high risk food.

Supervisors and managers are the third group who will not necessarily carry out direct food handling, but they will have a direct influence on food safety and therefore need to receive appropriate training. Some individuals in this category may be responsible for food hygiene training and will therefore need to be trained to carry out this part of their job. Personnel with special responsibilities such as food technologists, quality assurance employees and senior chefs may require specialist training in order that they can keep up with trends that may affect their work.

A fourth category are staff not in direct contact with food but who could affect its safety. Examples could be cleaning, maintenance, contract and administrative staff. Whilst this is not a legal requirement, it should be regarded as good practice.

Finally, agency and casual staff should be appropriately trained as they may represent a greater risk to food safety.

All staff should undertake update or refresher training sessions at intervals. The frequency should be related to the risk and nature of the business and the food handled; also the skill, competence and experience of the individual employee. The key points of hygiene principles can be reinforced. In addition, this training can take account of any changes in the business, for example changes in menu or production systems may raise new hygiene issues and controls. Any faults that have been identified can also be addressed. Refresher training must be both relevant and interesting and should not consist of the replay of the same video every 12 months. Such sessions could include a hazard spotting exercise utilizing slides or carrying out an annual inspection.

Stage 5: Evaluating and reviewing training ⁛ ⁛ ⁛

All training sessions should be evaluated by management to ensure that objectives of the session were achieved, knowledge was assimilated and, where appropriate, if this knowledge can be put into practice without difficulty. Evaluation techniques include comprehensive questionnaires, group discussion, individual feedback or on-the-job monitoring of the practical aspects. Where there may be special problems, e.g. language barriers, it is important to obtain individual feedback. Obviously any negative feedback must be acted upon and any necessary variation to the course programme or presentation implemented.

Periodic monitoring of hygiene standards will identify any training deficiencies or failure to maintain appropriate standards. Such deficiencies or failures can form the basis of refresher training.

Any instruction/training should be supported on-the-job by guidance and assistance from managers and supervisors. Management should lead by example in all aspects of food hygiene and safety, e.g. by wearing appropriate overalls and headgear in food rooms. Posters and suitably laminated signs can be utilized to reinforce the hygiene message, but posters should be changed frequently to maintain interest.

It is good practice to keep records of the training completed by every member of staff. Records are not needed to comply with the law. However, written evidence of hygiene training may be very important in demonstrating compliance to an enforcement officer. Records may also be relevant when attempting to establish a 'due diligence' defence.

Infectious diseases

Food and water can act as vehicles for a number of infections other than those which cause typical food poisoning. The agents that cause these infections include bacteria, viruses, protozoa (single celled organisms which live in water) and parasitic worms. Although some of these infections result in diarrhoea or vomiting, many also cause other, more general symptoms and may result in very serious illnesses.

Food-borne infections fall into two main groups:

- those that are now rarely contracted in this country but which may be caught abroad and brought back by the infected person; and
- those that have only recently been recognized as a cause of human illness and which can be transmitted by food.

Some of the most serious infections are described below.

Many of the infections known as 'imported infections' were once common in this country but are now usually contracted abroad. They are particularly associated with poor sanitary conditions or poor food quality and are most likely to be caught in countries where such conditions are common.

Food handlers should report any illness, including diarrhoea or vomiting, which occurred while they were abroad or within 3 weeks of return. It is good practice for employees to complete a review health questionnaire.

Typhoid and paratyphoid infections are due to bacteria in the Salmonella group (*Salmonella typhi* and *Salmonella paratyphi*). They cause a more severe illness than other salmonellae. The illness is characterized by a high fever lasting 2–3weeks or more. Death may result if not treated, although this is a rare occurrence in the UK. Unlike other salmonellae, man is the natural source of these bacteria and infection is passed on via food or water contaminated by human faeces or sewage. Even after recovery from illness, bacteria may continue to be found in the faeces of the infected person for months or years. These people are called carriers and it would be very unwise for them to continue work as food handlers.

Between 200 and 400 cases of typhoid and paratyphoid fever are reported each year in the UK; most people either catch their illness abroad or from a family member or friend who had been abroad.

Some infections have only been recognized as causes of human food-borne illness during the past 20 years and for some there are still gaps in what is known about their exact routes of transmission. Most are known to exist in the environment or have animal reservoirs, i.e. they are commonly found in animals. Their emergence as food-borne pathogens may be linked to changes in the ways animals are reared, e.g. intensive farming, including the use of unnatural foodstuffs for the animals or changes in the way food is stored and processed which have made human infection more likely.

First reported in England and Wales in 1977 as a cause of human gastro-enteritis, Campylobacter is now the most commonly recorded cause of diarrhoea. Symptoms may start suddenly with abdominal pains followed by smelly, sometimes blood-stained diarrhoea; fever, headaches and dizziness are also common. The diarrhoea may last up to three days and the other symptoms may persist for several days more.

Cattle and other animals including cats and dogs are known sources of these bacteria. Human infection has been linked to drinking contaminated water and unpasteurized milk and to contact with domestic pets with diarrhoea. Contaminated poultry meat may be one of the commonest sources of human infection. Campylobacters have frequently been isolated from chicken and chicken carcasses, which may carry the bacteria into the kitchen and thereby contaminate surfaces (including hands) and ultimately other foods. Although campylobacters do not multiply on food, the number that need to be swallowed to cause infection is low.

Food-borne listeriosis (infection with Listeria bacteria) is a disease of the 1980s and a particular increase in recorded cases occurred between 1987 and 1989. It can cause septicaemia or meningitis and abortion in pregnant women. People most at risk of serious illness are the elderly, people whose normal bodily protection against infection does not function properly and unborn babies. Obviously with such serious symptoms recovery may take some time and a proportion of cases may die.

Listeria are able to grow at temperatures below 8 °C and will multiply on foods in a refrigerator when other bacteria stop growing.

Milk and dairy products, in particular soft cheeses, have been shown to be sources of human infection. Other risk foods include prepared salads such as coleslaw and possibly pâté. Listeria have been shown in surveys to contaminate a number of foods, but they may only become a problem when the food is kept at refrigeration temperatures for long periods thereby allowing the bacteria to multiply.

Yersinia may be more common in England and Wales than current reporting suggests and it is frequently recorded as a cause of diarrhoea in some Scandinavian and European countries. Symptoms can also include severe abdominal pain, sometimes mistaken for appendicitis. Many animals carry Yersinia in their digestive tract and this bacterium has been found in milk and dairy products, meats (particularly pork) and vegetables. Like Listeria, Yersinia can also grow at the normal operating temperature of a refrigerator.

In the 1970s in North America some types of the bacterium *Escherichia coli* were shown to produce a toxin (verotoxin) which can cause mild to very severe bloody diarrhoea, as well as kidney damage which may result in renal failure. Increasing numbers of these infections have been recorded in the UK in the past few years. At the end of 1996 an outbreak in Scotland had caused 16 deaths and 633 reported cases. While ground beef used in making beefburgers was associated with outbreaks in the United States, Canada (and recently in the UK), there is still very little information about the way VTEC is transmitted in the UK. Some evidence has, however, been found that spreading from person to person may be an important mechanism for transmitting this illness. Cases have also been linked to direct contact with animals.

Cryptosporidium and Giardia are now major causes of gastro-enteritis and infection can result in watery diarrhoea lasting up to 2 weeks. Both are commonly found in animals including sheep, calves and domestic pets. Direct contamination of food due to poor hygiene standards is a possible method of spreading infection. Although food-borne outbreaks are rare, milk and sausage meat have been reported as possible vehicles of infection. Large outbreaks resulting from contamination of water supplies have also been recorded.

Personal hygiene

The personal hygiene of all persons engaged in catering is a fundamental factor in reducing the risks of food poisoning and maintaining high standards. The Food Safety (General Food Hygiene) Regulations 1995 and the Food Safety (Temperature Control) Regulations 1995 give food handlers direct responsibility in relation to hygiene and the prevention of contamination. Both managers and food handlers themselves can be prosecuted for not complying with the requirements of these regulations.

The job specifications and descriptions of all staff should clearly define the level of responsibility and staff required while underlining the importance of good personal hygiene.

Food handlers should be in good health and have an awareness of the need for hygiene. Potential employees who do not take the trouble to present a good appearance at an interview will also not respond to the high standards of hygiene required in the food environment. Previous evidence of a formal hygiene qualification is advantageous. Poorly presented staff may also mean a loss in customers with a subsequent loss in reputation and profits.

A commonsense approach to medical screening should be adopted, as it has been proven that routine medical and laboratory screening of food handlers is of no value. However a pre-employment medical questionnaire should be completed by all potential employees. These questionnaires should be screened by a doctor who may, depending on the results, follow this up with a further examination.

It is good practice for caterers who supply food to premises within the EU to medically screen all food handlers on an annual basis.

Staff illness

Under Regulation 5 of the Food Safety (General Food Hygiene) Regulations 1995, any person working in a food handling area who knows or suspects that he or she is suffering from, or is a carrier of, any disease that is likely to be transmitted through food or has an infected wound, skin infection, skin condition, sores or diarrhoea, in circumstances where they may directly or indirectly contaminate food with pathogenic micro-organisms, must inform the proprietor of the food business.

This requirement should be read in conjunction with Schedule I, Chapter VIII, paragraph 2, which requires the proprietor to consider excluding infected persons from all food handling areas. The regulation does not define food handlers, but the following are likely to fall within the scope of this regulation:

- those employed directly in the production and preparation of foodstuffs;
- those undertaking maintenance or repair work on equipment in food handling areas; and
- visitors, including enforcement officers, to food handling areas.

Diseases likely to be transmitted through food are similarly undefined. For practical purposes the following should be considered as reportable:

- Confirmed or suspected cases of Salmonella, Campylobactor, Shigella, Vibrio, Bacillus, *Staphylococcus aureus* and *Clostridium perfringens*.
- Confirmed or suspected cases of viral gastro-enteritis.
- Infection due to *Entamoeba histolytica*, *Cryptosporidium parvum* and *Giardia iamblia*, or with worms.
- Case or contact of typhoid or paratyphoid fever.
- Infection with verotoxin-producing *Escherichia coli* (VTEC).
- Infection with hepatitis A.

Should a food handler suffer from any of the above diseases, medical advice should be sought or contact made with the local authority Environmental Health Department. Infected persons should only return to work when it can be shown that they no longer present a risk to any food that they may handle. For those common illnesses listed in (a)–(c) above, this is likely to be 48 hours after any symptoms have stopped. In these instances, the provision of negative stool samples is not considered to be a necessary precondition before return to work. For the more serious conditions listed in (d)–(f) above, stool samples and a longer absence from work are appropriate.

Training in personal hygiene

An integral part of the induction training of all food handlers must be in personal hygiene. A high standard should be demanded and food handlers should be encouraged to bath or shower regularly and to wear clean clothing and footwear. Hygiene should form a part of any training, which should be a continuing process throughout employment.

Hands are one of the principal agents in transferring harmful bacteria to food. Handling raw food then cooked food is a particular danger. Hands should always be washed after the preparation of both raw and cooked food. As a matter of policy, handwashing should also take place before work starts and after:

- using the toilet;
- handling waste;
- blowing the nose or touching other parts of the body likely to harbour bacteria, e.g. nose, mouth, hair, ears, backside;
- smoking;
- carrying out cleaning duties.

Hands should be washed under hot running water (from elbow or foot-operated taps) with soap or a suitable bactericide.

Nailbrushes are no longer specifically mentioned in the Food Safety (General Food Hygiene) Regulations 1995, but if used, they should be made from plastic and cleaned and disinfected regularly. Nailbrushes must be used with care as excessive use may damage the skin and increase the risk of infection.

Food preparation or equipment sinks should not be used for hand washing. There should be a minimum of one wash-hand basin in each food preparation area, service area and toilet/ changing area, with sufficient soap and hand-drying facilities.

Hands should be dried using air driers, roller towels or, preferably, disposal paper towels. Foot-operated bins must be provided for the collection of soiled disposable towels.

There are differing opinions regarding the suitability of providing gloves for food handlers. As the hands are a frequent vehicle for passing bacteria to food, and gloves do form a barrier between the skin and the food being prepared, they may reduce the likelihood of food contamination. However, there is a danger of creating a false sense of security if gloves are viewed by food handlers as an alternative to frequent handwashing. Regular handwashing by food handling staff is vital to food hygiene regardless of whether gloves are used during food preparation or not.

Today, in some American states, legislators have even made the wearing of gloves by food handlers mandatory. Customers appear to like seeing them worn and food proprietors have seized upon the glove as a means of meeting their obligation to identify food hazards and control them. Now, instead of having to 'manage' handwashing in the food premises, train food handlers in handwashing techniques and monitor the success of any handwashing programme, it might appear that all the food proprietor has to do is to hand out the latex rubber gloves.

Gloves are able to prevent the bacteria that are normally resident on the hands from getting onto food. A glove's ability to prevent this from happening is solely dependent on its quality and the care the wearer has taken in washing and drying their hands beforehand. No glove is without its imperfections and very few claims are made about a glove's ability to prevent bacteria on the surface of the hand from being transferred to the food being handled. Whilst rubber latex gloves may be much better at preventing bacterial penetration (they are, after all, worn by surgeons), recent research has poured scorn on the vinyl glove, suggesting that as many as 4 per cent had defects, 34 per cent allowed the penetration of bacteria, and 53 per cent failed in use.

Gloves are just as capable of spreading bacteria around, as are hands. Like hands, they need to be washed periodically and a germicidal liquid soap is considered best. There is no evidence to suggest that gloves offer any more protection to food than simple but effective handwashing procedures.

There is, however, the following that can be said in favour of wearing rubber latex gloves:

- Their smoother texture allows fewer bacteria to be held on the surface of the glove, making them easier to clean.
- They can be said to have no 'residential' populations of bacteria in the way that hands do. The numbers of bacteria present when the gloves are new from the box should not be significant.
- Food handlers are usually made more aware of touching their face, mouths and hair if they are wearing rubber gloves and should, as a consequence, be less inclined to do so. However research has shown that glove wearers continue to touch other surfaces as well as contaminated raw food.

Hospitality, Leisure & Tourism Series

The food proprietor needs to take account of the following policy issues if the wearing of gloves is to add anything to the standards of food safety in the food business.

- They breed complacency amongst staff and the customers alike.
- Food handlers wash their hands less if wearing them.
- If hands are not washed well before putting on gloves, the gloves will get covered in bacteria anyway.
- Staff will continue to wear gloves even when dirty and torn.
- Water can get underneath the glove creating a warm, moist environment in which bacteria will thrive.
- Some people are seriously allergic to latex rubber gloves.

The following issues on using gloves should be considered.

- Wash, sanitize and dry hands well before putting on a pair of gloves.
- Put gloves on carefully so as not to tear them.
- Check first to make sure they are not damaged and discard them straight away if they are.
- Be able to distinguish between those gloves used for dirty operations (i.e. to protect the hands) and those gloves used to protect food from excessive handling.
- Remove gloves when food preparation ceases or before handling non-food items like coins.
- Exercise vigilance, and as soon as a hole or tear is noticed dispose of gloves. Wash and dry hands well before putting on a fresh pair of gloves.
- Dispose of all gloves safely; treat them as you might blood-soaked packaging.
- Wash, thoroughly sanitize and dry the hands after wearing gloves and always before putting on new gloves.
- Assess the health risks to those staff who may be, or become, allergic to latex rubber gloves. There are safer alternatives available, such as powderless rubber gloves.
- Training in proper handwashing technique is as important as ever. Evaluate the effectiveness of training regimes by observation and implement fresh training initiatives as required.

The latex rubber glove is here to stay but problems exist in the use of gloves in food preparation. The food proprietor must guard against the complacency the glove affords since cross-contamination is still very possible. Research has shown that food handlers wash their hands less if wearing gloves and tolerate worn and dirty gloves. Proper handwashing both before putting on gloves and whilst wearing them is extremely important and staff training should emphasize this need. There are health and safety implications associated with allergic reactions caused by exposure to natural latex rubber.

Additionally, under the Control of Substances Hazardous to Health Regulations 1999, the employer has a duty to assess the health risks to their employees arising from exposure to harmful substances whilst at work. Where latex rubber gloves are used routinely employers should take the following precautions:

- Adopt policies to protect workers from undue latex rubber exposure.
- Seek safer alternatives, such as powderless gloves or non-latex gloves.
- Enquire about an employee's sensitivity to latex rubber as part of their health history (questions like have they ever experienced itching, a rash or wheezing after wearing latex gloves or inflating a balloon may offer useful clues).
- Ensure that employees use good housekeeping practices.
- Provide employees with education programmes and training materials about latex allergy.
- Periodically screen high-risk employees for latex allergy symptoms (detecting symptoms early and removing symptomatic employees from latex exposure are essential in order to prevent long-term adverse health effects).
- Re-evaluate current prevention strategies whenever an employee is diagnosed with latex allergy.

It is vital to ensure that any open wound or abrasion is covered with a sterile, waterproof and detectable (often blue) dressing. Food handlers with septic cuts or boils should not handle food.

Hair is constantly falling out, and as hair also contains bacteria it may contaminate the food. It is therefore important that hair is kept clean and covered with a suitable hairnet. Hair should be combed or head coverings adjusted away from food preparation areas. Hair grips or clips must not be worn outside the head covering.

Touching the nose, mouth and ears during food preparation increases the danger of food contamination, especially by *Staphylococcus aureus*. Disposable tissues should be used when blowing the nose, followed by handwashing. Food handlers should be discouraged from eating sweets whilst working as the mouth is likely to harbour staphylococci bacteria. Food handlers with severe colds should not handle food as coughing or sneezing will dissipate droplets and particles over a wide area.

Strong-smelling perfume should not be worn by food handlers as it may taint food products.

The wearing of ornate rings or loose fitting jewellery should not be permitted as these are likely to harbour bacteria and also may present a safety hazard when handling knives or using machinery. As a rule only smooth wedding bands covered with a detectable dressing should be allowed in any food preparation areas.

Smoking, snuff-taking and associated tobacco products are no longer specifically prohibited by legislation. However, Schedule 1, Chapter VIII of the Food Safety (General Food Hygiene) Regulations 1995 requires every food handler to maintain a high degree of personal cleanliness which is taken to include hygienic practices and habits which, if unsatisfactory, may expose food to the risk of contamination. Apart from the physical contamination from ash or a cigarette end, the touching of lips during smoking can transfer harmful bacteria onto fingers and then onto food. Smoking also encourages coughing, creates an unpleasant atmosphere to work in and may also taint food products. For these reasons, the practice should be prohibited.

Protective clothing

All persons working in a food handling area are required to maintain a high degree of personal cleanliness and to wear suitable, clean and, where appropriate, protective clothing (Chapter VIII, paragraph 1, Food Safety (General Food Hygiene) Regulations 1995). Well-designed and ergonomic protective clothing will assist in increasing staff morale and promoting hygiene awareness. Its primary purpose, however, is twofold:

1 to prevent a person's outdoor clothing, which can become soiled, from coming into contact with food; and
2 to prevent food handlers from soiling their clothes through food preparation, pan washing etc.

Design

The clothing should be light in colour to improve the reflection of heat and encourage the wearer to change as and when the overall becomes dirty or soiled. Pockets should be kept to a minimum (preferably only a pen pocket) and with zip or pop stud fastenings rather than buttons. This will minimize the risk of foreign bodies finding their way into the food. The overall must be easily laundered and durable. In larger establishments, protective clothing could be colour coded to prevent cross-contamination between different working areas.

Changing facilities

Chapter I, paragraph 9 of the Food Safety (General Food Hygiene) Regulations 1995 states that adequate changing facilities must be provided for personnel where necessary.

Proper facilities for changing into protective clothing must be provided on catering premises (Offices, Shops and Railway Premises Act 1963, s.12). Arrangements should also be made to store working clothes that are not taken home. Staff should not be allowed to wear their protective clothing when travelling to and from work. If protective clothing is to be kept in 'food rooms' (i.e. where food or drink is handled) lockers or cupboards must be provided for its storage.

Regulations 23 and 24 of the Workplace (Health, Safety and Welfare) Regulations 1992 lay down certain requirements with regard to accommodation for clothing and facilities for changing clothing. For new workplaces taken into use after 1 January 1993, and modifications, extensions, conversions etc. started on or after that date, the requirements are effective from 1 January 1993. Existing workplaces (those in use prior to 1 January 1993) had until 1 January 1996 to comply.

Changing facilities should ideally be divided into dirty areas (outdoor clothing) and clean areas (clean overalls), separated in such a way as to discourage re-entry into the clean area with dirty overalls or outdoor clothing. All such areas should be clearly marked.

There should be sufficient numbers of overalls to enable staff to change as frequently as required. The use of aprons will greatly assist in keeping overalls clean and in better condition for longer periods, especially in areas where pan- and dishwashing is carried out. Tabards should be considered for cooking and service staff, as these will also help to keep overalls cleaner. Protective clothing should be available at the entrance to all food preparation premises and a notice to this effect should be displayed for all employees and visitors.

Head coverings

Head coverings must cover the hair completely but also be attractive in order to encourage their use by staff. They must be of a light colour and lightweight and preferably made with a material that washes easily and allows air to the head.

Footwear

The Health and Safety at Work etc. Act 1974 states that if protective footwear is provided, then all staff should be actively encouraged to wear it. Shoes should be well made, properly fitted, comfortable and in good repair. The wearing of safety (anti-slip) footwear should be encouraged but is not mandatory. If safety footwear is not available, then feet should be fully covered (no open toes), and the shoes should be of a design that is easily cleaned.

Disposable protective clothing

Although the use of disposable clothing may be expensive, it should be considered for those areas of work that involve the removal of heavily soiled or contaminated material, e.g. pan-wash, dishwash and heavy duty cleaning areas. They will not only help to keep overalls clean but also reduce the risk of cross-contamination from a dirty area to a clean one. Disposable aprons, hats, coats and poly gloves could also reduce the potential cost of replacement overalls through heavy soiling and wear.

PART 3

Food Hazard Analysis and Due Diligence

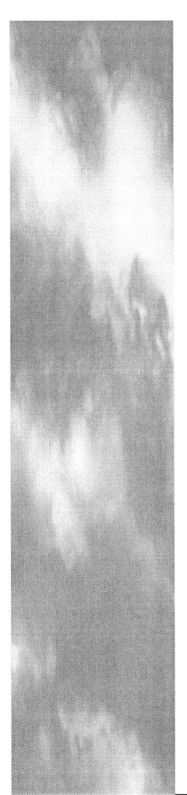

Food hazard analysis

Background

Many food businesses, particularly in the manufacturing sector, already use a system of food hazard analysis with the establishment and maintenance of critical control points, and the identification of hazards, in order to control raw materials and process operations. This chapter covers two main areas:

- The legislative basis for the implementation of food hazard analysis.
- The theory and practice of food hazard analysis.

Whilst a number of variations of food hazard analysis have been developed, including Assured Safe Catering and Hazard Analysis Critical Control Point (HACCP), they should be regarded as guidance on applying established principles in order to control food safety problems.

Legislation

The original basis for the implementation of food hazard analysis is the Directive on the Hygiene of Foodstuffs (93/43/EEC), usually referred to as the General Food Hygiene Directive. It introduced for the first time a requirement for food businesses to identify any steps in their activities that are critical to food safety, and to ensure that adequate control procedures are identified, maintained and reviewed. In the General Food Hygiene Directive, the five Codex principles (identified below) are incorporated into EU legislation. However, it was not considered necessary to lay down formal requirements regarding verification and documentation (principles six and seven). Whilst the latter two principles are not legislative requirements, they should be regarded as good practice.

Turning to the UK, the Food Safety (General Food Hygiene) Regulations 1995, Regulation 4 (3) states that:

> proprietors of food businesses must identify any steps in the activities of their food businesses which are critical for ensuring the safety of food and that adequate safety procedures are identified, implemented, maintained and reviewed.

This is an important legal requirement and is designed to make all businesses focus on food safety in their own operation and to make sure that it is under control. It tackles food safety from a different perspective. The old way was to start with the controls and try to fit the process around them. Food hazard analysis starts with processes and fits the controls to the business.

The law requires control and monitoring to be 'effective'. It is up to the food business to decide what is enough to be effective. In addition, a food hazard analysis policy should be regarded as an essential part of the defence of due diligence and all reasonable precautions, contained within section 21 of the Food Safety Act 1990.

Aim

The aim of food hazard analysis is to prevent food safety problems by careful planning. In this context, it would appear appropriate to give priority to ensuring that there is a coherent and consistent approach to matters relating to food hygiene. This goal can best be achieved by the application of food hazard principles and limiting detailed prescriptive provisions to cases where they are considered essential. Nevertheless, it should be noted that there is some flexibility in the manner in which food hazard analysis is conceived and applied in present legislation.

Need

Generally, all food hazard analysis systems are similar and involve hazard spotting, identification and prioritizing risks for action. This then leads on to the development of controls and the implementation of management systems. These systems then need to be monitored to assess compliance and check effectiveness.

Relating back to the legislation, the primary function of Regulation 4(3) of the Food Safety (General Food Hygiene) Regulations 1995 is the safety of food and not quality. Thus the need for food hazard analysis is compliance with the law, and the prevention of food poisoning, food contamination and food spoilage, which should then lead to a reduction in food complaints, improved quality and increased sales.

The proprietor/manager needs to think about the food operation systematically. He or she must look at the process step by step from the selection of suppliers and raw materials through to service of the food to customers. There will be steps at which hazards can occur and steps at which they can be controlled. Many of the controls will be simple commonsense practices that the business has followed for years, but the food hazard analysis approach should give a clearer focus on the controls that are really important to the business. It may also highlight some that have been missed.

The need for food hazard analysis can be summarized as follows:

- Prevention of food poisoning, food spoilage and food complaints.
- Improved quality, customer appreciation and increased sales.
- Less wastage and necessity to re-work products.
- Compliance with present and future statutes: due diligence should the need arise.
- Requirements of the Food Safety (General Food Hygiene) Regulations 1995 and the Food Safety (Temperature Control) Regulations 1995.
- Pressure from within the trade – the supplier/retailer relationship is often an important factor.

Principles

A difference can be identified between the seven Codex requirements (listed below) and the lesser requirement of regulation 4(3). The first five Codex requirements are a legal requirement, principles six and seven should be regarded as good practice. According to the Codex Alimentarius Guidelines for the Application of the Hazard Analysis Critical Control Point (HACCP) System, HACCP is a system that identifies specific hazards and preventive measures for their control.

The discussion in this section on food hazard analysis should be regarded as a variant of HACCP, which satisfies the requirements of the legislation. It is, however, useful to identify the approach from Codex, which consists of seven principles listed below.

1 Identify the potential hazards associated with food production at all stages, from growth, processing, manufacture and distribution, until the point of consumption.
2 Determine the points/procedures/operational steps that can be controlled to eliminate the hazards or minimize their likelihood of occurrence (i.e. critical control point or CCP).
3 Establish critical limits which must be met to ensure that the CCP is under control.
4 Establish a system to monitor control of the CCP by scheduled testing or observations.
5 Establish the corrective action to be taken when monitoring indicates that a particular CCP is not under control.
6 Establish procedures for verification, which include supplementary tests and procedures to confirm that the HACCP system is working effectively.
7 Establish documentation concerning all procedures and records appropriate to these principles and their application.

Each food business is left with the flexibility to decide what requirements are necessary, subject to the direction of the environmental health officer as a member of the enforcing authority, thus leaving an element of discretion. This approach illustrates flexibility in the design and implementation of a food hygiene policy to ensure the maintenance of a high level of consumer protection, while keeping the regulatory burden for business to a minimum.

Definitions

Central to the discussion so far has been the use of a number of terms which will now be explored in more detail.

Hazard

The team developing the food hazard analysis system needs to be able to recognize a hazard or get help from someone who can. A hazard is anything that may cause harm to a consumer. It may be:

• Microbiological, e.g. Salmonella in chicken.
• Physical, e.g. contamination by glass in any kind of food.
• Chemical, e.g. contamination by cleaning chemicals in any kind of food.

Food hazards do not tend to be as obvious as the falling object or unguarded machine and are therefore easily forgotten or ignored. Because, like bacteria, the dangers can be microscopic, they are often dismissed. With little to see in the way of hazard, the task of identifying them may appear theoretical or just plain irrelevant. Yet you do not need to be young, old, sick or pregnant for food hazards to cause serious harm or even death. Gone are the days when a kitchen could be run by intuition and common sense. Chemical, physical and microbiological food hazards are recognized for what they are: complex, subtle, mostly invisible and sometimes deadly.

Chemical hazards

The effects of chemical adulterants can be seen over the short term (acute) or long term (chronic). Food may become exposed to chemical hazards in a number of ways, including:

- cleaning chemicals;
- insecticides, rodenticides, herbicides and fungicides;
- reaction of acidic foods with certain metal containers;
- food additives when used in incorrect proportions;
- the solvents used in certain types of packaging;
- the addition of non-allowable chemicals by design or malice;
- the chemical reaction between two or more otherwise harmless chemicals.

Hazardous and/or inedible substances must be clearly labelled and separated from food. The practice of storing cleaning chemicals in old food containers must not be tolerated. Insecticides and rodenticides have also to be handled with considerable care within food establishments. Enamel, zinc, lead and copper containers will all react with acidic foods such as tinned tomatoes and pineapple.

Physical hazards

Food can become contaminated with all manner of foreign material from fingernails to mouse tails, dog hairs to cat teeth, fillings and filings. However, most foreign body contamination is easier to predict and causes usually fall into the following categories:

- A broken food container, or some constituent from the container or packaging, i.e. broken glass and rubber seals.
- Objects that fall from people or their clothing, i.e. buttons, hair and jewellery.
- The food environment, i.e. insects, rubber bands, machinery bits, dirt and old food.
- Malicious contamination.

Empty jars should be delivered both covered and inverted and visual checks can made prior to filling. The inside of the container must be washed or air blown. Staff must be provided with clothes that limit contamination risks, i.e. hairnets/hats, coats with inside pockets and fasteners. The food environment and equipment must be kept clean and free from extraneous items. Staff who take pride in the business are less likely to engage in malicious damage. Finally, in certain circumstances, management might consider not requiring an employee to work out his or her period of notice in order to avoid the possibility of malicious damage.

Microbiological hazards

Biological hazards may fall into several groups, including moulds (predominantly responsible for food spoilage) and viruses. But it is bacteria with their ability to grow invisibly on food which must be of most concern in the determination to make food safe.

If the conditions are right, bacteria will multiply exponentially to reach numbers that can cause infection. Some bacteria that cause food poisoning have a low infectious dose and hardly need to grow on food to cause illness. For instance, *E. coli* O157 (responsible for the outbreak in Lanarkshire, Scotland) results in an appalling number of deaths and incidence of renal failure in children. It is thought that as few as 10 organisms can cause illness. Infectivity is influenced not just by how many bacteria are ingested but also by how vulnerable the individual is to infection (whether they are young, old, pregnant or immunosuppressed) and whether the food eaten will protect the bacteria from the acid conditions of the stomach.

Certain types of bacteria may also cause illness by producing toxins either whilst growing on the food or once inside the body. Toxins are heat-stable and difficult or impossible to remove by cooking. Bacteria may be destroyed but their toxins can remain.

Other types of bacteria can survive adverse conditions (such as drying and cooking) by forming spores. These subsequently germinate and form new colonies when conditions are favourable.

Risks inherent in foods

Some foods do not need to be exposed to hazards but are inherently risky, presenting chemical, physical and biological dangers. These can be avoided altogether or processed so as to completely remove the hazard. Inherent risks include:

- naturally occurring toxins associated with certain foods;
- contamination of food by other harmful agents such as moulds, algae and heavy metals;
- foods prone to insects such as those which feed from within the growing plant;
- foods with inedible parts;
- bacteria associated with certain foods, i.e. Salmonella and spices.

Certain wild mushrooms are harmful, containing a number of toxins which can kill. *Amanita phalloides* (the Death Cap) is responsible for what can be a protracted death from liver and kidney failure. Fungi of the genus Aspergillus produce aflotoxin, a potent carcinogen, and may contaminate foods such as peanuts and cereal crops if damp. It also causes liver and kidney failure.

Nuts, potentially harmful to 1 in 200 people, will cause anaphylactic shock and can kill whilst foods such as the red kidney bean contain harmful toxins which must be removed by prolonged soaking and boiling. Green potatoes contain glycoalkaloids, which are not destroyed by cooking.

Shellfish may become contaminated with toxin-producing marine algae and cause diarrhoetic and paralytic shellfish poisoning (DSP and PSP). The protein in the brown flesh of some fish such as mackerel, tuna and pilchards contains histadines which can be changed by spoilage bacteria into harmful histamines.

Control measures

Control measures are those that can be used to eliminate or reduce to safe levels those hazards that have been identified. It is important to note that some hazards need not be controlled as they occur, because they may be better controlled at a later stage. For instance, buying raw poultry containing food poisoning organisms is a hazard at the purchase stage but it is better controlled by proper heat treatment at the cooking stage. Any control measure proposed must be capable of actually being carried out in the business or it may not be used.

Critical control points

The critical control point is the step in the preparation of the food which has to be carried out correctly to ensure that a hazard is eliminated or reduced to a safe level. In deciding whether there is a critical control point at any stage, the following question should be asked: Is it necessary to control the hazard at this stage, or will a subsequent step reduce or eliminate the hazard?

If a subsequent step will control the hazard, then that step is the critical control point and not the earlier stage. Another question that should be asked is: Can the hazard be eliminated or reduced to acceptable levels at all, at this step or any step? If the answer is 'no', consideration should be given to not serving this food at all, e.g. freshly prepared mayonnaise using raw eggs.

Of course, hazards should be controlled whenever possible, but some points in the process will be 'critical'. A point is critical if the lack of control measures at this point is likely to cause a health risk when the food is eventually consumed. Examples could be as follows:

- Cooking or reheating are usually critical. They should kill micro-organisms.
- Steps likely to lead to the contamination of food are usually critical, especially if the food is already cooked, for example juices from raw meat dripping onto a piece of cooked beef in a refrigerator.
- Steps that allow bacteria time to grow will also be critical as most food poisoning bacteria are more dangerous in larger doses.

High-risk foods

Food that is both suitable for the growth of bacteria and will be eaten as it is, e.g. cooked ham, is known as high-risk food. The protection of high-risk food involves preventing cross-contamination and restricting bacterial growth. This is mainly achieved using separation and strict time and temperature controls, i.e. keeping food outside the danger zone of between 8 and 63 °C.

Harmful bacteria may be introduced into the kitchen from the food itself – raw meats and their packaging, the soil surrounding dirty vegetables, shell eggs – pests, shoes and clothing and infected food handlers. Once in the kitchen, harmful bacteria may be transported to high-risk foods (cross-contamination) via the hands, dish cloths, clothing, packaging materials, work surfaces, equipment (i.e. slicing machines), ice and vermin.

In many, although not all cases, the emphasis of food hazard analysis is on high-risk foods. High-risk foods are those that do not receive another full cook before being served and which are thus prone to growth of food poisoning bacteria. Additional examples include cooked meats, fish and egg dishes. Hazard analysis does apply to other foods prepared in the business. For instance, other roast meats prepared from chilled raw material may well have the same steps and the same hazards and therefore the same controls (or may be largely the same, with a few extra steps). For example, if roast chicken were prepared from frozen chickens, the hazard analysis would have different steps at delivery and storage, and an extra 'thawing' step.

Other food categories may be completely different. For example, caterers may produce a whole range of dishes. Salad preparation or ice cream production is quite different to cooking chickens. They must be approached with a totally separate food hazard analysis. The test applied by the operator is: Do other foods have different steps, different hazards or different controls?

A note of caution: Weaknesses in the application of food hazard analysis can emerge since, to be effective, any system must cover the entire food chain, from primary production until the point of consumption. Most catering operators cover all stages of food production and distribution after primary agricultural production and some avoid the important requirement for documentation and verification. Whilst these latter two are not a legal requirement, they must be regarded as best practice.

Possible problems of food hazard analysis

Confusion can sometimes arise with HACCP as opposed to more generalized food hazard analysis discussed here because the former is usually used by large, often manufacturing, businesses and tends to be more product-based as opposed to multi-product orientated. However, the benefits of adopting food hazard analysis, namely greater assurance of product safety and increased operational efficiency, apply equally to all sectors of the catering trade.

The main difficulties for catering operations in applying food hazard analysis are likely to be the availability of adequate expertise and knowledge related to the wide range of products or meals produced and ensuring continuity in the analysis to be undertaken. Also, considerable resources will be required for developing the subsequent quality programme and for appropriate training to support this programme and the system itself.

An essential element of this whole discussion is the importance of teamwork. It is suggested that a food hazard system should be set up and introduced in phases over a period of time to avoid over-burdening staff with too many changes in one go. Staff will need to be made aware of changes and kept up to date as the system evolves. What is actually developed must be relevant to the nature and type of operation. In small businesses it may be practical for the system to be developed by just one person. In larger operations a team may be required. Team members must be able to demonstrate a complete understanding of the operation, identify hazards, suggest likely controls and have an understanding of food hygiene. There must be a team leader who takes responsibility for implementation of the system.

Operational flow

Explicit in developing a hazard approach to food production is the need to develop a flow chart of the operation. In larger catering outlets multiple flow charts will be necessary for the various sections of the department.

Purchase of food

Within this flow chart approach are various stages. For instance, high-risk foods could be contaminated with toxins or food poisoning bacteria. Buying from a reputable supplier and specifying temperature on delivery could rectify this contamination matter.

Receipt of food ⊛ ⊛ ⊛

At the receipt stage, toxins or food poisoning bacteria could contaminate high-risk foods. Checks on temperature, and sensory and visual checks would remedy this.

Storage of food ⊛ ⊛ ⊛

During storage, further contamination of high-risk foods (i.e. the growth of toxins/food poisoning bacteria) could occur. Processes to remedy this would be to store high-risk foods (wrapped) at safe temperatures. These foods should be date-labelled and the stock should be rotated and used by the date recommended.

Preparation of food ⊛ ⊛ ⊛

During preparation, pathogenic bacterial growth and high-risk food contamination is possible. The ambient temperature exposure of the food should be limited in the preparation process. Raw and cooked foods should be stored separately and all high-risk foods should be prepared with clean equipment. All food handlers should wash their hands before touching the food.

Cooking food ⊛ ⊛ ⊛

Pathogenic bacterial survival is a possibility during the cooking phase. It is important to ensure that the thickest part of all chicken, rolled joints etc. are cooked to at least 75 °C. Before other meats (e.g. steaks) are cooked, the outside should be seared.

Cooling food ⊛ ⊛ ⊛

The production of toxins, pathogenic bacterial contamination and/or the growth of pathogens or spores can happen at this stage. Staff should ensure that all food is cooled quickly. Unless the food has a short cooling period, it should not be left to cool at room temperature.

Hot holding of food ⊛ ⊛ ⊛

The further production of toxins and/or pathogenic bacterial growth can occur during hot holding. Operators should ensure that all hot holding food is kept hot (i.e. above 63 °C).

Reheating food ⊛ ⊛ ⊛

Possible occurrence of pathogenic bacterial survival during reheating. When reheating food, staff should ensure that the temperature reached is 75 °C or above.

Hospitality, Leisure & Tourism Series

Chilled storage of food ● ● ●

Pathogenic bacteria can grow at this stage in the process and the use of temperature control is particularly important. All high-risk foods should be date coded, used in rotation and within the shelf life for each product.

Serving food ● ● ●

Food can be contaminated, toxins produced and the growth of pathogens can occur during service. For hot foods, staff should ensure that high-risk foods are served as quickly as possible. For cold foods, high-risk foods should be removed from refrigeration and served as quickly as possible after this.

Monitor and control

An important aspect of any food hazard analysis system is monitoring and control, whereby critical control points must be monitored and, where helpful, recorded with appropriate documentation. The frequency of monitoring will depend on the nature of the control, practicality and the level of confidence given by the procedure. The methods adopted should be kept as simple as possible, e.g. visual checking of food on delivery, what it looks like, the condition of any packaging, and 'best before' or 'use by' dates. Another example should be temperature monitoring. Again, if records are to be kept, any recording sheet used should be simple and staff should be trained to ensure correct completion. Records also prove useful if there is a query from an environmental health officer or a customer.

Effectiveness

An essential part of food hazard analysis is that controls must be set for the critical points and monitored to ensure that such mechanisms are effective. In order to make it possible to monitor them, controls should have targets. For example, to prevent growth, the control is not just to 'keep meat in the fridge', the target is to keep meat below, say, +5 °C. It is important to remember that growth always has two elements, time and temperature.

There must also be targets about stock rotation using the 'use by' date marks, or for food for display, to work within the 'four hour rule'.

To prevent contamination from equipment, the control is not just to keep it clean. The target should be to clean and disinfect the equipment following a detailed schedule.

For food being cooked, the control is not simply to 'cook thoroughly', but a precise target should be set, for example 'cook to centre temperature of 75 °C'.

Hospitality, Leisure & Tourism Series

The critical points can be monitored whenever that process step is used. However, it may not be necessary to monitor every product every time. For example, if when checking the condition and date marks of deliveries there is not time to open every box, enough should be opened to give a reasonable idea of the load. Or if a batch of roast meat is being cooked, the temperature of a sample, perhaps the top and the bottom of the oven, should be checked.

Finally, setting control targets and monitoring the points is not enough. If a check shows that a target was not achieved, action must be taken to put it right, as without it the system is ineffective. Examples could be as follows:

- On inspection, food contact equipment is not clean – do not use it until it has been cleaned and disinfected properly.
- The fridge temperature is incorrect – adjust or repair it immediately. How warm did the contents get before you found the problem and for how long? They may have to be thrown away or reprocessed.
- After inspecting the contents of the fridge it is discovered that the juices from raw meat have dripped onto cooked meat. Discard the cooked meat immediately. Ensure that raw and cooked produce are separated; if possible install another fridge especially for raw produce.

Where a target is not achieved or if a routine check shows that something is wrong, the action and decisions taken should be recorded. At the planning stage, the sort of action that should be taken at each step in response to hazards should have been identified and staff involved in that step/process instructed as to what is expected of them. Some cases will be easier than others.

- If a delivery is out of code, there is no alternative but to refuse to accept it.
- If equipment has not been properly cleaned, it should not be used until it has been cleaned again.
- If staff are spotted about to return to work after a break without washing their hands, they should be stopped. Repeated defiance of hygiene rules should be a disciplinary offence.
- If raw and cooked meat is in direct contact in the storage fridge, the cooked meat must be discarded and staff instructed on the proper procedures.
- If, after normal cooking time, meat on the bottom rack has not reached target temperature, continue cooking the batch until it has.

Implementation

The next step in food hazard analysis is implementation. Any necessary record sheets should be prepared along with any instructions for controls and checking procedures that staff may need to refer to. Procedures should be unambiguous. References like 'complete separation between raw and cooked foods should be achieved wherever possible' should include procedures as to what to do if complete separation is not possible in a particular case. Procedures and instructions should state:

- What is to be done.
- How it is to be done.
- When it is to be done.
- Where it is to be done.
- Who is to do it.

It is important that procedures, instructions and training cover what to do if a critical control point is not achieved. For example, staff should know when to:

- place food back into the oven if the cook temperature is not achieved;
- inform the manager immediately;
- throw the food away.

Review

Once the hazard system is operational, it will need to be checked to ensure that:

- it is running as it was planned to run; and
- the checking of the critical control points is satisfactory.

This will mean establishing that the critical control points identified are:

- being correctly applied;
- being adequately monitored; and are
- accompanied by adequate work instructions.

Additionally, this check should establish that:

- the system is understood; and
- all parts of the system are working compatibly.

A full review of the system should be carried out fairly soon after it has been put fully into operation to correct any teething problems that may arise. The whole system may need to be looked at in any of the following circumstances.

- When checks show that the system is not working correctly.
- When there are changes to the type of food being served.

- When there are changes to the design or layout of premises.
- When there are changes to the way food is brought or prepared.
- From time to time to see that the system is working.

Controls must be kept up to date (legislation for instance can change frequently). No matter how good a system appears to be, it must be reviewed from time to time and changes to procedures made as necessary. Changed circumstances might include the following, for example:

- The current controls are impracticable or are not effective.
- New products are introduced with different hazards or controls.
- The method of processing is changed.
- New equipment is introduced.

Strictly speaking, food hazard analysis does not have to be written down, nor do there have to be written records of any routine checks. However, all businesses should have a written system and records as a matter of good practice for three reasons:

1 It is the best way of doing it.
2 It will show an enforcement officer that the law has been complied with.
3 It may provide evidence of due diligence in a legal defence.

Once set up, this food hazard approach should be underpinned by good hygiene standards. General policies could be produced to cover areas such as personal hygiene, hand washing, cleaning, buying ready prepared vegetables, prevention of glass or packaging materials entering preparation areas.

Practical application

Who does it?

Proprietors must lead the way: it is their responsibility to have controls in place. Input will be needed from someone who understands food safety and hazard analysis. If the proprietor lacks the appropriate knowledge, a member of staff may have the right training to assume responsibility on a day-to-day basis. If no one in the business has the right skills, training will be required. Alternatively, a consultant could be employed. If employing a consultant, it is important that the system is right for your business and has been 'made to measure'.

Involving key members of staff

Involving key members of staff is very important. They should know the processes involved and may be able to suggest practical ways of tackling issues that arise. Eventually, the results of the food hazard analysis must be put to work in the business, so if staff are involved from the start, they are more likely to understand any need for change and/or training.

How to start

Start with one of the most important dishes or product lines. First think about all the steps that the food goes through from the time it is delivered as a raw material, until it is served to a customer. Take a blank hazard analysis chart and fill out the left-hand column. Write one handling or process step in every box.

Identifying hazards and implementing control systems

Once the steps in handling or processing have been identified, the other columns should be filled in, for example:

- Column 2, Hazards – decide on the hazards for each step.
- Column 3, Controls and Targets – if hazards were identified under column 2, consider how they can be controlled and what targets are needed.
- Column 4, Monitor – once control measures and targets have been set, they need to be checked; decide on the frequency according to the step.
- Column 5, Action – if targets have not been met for each step, decide on the action that needs to be taken.

Staff training

Staff need to understand the controls to put them into action. Each staff member should know about the controls that are part of the job they do. Staff training is essential to any catering business in implementing this food hazard analysis system.

Summary

Although food hazard analysis was a new legal requirement in the Food Safety (General Food Hygiene) Regulations 1995, it is not a new idea, having first been introduced into food processing in the USA over 30 years ago, with food hazard analysis being applied to catering operations in the late 1970s. Since its inception, food hazard analysis has highlighted the same few basic controls over and over again:

- Selecting good raw materials and good suppliers.
- Proper equipment sanitation (especially equipment and tools used with cooked foods)
- Good personal hygiene standards (especially when handling cooked foods).
- Keeping raw and cooked foods separate.
- Time and temperature controls in storage, during cooking or reheating, and during chilling after heating.

Even though food hazard analysis is not new, and the hygiene principles are even older, the approach it takes is that hazard analysis starts with *your* operation and *fits to it* the controls that are necessary.

Due diligence

Background

The defence commonly known as the due diligence defence is to be found in section 21 of the Food Safety Act 1990 and represents an important development in food law. To explain the due diligence defence it is first necessary to understand the legal principle of strict liability.

The Food Safety Act 1990 is a criminal statute and as such it creates criminal offences. The usual principle of criminal law is that there are two elements to a crime:

- Actus reus – the prohibited conduct or action, representing the facts that must be proved by the prosecution.
- Mens rea – the state of mind of the accused; his or her intention to commit the crime.

In the case of theft, for example, it is necessary for the prosecution to show not only that the accused took the goods (actus reus) but also that he or she dishonestly intended to keep them (mens rea). So if the accused took the goods by mistake (for example taking the wrong coat from a cloakroom in error) no criminal offence has been committed.

Sometimes criminal law omits the burden on the prosecution to prove the criminal intent, so that the action alone is the criminal offence. This is known as strict liability.

The following offences in the Food Safety Act 1990 are all strict liability offences:

- rendering food injurious to health (s.7);
- selling food not complying with food safety requirements (s.8);
- selling food not of the nature, substance or quality demanded (s.14);
- falsely describing or presenting food (s.15).

Taking as an example the offence in section 8 of selling any food for human consumption which fails to comply with the food safety requirements, the prosecution only has to prove two facts:

- that the accused sold the food; and
- that the food failed to comply with the food safety requirements.

The third fact (namely that the food was for human consumption) is presumed by section 3 of the Act. Those facts are the actus reus of the crime.

The prosecution does not have to go to the next stage to prove that the accused intended to sell the food dishonestly or indeed that the accused even knew the food failed to comply with food safety requirements. Therefore the knowledge, fault or state of mind of the accused is irrelevant; if the prosecution proves the facts then the accused will be convicted of the crime unless he or she can prove the due diligence defence set out in section 21.

This concept of strict liability is made applicable to food safety because of the philosophy of the Act, which is to protect the public. If a customer is served with food that causes food poisoning or buys food containing a foreign body that causes injury, then the fact that no one was at fault is of little comfort to the customer. Each customer is entitled to expect that the food they buy is safe to eat.

A balance must, of course, be made between the rights of the customer and the responsibilities of the caterer. While caterers are responsible for the safety of the food they sell, it is not reasonable for caterers to be convicted of a criminal offence without some degree of blame or fault on their part. The due diligence defence introduces that element of balance; if the accused can satisfy the due diligence defence then he or she is entitled to be acquitted; if the accused fails to satisfy the due diligence defence, he or she is blameworthy and will be convicted.

The main due diligence defence

The main due diligence defence in section 21(1) states that in any court proceedings for an offence under sections 7, 8, 14 and 15 of the Act, it is a defence for the accused to prove that he or she took all reasonable precautions and exercised all due diligence to avoid commission of the offence. This main due diligence defence is extended by the Food Safety Act 1990 (Consequential Modifications) (England and Wales) Order 1990 to cover offences under Regulations pre-dating the Food Safety Act 1990. In Scotland, the Food Safety Act 1990 (Consequential Modifications) (Scotland) Order 1990 covers offences under Scottish food legislation pre-dating the Food Safety Act 1990. Regulations post-dating the Food Safety Act 1990 generally make provision for incorporating the due diligence defence, in particular regulation 7 of the Food Safety (General Food Hygiene) Regulations 1995.

To understand how the main due diligence defence operates it is instructive to examine its constituent parts in some detail.

'It is a defence for the person charged to prove . . .'

Once the unlawful act (or omission of a legal requirement) has been proved by the prosecution beyond reasonable doubt, the onus of proof shifts to the accused. The accused must prove he or she was not responsible for the offence, but only on the balance of probabilities.

'. . . that he took all reasonable precautions . . .'

The courts expect to see some initial assessment of the risk areas and some systems set up for avoiding or dealing with those risks. In the case of offences arising under the Food Safety (General Food Hygiene) Regulations 1995 this should include the assessment under Regulation 4(3) of those regulations.

'. . . and exercised all due diligence . . .'

'Due diligence' and 'reasonable precautions' are not the same thing. Due diligence means ensuring that the systems work in practice. It is not enough to set up systems (and therefore take 'reasonable precautions') merely to allow them to lapse into disuse. It is important to be vigilant and make certain that the systems operate effectively (and show due diligence).

'. . . to avoid commission of the offence . . .'

This means the precautions and diligence must be aimed at preventing the offence charged. As it is obviously not known in advance what offence will be charged, it is therefore necessary to have systems in place and to monitor them in order to avoid all offences under the Food Safety Act 1990 and Regulations made under the Act or previous food legislation.

'. . . by himself or by a person under his control.'

The offence may be committed by the caterer personally (whether the caterer is an individual or a company), or it may be due to the fault (or default) of an employee. Caterers must ensure that their reasonable precautions and due diligence are designed to avoid the commission of the offence not only personally but also by the action or inaction of an employee. The diligence may therefore need two levels of monitoring designed to prove the effectiveness of both the systems and the monitoring of those systems.

The main due diligence defence therefore involves taking all reasonable precautions and exercising all due diligence to avoid commission of the offence. How the courts have interpreted that duty in practice is considered below.

If the two third party fault defences (explained below) are not available (because, for example, the food was prepared by the caterer or he or she imported it into the UK – such as buying and importing cheese or wine direct from a producer in France), then the only defence available is the main due diligence defence.

Attached to the main due diligence defence are two subsidiary 'third party fault defences', unique to food safety laws. These defences allow caterers to escape conviction in certain circumstances where some other person is the real culprit. These two 'third party fault defences' are in section 21(2–4). They can only apply if three pre-conditions are first satisfied.

1 The third party defences can only be used in response to prosecutions under section 8 (selling food not complying with food safety requirements), section 14 (selling food not of the nature, substance or quality demanded), section 15 (falsely describing or presenting food) and most offences created by Regulations made under the Act or pre-dating the Act.
2 The accused must neither have prepared the food in question nor imported it into the UK. 'Prepared' in this context includes subjecting the food to heat or cold but does not include merely slicing the food (*Leeds City Council* v. *Dewhurst*, 1990 – a case involving the slicing of cooked meats).
3 The accused must be able to prove that the offence was committed:
    (a) due to the act or default of some other person, or
    (b) because he or she had relied on information supplied by some other person.

'Some other person' does not include someone under the accused's control, such as an employee.

Once these pre-conditions are satisfied, caterers may be able to rely on one of the two third party fault defences. This defence will be satisfied if:

(a) the sale (or intended sale) was not under the accused's brand name or mark; and

Hospitality, Leisure & Tourism Series

(b) the accused did not know, and could not reasonably be expected to know, that his or her action (or default) would lead to an offence.

Of the three constituent parts to the due diligence defence, the *brand names third party defence* is the simpler for caterers to prove. Caterers should therefore take steps to be able to use that defence wherever possible. This means taking action to ensure that food is sold (or given as a gift, reward or prize) under the brand name of someone else.

If caterers have a wine/drinks list, it is preferable to describe drinks by their brand names. This can easily be done for most kinds of beer, ciders, spirits, fortified wines, colas, mineral waters etc. For the menu this is more difficult, but it could be possible with food such as pâté, cheese, after-dinner mints, biscuits etc. Some thought needs to be given as to how products are described but it must be stressed that if the brand names are not given, it is not possible to rely on the brand names defence.

The second available defence requires more vigilance on the part of caterers than the brand names defence because:

(a) the accused must have previously carried out all checks on the food in question as were reasonable in the circumstances, or it must have been reasonable in the circumstances for the accused to rely on checks carried out by the supplier; and

(b) despite such checks, the accused did not know and had no reason to suspect that he or she was committing an offence.

This *non-brand names third party defence* requires caterers to carry out checks (either personally or arranging for this to be done by, for example, a specialist food examiner or analyst), or to rely on the checks of suppliers where such reliance is reasonable. If it is reasonable in the circumstances to rely on the checks of the suppliers, caterers should satisfy themselves that these checks are thorough. It can be said with certainty that unless caterers either carry out their own checks or have knowledge of their suppliers' quality control systems, a non-brand names third party defence will fail.

Checks may be sophisticated or simple depending on a combination of the following:

• the size and resources of the company;
• the nature of the supplied produce; and
• the potential for the product to vary from a standard.

As both these third party fault defences are new and unique to food safety laws it is not possible to give detailed guidance on their application until the courts have made judgments on a number of cases. It is clear, however, that the brand names defence is basically factual, whereas in the non-brand names defence, the individual circumstances of each case are likely to decide the issue.

Due diligence in practice

Whilst the due diligence defence is new to food safety law it is not a new concept. The main due diligence defence can be found in near identical form in other criminal consumer protection legislation, in particular:

- The Trade Descriptions Act 1968 (s.24)
- The Weights and Measures Act 1985 (s.34)
- The Consumer Protection Act 1987 (s.38).

Due diligence defences under these Acts have given rise to many cases which have established certain ground rules and it is reasonable to assume that the same ground rules will apply to the due diligence defence under the Food Safety Act 1990.

The main principles which can be gleaned from these cases are listed below.

1 Only in extremely rare circumstances can doing nothing be adequate

Sutton London Borough Council v. Perry Sanger & Co Ltd (1971)
Dealers in dogs bought in a dog stated to be of a rare breed with which they were not familiar and then sold it on as a pedigree. As no precautions had been taken to check that it was a pedigree they could not rely on the due diligence defence when it was found that the dog was a cross-breed.

Denard v. Smith & Dixons (1991)
Computer packages were advertised for sale containing certain specified games programs. The advertised games were out of stock and were replaced by substitute games but the advertisements were not altered. Nothing was done to inform customers of the change – the due diligence failed.

Gale v. Dixon Stores Group Ltd (1994)
There was no evidence of any procedure to avoid returned faulty goods being sold as 'new' until after the event. The due diligence defence failed.

Hurley v. Martinez & Co Ltd (1990)
German wine was sold by UK retailers. The wine was labelled in Germany as 8% alcohol but was actually 7.2%. The retailers carried out no checks but relied on the label. In this case the defence was proved. (See more on this case later.)

2 Failure to take obvious tests or precautions will result in conviction

Sherratt v. *Geralds the American Jewellers Ltd* (1970)
Failure to immerse so-called divers' watches in water led to a conviction when the watches were found not to be waterproof.

Turtington v. *United Cooperatives Ltd* (1993)
Staff were instructed not to accept furniture without a label with the batch number for the foam filling. Even if the furniture had such a number, the batch was not checked to see if it complied with the furniture fire safety rules. Failure to make such enquiries was fatal to a due diligence defence.

R v. *F & M Dobson Ltd* (1994)
Failure to install a metal detector at the end of the production line for confectionery enabled a chocolate covered knife blade to get into the final product. Due diligence failed.

3 The precautions taken must be reasonably adequate

Rotherham Metropolitan Borough Council v. *Raysun (UK) Ltd* (1988)
Testing a single packet of crayons from a batch of 10,000 dozen packets was insufficient.

P & M Supplies (Essex) Ltd v. *Devon County Council* (1991)
Out of over 76,000 toys only 0.5 per cent were random tested. The accused had failed to show that the number (and type) of tests were adequate to support a due diligence defence.

Dudley Metropolitan Council v. *Robert Firman Ltd* (1992)
Manufacturer could not show it had taken all reasonable precautions to ensure that foam and fabric used in cushions complied with fire safety rules when random sampling consisted of only three separate laboratory certificates.

Sutton LBC v. *David Halsall plc* (1994)
To establish a defence, the evidence must show that in-house testing is adequate as to sample size and nature of the testing and, if purported to comply with a British Standard, that the standard is met or bettered.

Warwickshire CC v. *Verco* (1994)
If a purchaser has doubts about the authenticity of products supplied to him he should make further enquiries of his supplier or contact his local enforcement authority for guidance.

4 The precautions to be taken may increase in proportion to the resources available

Garret v. *Boots the Chemist Ltd* (1980)

Large retailers such as Boots the Chemist may need to carry out random testing in circumstances where the same tests by the proprietors of a village shop would not be considered necessary.

5 Contractual warranties from suppliers can form part of the reasonable precautions

Riley v. *Webb* (1987)

Wholesalers of fancy goods and toys failed to impose contract conditions on their suppliers to ensure compliance with safety legislation and could not rely on the due diligence defence.

Hicks v. *S D Sullam Ltd* (1983)

Bulbs were falsely described as 'safe'. Reliance on the verbal assurances sought and obtained from the overseas purchasing agent was inadequate.

Riley v. *Webb* (1987)

Even an assurance (as to compliance with statutory obligations) which is a term of the contract may be inadequate without further checks.

6 If reliance is made on suppliers' checks then it must be known what those checks are

Amos v. *Melcon (Frozen Foods) Ltd* (1985)

Frozen silverside was misdescribed as rump steak. No enquiries had been made of the suppliers as to the precautions they took to avoid this common problem.

Coventry City Council v. *Ackerman Group plc* (1994)

The manufacturer or importer is responsible for ensuring that a retailer is properly instructed as to any relevant measures (e.g. essential instructions to render a product safe in use) which need to be passed on to users.

7 Requesting the enforcing authority to inspect cannot evade responsibility

Taylor v. *Lawrence Fraser (Bristol) Ltd* (1987)

No attempts were made to check that toys complied with safety legislation other than to ask the local trading standards department to take samples for analysis. Such an invitation cannot support a due diligence defence.

8 If all food leaving the premises is inspected by the enforcing authority, a due diligence defence may be established

Carrick District Council v. *Taunton Vale Meat Traders Ltd* (1994)
All meat leaving the slaughterhouse was inspected by the local authority meat inspector and no meat left the premises unless certified as fit for human consumption by the inspector (see below for more commentary on this case).

9 The precautions must be directed at avoiding the offence charged

Haringey London Borough Council v. *Piro Shoes Ltd* (1976)
A circular letter was sent to all branch managers warning that a batch of shoes was incorrectly described as 'all leather' and instructing that the word 'all' should be deleted at the till. The offence was committed when the shoes were put on display with the offending description hence the precautions taken were too late to avoid the offence.

10 The maxim 'res ipsa loquitur' is not applicable in criminal cases

Cow & Gate Nutricia Ltd v. *Westminster City Council* (1995)
A small piece of bone was found in a jar of baby food. This fact was not, in itself, sufficient to negate the statutory due diligence defence.

Carrick District Council v. *Taunton Vale Meat Traders Ltd* (1994)
This is an important case because it is the first (and as yet only) case reported as a law report in which the adequacy of precautions to satisfy the due diligence defence in the Food Safety Act 1990 has been considered.

The facts were simple. Taunton Vale Meat Traders operated a slaughterhouse at Honiton in Devon. All meat leaving the premises was inspected by the meat inspector employed by East Devon District Council.

On 20 February 1991, the meat inspector inspected carcasses killed the evening before and stamped four quarters of beef from one animal as being fit. The meat was transported to Redruth in Cornwall where it was inspected again and was found to be unfit.

Taunton Vale Meat Traders had no separate system of checking or verifying that any meat was fit for consumption, but no meat left the premises unless it had been certified by the meat inspector. In other words, the company relied entirely upon the local authority meat inspector to say whether the food was fit. A prosecution followed initiated by Carrick District Council (the local authority covering Redruth). The case went on appeal to the High Court.

The case for the prosecution was that merely relying upon the meat inspector was not sufficient to satisfy a due diligence defence under section 21 of the Food Safety Act 1990. In other words the prosecution alleged that Taunton Vale Meat Traders should have had their own due diligence systems in place to run alongside, and independent of, those operated by the meat inspector. This would pick up the remote chance that the meat inspector might get it wrong.

The defence case was that reliance on the meat inspector's certificate was sufficient due diligence because it was reasonable for the company to place reliance on that certificate.

The court, in essence, approached the case by asking what more could the company have reasonably done to avoid committing the offence? That is a vital question because it would be quite wrong to punish the company if in reality there was nothing more the company could have done than it had already had done to avoid the offence.

The due diligence defence succeeded and the prosecution failed. The appeal court made two very important observations:

1 Every case will depend on its own facts as to whether a due diligence defence has been established.
2 In this case the accused acted quite reasonably in relying entirely upon the inspection by the meat inspector and the company was not obliged to duplicate that system.

That second observation was the clue to the outcome of the appeal because what the court did was to answer its own question by saying that the company really could not have done anything more than it was already doing to avoid the offence. It would be unreasonable for the law to expect Taunton Vale Meat Traders to employ its own meat inspector to do exactly the same job as the local authority meat inspector, especially bearing in mind the fact that the local authority meat inspector was highly experienced and competent.

The first observation by the appeal court is of more general interest because there are few food premises where every product is inspected by a local authority inspector. Accordingly, for most food businesses it will be important to look at the operation from the point of view of what more can reasonably be done to avoid committing a food safety offence.

11 Powers of EHOs to search premises and inspect records

Walkers Snack Foods Ltd v. Coventry City Council (1997)
The company appealed against conviction on two charges of failing to give an environmental health officer the assistance

reasonably required (s.33(1) of the Food Safety Act 1990) and causing food to be sold which was not of the substance demanded. The company argued that:

(i) It was entitled to prevent inspection of documents or areas of the premises which it would rely on for a due diligence defence.
(ii) It relied on a consultant's advice that because the EHO was acting outside her home area she was not entitled to examine the production line and this provided reasonable cause for its failure to assist.
(iii) Evidence obtained in breach of PACE Codes of Practice should be excluded.
(iv) Privilege against self-incrimination supported a defence of reasonable cause.

The appeal was dismissed, with the court finding that: (i) and (ii) EHOs were empowered under section 32 (1)(b) of the 1990 Act to enter business premises, whether within or without the authority's area, for the purpose of determining whether an offence had been committed, and under section 32(5) of the Act they could inspect any records relating to a food business for that purpose. EHOs would be unable to carry out their functions properly under section 32 to assess the prospects of a defence made out prior to deciding whether to prosecute unless they had free access to documents and premises. (iii) Requests for information from EHOs acting under section 32 fall outside the scope of PACE. (iv) No privilege against self-incrimination under section 33(3) attached to an employee, who was not authorized to speak for the company, responding to an EHO's questions which might incriminate the employer.

In every case where the accused:

(a) intends to rely on one of the 'third party fault defences'; or
(b) intends to rely on the main due diligence defence on the basis of allegations that the offence was due to the fault of some other person or in reliance on information supplied by some other person the accused must serve on the prosecutor a written notice identifying or helping to identify that other person.

There is a strict time limit for serving that notice prior to the court hearing. If the notice is not served, the accused cannot rely on that defence without the consent of the court. Such consent is unlikely to be given without a good reason why the notice was not served within the specified time.

Risk assessment

It is clear from an analysis of the due diligence defence (both main and third party) that catering control systems must be initiated or reviewed in the light of the responsibilities created under the Food Safety Act 1990. Such control systems must be based on an identification of risk areas throughout the catering processes and procedures. This is all the more important in the light of the requirement in Regulation 4(3) of the Food Safety (General Food Hygiene) Regulations 1995.

The purpose of risk assessment is to identify each hazard (the circumstance with potential to cause harm) and the risk (the probability of that harm happening). Typical areas that will be identified by a risk assessment will be as follows:

• Cleaning and pest control.
• Taking delivery of food.
• Storage and stock rotation.
• Food preparation including cooking and temperature control.
• Refuse disposal.
• Personal hygiene and training.

This assessment should not be seen as a one-off process but should be kept under review, especially when any changes are made to ingredients, processes, equipment, staffing etc.

Having identified the risk areas through the assessment, it is necessary to create systems to control those identified risks. There is no legal requirement for these systems to be written down, but the existence of records will assist in any due diligence defence, whilst also providing a framework for good catering practice.

Management control

It is necessary to set up a programme of monitoring, control and surveillance to ensure the due diligence systems which have been instituted actually operate in practice and do not fall down through familiarity. For a large organization, in particular one with a wide geographical spread, it may be important to have two levels of monitoring, both at local and head office level. Again, it is recommended that records be kept of all monitoring for a period of approximately 6 months. All results should be recorded, with an investigation of any that require remedial action.

It is also advisable to consider whether a particular person in the organization should have the responsibility of 'compliance officer' for ensuring compliance with all food legislative controls and whether this person has sufficient authority and resources to do the job.

The job of designing the necessary systems to comply with reasonable precautions and the setting up of the monitoring controls to comply with due diligence should not be delegated. The proprietor or a senior person in the company should take responsibility. Delegation of the task to a more junior level may result in the delegation of the task itself being regarded as a lack of due diligence.

It should be borne in mind that complaints by the public can often lead to action by the enforcement authorities. It is important to have management controls for complaints to be reported to and considered by an appropriate senior member of staff. Analysis of complaints may show trends that could pinpoint problem areas.

Staff and due diligence

The leading case on the question of how the default of a member of staff affects the criminal liability of the employer is a House of Lords case in 1971, *Tesco Supermarkets* v. *Nattrass*. The prosecution against Tesco Supermarkets was under the Trade Descriptions Act 1968 and the offence was of advertising a lower price than the price at which the goods were available in the shop. The company pleaded the classic due diligence defence.

The court considered that Tesco had taken all reasonable precautions and exercised all due diligence by setting up management systems to ensure that incorrectly priced goods were not put on the shelves. This was coupled with a monitoring system involving daily reports to head office by each store manager. Due, however, to the fault of the manager at one of Tesco's stores, some washing powder was put on that store's display shelves marked at a higher price than advertised in the window. The question arose, 'Did the fault of the manager mean that Tesco had failed to take all reasonable precautions and had failed to exercise due diligence?' The answer was 'No' and so Tesco was duly acquitted. The court decided that a company such as Tesco operates through a 'controlling will'; namely a body of senior directors, executives etc., who decide the company policy and ensure that it is put into operation. They effectively control the company and any act or default by them is the act or default of the company. A manager of one of some 800 stores around the country could not be regarded as within that top echelon of management and therefore his or her default is not the company's default. The company had done all it could in order to comply with the requirement for all reasonable precautions and due diligence; it was merely that the manager on this occasion had failed to do his job.

In *Westminster City Council* v. *Turner Gow* (1984) the accused was a company which was in business as a coal merchant. The company had devised systems to avoid short weight offences. Those systems included written instructions given to all drivers and a system of checking at the weighbridge. Despite this, a short weight offence occurred as the result of a driver disobeying these widely known orders. The company's defence of due diligence succeeded.

If, however, the top management does fall down in its task not only will the company be prosecuted but also the senior managers/executives responsible (s.36 of the Food Safety Act 1990).

In the case of an employee who, deliberately or otherwise, fails to comply with the company instructions, the individual employee can be prosecuted under section 20 of the 1990 Act.

There are three other points to note about staff and the due diligence defence.

1 It is important to remember that staff fault can never be the basis of a third party due diligence defence.
2 The systems (precautions) and monitoring (due diligence) which are established by the employer must be such as to avoid not only the employer committing the offence, but also the employee. This means that the controls must take some account of the possibility of staff aberrations.
3 The fact that staff were not properly trained or supervised, or did not know what to do or were just plain incompetent for the job, may tend to show that the employer has not taken all proper steps to be able to prove the due diligence defence.

Two cases illustrate this last point.

Baxters (Butchers) v. Manley (1985)
The charge was of short weight and mis-pricing. The accused relied on the due diligence defence. Although rules had been issued to shops, no instructions had been given to managers and the shop manager had been given insufficient training. The defence failed.

Knowsley Metropolitan Borough Council v. Cowan (1991)
Written instructions had been given to managers of a chain of butchers' shops, including the direction that they were responsible for recruitment and training. No training or supervision of staff selection and training existed. A 15-year-old boy was taken on as an assistant and on more than one occasion sold underweight food. The due diligence defence failed because of inadequate personnel practices.

Personnel and training policies may need to be reviewed in the light of these cases.

The risk of prosecution

If the worst happens and a prosecution against a caterer is under consideration because, for example, he or she has served food to customers which happens to be so contaminated as to be unfit to eat, then the question arises as to whether the prosecuting authority must prosecute as a matter of course, or if it has discretion whether to prosecute. Furthermore, in exercising that discretion, will the prosecuting authority take into account the management control systems of that caterer? The answer to these questions is to be found in Code of Practice No. 2 (issued under section 40 of the 1990 Act) giving guidance to enforcement authorities. In the Code, it states that before deciding whether a prosecution should be initiated, the authority should consider a number of factors including the likelihood of the accused being able to establish a due diligence defence.

This means that if caterers can demonstrate to the enforcement officers that they can either satisfy the conditions for one of the 'third party fault defences', or have sufficient management control systems to convince a court (on the balance of probabilities) that they have complied with the main due diligence defence, then a prosecution is unlikely.

If caterers intend to rely upon the main due diligence defence, then they should be able to produce sufficient evidence to convince a sceptical enforcement officer of the adequacy of their systems, checks etc. It is, of course, always much easier to prove these matters if the systems are written, the checks are properly recorded and the staff training logs kept up to date.

If the enforcement authority does proceed with a prosecution and the caterer relies on the due diligence defence, it is an easier task to convince a court of the adequacy of the precautions and due diligence in operation if records are available. If the due diligence defence involves an allegation that a member (or ex-member) of staff was responsible then it is obviously easier both to support that defence and identify that member of staff if written systems clearly identify responsibilities.

Relying on the due diligence defence in court

Even the most cursory glance of cases before the courts reveals a reluctance to acquit an accused who is prosecuted for a food offence. The courts tend to consider that their job is to protect the public and that an acquittal is a precedent which will lead to lower protection. Such considerations by the courts are fallacies.

The primary job of the courts in these situations is to punish an offender. The existence of the law coupled with the liability to be punished for breach is the protection for the public.

The accused is in court either because he or she has no due diligence system at all or because, despite having such a system, an incident has happened which, on the face of it, is an offence. The accused who has no due diligence system will be convicted.

The difficulty facing the accused who has a due diligence system and who relies upon the due diligence defence is to persuade the court that despite what has happened, he or she should not be convicted.

There are a number of important preliminary points:

1 Some apparent breaches of the food legislation will occur without anyone necessarily being criminally liable.
2 The court's role is to decide the guilt or innocence of the particular person in front of them. In coming to that decision they ought to be looking for the accused's fault, i.e. was there a foreseeable risk and a failure by the accused to address it properly?
3 The purpose of the due diligence defence is to distinguish the conscientious caterer/food producer from others.
4 No system can be perfect and so, inevitably, even in the best of systems there will be problems which slip through the net. That does not attract criminal sanctions.
5 The duty is to take all 'reasonable' steps. That involves a degree of assessment both of the risk and the measures needed to cope. If the risk was not foreseeable in the first place then it is not 'reasonable' to expect any steps to be taken. Furthermore, the duty is to take all reasonable steps, not all practicable steps or possible steps, so if it was possible to do more, but not reasonable to do more, then it is not necessary to do more.
6 The realities of commercial life should not be ignored.
7 The customer may have adequate remedies in civil law, i.e. be able to sue the accused and succeed even though the accused may not be criminally liable.

Paragraphs 1 and 4 above are well demonstrated by the case of *R* v. *Bow Street Magistrates Court ex parte Cow and Gate Nutrition plc* (1995). The prosecution was under section 14 of the Food Safety Act 1990 and followed from the discovery of a piece of bone in a jar of baby food manufactured by the accused. The company did not dispute that the bone was in the jar, but relied on the due diligence defence and gave evidence of its sophisticated production process. The magistrate convicted the company because, in his view, the mere presence of the bone must mean that all due diligence had not been exercised. The case was appealed to the High Court. The appeal judge pointed out that the magistrate's logic was flawed, because if that logic was correct, it would mean that no due diligence defence could ever succeed. A due diligence defence only arises once the primary facts of the offence exist and to say that the presence of the bone itself was evidence of failure to exercise due diligence was incorrect.

Having said that, it is for the accused to prove the due diligence defence but on the balance of probabilities (i.e. not beyond all reasonable doubt). Failure to prove the due diligence defence before the court in the first instance (usually the Magistrates or Sheriff) will usually mean that the conviction will not be reversed on appeal. Appeal courts will generally not interfere with the lower court's view of the adequacy of the accused's systems. Getting the defence right first time, therefore, is important.

Looking at the key issues:

1 Was the risk reasonably foreseeable in the first instance? In the case of *Hurley* v. *Martinez & Company Ltd* the question arose as to whether a wine wholesaler in the UK could reasonably foresee that an error in preparing the wine label in Germany would result in the alcoholic strength being mis-stated. In that case it was not reasonably foreseeable and so the wine wholesaler was entitled to be acquitted.

2 If the accused relies upon the verification regimes at an earlier stage in the chain of supply are those regimes known to the accused? If so, there must be evidence of that knowledge. In *Rotherham MBC v. Raysun (UK) Ltd* the sampling of crayons was carried out by agents in Hong Kong and adverse reports were to be sent to the company in the UK. No reports were received. As the satisfactory reports were not to be sent to the company, there was no check that the analyses were taking place at all. The accused was convicted.

3 If the accused carries out his or her own tests are those adequate? That is a question for the accused to prove. In *P & M Supplies (Essex) Ltd* v. *Devon County Council* the conviction was not reversed on appeal. The Appeal Court said that it was for the accused to show that the number of tests was adequate and this may mean independent statistical evidence as to what should be done by a reasonable trader.

4 If the systems involve staff instruction and training, it is for the accused to prove the existence of adequate instructions, training programmes, supervision etc. Inability to do so will result in conviction. In *Knowsley MBC v. Cowan* the magistrates originally acquitted on evidence of duties listed in the contracts of employment of individual managers but on appeal a conviction was substituted because such a list was inadequate. There should have been evidence of instructions (written or otherwise), training programmes etc.

Each case must be approached on its facts and merits but for those caterers and food producers who have due diligence systems in place, the task is to persuade the court to strike the right balance so that the burden on a business is commensurate with the risk involved.

Due diligence and the European Union

The Food Safety Act 1990 was not enacted to implement any European Directive, but it does specifically provide (in section17) for the implementation of European Union (EU) laws. Food safety is increasingly being regulated through EU laws to ensure that food produced, manufactured, packaged etc. in one member state is acceptable in another member state without a further layer of checks and tests.

The problem is that the due diligence defence in the Food Safety Act 1990 encourages such further checks and tests. The result is that to the extent that the due diligence defence imposes a further level of verification, it may be in breach of Article 30 of the Treaty of Rome as an unjustified barrier to trade. The case already mentioned of *Hurley v. Martinez & Co Ltd*, recognized that if the food has been produced, labelled etc. in accordance with EU consumer protection laws in a member state, it is inappropriate to require a retailer in another member state to check compliance with those laws.

There are cases on this aspect of European law. In *Ministère Publique v. Bouchara* (1991), laws which made an importer liable for goods manufactured in another country only survived the Article 30 challenge because the law was reasonably required for consumer protection. In the case of *EC Commission v. Belgium* (1993), the Belgium Government did not dispute that a Belgian law requiring sterile medical supplies to be subjected to tests which had already been carried out in the EU country of manufacture, was a breach of Article 30.

It can be seen, therefore, that there is an argument to say that the Food Safety Act 1990 has its limits and those limits are where it strays into the area covered by Article 30.

However, alleging a breach of Article 30 of the Treaty of Rome is a somewhat heavyweight defence which may not be necessary. The decision in *Hurley* v. *Martinez & Co Ltd* was largely as to what tests and checks are reasonable for a due diligence defence and in the circumstances of that case (labelling of the alcoholic content of wine), it was reasonable for a small retailer with an extensive range of stock to rely entirely on the fact that the German producers of the wine were required by European law to carry out tests before labelling the wine. The wine label was not so wrong as to alert the retailer, and in the circumstances, the due diligence defence was satisfied by merely checking that the label appeared to show compliance with EU laws.

Furthermore, the decision in *Hurley* v. *Martinez & Co Ltd* does not just protect retailers selling food imported from another member state. If the rule is that apparent, compliance with EU food laws at an earlier stage in the chain is sufficient to satisfy a due diligence defence then that defence applies, whether the food is produced in the UK or in any other member state.

This aspect of the due diligence defence is likely to become increasingly important as EU food safety laws become more comprehensive.

References

Act (1860) *An Act for Preventing the Adulteration of Articles of Food or Drink*, 23 & 24 Vict. Ch 84, London: HMSO.

Act (1872) *Public Health Act 1872*, 35 & 36 Vict. Ch 79, London: HMSO.

Act (1905) *French Law of 1st August 1905, Frauds and Attempted Frauds*, translated by Leatherhead Food Research Association.

Act (1938) *Food and Drugs Act 1938*, 1 & 2 Geo.VI Ch 56, London: HMSO.

Act (1955) *Food and Drugs Act 1955*, Eliz. II Ch 16, London: HMSO.

Act (1956) *Food and Drugs (Scotland) Act 1956*, Eliz. II Ch 30, London: HMSO.

Act (1968) *Trades Description Act 1968*, London: HMSO.Act (1973) *Denmark Food Act etc., Act No. 310 of the 6th June*, translated by Leatherhead Food Research Association.

Act (1974a) *Health and Safety at Work Act 1974*, 19 Halsbury's Statutes (4th edn) 620, London.

Act (1974b) *German Act to Record and Clarify the Law on Trade in Foodstuffs, Tobacco Products, Cosmetics and Certain Necessities*, translated by Leatherhead Food Research Association.

Act (1983) *French Law of 21st July Consumer Safety*, translated by Leatherhead Food Research Association.

Act (1984) *Food Act 1984*, Eliz. II Ch 30, London: HMSO.

Act (1987) *Consumer Protection Act 1987*, London: HMSO.

Act (1988) *Netherlands Food and Drugs Act*, Statute Book 1935, 793, translated by Leatherhead Food Research Association.

Act (1990a) *The Food Safety Act 1990*, London: HMSO.

Act (1990b) *French Draft Act Relating to the Health Regulations Governing Foodstuffs, Products or Drinks Intended for Human Consumption*, 15th March 1990, translated by Leatherhead Food Research Association.

Act (1992) *Netherlands Food and Drugs Act Preparation and Treatment of Food Products*, translated by Leatherhead Food Research Association.

Act (1993) *Denmark Act Amending the 1973 Act on Foodstuffs etc.*, 6th June 1993, translated by Leatherhead Food Research Association.

Agra Europe (1992) *EC Food Law Monthly*, January, London: Agra Europe Ltd.

Agra Europe (1993) *EC Food Law Monthly*, December, London: Agra Europe Ltd.

Agra Europe (1994) *EC Food Law Monthly*, November, London: Agra Europe Ltd.

Anderson KG (1991) The Official Control of Foodstuffs Directive 89/397/EEC-Article 13: A Food Industry View, *Food Science & Technology Today*, 5 (2), pp 79–82.

Anonymous (1990) *Lebensmittelrecht; Europaeische Hygieneregelungen*, Lebenesmitteltechnik, Germany, 22 (10), p 544.

Anonymous (1992a) United Kingdom Food Advisory Committee Review of Food Labelling and the Government's Response, *European Food Law Review*, 1 (1), pp 81–91.

Anonymous, (1992b) A £30,000 Take-Away, *The Advertiser*, Newbury, Berkshire, 1 December.

Anonymous (1992c) Chinese Take-away Family Devastated, *Newbury Weekly News*, Berkshire, 3 December.

Anonymous (1992d) Co-op's Milk Production Defective: Magistrate, *County Down Spectator and Ulster Standard*, Northern Ireland, 28 May.

Anonymous (1992e) The Codex Food Labelling Committee: Maintaining International Standards Relevant to Changing Consumer Demands, *European Food Law Review*, 3 (1), pp 70–80.

Arthur Anderson (1997–2001) *Arthur Anderson Hospitality Industry Benchmark Survey*, London: Anderson Consulting.

Aston G and Tiffney J (1993) *The Essential Guide to Food Hygiene*, London: Eaton Publications.

Bohl A (1991) Verkehrsauffassung und Verbrauchererwartung im Lebensmittelrecht, Anspruch und Wirklichkeit, *Lebensmittelkontrollur*, Germany, 6 (2), p 31.

Booker C (1993) Spreading Fear and Confusion, Here Comes the Hygiene Police, *Daily Telegraph*, 20 April.

Cecchini P (1988) *The European Challenge 1992: The Benefits of a Single Market*, Brookfield, VT: Gower.

Cecchini P (1989) *Europe 92: The Advantage of the Single Market*, EC Commission, Brussels.

CECG (1987) *A Hot Potato? Food Policy in the EEC*, Consumers in the European Community Group, London.

CECG (1991a) *Food Labelling and 1992*, Consumers in the European Community Group, London.

CECG (1991b) *Proposed Reform of the Scientific Committee for Food*, Consumers in the European Community Group, London.

CECG (1991c) *Food Hygiene in the Single Market*, Consumers in the European Community Group, London.

Clarke D (1993) Food Labelling and the Caterer, *The Voice of the British Hospitality Association*, September, pp 14–15.

Code of Practice No. 1 (1990a) *Responsibility for the Enforcement of the Food Safety Act 1990*, London: HMSO.

Code of Practice No. 4 (1990b) *Inspection, Detention and Seizure of Suspect Food*, London: HMSO.

Code of Practice No. 5 (1990c) *The Use of Improvement Notices*, London: HMSO.

Code of Practice No. 6 (1990d) *Prohibition Procedures*, London: HMSO.

Codex (1985) *Volume A, Recommended International Code of Practice, General Principles of Food Hygiene, Second Revision*, Food and Agricultural Organization of the United Nations World Health Organization, Rome.

Codex (1989) *Codex Alimentarius Guidelines for the Application of the Hazard Analysis Critical Control Point System*, Food and Agricultural Organization of the United Nations World Health Organization, Rome.

COM (83) (1983) *Draft Technical Regulations Relating to Foodstuffs*, Directive 83/189/EEC, EC Commission, Brussels.

COM (93) 632 final (1993) *Making the Most of the Internal Market*, 22 December, EC Commission, Brussels.

COM (93) 669 final (1993) *Management of the Mutual Recognition of National Rules after 1992*, 15 December, EC Commission, Brussels.

COM (94) 29 final (1994) *Development of Administrative Co-operation for the Implementation and Application of Community Legislation in the Framework of the Internal Market*, 16 February, EC Commission, Brussels.

COM (97) 184 (1997a) *The Action Plan for the Internal Market*, EC Commission, Brussels.

COM 97 (1997b) *Results of the Official Control on Foodstuffs: EU Summary of the Inspection and Sampling Statistics 1994*, Febuary, EC Commission, Brussels.

Crawford A (1987) Salmonella Poisoning on the Increase, *Health & Safety at Work*, January, pp 23–4.

Dauer K (1991) Europaeisches Lebensmiielrecht, *Verbrauche – Rundschau*, No. 12, pp 1–31.

Dehove RA (1986) *Lamy – Dehove Reglementation des Produits Qualite Repression des Fraudes*, Paris: Lamy SA.

Deutsches Lebensmittelbuch (1992) *Leitsatze 92*, Bundesanzeiger Verlagsges mbH, Cologne, Germany.

Docksey C and Williams K (1994) The Commission and the Execution of Community Policy, in Edwards G and Spence D (eds), *The European Commission*, London: Longman.

DOH (1992a) *Government Outlines Food Hygiene Training Requirements*, Department of Health Press Release H92/247, 28 July, London.

DOH (1992b) *Food Hygiene Training*, Department of Health Consultation Document, 17 December, London.

DOH (1993a) *Food Safety Act 1990 – Code of Practice No. 5 on the Use of Improvement Notices and No. 9 on Food Hygiene Inspections*, Department of Health Consultation Document, 20 August, London.

DOH (1993b) *Food Hygiene Training, Annex C*, Department of Health Consultation Document, 17 December, London.

DOH (1993c) *Draft Regulations Amending Certain Food Temperature Controls Contained in the Food Hygiene (Amendment) Regulations 1990 and 1991*, Department of Health Consultation Document, 1 April, London.

DOH (1993d) *Food Temperature Controls Review*, Department of Health Consultation Document, 4 October, London.

DOH (1993e) *Review of the Food Hygiene (Amendment) Regulations 1990 and 1991*, Department of Health Consultation Document, 22 February, London.

DOH (1993f) *Review of the Food Hygiene (Amendment) Regulations 1990 and 1991*, Department of Health Consultation Document, 1 April, London.

DOH (1996) *Enforcement of the Temperature Control Requirements of Food Hygiene Regulations*, Department of Health Consultation Document, London.

EC Commission (1962) *Colouring of Foodstuffs Directive*, 2645/62, OJ No. L115, November, as amended, EC Commission, Brussels.

EC Commission (1971a) *Health Problems Affecting Trade in Fresh Poultry Meat Directive*, 71/118/EEC, OJ No. L055, EC Commission, Brussels.

EC Commission (1971b) *Compositional Standards and Lawful Names for Milk as Amended*, Council Regulation No. 1411/71, OJ No. L148,03.07.71; 74/1556, OJ No. L167, 22.06.74; 76/566, OJ No. L067,15.03.76; 88/222, OJ No. L028, 01.02.88, EC Commission, Brussels.

EC Commission (1977) *Health Problems Affecting Intra Community Trade in Meat Products*, Council Directive 77/99/EEC, OJ No. L26 January 1977 – amended directive OJ No. L57 March 1992, EC Commission, Brussels.

EC Commission (1979) *The Labelling of Foodstuffs*, Council Directive 79/112/EEC, OJ No. L033, February, EC Commission, Brussels.

EC Commission (1983) *Procedures for the Provision of Information Set Out in Directive 83/189/EEC*, draft technical regulations relating to foodstuffs, EC Commission, Brussels.

EC Commission (1985a), *Completion of the Internal Market; Community Legislation on Food Stuffs*, Communication from the Commission to the European Parliament, COM (85) 603, Final, Luxembourg.

EC Commission (1985b) *Product Liability Directive*, 85/374/EEC, EC Commission, Brussels.

EC Commission (1986) *Single European Act 1986* (Cmnd 9758(1986) Bull EC Supp 2/86, EC Commission, Brussels.

EC Commission (1989a) *Official Control of Foodstuffs*, Council Directive, 89/397/EEC, OJ No. L 186, June, EC Commission, Brussels.

EC Commission (1989b) *Materials and Articles in Contact with Food-General Requirement*, Council Directive 89/109/EEC, OJ No. L40, February, EC Commission, Brussels.

EC Commission (1989c) *Food Additives Framework*, Council Directive, 89/107/EEC OJ No. L40, February, EC Commission, Brussels.

EC Commission (1990a) *Nutrition Labelling of Foodstuffs, Council Directive*, 90/496/EEC, OJ No. L 276, October, EC Commission, Brussels.

EC Commission (1990b) *Genetically Modified Organisms*, 90/220/EEC, EC Commission, Brussels.

EC Commission, (1991a) *The Farmed Game Council Directive*, 91/495/EEC, OJ L268 24.9.91 and The Wild Game Directive, 92/45/EEC, OJ L268, September, EC Commission, Brussels.

EC Commission (1991b) *Quantitative Declarations of Characterising Ingredients*, Draft Council Directive, COM 1991 536, File, Amending Directive 79/112/EEC, OJ No. L033 on Food Labelling, EC Commission, Brussels.

EC Commission (1991c) *The Hygiene of Foodstuffs*, Draft Proposal for a Council Directive, COM (91) 525 (final) OJ, February, EC Commission, Brussels.

EC Commission (1991d) *Health Problems Affecting Intra Community Trade in Fresh Meat to Extend it to the Production and Marketing of Fresh Meat*, Council Directive 64/433/EEC 91/497/EEC, OJ No. L 268, September, EC Commission, Brussels.

EC Commission (1991e) *Directive 91/493/EEC Laying Down Health Conditions for the Production and the Placing on the Market of Fishery Products*, OJ No. L268, September, EC Commission, Brussels.

EC Commission (1992a) Sutherland Report: *The Internal Market after 1992; Meeting the Challenge*, EC Commission, Brussels.

EC Commission (1992b) Product Safety Directive, 92/59/EEC, EC Commission, Brussels.

EC Commission (1993a) *The Hygiene of Foodstuffs*, Council Directive, OJ No. L 175/1, June, EC Commission, Brussels.

EC Commission (1993b) *Protection of Geographical Indications and Designations of Origin, EEC/2081/92, and Certificates of Special Character*, EEC2082/92, OJ, EC Commission, Brussels.

EC Commission (1993c) *The Treaty on European Union*, Council and Commission, Brussels.

EC Commission (1996) *The Study of the Impact and Effectiveness of the Internal Market Programme on the Processed Foodstuffs Sector*, The Sutherland Report, EC Commission, Brussels.

EC Council (1992) *European Communities to the Council, Common Position Adopted by the Council with a View to the Adoption of a Directive on the Hygiene of Foodstuffs*, 16 December, EC Commission, Brussels.

EC Presidency (1992) *Draft Proposal for a Council Directive on the Hygiene of Foodstuffs*, Draft Presidency Compromise Text, July, EC Commission, Brussels.

Eckert D (1991) Gestaltungsfragen des Lebensmittelrechts in Deutschland und Europa, Chancen und Risiken, Zeitschrift fuer das gesamte, *Lebensmittelrecht*, No. 3, pp 221–41.

Economic and Social Committee (1992) *Opinion on the Proposal for a Council Directive on the Hygiene of Foodstuffs*, OJ, August, EC Commission, Brussels.

European Parliament (1992) *Committee on the Environment Public Health and Consumer Protection. Report on the Commission Proposal for a Council Directive on the Hygiene of Foodstuffs* (COM910525) Final C30058/92/SYN/376, Reporter, Mrs Pauline Green, June, Strasbourg.

EUROSTAT (1996) *Basic Statistics of the Community, The Statistical Office of the European Communities*, Brussels.

Fallows SJ (1988) *Towards 1992: Completing the EEC Internal Market for Food*, Doncaster: Horton Publishing.

Fallows SJ (1991) European Food Law: Trends and Actions, *Food Science & Technology Today*, 5 (2), pp 79–82.

Fedsted J, Bockhahn K and Ostergaard K (1995) Food Legislation in Denmark, *European Food Law Review*, 1 (2), pp 43–52.

Fogden M (1995a) European Community Food Hygiene Legislation Part 5: Processing controls, *European Food Law Review*, 1 (1), pp 61–75.

Fogden M (1995b) European Community Food Hygiene Legislation Part 6: Controls on Finished Products, *European Food Law Review*, 1 (2), pp 55–63.

Food Hygiene Briefing (1994) Due Diligence: Case Developments, *Food Hygiene Briefing*, No. 24, Kingston upon Thames: Croner Publications.

Freidhof E (1991) *Folgen des EG-Lebensmittelrechts aus Verbrauchersicht*, *Verbraucherdienst*, 36 (11), pp 223–232.

FSD (1993a) *Enforcing Food Law*, Food Safety Directorate, Information Bulletin No. 33, MAFF, London, pp 7–8.

FSD (1993b) *Enforcing Food Law*, Food Safety Directorate, Information Bulletin No. 34, MAFF, London, pp 7–8.

FSD (1993c) *Enforcing Food Law*, Food Safety Directorate, Information Bulletin No. 35, MAFF, London, pp 7–8.

FSD (1993d) *Enforcing Food Law*, Food Safety Directorate, Information Bulletin No. 36, MAFF, London, pp 7–8.

FSD (1993e) *Food Poisoning and E. coli 057*, Food Safety Directorate, Information Bulletin No. 35, MAFF, London.

Gorny D (1992) European Food Quality – the Prospective Importance of ISO9000/EN29000, *European Food Law Review*, 3 (1), pp 13–25.

Govern Balear (1992) *Legislacion Comedores Colectivos, Conselleria de Sanitat i Seuretat Social Direccio General de Sanitat*, Palma de Mallorca.

Gray PS (1993) 1993 and European Food Law, an end or a new beginning?, *European Food Law Review*, 1 (2), pp 14–22.

HMSO (1993) *Assured Safe Catering*, London: HMSO.

IEHO (1992) *Draft Guidelines on the Hygienic, Design and Construction of Food Premises*, Institute of Environmental Health Officers, April, London.

Inglis KM and Amaducci S (1994) The Application of EEA Food Law, *European Food Law Review*, 4 (2), pp 65–78.

Italian Ministry of Health (1994) *Uniform Criteria for the Elaboration of Food and Beverage Safety Control Programs*, Decree of the President of the Italian Republic, General Direction for Food Safety and Nutrition, Central Security Office, Rome 18 March.

Jackson C (1990) The Role of the European Parliament in the Control of Foodstuffs Legislation, *European Food Law Review*, 1 (1), pp 53–71.

Joint Hospitality Industry Congress (1994) *EC Food Hygiene Directive Voluntary Guides to Good Hygiene Practice*, Internal document, January.

Jukes DJ (1988a) Approaching 1992 – European Community Developments, *British Food Journal*, 91 (2), pp 12–21.

Jukes DJ (1988b) Food Law Harmonisation Within the European Community, *British Food Journal*, 90 (4), pp 147–54.

Jukes DJ (1989) European Developments in the Foodstuffs Sector, *British Food Journal*, 92 (5), pp 3-10.

Jukes DJ (1991) *Food Law Enforcement in the UK – Time for Change?*, Doncaster: Horton Publishing.

Jukes DJ (1993) *Food Legislation of the UK*, 3rd edition, Oxford: Butterworth-Heinemann.

Knowles TD (1992) *Effect of the EC Law on the Hospitality Industry*, Discussion Paper, Leeds Metropolitan University.

Knowles TD (1994) Some Aspects of UK and European Food Legislation, *Hygiene and Nutrition in Foodservice and Catering*, 1 (1), pp 49–62.

Knowles TD (1999) Attitudes towards Food Safety within Selected Countries of the European Union, Unpublished Phd thesis, University of Luton.

LACOTS (1989) *European Metrology; Inspection Protection and Control*, Local Authorities Co-ordinating Body on Trading Standards, Croydon.

LACOTS (1990) *Food Inspection in the EEC*, Local Authorities Co-ordinating Body on Trading Standards, Croydon.

LACOTS (1991a) *European Directory; Consumer Protection Control Bodies*, Local Authorities Co-ordinating Body on Trading Standards, Croydon.

LACOTS (1991b) *European Directory; Consumer Product Safety*, Local Authorities Co-ordinating Body on Trading Standards, Croydon.

Leible S and Losing N (1993) Principos Fundamentales del Derecho Alimentario Espanol, *European Food Law Review*, 1 (2), pp 12–22.

Lister C (1992) *Regulation of Food Products by the European Community*, Oxford: Butterworth-Heinemann.

Lugt M (1994) Enforcement of Food Law in the Netherlands and its Future, *European Food Law Review*, 3 (2), pp 16–26.

Lugt M (1995) Implementation of Hygiene Directive 94/43/EEC in the Netherlands, *European Food Law Review*, 4 (1), pp 35–44.

Lundberg CC and Woods RH (1981) Modifying Restaurant Culture: Managers as Cultural Leaders, *International Journal of Contemporary Hospitality Management*, 2 (4).

MAFF(1976) *Food Quality and Safety – A Century of Progress*, London: HMSO.

MAFF (1989) *Food Safety Protecting the Consumer*, CM732, HMSO, London.

MAFF (1993a) *Food from Britain to Run Registered Denomination System for Food*, MAFF Press Release 364/92, 18 November, London.

MAFF (1993b) *Nutrition Labelling Directive (90/496/EEC): Draft Implementing Regulations*, MAFF consultation document, 22 December, London.

MAFF (1993c) *Nutrition Labelling: Graphical (Diagrammatic or Descriptive) Formats*, MAFF consultation document, 29 January, London.

MAFF (1993d) *The Food Advisory Committee Review of Food Labelling in Catering Establishments*, MAFF consultation document, 9 March, London.

MAFF (1998) *Food Standards Agency: A Force for Change*, London: HMSO.

Mathijsen PSRF (1990) *A Guide to European Community Law*, 5th edn, London: Sweet and Maxwell.

Middlekauff RD and Shubik P (1989) *International Food Regulation Handbook*, Marcel Dekkar.

Morris EM (1991) Nutrition Labelling, *European Food and Drink Review*, Spring, pp 77–79.

North R (1996) Food Safety Policy, in Thomas R (ed.), *The Hospitality Industry, Tourism and Europe*, London: Cassell.

O'Connor B (1993) Free Movement of Foodstuffs in EC Law, *European Food Law Review*, 3 (2).

Order (1980) *Denmark Promulgation Order on Retail Sale of Food Products*, 28 March, translated by Leatherhead Food Research Association.

Order (1990) *The Designation of Monitoring Authorities Commodities Act and Meat Inspection Act*, The State Secretary of Welfare, Public Health and Culture of 7 September, No. 688973, *Staatscourant, No. 180*

Owen R and Dynes M (1992) *The Times Guide to the Single European Market*, Times Books, London: Harper Collins.

Painter AA (1991) The Origin of Food Products, *European Food Law Review*, 2 (4), pp 282–90.

Pannell Kerr Forster (1997–2001) *Euro City Survey*, London: Pannell Kerr Forster Associates.

Pennington Report (1997) *The Pennington Group: Report on the Circumstances Leading to the Outbreak of Infection E. coli 0157 in Central Scotland, the Implication Food Safety and the Lessons to be Learned*, London: HMSO.

Regulation (1959) *Food Hygiene Scotland Regulations 1959*, London: HMSO.

Regulation (1966) *Food Hygiene (Market, Stalls and Delivery Vehicles) Regulations 1966, Statutory Instrument 1966/791*, London: HMSO.

Regulation (1970) *Food Hygiene General Regulations 1970, Statutory Instrument 1970/1172*. London: HMSO.

Regulation (1980) *French Food Hygiene Regulations*, Decree of September 26, Official Journal NC of the 15 October, Paris.

Regulation (1990a) *Food Safety (Sampling and Qualifications) Regulations 1990*, London: HMSO.

Regulation (1990b) *Detention of Food (Prescribed Forms) Regulations 1990*, London: HMSO.

Regulation (1990c) *Food Labelling (Amendment) (Irradiated Food) Regulation 1990*, Statutory Instrument 1990/2489, London: HMSO.

Regulation (1990d) *Food Hygiene (Amendment) Regulations 1990*, Statutory Instrument 1990/1431, London: HMSO.

Regulation (1990e) *Food (Control of Irradiation) Regulations 1990*, SI 1990/2490, London: HMSO.

Regulation (1991a) *Food Safety (Improvement and Prohibition-Prescribed Forms) Regulations 1991*, London: HMSO.

Regulation (1991b) *Food Premises (Registration) Regulations 1991*, Statutory Instrument 1991/2825, London: HMSO.

Regulation (1991c) *Food Hygiene (Amendment) Regulation 1991*, Statutory Instrument 1991/1373, London: HMSO.

Regulation (1993) *Netherlands Food and Drugs Act Regulation Food Hygiene, No. DGVgz/VVP/L 93272*, translated by Leatherhead Food Research Association.

Regulation (1995a) *Food Safety (General Food Hygiene) Regulations 1995*, London: HMSO.

Regulation (1995b) *Food Safety (Temperature Control) Regulations 1995*, London: HMSO.

Richmond Committee Report on the Microbiological Safety of Food (1989) London: HMSO.

Roberts D (1991) 1992 and all that!, *British Food Journal*, 93 (1), pp 25–6.

Roberts D (1992) European Enforcement, *European Food Law Review*, 1 (2), pp 62–72.

Roberts D (1993a) Level Playing Fields in Europe, *European Food Law Review*, 4 (1), pp 32–44.

Roberts D (1993b) Food Enforcement in the United Kingdom, *European Food Law Review*, 4 (2), pp 44–51.

Roberts D (1994) The Defence of Reasonable Precautions and Due Diligence in the Administration of the United Kingdom and European Food Legislation, *European Food Law Review*, 4 (1), pp 31–43.

Saunders B (1991) Quality, Safety and Choice: A European Food Policy for the 1990s, *BNF Nutrition Bulletin*, 16 (3), pp 147–59.

Shepard J, Kipps M and Thomson J (1990) Hygiene and Hazard Analysis in Food Service, in Cooper CP (ed), *Progress in Tourism, Recreation and Hospitality Management*, Vol. 2, London: Belhaven Press, pp 192–226.

Sherman J (1988) Resign Calls over Currie Egg Alert, *The Times*, 5 December, p 1.

Smith J and Drandfield J (1991) European and US Federal Food Regulations: Current Issues, *Trends in Food Science and Technology*, 2 (10), pp 236–40.

Thomas WH (1992) United Kingdom Food Advisory Committee Review of Food Labelling and the Governments Response, *European Food Law Review*, 3 (1), pp 81–92.

Thomas WH (1993) Registration of Food Premises in the United Kingdom, *European Food Law Review*, 3 (2), pp 71–83.

Toner M (1993) Bazil Forte Takes on the Beaurocrats, *Daily Mail*, 27 February.

WHO (1988) *Food Safety Services*, 2nd edn, World Health Organization, Rome.

Wittekindt E (1991) Sind Sie Über Food Design Informiert ? *Anhaltspunkte*, No. 1 pp 14–19.

Woods RH (1989) More Alike than Different: the Culture of the Restaurant Industry, *Cornell Hospitality and Restaurant Association Quarterly*, 30 (2), pp 82–97.

WTO (1992) *Food Safety and Tourism*, Hospitality Abou Nawas, Tunis, Tunisia, 25–27 November 1991, World Tourism Organization, Madrid.

APPENDIX

Useful Internet addresses

www.foodstandards.gov.uk Home page of the Food Standards Agency, UK

www.open.gov.uk/doh/dhhome.htm Home page of the Department of Health (DH), UK

www.open.gov.uk/scotoff/scofhom.htm Home page of the Scottish Office

www.the-stationery-office.co.uk/ Home page of The Stationery Office

www.Parliament.uk/hophome.htm Home page of the UK Parliament

The following sites are concerned with enforcement work:

www.cieh.org.uk/cieh/ Chartered Institute of Environmental Health (CIEH)

www.xodesign.co.uk/tsnet/ Trading Standards Net

http://dspace.dial.pipex.com/town/square/ac140/index.html Environmental Health

www.bsi.org.uk/ Home page of the British Standards Institute (BSI)

www.cec.org.uk/ Home page of the European Commission UK Office. This site gives access to:

www.europa.eu.int/ Europa home page

www.fao.org/ Home page of the Food and Agriculture Organization, based in Italy

www.who.ch/ Home page of the World Health Organization, based in Switzerland

www.fda.gov/ Home page of the Food and Drug Administration (FDA)

www.iso.ch/ Home page of International Organization for Standardization (ISO)

Index

Hospitality Leisure & Tourism Series

Hospitality Leisure & Tourism Series

Hospitality Leisure & Tourism Series

Printed in the United Kingdom
by Lightning Source UK Ltd.
116979UKS00001B/13